LICENSING
THE NEW LAW

LICENSING
THE NEW LAW

Kerry Barker LLB, *Barrister*
Guildhall Chambers, Bristol

Susan Cavender
Bristol

JORDANS
2003

Published by
Jordan Publishing Limited
21 St Thomas Street
Bristol BS1 6JS

British Library Cataloguing-in-Publication Data
A catalogue record for this book is available from the British Library.

ISBN 0 85308 880 2

Typeset by MFK-Mendip, Frome
Printed and bound in Great Britain by The Cromwell Press

In memory of Eric Barker (1917–1993)
'A good man'

PREFACE

In this book we aim to explain the new laws, drawing, where appropriate, on experience and authorities in relation to the old laws, and to provide guidance to those working in the hospitality and leisure industry, their legal advisers, the police, local authorities and local justices and their advisers (who will hear appeals) and those members of the public (local residents) who might feel the need for help with problems arising in their areas. We hope that we have done so in a form that is readily understandable but which meets the needs of specialist lawyers, police and local government officers, justices and their advisers, and local councillors or residents.

The Licensing Act 2003 (LA 2003) can be found, in full, in the appendix to this book. It is now the case that where there is difficulty with interpretation of a statute, regard can be had to the Explanatory Notes issued by the relevant government department and published by The Stationery Office.[1] The Notes are published to assist non-lawyers to understand the legislation. We have taken into account the Explanatory Notes where appropriate.

At the time of going to print there was a significant amount of secondary legislation (regulations etc) still to be published. Nevertheless, the scheme of the LA 2003 and the Guidance given by the Government was more than sufficient to enable a comprehensive review of the legislation to be undertaken. References to the Guidance issued by the Secretary of State are to the final draft (version 2.6). The law is stated as it stood at the time that the Licensing Bill 2002 was given Royal Assent and became the Licensing Act 2003 (10 July 2003).

We are extremely grateful to Martin West and Jo Morton of Jordans for their help and guidance. Should this book contain any error, however, it is entirely of our own making and for which we accept full responsibility.

Kerry Barker
Guildhall Chambers
Bristol

Susan Cavender
Bristol

September 2003

---

[1] *Westminster City Council v National Asylum Service* [2002] UKHL 38.

CONTENTS

Preface   vii
Table of Cases   xv
Table of Statutes   xix
Table of Statutory Instruments, Statutory Guidance etc   xxvii
Table of European Material   xxix

Chapter 1   **HISTORY AND BACKGROUND TO**
             LICENSING LAW
             Introduction   1
             Sale and supply of alcohol   1
             Provision of public entertainment   4

Chapter 2   **HOW THINGS WILL CHANGE**
             Introduction   7
             Licensing authorities   9
             Changes   10
               Justices' licences   10
               Renewals   10
               Transfers   10
               Protection orders   10
               Removals   10
               Demand   11
               Permitted hours   11
               Occasional licences and occasional
                 permissions   11
               Personal licences   11
               Closure powers   12
               Review and revocation   12
               Sunday closing in parts of Wales   12
               Late night refreshments   12
               Theatres and cinemas   13
               Public entertainments licences   13
               Registered clubs   13
               Offences   13
               Supply of alcohol to children   13
               Wholesale supplies   14
               Fees   14

Chapter 3   **LICENSING OBJECTIVES**
             Introduction   15

The licensing objectives   16

Chapter 4   **LICENSABLE ACTIVITIES**
             Introduction   19
             Definition of licensable activities   21
             The sale or supply of alcohol   21
             Regulated entertainments   22
             Exemptions relating to regulated
                 entertainments   24
                 Films – advertising and educational or
                     information activities   24
                 Incidental music   24
                 Television and radio   24
                 Religious services and places of worship   25
                 Garden fêtes etc   25
                 Morris dancing   26
                 Vehicles in motion   26
                 Vessels   26
                 General point   26
             Late night refreshments   26
             Exemptions relating to late night refreshments   27
                 Hotels, clubs and other places providing
                     overnight accommodation   27
                 Employees   27
                 Exhibition halls and 'near beer' premises   28
                 Certain types of food and drink   28
                 General point   28

Chapter 5   **THE NEW LICENSING AUTHORITIES**
             Introduction   29
             Duties of licensing authorities   30
             Licensing committees   31
             Delegated powers   32
             Records   33
             Proceedings before licensing committees   34

Chapter 6   **LICENSING POLICIES AND GUIDANCE
             ISSUED BY THE SECRETARY OF STATE**
             Introduction   35
             Licensing statement   35
             Consultation   35
             Revision   37
             Regulations   37
             Licensing guidance   38
             The law relating to licensing policies   39

Chapter 7   **PREMISES LICENSES**
             Introduction   41
             The relevant licensing authority   42

Definition of 'premises' 42
Who can apply 42
Application for a premises licence 43
The operating schedule 44
The relevant licensable activities 45
The intended times when the licensable
activities will take place 45
Any other times that the premises will be
open to the public 46
If the licence is for a limited period only 46
Information as to the proposed designated
premises supervisor 47
The supply of alcohol 47
The steps that will be taken by the applicant
to promote the licensing objectives 47
The plan 47
Consent of the designated premises supervisor 47
Fees 47
Determination of application for premises
licence 48
Relevant representations 49
Conditions 50
Provisional statement 51
Determination of applications 52
Form of premises licence 53
Duration of licence 54
Variation of a premises licence 55
Variation of designated premises supervisor 56
Request to be removed as a designated premises
supervisor 57
Transfer of premises licence 58
Reviews of premises licences 59
Powers of entry 62
Excluded premises 62
Small premises 63

Chapter 8 **CLUBS**
Introduction 67
Application for a club premises certificate 68
Inspection 69
Qualifying clubs 69
Qualifying club activities 70
Sales to a guest 71
Test of good faith 72
Determination of application 72
Conditions 73
Form of club premises certificate 74
Duty to keep and produce certificate 74
Duration 75

Variation   75
Review of the club premises certificate   76
Powers of entry   78
Industrial and provident societies, miners'
    welfare institutes and friendly societies   79

Chapter 9   **TEMPORARY EVENTS**
Introduction   81
Permitted temporary activities   82
Temporary event notice   82
Restrictions on the use of premises for
    temporary events   84
Objections to temporary event notices   85
Control of temporary events   87

Chapter 10   **PERSONAL LICENCES**
Introduction   89
Application for a personal licence   91
Determination of application   91
Qualifications   93
Form of personal licence   93
Duration   94
Renewal   94
Determination of application for renewal   95
Convictions   96
Powers of the criminal courts upon conviction   97
Duties of the licensing authority   97
Surrender of a personal licence   98

Chapter 11   **OFFENCES**
Introduction   99
Bodies corporate and associations   101
Unauthorised licensable activities   101
Unauthorised sale of alcohol   102
Drunkenness and disorderly conduct   103
Smuggled goods   104
Children and alcohol   105
Unaccompanied children prohibited from
    certain premises   107
Confiscated of alcohol by constables   108
Vehicles and trains   109
False statements   109

Chapter 12   **CLOSURE OF PREMISES**
Introduction   111
General closure orders   111
Specific closure orders   113
    Decision making by police   113
Extension of closure orders   114

Cancellation of a closure order 115
Powers of the magistrates' court 115
Review by the licensing authority 117
Exemption of the police from liability for
   damages 119

Chapter 13 **HEARINGS**
Introduction 121
Rules and regulations 122
Bias 123
Right to a fair hearing 124
Discretion 127
Guidance 128
Representations by interested parties 130
Admission of the public and provision of
   information 131

Chapter 14 **APPEALS**
Introduction 133
Powers of magistrates courts 134
Premises licence 137
Club premises certificate 139
Temporary event notice 139
Personal licence 140
Review following closure order 141

Chapter 15 **TRANSITIONAL PROVISIONS**
Introduction 143
Conversion of existing licences 144
   Permitted hours 148
   Provisional grants 148
Club certificates 149
Personal licences 150
Miscellaneous provisions 152

Appendix **LICENSING ACT 2003** 153

Index 347

TABLE OF CASES

References are to paragraph numbers.

A-G v Barker [2000] 1 FLR 759, (2000) 97(10) LSG 37; *sub nom* A-G v
    B [2000] Fam Law 400, QBD   13.7.4
A-G v PYA Quarries Ltd [1957] 2 QB 169, [1957] 2 WLR 770; *sub*
    nom A-G (on the relation of Glamorgan County Council and
    Pontardawe RDC) v PYA Quarries Ltd [1957] 1 All ER 894, CA   3.2.6
Adams v Licensing Division No 3 of the South Lanarkshire Council
    [2002] LLR 271   13.4.7
Anisminic v Foreign Compensation Commission [1969] 2 AC 147,
    [1969] 2 WLR 163, [1969] 1 All ER 208, HL   13.5.1
Associated Provincial Picture Houses Ltd v Wednesbury Corporation
    [1948] 1 KB 223, [1948] LJR 190, [1947] 2 All ER 680, CA   13.5.2

Barclay v Renfrewshire Council [2002] LLR 603   15.1.3
Boddington v British Transport Police [1998] 2 WLR 639, [1998] 2
    All ER 203, (1998) 162 JP 455, HL   6.6.4
Breen v Amalgamated Engineering Union [1971] 2 QB 175, [1971] 2
    WLR 742; *sub nom* Breen v Amalgamated Engineering Union
    (now Amalgamated Engineering and Foundry Workers Union)
    [1971] 1 All ER 1148, CA   13.4.5

Camec (Scotland) Ltd v City of Glasgow Licensing Board and Others
    [2003] LLR 389, 2002 GWD 33-1097, Sh Ct (Glasgow)   14.2.8
Catscratch Ltd and Lettuce Holdings Ltd v City of Glasgow Licensing
    Board [2001] LLR 610, 2001 SLT 344, Ct of Sess   13.4.8
Chief Constable of Derbyshire v Goodman and Newton [2001] LLR
    127   14.2.9
Chief Constable of West Midlands Police v Coventry Crown Court
    and Tubman [2001] LLR 144   14.2.9
City of Bradford Metropolitan District Council v Booth [2001] LLR
    151   14.2.9
Collins v Lane, Cornish and Worcester Norton Sports Club Ltd
    [2003] LLR 19   11.2.4
Crompton (T/A David Crompton Haulage) v Department of
    Transport North Western Area [2003] EWCA Civ 64, [2003]
    LLR 237, [2003] TLR 62, (2003) *The Times*, February 7, CA   13.4.7

Di Ciacca v Scottish Ministers [2003] LLR 426   13.4.8

English v Emery Reimbold & Strick Ltd [2002] EWCA Civ 605,
    [2002] 1 WLR 2409, [2002] 3 All ER 385   14.2.8, 15.4.7

Fleury and Others v Westminster City Council [2003] EWCA Civ
    1007, [2003] LLR 456, CA   14.1.5

Garrett v Middlesex Justices (1884) 12 QBD 620   12.6.10
Green v Inner London Licensing Justices (1994) *Licensing Review*
    (October)   7.23.3

Howker v Robinson [1973] QB 178, [1972] 3 WLR 234, [1972] 2 All
    ER 786, DC   11.3.4

McInnes v Onslow-Fane [1978] 1 WLR 1520, [1978] 3 All ER 211,
    (1978) 122 SJ 844   13.4.7
McCool v Rushcliffe Borough Council [1998] 3 All ER 889, (1998)
    162 JPN 883, QBD   13.6.7
Michael v Gowland [1977] 1 WLR 296, [1977] 2 All ER 328, (1976)
    Fam Law 109, DC   14.1.6

R v Andover Justices (1886) 16 QBD 71   12.6.10
R v Barnsley Metropolitan Borough Council ex parte Hook [1976] 1
    WLR 1052, [1976] 3 All ER 452, 120 SJ 182, CA   13.4.7
R v Birmingham City Council and Others ex parte Quietlynn Ltd
    [1985] 83 LGR 461   13.4.10
R v Chester City Council and Others ex parte Quietlynn Ltd (1983)
    The Times, October 19   13.1.5
R v Chester Crown Court ex parte Pascoe and Jones (1987) 151 JP
    752, (1987) 151 JPN 574, DC   6.7.1, 13.5.5
R v Diggines ex parte Rahmani [1985] QB 1109, [1985] 2 WLR 611,
    [1985] 1 All ER 1073, CA   13.4.10
R v Essex Quarter Sessions ex parte Thomas [1966] 1 WLR 359,
    [1966] 1 All ER 353, 130 JP 121, DC   14.2.3
R v Gloucester Crown Court ex parte Warner; sub nom R v Licensing
    Justices for Gloucester ex parte Warner [2001] LLR 687, [1999]
    COD 90, QBD   14.2.8
R v Greater London Council ex parte The Rank Organisation [1982]
    LS Gaz R 643, (1982) *The Times*, February 18, DC   13.4.11
R v Hastings Magistrates' Court ex parte McSpirit (1994) 162 JP 44,
    (1994) *The Times*, June 23   10.3.4
R v Hereford Magistrates' Court ex parte Rowlands; R v Hereford
    Magistrates' Court ex parte Ingram; R v Harrow Youth Court ex
    parte Prussia [1998] QB 110, [1997] 2 WLR 884, [1997] 2 Cr
    App R 340, QBD   14.2.6
R v Huntingdon District Council ex parte Cowan [1984] 1 WLR 501,
    [1984] 1 All ER 58, (1984) 82 LGR 342, DC   13.4.10
R v Knightsbridge Crown Court ex parte Aspinall Curzon Ltd (1982)
    The Times, December 16, DC   14.2.3

R v Liverpool Corporation ex parte Liverpool Taxi Fleet Operators'
  Association [1975] 2 QB 299, [1972] 2 WLR 1262; *sub nom*
  Liverpool Taxi Fleet Operators' Association, Re [1972] 2 All ER
  589, CA   13.4.9
R v Liverpool Crown Court ex parte Goodwin [2002] LLR 698   7.23.3
R v London County Council, ex parte Akkersdyk, ex parte Fermenia
  [1892] 1 QB 190, 56 JP 8, [1891-4] All ER Rep 509, DC   13.3.5, 13.4.1
R v Merthyr Tydfil Crown Court ex parte Chief Constable of Dyfed
  Powys Police [2001] LLR 133, (1998) 95(46) LSG 35, (1998) 142
  SJLB 284, QBD   14.2.9
R v North West Suffolk (Mildenhall) Magistrates ex parte Forest
  Heath District Council; *sub nom* R v Mildenhall Magistrates ex
  parte Forest Heath District Council [1997] COD 352, (1997) 161
  JP 401, (1997) *The Times*, May 16, CA   13.7.5
R v Ruffel (David Ian) (1992) 13 Cr App R (S) 204, CA   3.2.6
R v Sheffield Crown Court ex parte Consterdine (1998) 34 *Licensing
  Review* 19, [2002] LLR 712   6.7.1
R v Somerset County Council ex parte Fewings [1995] 1 WLR 1037,
  [1995] 3 All ER 20, (1995) 7 Admin LR 761, CA   13.5.4
R v Stafford Crown Court ex parte Wilf Gilbert (Staffordshire) Ltd;
  sub nom R v Stafford Crown Court ex parte Wilf Gilbert (Staffs)
  Ltd [1999] 2 All ER 955, [2001] LLR 138, [1999] COD 262,
  QBD   14.2.9
R v Teeside Crown Court ex parte Ellwood (1990) 154 JP 496   14.2.8
R v Torquay Licensing Justices ex parte Brockman [1951] 2 KB 784,
  [1951] 2 All ER 656, 115 JP 514, DC   6.7.1
R v Totnes Licensing Justices ex parte Chief Constable of Devon and
  Cornwall (1990) 156 JP 587, [1990] COD 404, (1992) 156 JPN
  538   14.2.9
R v Windsor Licensing Justices ex parte Hodes [1983] 1 WLR 685,
  [1983] 2 All ER 551, (1983) 187 JP 353, CA   13.4.7
R v Winson [1969] 1 QB 371, [1968] 2 WLR 113, [1968] 1 All ER
  197, CA   11.3.4
R (Alconbury Developments Ltd and Others) v Secretary of State for
  the Environment, Transport and the Regions [2001] UKHL 23,
  [2002] 2 WLR 1389   13.4.3
R (Chattington) v Chief Constable of South Wales and Others
  [2001] EWHC Admin 887, [2003] LLR 298   6.3.8
R (Chief Constable of Lancashire) v Preston Crown Court and
  Gosling [2001] EWHC Admin 928, [2002] LLR 14   14.2.3
R (Crew) (Chief Constable of the West Midlands Police) v
  Birmingham Licensing Justices [2001] EWHC Admin 1113,
  [2002] LLR 293   13.6.7
R (Cunningham) v Exeter Crown Court [2003] EWHC 184 (Admin),
  [2003] LLR 325, [2003] TLR 44, (2003) *The Times*, January 30,
  QBD   14.2.9
R (Grundy and Co) v Halton Magistrates' Court [2003] EWHC 272
  (Admin), [2003] LLR 335   11.1.10
R (Spearing) v London Borough of Hammersmith and Fulham and
  Ablethird Ltd [2001] EWHC Admin 1109, [2002] LLR 401   13.4.4

R (Westminster City Council) v Middlesex Crown Court and Chorion
     plc [2002] EWHC 1104 (Admin), [2002] LLR 538   6.7.1, 6.7.3, 13.5.5,
                                                                    14.2.2
Rushmoor Borough Council v Richards (1996) 160 LG Rev 460,
     [1996] COD 313, (1996) *The Times*, February 5, QBD   14.2.7

Sagnata Investments Ltd v Norwich Corporation [1971] 2 QB 614,
     [1971] 3 WLR 133, [1971] 2 All ER 1441, CA   13.5.5, 14.2.3
Secretary of State for Education v Tameside Metropolitan Borough
     Council [1977] AC 1014, [1976] 3 WLR 641; *sub nom* Secretary
     of State for Education v Metropolitan Borough of Tameside
     [1976] 3 All ER 665, HL   13.5.3
Sharp v Wakefield [1891] AC 173, 55 JP 197, 39 WR 561, [1886–90]
     All ER Rep 651, HL   13.4.1
Sheldrake v DPP [2003] EWHC 273 (Admin), [2003] TLR 107,
     (2003) *The Times*, February 25, QBD   11.1.10
Southwark London Borough Council v Allied Domecq Leisure Ltd
     (1998) 162 JP 1010, [1999] EHLR 231, (1998) *The Independent*,
     November 30, QBD   11.3.4
Sporrong and Lonroth v Sweden (1983) 5 EHRR 35, ECHR   12.6.8, 13.4.7
Stepney Borough Council v Joffe; Same v Diamond; Same v White
     [1949] 1 KB 599, [1949] LJR 561, 113 JP 124, DC   14.2.3

Tehrani v Rostron [1972] 1 QB 182, [1971] 3 WLR 612, 115 SJ 641,
     CA   14.1.5
Tre Traktorer AB v Sweden (1991) 13 EHRR 309   12.6.8, 13.4.7
Tudor v Ellesmere Port and Neston Borough Council (1987) *The
     Times*, May 8   13.4.10

Westminster City Council v Lunepalm (1985) *The Times*, December
     10   14.1.5
Westminster City Council v National Asylum Service [2002] UKHL
     38   *preface*
Westminster City Council v Zestfair (1989) 153 JP 613, 88 LGR 288,
     (1989) 133 SJ 1262   14.2.7
William Hill (Caledonia) Ltd v City of Glasgow Licensing Board and
     Ladbrokes Ltd [2003] LLR 549, 2003 GWD 9-241   14.2.8

TABLE OF STATUTES

References are to paragraph numbers.

Alehouse Act 1828	1.2.2
Betting Gaming and Lotteries Act 1963	4.1.3
Cinematograph Act 1909	1.3.4
Cinematograph Act 1952	1.3.4
Cinematograph (Amendment) Act 1982	1.3.4
Cinemas Act 1985	1.3.4, 4.1.2, 15.2.1, 15.5.4
s 3(1A)	2.1.7
s 9	2.1.7
s 17	2.1.7
s 18	2.1.7
Civic Government Scotland Act 1982	15.1.3
Confiscation of Alcohol (Young Persons) Act 1997	1.2.14, 11.9.1
Criminal Justice and Police Act 2001	12.1.1
Deregulation and Contracting Out Act 1994	1.2.14
Disorderly Houses Act 1751	1.3.1
Finance Act 1967	1.2.11
Finance Act 1995	15.5.2
Fire Precautions Act 1971	7.24.5
Gaming Act 1968	4.1.3
Greater London Council (General Powers) Act 1966	4.7.3
Pt IV	2.1.7

Greater London Council (General Powers) Act 1986	4.1.3
Greater London Government Act 1968	4.1.2
Greater London Government Act 1976	4.1.2
Greater London Government Act 1978	4.1.2
Greater London Government Act 1979	4.1.2
Greater London Government Act 1982	4.1.2
Greater London Government Act 1986	4.1.2
Human Rights Act 1998	14.2.8
s 3(1)	11.1.9
s 6(1)	12.8.3
Hypnotism Act 1952	4.5.5
Late Night Refreshment Houses Act 1969	1.3.5, 2.1.7, 4.1.2, 15.2.1
Licensing Act 1872	1.2.4, 1.2.5
Licensing Act 1902	1.2.6
Licensing Act 1961	1.2.9
Licensing Act 1964	1.2.10, 2.1.7, 4.1.2
Pt I	15.1.5, 15.4.1
Pt 2	15.3.1
s 6	15.2.18
s 21	14.1.5
s 23	14.1.5
s 66	2.3.14
s 67	2.3.14
ss 179A–179K	12.1.1
s 182	7.24.1, 13.5.6, 13.6.1, 13.6.2
s 188	12.1.1

Licensing Act 1964 – *cont*		s 8(1)	5.5.1
s 199(c)	15.2.1	(2)	5.5.2
Sch 8	2.3.14	(3)–(5)	5.5.3
Licensing Act 2003	1.3.8, 2.1.2,	(6), (7)	5.5.6
	2.1.3, 2.1.4, 2.1.5, 2.3,	s 9	5.6.1, 13.1.4
	2.3.15, 2.3.21, 3.1.5,	(1)	5.4.1
	3.2.5, 4.1.1, 4.1.3, 4.1.7,	(2)	13.8.1
	4.4.2, 4.4.3, 4.5.3, 4.5.4,	(3)	5.6.2, 7.23.3, 13.1.4
	4.5.6, 5.1.1, 5.2.1, 5.2.2,	(4)	7.23.3
	5.3.6, 6.1.2, 6.3.7, 6.6.4,	(4A)	7.23.3
	6.6.5, 6.7.2, 6.7.3, 7.5.1,	(4B)	7.23.3
	7.5.2, 7.6.5, 7.6.8, 7.6.17,	s 10(1)	5.4.1
	7.9.1, 7.11.5, 7.21.3,	(3)	5.4.1
	7.21.8, 7.22.1, 7.24.6,	(4)	5.4.2, 5.4.4
	8.1.4, 8.7.3, 8.10.1, 9.3.5,	(b)–(d)	5.4.3
	9.6.2, 10.1.1, 11.1.2,	(5)	5.4.1
	11.4.2, 11.4.3, 11.5.1,	s 11	7.1.4, 15.2.13
	12.3.3, 13.1.4, 13.4.6,	s 12	7.2.1, 7.5.4
	13.4.9, 13.4.10, 13.5.4,	s 13	7.22.3, 13.4.9
	13.6.1, 13.6.7, 13.7.3,	(2)	11.1.3
	13.8.3, 14.1.1, 14.1.3,	(3)	7.11.2, 8.10.2, 13.7.1
	14.1.4, 14.1.6, 14.2.4,	(4)	7.5.6, 8.10.2
	14.2.8, 14.2.10, 15.1.7,	s 16	7.4.1, 7.4.2
	15.1.8, 15.2.4, 15.2.18,	s 17	7.5.4
	15.5.2	(4)	7.6.6
Pt 1	14.3.2	s 18	7.5.3, 7.11.1
Pt 2	14.4.2	(1), (2)	7.10.1
Pt 3	2.3.1	(3)	7.10.2
Pt 4	8.1.5, 8.1.6	(b)	7.13.5, 7.14.2
Pt 5	2.3.8, 9.1.4, 9.2.1	(4)	7.10.4
Pt 6	2.3.11, 14.6.4	(6), (7)	7.11.1
Pt 7	2.3.19, 11.1.1	(8)	7.11.4
Pt 8	2.3.12, 9.6.6, 12.1.1	(9)(b)	7.11.6
s 1(1)	4.2.1	(10)	7.12.1
(2)	8.4.1	s 19	7.10.1, 7.12.2, 10.1.2, 12.7.5,
s 3(1)	5.1.1		15.2.13
(f), (g)	5.1.2	s 20	7.10.1, 7.12.3, 12.7.5, 15.2.13
s 4	2.3.6, 3.1.1, 3.1.3, 5.2.1, 5.2.3	s 21	7.10.1, 7.12.4, 15.2.13
(1)	3.1.3, 5.2.1	(2)	7.12.4
(3)	5.2.2, 13.6.2	s 22	7.12.7
s 5	3.2.2, 5.2.3, 6.1.1, 13.6.2	s 23	5.5.4
(1)	6.1.1, 6.2.1	(2)	7.14.2
(2)	6.2.1	(3)	7.14.3
(3)	6.3.1	s 24	7.15.1
(6)	6.4.1	s 27	7.16.2
(7)	6.5.1	s 28	7.16.4
s 6(1)	5.3.1	ss 29–32	7.13.6
s 7(1)	5.3.2	s 29	7.13.1, 7.13.3
(3)–(7)	5.3.3	s 32	7.13.4
(9)	5.3.4	s 33	7.15.3

Licensing Act 2003 – *cont*		s 74	15.3.8
ss 34–39	15.2.14	s 75	8.6.5, 15.3.8
s 34	7.17.1	s 76	8.6.5
s 35(1), (2)	7.17.2	s 77	5.5.4, 8.6.6
(4)	7.17.4	s 78	8.7.1
s 36(5)	7.17.6	s 80	8.8.1
(6), (7)	7.17.7	s 81	8.8.2
s 37(5)	7.18.2	s 82	8.7.4
s 38	7.18.3	s 83	8.7.4
s 39	7.18.2	ss 84–86	15.3.9
s 40	7.18.4	s 84	8.9.1
s 41	7.19.1	s 85	8.9.4
s 42	7.16.5, 7.20.1	(2)	8.9.4
(6), (7)	7.20.2	(6)	8.9.3
s 43	7.16.5	s 86	8.9.5
s 44	7.20.3	(2)	8.9.5
(5)	7.20.4	s 87	8.10.2
s 46	7.20.6	s 88	8.10.5
s 47	7.16.6, 7.20.10	(3)	8.10.7
s 48(1)	7.16.8	(4)	8.10.7
s 49	7.16.7	(6)	8.10.7
s 50	7.16.5, 7.20.10	(7), (8)	8.10.6
s 51	7.21.4	(10)	8.10.8
(4)	7.21.6	(11)	8.10.9
(5)	7.21.7	s 89	8.10.10
s 52	7.21.9	s 90	8.4.8
(7), (8)	5.4.3	(2)	8.3.1, 8.4.8
(10)	7.21.11	s 93	3.2.5, 5.5.5
s 53	7.21.14, 13.4.3	s 94	8.7.5, 8.7.6
s 55(2)	7.9.1	s 96	8.2.5, 8.11.2
s 56	5.5.5	(1)	8.11.2
s 57	7.15.4	s 97	8.11.1
(4)	7.15.5	s 98	9.2.1
s 59	7.22.2	s 100	9.2.1
s 60	8.1.6, 15.1.4, 15.3.1	(1)	9.3.1
s 62	4.7.1, 8.3.1, 8.4.5	(2), (3)	9.3.2
s 63	8.5.1	(4), (5)	9.3.3
(3)	8.5.2	(6)	9.3.4
s 64	8.3.2	(7)	9.3.6
s 65	8.12.1	s 101(1)	9.4.1
s 66	8.12.1	(2)(b)	9.4.3
s 68	8.2.1, 8.4.5	(d)	9.4.2
s 70	4.3.4	(3), (4)	9.4.3
s 71(1)	8.2.1	s 102	9.5.1
s 72(1), (2)	8.6.1	s 103	9.3.8
(3)	8.6.2	s 104	9.3.7, 9.5.2
(4)	8.6.4	s 105(2)	9.5.3
(8), (9)	8.6.3	(3)	9.5.4
(10)	8.6.5	(5)	9.5.5
s 73	8.4.3, 8.4.4, 15.3.8	s 106	9.5.6

Licensing Act 2003 – *cont*

s 106(5)	9.5.7
s 107(1)	9.4.8
(2)	9.4.5
(3)	9.4.6
(4), (5)	9.4.4
(6)	9.4.7
(8)	9.4.8
s 108	9.6.1
s 109	9.6.3
(8)	9.6.4
s 110	9.6.5
s 111	10.2.2
(2)	10.2.3
s 113	10.3.3
s 114	10.3.4
s 115(1)	10.6.1
(2)	10.6.2
s 116	10.12.1
(3)	10.12.2
s 117	10.1.5, 10.2.1, 15.4.2
(2)	10.2.4
(3)	10.7.1
(4)	10.7.2
(6)	10.7.3
s 118	10.2.5
s 119	10.6.3, 10.7.4
s 120	10.3.1, 10.4.1, 15.4.3
(3)	10.3.2
(4)	10.3.2, 10.3.6
(5), (6)	10.3.6
(7)	10.3.7
(8)	10.4.1
s 121	10.11.1
(2)	10.8.2, 10.8.3, 10.8.4
(4)	10.8.3
(5), (6)	10.8.4
s 122	10.8.5, 15.4.7
(1), (2)	10.3.8
s 123	10.3.5
(1)	10.11.1
s 124	10.3.5, 10.8.3
(4)	10.11.1
s 125	10.3.8
(4)	10.5.1
s 126	10.5.2
s 127	10.5.3, 10.11.1
s 128	10.9.1, 10.9.4
(2)	10.9.2
(4), (5)	10.9.3

s 128(6)	10.9.4
s 129	10.10.1, 10.10.3, 14.6.4
(3)	10.10.1
(4), (5)	10.10.2
s 130	10.10.2, 14.6.4
s 131	10.10.3, 10.11.1
s 132	10.10.4, 10.11.1
s 133	10.2.1
s 134	5.5.5, 10.11.1
(4)	10.11.2
s 135	10.5.4
s 136(1)(a)	11.1.7, 11.3.1
(b)	11.3.3
(2)	11.3.2
s 137	11.1.7, 11.4.1
s 138	11.1.7, 11.4.3
s 139	11.1.7, 11.3.1
(1)	11.1.8
s 140	11.5.2
s 141	11.5.3
(3)	11.5.3
s 142	11.5.4
s 143	11.5.1, 11.5.5
(4)	11.5.6
s 144	11.6.1
s 145	11.8.1
(3)	11.8.3
(5)	11.8.4
(6)	11.8.5
(7)	11.8.6
s 146(1)	11.7.1
(2)	11.7.5
(4)	11.7.2
(5)	11.7.3
(6)	11.7.4
s 147	11.7.6
s 148	11.7.8
s 149(1)	11.7.9
(3)	11.7.10
(4)	11.7.11
(5)	11.7.11
(6)	11.7.12
s 150(1), (2)	11.7.14
s 151	11.7.15, 11.7.16
s 152	11.7.15, 11.7.17
s 153	11.7.15, 11.7.18
s 154	11.7.13
(2)	11.7.13
s 155	11.9.1
s 156	4.3.8, 11.10.1

Licensing Act 2003 – *cont*

s 157	11.10.3
s 158	11.11.1
s 159	11.7.19
s 160(1), (2)	12.2.1
(3)	12.2.2
(4), (5)	12.2.5
s 161(1)	12.3.2
(3)	12.3.4
(4)	12.3.5
(8)	12.6.6
ss 162–168	12.3.5
s 162	12.4.1
(4)	12.4.4
s 163(1)	12.5.1
(2)	12.5.2
(3)	12.5.3
s 164	12.6.1
s 165	14.1.3
(1)	12.6.2
(2)	12.6.3
(3)	12.6.4
(5)	12.6.6
(9)	12.6.7
s 166	12.6.10, 14.1.3
s 167(1)–(3)	12.7.2
(4)	12.7.3
(6)	12.7.5
(8)	12.7.5
(9), (10)	12.7.6
(12)	12.7.7
s 168(5)	12.7.8
(7)	12.7.8
(8), (9)	12.7.11
s 169	12.3.10
s 170	12.8.1
s 171(2)	12.3.8
(3)	12.3.9
(4)	12.3.8
(5)	12.3.6
s 173(1)(e)	5.1.2
s 175	4.3.6, 9.1.1
s 176	7.23.1
(2)	7.23.1, 7.23.2
(4)	7.23.2
s 177	7.24.3
(8)	7.24.5
s 178	7.20.8
s 179	11.1.3
s 180	11.1.4

s 181	6.7.3, 14.1.7
(2)	14.2.1, 14.2.9
s 182	3.1.1, 3.2.2, 5.2.2, 5.2.3, 6.1.1, 6.6.1
(3)	6.6.2
s 183	5.6.1, 13.1.4
(1)	13.2.1
(2)	13.2.2
s 184	9.3.5
s 185	13.8.3
s 186	11.1.5
s 187(1)	11.2.1
(4)	11.2.2
(6), (7)	11.2.3
s 188	11.2.5
(1)	11.2.4
s 189(1)	4.5.10
(2)	4.5.9
s 190	4.3.5, 11.1.6
s 191	4.3.1
s 192	4.3.2
s 193	4.3.8, 7.3.1, 8.4.5, 11.10.2, 15.1.6
s 195	5.1.2
s 196	5.1.2
s 199	2.3.14
s 200	15.1.1
Sch 1	4.4.1
Pt 1, para 1(5)	4.1.6
para 3	4.4.2
Sch 1, Pt 2	4.5.1
paras 5, 6	4.5.2
para 7	4.5.3
para 8	4.5.5
para 9	4.5.6
para 10	4.5.7
para 11	4.5.9
para 12	4.5.8
Sch 1, Pt 3	4.4.1
paras 14–18	4.4.1
Sch 2	4.6.1, 12.3.9
para 1(1)(a)	4.6.1
(b)	4.6.2
para 2	4.6.3
para 3(2)(a), (b)	4.7.1
(c)	4.7.2
(d)	4.7.2
(e)	4.7.1, 4.7.2
para 4	4.7.3
para 5	4.7.4

Licensing Act 2003 – *cont*	
Sch 3	5.5.1
Sch 4	10.3.1, 10.3.3, 10.8.2,
	10.8.4, 15.4.2, 15.4.3
Sch 5	14.1.7, 14.6.4, 15.4.8
Sch 5, Pt 1	14.3.1
Pt 2	14.4.1
paras 1–8	14.3.1
para 9(1), (2)	14.3.2
(3), (4)	14.3.3
paras 10–14	14.4.1
para 15	14.4.2
(3)	14.4.3
Pt 3, para 16	14.5.1
para 16	9.5.8
(6)	14.5.2
para 17	10.8.7
(2), (3)	14.6.2
(5)	14.6.2
(10)	14.6.3
Pt 3, para 18	14.6.1, 14.7.1
para 18(3)	12.7.10, 14.7.2
(4)	12.7.10
(6)	14.7.3
Sch 7	2.3.14
Sch 8	15.1.1, 15.2.9
Pt 1	15.1.2
Pt 1, para 1(1)	15.2.1
para 2	15.2.3
(5), (6)	15.2.5
para 3	15.2.7
(2), (3)	15.2.8
para 3(5)	15.2.7
para 4	15.2.11
(2)	15.2.12
(4)	15.2.12
(5)	15.2.10
para 5	15.2.11
(1)	15.2.12
para 6(5)–(7)	15.2.13
(9)	15.2.13
para 7	15.2.14
(2), (3)	15.2.14
para 9	15.2.15
(3)	15.2.15
para 11(1), (2)	15.2.16
(3)	15.2.17
para 12	15.2.18
Pt 2	15.1.4
para 13(1)	15.3.1
para 14	15.3.3

Sch 8, para 14(1), (2)	15.3.2
para 15	15.3.4
para 16	15.3.5
(2)	15.3.6
(4)	15.3.6
para 17	15.3.5, 15.3.8
para 18	15.3.8
para 19	15.3.9
para 20	15.3.7
para 21	15.3.5, 15.3.10
Pt 3	15.1.5, 15.4.1
para 23	15.4.1
(1)(c)	15.4.3
(3)	15.4.2
para 24	15.4.3
para 25	15.4.3
para 26	15.4.4, 15.4.7
(1)	15.4.5
(4)	15.4.6
(6)	15.4.7
para 27	15.4.8
para 29	15.5.1
para 30	15.5.2
paras 31, 32	15.5.3
para 33	15.5.4
Pt 4, para 29	6.3.3
Licensing (Amendment) Act 1980	1.2.12
Licensing (Consolidation) Act 1910	1.2.7
Licensing (Consolidation) Act 1953	1.2.8
Licensing (Occasional Permissions) Act 1983	2.1.7
Licensing (Young Persons) Act 2000	1.2.14
Local Government Act 1972	
s 94(1)	13.3.1
s 95(1)	13.3.1
(3)	13.3.2
s 97(4)–(6)	13.3.3
s 100	13.8.2
Sch 12A	13.8.2
Local Government (Access to Information) Act 1985	
s 1	13.8.2
Local Government (Miscellaneous Provisions) Act 1982	1.3.1, 1.3.5, 2.3.17, 4.1.2
Sch 1	2.1.7, 15.2.1
Sch 3	4.1.3

London Government Act
1963   4.1.2
Sch 12   1.3.1, 2.1.7, 15.2.1
    para 10(1)(a)   11.3.4
London Local Authorities
Act 1990   1.3.5
Pt 2   15.2.1
ss 4–17   2.1.7
s 19   2.1.7
s 20   2.1.7
London Local Authorities
Act 1995   4.7.3
Lotteries and Amusements
Act 1976   4.1.3
s 3(1)   9.1.1
s 22   4.5.7

Magistrates' Courts Act 1980
ss 11–114   14.1.6
Middlesex County Council
Act 1944   1.3.1

Police Act 1996   7.22.2, 9.6.2
Private Places of
Entertainment Act 1967   4.1.2
Private Places of
Entertainment
(Licensing) Act 1967   1.3.2, 2.1.7, 15.2.1
Public Bodies (Admission to
Meetings) Act 1960   13.8.2
Public Entertainments
Licenses (Drug Misuse)
Act 1997   2.1.7, 12.1.1, 12.1.3

Public Health Acts
Amendment Act 1890
Pt IV   1.3.1

Refreshment Houses Act
1860   1.3.5
Refreshment Houses Act
1964   1.3.5, 2.1.7, 4.1.2
Refreshment Houses Act
1967   1.3.5
Rehabilitation of Offenders
Act 1974   10.3.4

Sporting Events (Control of
Alcohol) Act 1985   4.1.2
Sunday Entertainment Act
1932   2.1.7
Sunday Observance Act 1780   2.1.7
Sunday Theatre Act 1972   2.1.7
Supreme Court Act 1981
s 18(1)(c)   14.1.5
s 28   14.1.5

Theatres Act 1843   1.3.8
Theatres Act 1968   1.3.8, 4.1.2, 15.2.1
s 15(6)   2.1.7
s 17   2.1.7

Video Recordings Act 1984   7.12.3

Wine and Beerhouses Act
1869   1.2.3

TABLE OF STATUTORY INSTRUMENTS, STATUTORY GUIDANCE ETC

References are to paragraph numbers.

Cinematograph (Safety) Regulations 1955, SI 1955/1129 .... 1.3.4
Cinematograph (Safety) Regulations 1965, SI 1965/282 .... 1.3.4
Cinematograph (Safety) (Amendment) Regulations 1982,
    SI 1982/1856 .... 1.3.4
Civil Procedure Rules 1998, SI 1998/3132
    Part 52 (Appeals) 14.1.6
    PD Appeals 14.1.6

D of E Circular 94/75 National Code of Local Government
    Conduct 13.3.4
Department of Culture Media and Sport Press Notice 091/03
    (31 July 2003) 10.1.4
Department of Culture Media and Sport Regulatory Impact
    Assessment 15 November 2002 .... 7.9.1

Guidance issued under the Provisions of LA 2003, s 182 .... 2.3.6, 3.2.4,
    5.2.2, 5.4.4, 6.1.2, 6.3.7, 6.6.1, 6.6.2, 6.6.4, 7.21.8, 13.5.6,
    13.6.2, 13.6.7
    foreword 3.1.1
    para 2.3 .... 13.6.2
    para 3.7 .... 6.3.4
    paras 3.12, 3.13 .... 2.3.6
    para 3.49 .... 5.4.4
    para 5.23 .... 13.4.9
    para 5.32 .... 7.6.5
    para 5.50 .... 7.5.1
    para 5.52 .... 13.6.3
    para 5.53 .... 13.6.4
    paras 5.55–5.57 .... 13.7.2
    para 5.57 .... 5.4.4, 13.7.6
    paras 5.78–5.80 .... 13.6.5
    paras 5.89, 5.90 .... 13.6.6
    Pt 6 .... 2.3.7
    Pt 7 .... 7.12.6, 13.6.4
    para 7.4 .... 7.6.3
    para 7.5 .... 7.12.5
    para 7.7 .... 7.6.9
    para 7.9 .... 7.6.12

Guidance issued under the Provisions of LA 2003, s 182 – *cont*
    para 10.7   6.7.4, 14.2.4
    para 10.8   6.3.7, 6.6.4, 6.7.4, 14.2.4
    Annexes D to H   7.12.6

Licensing Act 2003 (Commencement) Order 2003, SI 1911/2003   2.3.14

Magistrates' Courts Rules 1981, SI 1981/552   12.6.7
    rr 76–81   14.1.6

TABLE OF EUROPEAN MATERIAL

References are to paragraph numbers.

European Convention for the Protection of Human Rights and
    Fundamental Freedoms 1950   11.1.9, 12.6.8, 12.8.3, 13.1.3
    Art 6   13.4.2, 13.4.3, 15.4.7
        (1)   13.4.2, 13.4.3
    First Protocol, Art 1   12.6.8, 13.4.7, 13.4.8

Chapter 1

HISTORY AND BACKGROUND TO LICENSING LAW

'History, Karl Marx tells us, repeats itself, first as tragedy then as farce. It isn't necessary to be a Marxist to appreciate the truth of the observation. Supporting Manchester City leads to much the same conclusion.'

Colin Shindler
(*Father, Sons and Football*)

1.1 INTRODUCTION

1.1.1 The history of legislation to control the sale and supply of alcohol and the provision of public entertainment is long and convoluted. Uppermost in the minds of the legislators seem to have been the mixed purposes of quality control, price control, the need for a sober workforce and the prevention of public disorder (which included immorality). From the second half of the seventeenth century can be added the raising of revenue through taxation.

1.2 SALE AND SUPPLY OF ALCOHOL

1.2.1 At first beer was taxed but spirits were not. The consequent surge in the sale of spirits and all-round drunkenness led to the imposition of high duties on spirits and the requirement that retailers and premises be licensed. In turn these high duties led to illegal sales from unlicensed premises. The powers and discretion afforded to local justices were increased and licence fees reduced. The concept of controlling supply to meet demand was introduced but failure to enforce the various laws led to even greater numbers of taverns and gin houses. It was not until 1787, when the Home Secretary circulated a Royal Proclamation on vice and immorality, which led to the closure of public houses on a wide scale without compensation on the grounds that they were disorderly, or ill-constructed, or improperly situated, or superfluous, that the authorities began to regain control.

1.2.2 In 1828 the first of the modern Acts, the Alehouse Act 1828, regularised the proceedings before justices bringing in powers of grant, transfer and renewal of licences on an annual basis. The General Annual Licensing Meeting – the Brewster Sessions – became the focus of attention on the need for premises on which alcohol was consumed to have a premises licence to go with the excise licence for the retail sale of the alcohol. No more than eight nor fewer than four special sessions were to be held during the year for the purpose of transferring licences. Conditions were imposed upon the holders of justices' licences to prevent drunkenness or disorderly conduct, unlawful games and the use of the premises by persons of bad character. In 1842 the power to grant temporary licences or 'protection orders' was given.

1.2.3 Off-licences, that is licences for the sale of alcohol for consumption away from the premises of the retailer, came into being through a series of Acts dealing with beerhouses, refreshment houses and shops selling bottled foreign wines. At the time, the retailer of alcohol for consumption off the premises needed only an excise licence and it was not until the Wine and Beerhouses Act 1869 that, in effect, all retail sales came under the control of the local justices.

1.2.4 In 1872 the Licensing Act introduced more uniformity including standard forms of application, the removal of licences from one part of the district to another, and the replacement of conditions on licences by statutory offences. Since that time the basic principles governing the licensing of the sale and supply of alcohol have changed very little.

1.2.5 In 1872 it was made illegal to sell spirits to children under the age of 16 years. In 1886 the sale of any alcoholic drink for consumption by a child under 13 years in licensed premises was forbidden. In 1901 the sale of any alcohol to children under 14 was prohibited and the present age limit of 18 years was introduced in 1923.

1.2.6 The Licensing Act 1902 gave powers to the police to arrest a person found drunk in a public place or on licensed premises, or in charge of a child under 7 years of age. The sale of alcohol to habitual drunkards was forbidden. Any conviction of a licensee was to be entered in the licensing register and the 'off-licence' as such was introduced giving justices a very wide discretion to grant or refuse. The structure of licensed premises was brought within the justices' jurisdiction, with their consent being required for structural alterations of certain kinds. For all new premises, a plan had to be deposited and approved.

1.2.7 The Licensing (Consolidation) Act 1910, as its name implies, was a consolidating measure bringing together and repealing most of the previous legislation. During the First World War various emergency statutes controlled drinking hours. These were replaced in 1921 by the introduction of permitted hours across the country. At that time only 9 drinking hours per day were allowed outside London (which had an extra hour). Those hours had to be fixed between 11 am and 10 pm (11 pm in London) and there had to be a 2-hour break in the afternoon. On Sundays only 5 hours were permitted, whilst Wales and Monmouthshire were 'dry'. Sales on credit were also prohibited, unless alcohol was bought with a meal. To the surprise of many, that restriction remains in force today.

1.2.8　A further consolidating Act was passed in 1953. Several minor amendments were made and, in particular, the provisions governing appeal to Quarter Sessions were brought into line with those governing magistrates' courts. Persons under the age of 18 years were no longer allowed to be employed in bars.

1.2.9　New legislation was introduced in the Licensing Acts of 1955 and 1961. Restaurant, residential and the combined restaurant and residential licences were introduced, with provisions which limited the powers of the justices to refuse an application. Clubs wishing to supply alcohol to their members now had to apply to the magistrates' court for a certificate of registration. Qualification limited such clubs to those of a bona fide nature. The operators of many previous 'clubs' had to apply for a justices' licence. People were allowed to vote in Wales and Monmouthshire as to the continuation of 'dry' Sundays. A new activity provided by the Act was 'drinking up' time – then only 10 minutes – and 'special hours' were introduced allowing late night drinking in restaurants and clubs providing music, singing and dancing.

1.2.10　The current Act, the Licensing Act 1964, was a consolidating measure, bringing together the various statutes controlling the sale and supply of intoxicating liquor.

1.2.11　The Finance Act 1967 removed the requirement for an excise licence for retail sales or supply to club members. An excise licence is still required for wholesale supplies but wholesalers do not need a justices' licence.

1.2.12　In 1980 the courts were empowered to order the exclusion of certain categories of convicted persons from licensed premises. The Licensing (Amendment) Act 1980 enabled the justices to limit the opening hours permitted under a special hours certificate in order to prevent disorder or the disturbance of residents.

1.2.13　In 1983 justices were given the power to grant occasional permissions (as opposed to occasional licences which could only be granted to an existing licensee) to persons organising certain classes of function for charitable or similar purposes. In 1985 new laws were introduced to prevent or control the sale of alcohol to football supporters attending designated sports grounds. All-day opening was allowed in 1988 by the abolition of the afternoon break, and since 2000 licensed premises have been allowed to remain open for 36 hours over the New Year and for the Queen's Jubilee celebrations.

1.2.14　Following the Deregulation and Contracting Out Act 1994 several measures have been introduced in a piecemeal fashion to overcome problems created by tensions between fundamentally nineteenth century legislation and late twentieth century leisure activities. Still traditional legislation was needed to overcome difficulties in prosecuting those who allowed the sale of alcohol to young persons and who bought alcohol for persons under 18 for consumption off the premises.[1]

1.3   PROVISION OF PUBLIC ENTERTAINMENT

1.3.1   The control of music and dancing was transferred from local justices to local authorities by the Local Government (Miscellaneous Provisions) Act 1982. It did not apply to Greater London, however. Prior to the 1982 Act, outside London the control of music, singing and dancing, through the issue of licences, rested with the local justices but only if the provisions of the Public Health Acts Amendment Act 1890, Part IV had been adopted by the local authority. There had been, therefore, a patchwork quilt of controls across the country. In London such activities as music and dancing had been controlled by the local authorities through the Disorderly Houses Act 1751 and the Middlesex County Council Act 1944 before their repeal and consolidation within the London Government Act 1963, Sch 12. The codes under the Local Government (Miscellaneous Provisions) Act 1982 and the London Government Act 1963 were similar but not identical.

1.3.2   The Private Places of Entertainment (Licensing) Act 1967 gave the power to local authorities to apply to their area provisions for the control by licensing of premises used for entertainment promoted for private gain, but escaping the existing music and dancing legislation because the entertainment was not open to the public. Again many local authorities did not adopt the provisions.

1.3.3   The Theatres Act 1968 repealed the Theatres Act 1843 and abolished the censorship of theatres by the Lord Chamberlain. Licensing control over theatres was given to the local authorities, and the censorship was replaced by provisions preventing obscene performances analogous to those relating to the publication of books and by other measures for the control of performances by the courts, instead of by local administrative or executive action.

1.3.4   Control of cinemas was first introduced in 1909 because of the danger to the public caused by highly inflammable celluloid film catching fire. The provisions of the Cinematograph Act 1909 were extended to non-inflammable and cinematograph exhibitions and television (involving the projection of light) by the Cinematograph Act 1952. Those Acts were further amended and extended by the Cinematograph Act 1982 and in turn consolidated within the Cinemas Act 1985. The licensing authority was the local authority and there had to be strict compliance with the Cinematograph (Safety) Regulations of 1955, 1965 and 1982. The requirement for a licence

---

[1]   The Confiscation of Alcohol (Young Persons) Act 1997 and the Licensing (Young Persons) Act 2000.

under the Cinemas Act 1985 did not apply to the simultaneous reception and exhibition of a television broadcast.

1.3.5   Places that provided late night refreshments were also subject to different controls depending upon their location. In London, save for the borough of Merton and the City of London, the sale of meals and refreshments for consumption both on and off the premises after 11 pm was controlled under the provisions of the London Local Authorities Act 1990. Outside London the Late Night Refreshment Houses Act 1969, which consolidated the provisions relating to refreshment houses outstanding from the 1860, 1964 and 1967 Acts, applied but only to premises selling such refreshments after 10 pm for consumption on the premises. Takeaways (premises selling food for consumption off the premises) could be the subject of a closure order under the Local Government (Miscellaneous Provisions) Act 1982 to prevent the unreasonable disturbance of residents in the neighbourhood, but were not licensable. None of these provisions applied to the mobile hot-dog stall or burger van that operated in the street.

1.3.6   Having pledged to reform the 'antiquated' licensing laws, the Labour Government published a White Paper in April 2000, *Time for Reform: Proposals for the Modernisation of Our Licensing Laws*.[2] In the foreword, Jack Straw, the Home Secretary, wrote:

> 'The current alcohol licensing system is an amalgam of 19th century legislation, intended to suppress drunkenness and disorder, and later additions. The law is complex, and involves a great deal of unnecessary red tape for business. We owe the magistrates and police a large debt of gratitude for doing their best to make the system work; but it has been impossible to prevent inconsistencies and arbitrary decisions from arising. At the same time, there are too few effective sanctions against premises attracting trouble. The rules governing the admission of children to licensed premises are obscure and deeply confusing. The controls on under-age "off sales" are inadequate. It is also difficult to find in the present arrangements for licensing the sale of alcohol any real accountability to local residents whose lives are fundamentally affected by the decisions taken. The time has come to develop a better system.'

1.3.7   In bringing forward new legislation, the Government's aim, whilst relaxing the burdens on the industry, was said to be:

> '... to bring about reform which assures the safety of the public, better protects children and safeguards all against crime, disorder and disturbance; the decisions we make on these issues will in turn help to shape the future of our villages, towns and cities.'

1.3.8   What was proposed, and what the new Licensing Act 2003 (LA 2003) seeks to impose, is a new system for licensing and controlling the sale and supply of alcohol, the provision of all forms of public

---

[2]   Cm 4696.

entertainment and the provision of refreshment late at night where alcohol may not be involved. The greater freedom and flexibility provided to the hospitality and leisure industry was to be offset, or balanced, by tougher powers for the police, the courts and licensing authorities to deal in an uncompromising way with anyone trying to exploit the greater freedoms against the interests of the public in general.

Chapter 2

HOW THINGS WILL CHANGE

'The past is a foreign country; they do things differently there.'

LP Hartley
(*The Go-Between*)

2.1 INTRODUCTION

2.1.1 When introducing the Licensing Bill 2002 to the House of Lords, Baroness Blackstone, the Minister of State at the Department for Culture, Media and Sport, said:[1]

'Citizens of and visitors to this country want greater flexibility to be able to enjoy a drink or a meal at a time they choose. More than 90 per cent of men and 85 per cent of women enjoy alcoholic drinks. The vast majority behave responsibly. If they want to go for a drink after watching a film or a play at 11 pm they should have that option. This Bill will deliver greater choice for customers, those with families in particular. It will make our country more attractive to tourists and our great cities better able to compete for international events with cities such as Berlin, Rome and Tokyo. It will also remove perverse influences on drinking culture, such as fixed, artificially early closing times that can lead to problems of violence and binge drinking.

At the same time we recognise that issues of public disorder and anti-social behaviour have always arisen when large groups of people gather for popular pastimes, especially late at night. The Bill's aim to provide greater choice is tempered by its provision of strengthened protection. Modern laws are required to ensure that people may enjoy their leisure time while being adequately protected, without fear of violence, intimidation or disorder. The Bill provides measures to deliver strengthened public protection and complements other schemes across central Government and the public and private sectors.

The current system for the licensing of alcohol, public entertainment and late-night refreshment in England and Wales is an outdated amalgamation of legislation dating back centuries. It is complex, difficult and contains much unnecessary red tape. The Bill represents the first wholesale reform of the licensing regime for 40 years. It will benefit business across the piece, from restaurants and cafes, traditional pubs and clubs to theatres and cinemas. It will make it easier for

---

[1] *Hansard*, HL Deb, vol 641, col 640 (26 November 2002).

operators to provide a wide range of leisure options within a single premises.'

2.1.2   In her foreword to the Guidance issued to local authorities, Tessa Jowell, the Secretary of State for Culture, Media and Sport, said:

> 'The Licensing Act 2003 marks the end of the existing outdated licensing regimes. The legislation reflects that the activities it covers are to be carried on in a modern, vibrant society that deserves a more responsive and flexible system.'

2.1.3   The Licensing Act 2003 (LA 2003) does indeed bring about wholesale change. Vast tracts of legislation, and with them ways of acting, thinking and planning, are repealed. Old terminology disappears. There is to be a new way of doing things.

2.1.4   There are also some ill-considered parts of the LA 2003 – some the result of last-minute compromises to ensure that the Bill completed its passage through Parliament before the summer recess.

2.1.5   Further, and unusually, in order to meet many of the concerns expressed by those lobbying Parliament on behalf of the various interest groups, ministers promised that consistency of approach and the expected outcomes could be achieved by the issue of detailed guidance which the new licensing authorities, local councils, would have to follow. Tessa Jowell, in the foreword to the Guidance, said:

> 'This guidance is intended to aid licensing authorities in carrying out their functions under the 2003 Act and to ensure the spread of best practice and greater consistency of approach. This does not mean that we are intent on eroding local discretion. On the contrary, the legislation is fundamentally based on local decision-making informed by local knowledge and local people. Our intention is to drive out unjustified inconsistencies and poor practice, while building on good practice adopted in recent years by licensing justices and some local authorities.'

2.1.6   The tensions between the aspirations of the alcohol and entertainment industries on the one hand, and residents on the other, are well recognised. The Government's perhaps over-optimistic hope is for businesses and residents to work together for the benefit of the community. Again, Tessa Jowell:

> 'Deregulation inevitably brings with it a higher degree of self-regulation by licence and certificate holders. This shift means that the primary responsibility for controlling activities on licensed premises firmly rests on these holders and the managers of such premises. The licensing authorities, supported by the enforcement authorities, will in future keep the activities of these holders under review to ensure minimum standards are met instead of seeking to exercise control by setting prescriptive and all-encompassing licence conditions. This means that all concerned must work closely together in partnership for the community of which both businesses and residents form a part.'

2.1.7 Amongst other legislation, the principal statutes repealed by the LA 2003, in chronological order, are:

- Sunday Observance Act 1780 (the whole Act);
- Sunday Entertainments Act 1932 (the whole Act);
- London Government Act 1963, Sch 12;
- Licensing Act 1964 (the whole Act);
- Refreshment Houses Act 1964 (the whole Act);
- Greater London Council (General Powers) Act 1966, Part IV;
- Private Places of Entertainment (Licensing) Act 1967 (the whole Act);
- Theatres Act 1968, ss 15(6) and 17;
- Late Night Refreshment Houses Act 1969 (the whole Act);
- Sunday Theatre Act 1972 (the whole Act);
- Local Government (Miscellaneous Provisions) Act 1982, Sch 1;
- Licensing (Occasional Permissions) Act 1983 (the whole Act);
- Cinemas Act 1985, ss 3(1A), 9, 17 and 18;
- London Local Authorities Act 1990, ss 4–17, 19 and 20;
- Public Entertainments Licences (Drug Misuse) Act 1997 (the whole Act).

2.2 LICENSING AUTHORITIES

2.2.1 After hundreds of years the role of local licensing justices is abolished. Their functions are transferred to the local authorities. The purpose is to give power to committees of democratically accountable councillors. Local authorities already had control of activities such as the provision of public entertainment and so had significant experience with regard to regulation of entertainment activities. From henceforth local authorities will be responsible for the licensing or regulation of all forms of entertainment (including the sale and supply of alcohol) except for the various forms of betting and gaming which, for the moment remain with the magistrates sitting in betting and gaming licensing committees and the Gaming Board.

2.2.2 Justifying the change on behalf of the Government, Lord Davies of Oldham said:[2]

> '... we see the advantage of bringing the whole of licensing under one regime. The local authorities do not lack experience as regards licensing and they will have additional functions as a result of this measure ... we are consolidating under one body ... We are transferring to licensing authorities the advantage of local accountability, which is an important role in local life.'

2.2.3 The safeguard, for all parties, is the right to appeal against a decision of a licensing authority to the magistrates' court (not the licensing justices, who will no longer exist). There will be no onward

---

[2] *Hansard*, HL Deb, vol 642, col 427 (12 December 2002).

appeal to the Crown Court, however. Decisions of licensing authorities and magistrates' courts will still be subject to judicial supervision through claims for judicial review, and points of law will still be the subject of appeals by case stated from the magistrates' court.

2.3   CHANGES

The more significant changes made by the LA 2003 are as follows.

Justices' licences

2.3.1   The justices' licence – either for the sale of alcohol both on and off the premises, or just off the premises – is abolished. So are 'Part IV' restaurant and/or residential licences. They are replaced by the all-embracing premises licence.[3] A premises licence will be able to be held by a body corporate and not just by an individual. In order to sell alcohol in premises with the benefit of a premises licence, there will have to be a designated premises supervisor, who must also hold a personal licence.

Renewals

2.3.2   Premises licences are almost 'permanent'. They are not renewable and will continue indefinitely unless revoked by the licensing authority. There are certain circumstances involving the death, disability or insolvency of the owner in which a premises licence will lapse, and they can be surrendered, but otherwise they are 'permanent'.

Transfers

2.3.3   The ability to transfer a premises licence from one holder to another is retained.

Protection orders

2.3.4   Protection orders will cease. There are provisions to allow premises with a premises licence to carry on trading in the event of a change of the designated premises supervisor and for a licence to be reinstated following its lapse.

Removals

2.3.5   The old power to 'remove' a licence from one premises in an area to other premises in that area is abolished.

---

[3]   LA 2003, Part 3.

Demand

2.3.6 The concepts of need or demand become irrelevant. The only matters to be taken into account when determining whether or not to grant a premises licence are the four licensing objectives set out in LA 2003, s 4. There may be circumstances where in a particular area saturation point has been reached so that the grant of a further premises licence would undermine one of the new licensing objectives. This is referred to in the Guidance issued by the Secretary of State as 'Cumulative Impact' and is a proper matter for a licensing authority to consider in terms of policy. Quotas cannot be fixed, however, and each application would have to be considered on its merits.[4]

Permitted hours

2.3.7 The concepts of permitted hours, extended hours and special hours are also abolished. Licensing authorities may not fix permitted hours in their area or parts of their area. The Government's idea was to allow flexibility to overcome a culture of binge drinking and the disorder caused when large numbers of customers leave premises simultaneously. This means that fixing permitted hours in an area, sometimes referred to as 'zoning', is not permitted. Conditions can be attached to a premises licence limiting the opening hours but will have to be determined on a case-by-case basis.[5]

2.3.8 There is no provision whereby the holder of a premises licence can extend the opening hours for a special occasion. It is possible, however, to make an application for a temporary 'licence' by giving a temporary event notice.[6]

Occasional licences and occasional permissions

2.3.9 Both these forms of licence, one applied for by the holder of a justices' licence and the other by the organiser of a charitable or similar event, are replaced by temporary event notices which permit licensable activities on a temporary basis.

Personal licences

2.3.10 Whilst held by an individual, body corporate or association, a premises licence relates to the premises and not the holder. In order to sell alcohol in or from premises with the benefit of a premises licence there must be a holder of a personal licence.[7] By this means

---

[4] Paragraphs 3.13–3.12 of the Guidance.

[5] Part 6 of the Guidance.

[6] LA 2003, Part 5.

[7] Every supply of alcohol under a premises licence must be made by a personal licence holder or an individual authorised by a personal licence holder.

the Government seeks to ensure the proper control and supervision of the sale of alcohol.

2.3.11   The 'fit and proper' person test has gone. The only matters for consideration in determining whether or not a person is suited to be a holder of a personal licence are: age (minimum 18 years); qualifications (through a recognised course); convictions for relevant offences (if any); and whether or not a personal licence relating to the individual has been forfeited within the previous 5 years. The only relevant licensing objective is the crime prevention objective.[8]

Closure powers

2.3.12   The existing powers of the police and local authorities to close down licensed premises in certain circumstances are replaced by new powers afforded to either the police or magistrates' courts.[9]

Review and revocation

2.3.13   Licensing authorities will be able to review premises licences or club premises certificates following representations made by either the police (or other enforcement agencies) or local people. Such representations can be made at any time, although there can be restrictions placed upon repeated representations made by local residents and businesses. Reviews of premises licences will automatically follow closure orders made by magistrates' courts. Upon review the licensing authority will have new powers to modify conditions and suspend premises licences as well as the power to revoke a licence.

Sunday closing in parts of Wales

2.3.14   The first sections of the new LA 2003 to be brought into force were s 199 and Sch 7 (repeals) so far as relating to the Licensing Act 1964, ss 66 and 67, Sch 8. On 16 July 2003 those provisions were repealed, thus bringing to an end polls to decide whether licensed premises should be permitted to be open on Sundays in Wales and Monmouthshire.[10]

Late night refreshments

2.3.15   The provisions relating to 'night cafes' in London and late night refreshments in all other parts of the countries of England and Wales are brought together by making the provision of late night refreshment a licensable activity. Also brought under the umbrella of the new LA 2003 are hot-dog stands or burger vans, thus giving

---

[8]   LA 2003, Part 6.

[9]   Ibid, Part 8.

[10] Licensing Act 2003 (Commencement Order) 2003, SI 1911/2003.

licensing authorities comprehensive control of all late night entertainment and associated activities.

Theatres and cinemas

2.3.16   Theatre and cinema licences are abolished – and with them the right, for example to sell alcohol. Both activities now come within the definition of licensable activities for which a premises licence will be required.

Public entertainments licences

2.3.17   The old 'music, singing and dancing' licences, which were renamed 'public entertainments' licences in the Local Government (Miscellaneous Provisions) Act 1982 when responsibility was passed from local justices to local authorities, are abolished. The provision of music and dancing, or music and dancing facilities, are licensable activities for which a premises licence or club premises certificate will be required in future.

Registered clubs

2.3.18   Registered members' clubs are to be replaced by clubs having the benefit of a club premises certificate. The certificate will be able to cover any licensable activity. Qualification for a certificate is similar to current qualifications. One of the main changes with regard to clubs is that the restrictions on the supply of alcohol to children (those under 18 years of age) are brought into line with sales through licensed premises.

Offences

2.3.19   Whilst some of the old offences relating to personal behaviour have not been replaced, the LA 2003 sets out in Part 7 a series of offences relating to unauthorised licensable activities, sales or supplies to drunks, and the sale or supply of alcohol to children. Gone, however, are offences such as those relating to the presence of prostitutes in licensed premises, or the sale of alcohol to police officers in uniform.

Supply of alcohol to children

2.3.20   As well as bringing members clubs into line with other premises when it comes to the sale or supply of alcohol to children, an attempt has been made to clear up the confusing laws relating both to the presence of children in licensed premises and the consumption of alcohol by children. In future, unaccompanied children (under the age of 16 years) will not be allowed in premises used primarily or exclusively for the supply of alcohol on those premises. No sale or supply of alcohol to or for children will be allowed, save that there are provisions to allow the consumption by children aged 16 and 17 of beer, wine or cider provided that they are accompanied by an adult and having a table meal.

Wholesale supplies

2.3.21   Under the new law the only sales or supplies of alcohol for which a premises licence or club premises certificate will not be required are sales or supplies to traders – that is, those responsible for premises with premises licences, club premises certificates, or organising temporary events. All sales or supplies of alcohol to private individuals, no matter what the quantity, will come under the new Act.

Fees

2.3.22   Whilst fees payable to magistrates' clerks were fixed by secondary legislation, those payable to local authorities in relation to public entertainments licences were not. This led to the charging of sometimes very high fees in relation to nightclubs and similar premises. Following many complaints from businesses, the Government determined that, whilst fees will be intended to meet the costs incurred by local authorities, those costs will be fixed centrally and not subject to local variations.

Chapter 3

LICENSING OBJECTIVES

'It doesn't much signify whom one marries, for one is sure to find next morning that it was someone else.'

Samuel Rogers
(*Table Talk*)

3.1 INTRODUCTION

3.1.1 Somewhat obscurely, the objectives of the legislation and primary considerations for all decisions made in accordance with it are hidden away in LA 2003, s 4, 'General duties of licensing authorities'. Throughout the LA 2003 various references are made to the objectives with different emphases, but it is the achievement of them that is the justification for the whole framework of the LA 2003. In her foreword to the Guidance issued under the provisions of LA 2003, s 182, Tessa Jowell, the Secretary of State for Culture, Media and Sport, said:

> 'The purpose of the legislation is to provide a clear focus on the promotion of four objectives which must now form the central purpose when licensing functions are carried out ...'

3.1.2 During the debates in the House of Lords, Lord Davies of Oldham, speaking on behalf of the Government, raised a fifth objective:

> '... we have a balance between the need to prevent crime, disorder and public nuisance, to ensure public safety and to protect children from harm, and to reduce the regulatory burden on industry – an express objective of the Bill.'[1]

3.1.3 Each licensing authority must carry out its functions under the LA 2003 'with a view to promoting the licensing objectives'.[2] The use of the word 'must' in s 4 makes this a mandatory provision, and the scheme of the Act is such as to make it virtually impossible for a court to regard any provision relating to these objectives as directory rather than mandatory.

3.1.4 The rule is expressed by Bennion as follows:[3]

---

[1] *Hansard*, HL Deb, vol 643, col 70 (13 January 2003).

[2] LA 2003, s 4(1).

[3] Bennion, *Statutory Interpretation* (Butterworths, 3rd edn), at p 30.

'Section 10. Mandatory and directory requirements.

(1) This section applies where—

   (a) a person ("the person affected") may be affected by a thing done under an enactment, and

   (b) the legal effectiveness of that thing is subject to the performance by the same or any other person ("the person bound") of some statutory requirement ("the relevant requirement"), and

   (c) the relevant requirement is not complied with, and

   (d) the intended consequence of the failure to comply is not stated in the legislation.

(2) In ascertaining, in a case where this section applies, the effect of the failure to comply with the relevant requirement, it is necessary to determine whether the requirement was intended by the legislature to be mandatory or merely directory. For this purpose it may be relevant to consider whether the person affected and the person bound are the same, and whether the thing done under the enactment is beneficial or adverse to the person affected.

(3) Where the relevant requirement is held to be mandatory, the failure to comply with it will invalidate the thing done under the enactment.

(4) Where the relevant requirement is held to be merely directory, the failure to comply with it will not invalidate the thing done under the enactment; and the law will be applied as nearly as may be as if the requirement had been complied with.'

3.1.5 It is likely that decisions relating to premises and licences will be treated as interferences with property. If so, the statutory conditions relating to decision-making with regard to those premises or licences are likely to be regarded as mandatory. The provisions of the LA 2003, and regulations dealing with such matters as the giving of notices and compliance with time limits, are more likely to be regarded as directory unless failure to comply leads to a party being at a significant disadvantage or not having the opportunity to have a fair hearing.

3.2 THE LICENSING OBJECTIVES

3.2.1 The licensing objectives are:

– the prevention of crime and disorder;
– public safety;
– the prevention of public nuisance; and
– the protection of children from harm.

3.2.2 In addition to having to carry out its licensing functions with a view to the promotion of the licensing objectives, a licensing authority has to have regard to:

- its licensing statement (as published under LA 2003, s 5); and
- any guidelines issued by the Secretary of State (under LA 2003, s 182).

3.2.3 The difference between the expressions 'must carry out its functions with a view to' and 'must also have regard to' is significant in that, whilst the licensing authority has to make its decisions with a view to promoting the licensing objectives, and with no ulterior motive or purpose therefore, the requirement to have regard to its licensing statement and Government Guidance leaves the licensing authority with a wide discretion. It will be permissible for a licensing authority not to follow its statement or ministerial guidance where circumstances might justify an exception provided that the authority's decision is made with a view to promoting the licensing objectives.

3.2.4 This interpretation is consistent with what Lord McIntosh of Haringey said in the House of Lords:[4]

> 'The guidance is not legislation; it is a document produced by the Secretary of State that is designed to secure that no unnecessary conflicts exist between the licensing policies set out by different licensing authorities. It also sets out the kind of issues that licensing authorities must consider when they are producing such a policy. The phrase for that is quite deliberately "have regard to"; in other words, when we are talking about guidance, which is neither legislation nor an instruction, the words 'have regard to' are appropriate because the authority retains an ultimate discretion to depart from the guidance.

> If an authority departs from the guidance, it has a public duty to show that it has had regard to the guidance – that is to say, that it has taken it seriously and used it in the process of formulating its objectives.'

3.2.5 The terms 'crime and disorder', 'public safety' and 'public nuisance' are not defined in the LA 2003. In various parts of the Act there are references to the 'crime prevention objective', which is to be interpreted as a reference to the prevention of crime and disorder.[5] In the debates in the House of Lords the Government was said to have intended to rely upon the common law as to the meaning of 'public nuisance'. Baroness Blackstone said:[6]

> 'We are not focusing on all the unpleasant behaviour, either during the day or late at night, that has been referred to. If customers behave badly after they leave the licensee's control, they are personally responsible for their actions and have to be dealt with in various other ways, with which I shall deal in a moment. Licensing law concerns the placing of duties on licensees. Therefore, we have to understand that it does not make any sense to require licensees to deal with nuisance once customers are outside their control.

---

[4]　*Hansard*, HL Deb, vol 642, col 629 (17 December 2002).

[5]　LA 2003, s 193.

[6]　*Hansard*, HL Deb, vol 642, col 560 (17 December 2002).

I turn to the legal points raised by the noble Baroness, Lady Buscombe. The judgments that she cited have developed on a case by case basis. Yes, we do expect case law developed to date to be applied here. I say to the noble Viscount, Lord Falkland, that it would not be appropriate to provide a rigid meaning as to what constitutes a public nuisance ...

What may constitute a public nuisance will obviously vary from case to case. It would be quite inappropriate to give it a completely rigid meaning. Being precise would either exclude a case which, on any analysis, would give rise to public nuisance or might include an instance which the public – residents living in the vicinity of licensed premises – do not consider causes a nuisance. It is right that the objective of the prevention of public nuisance can be considered against individual circumstances.'

3.2.6   The authorities on public nuisance referred to by Baroness Buscombe were:

–   *Ruffell*[7] – which concerned the criminal offence of 'public nuisance' caused by those attending an illegal acid-house party who blocked the road, disturbed residents with noise and deposited litter and excrement in adjoining woodlands; and
–   *A-G v PYA Quarries Ltd*[8] – in which Romer LJ said:[9]

> 'Any nuisance is public which materially affects the reasonable comfort and convenience of life of a class of Her Majesty's subjects. The sphere of the nuisance may be described generally as "the neighbourhood", but the question whether the local community within that sphere comprises a sufficient number of persons to constitute a class of the public is a question of fact in every case.
>
> It is not necessary in my judgment to prove that every member of the class has been injuriously affected. It is sufficient to show that a representative cross-section of the class has been so affected for an injunction to issue.'

---

[7]   [1992] 13 Cr App R (S) 204.

[8]   [1957] QB 169.

[9]   Quoted by Baroness Buscombe – *Hansard*, HL Deb, vol 642, col 546 (17 December 2002).

Chapter 4

LICENSABLE ACTIVITIES

'Life without industry is guilt and industry without art is brutality.'

John Ruskin

4.1 INTRODUCTION

4.1.1 The LA 2003 brings together the legislation concerning the following activities:

– the sale by retail of alcohol;
– the supply of alcohol to members of a club;
– entertainment provided to members of the public, to members of a club or for consideration and with a view to profit in any of the following forms:
  – performance of a play;
  – showing of a film;
  – indoor sporting events;
  – boxing and wrestling;
  – performance of live music;
  – playing of recorded music;
  – performance of dance;
  – entertainment facilities provided to members of the public, to members of a club or for consideration and with a view to profit;
– the provision of late night refreshment.

4.1.2 The corresponding pieces of legislation which have been either repealed or amended by the repeal of significant parts are:

– the Licensing Act 1964;
– the Refreshment Houses Act 1964;
– the Private Places of Entertainment Act 1967;
– the Theatres Act 1968;
– the Late Night Refreshment Houses Act 1969;
– the Local Government (Miscellaneous Provisions) Act 1982;
– the Cinemas Act 1985;
– the Sporting Events (Control of Alcohol) Act 1985;
– the London Government Act 1963;
– the Greater London Government Acts 1968, 1976, 1978, 1979, 1982 and 1986.

4.1.3 What are not covered by the new LA 2003 are provisions relating to:

– sex establishments and sex encounter establishments (covered by the Local Government (Miscellaneous Provisions) Act 1982, Sch 3, and the Greater London Council (General Powers) Act 1986);

– betting (controlled by the Betting Gaming and Lotteries Act 1963);

– gaming (controlled by the Gaming Act 1968);

– lotteries (controlled by the Lotteries and Amusements Act 1976);

– most outdoor sporting events (save insomuch as alcohol is supplied to those attending them).

4.1.4 In relation to entertainment, or entertainment facilities, there should be little difficulty in determining whether or not they are provided to members of the public or members of a qualifying club.

4.1.5 In other circumstances the activities will still be regarded as regulated entertainment and, therefore, licensable if they are provided for consideration and with a view to profit. Activities will only be regarded as provided for consideration if a charge is made by any person concerned in the organisation or management of the entertainment or the entertainment facilities, and which is paid by or on behalf of some or all of the persons for whom the entertainment or entertainment facilities are provided.

4.1.6 'Charge' includes any charge for the provision of goods or services.[1] The musicians or disk jockeys providing the music are not caught by the charging provisions.

4.1.7 Thus, it will matter not that a charge is made, say, for food or soft drinks rather than admission, if entertainment is provided. What will determine the issue is whether or not the activity was organised with a view to profit. In other words, was a profit intended from the outset? A group of friends, a society or guests at a wedding sharing the cost of entertainment would not be regarded as the providers of regulated entertainment. If, however, the society, for example, was hoping to raise funds, and therefore make a profit, then even though the function was private, in that it was restricted to members of the society, the organisers would still be involved in the provision of regulated entertainment and so would need to comply with the provisions of the LA 2003.

---

[1] LA 2003, Sch 1, Part 1, para 1(5).

4.2 DEFINITION OF LICENSABLE ACTIVITIES

4.2.1   The LA 2003 sets up a regime to deal with 'licensable activities' which are defined[2] as:

(a) the sale by retail of alcohol;
(b) the supply of alcohol, by or on behalf of a club, to or to the order of a member of the club;
(c) the provision of regulated entertainments; and
(d) the provision of late night refreshment.

4.3 THE SALE OR SUPPLY OF ALCOHOL

4.3.1   'Alcohol' is defined in LA 2003, s 191. It means spirits, wine, beer, cider or any other fermented, distilled or spirituous liquor, but does not include:

(a) alcohol which is of a strength not exceeding 0.5% at the time of sale or supply;
(b) perfume;
(c) flavouring essences;
(d) Angostura Bitters;
(e) alcohol included in a medicinal product;
(f) denatured alcohol;
(g) methyl alcohol;
(h) naphtha; or
(i) alcohol contained in liqueur confectionery.

4.3.2   The 'sale by retail' of alcohol is a sale to any person other than off sales made to:

(a) a trader for the purposes of his trade;
(b) a club which holds a club premises certificate for the purposes of that club;
(c) the holder of a personal licence for the purposes of making sales authorised by a premises licence;
(d) the holder of a premises licence for the purpose of making sales authorised by that licence; or
(e) the premises user in relation to a temporary event notice for the purpose of making sales authorised by that notice.[3]

4.3.3   This means that sales of alcohol by a wine broker or wholesaler to a private individual are licensable activities, requiring a premises licence, no matter what the quantity.

4.3.4   The 'supply of alcohol to members or guests' means, in the case of any club, the supply of alcohol by or on behalf of a club to, or to the order of, a member of the club, or the sale by retail of alcohol by or

---

[2] LA 2003, s 1(1).

[3] Ibid, s 192.

on behalf of the club to a guest of a member of the club for consumption on the premises where the sale takes place.[4]

4.3.5   In relation to sales made by telephone, written order (fax etc) or the Internet, where the alcohol is stored at a different location, the place where the alcohol is appropriated to the contract – or in other words put onto the delivery van – is deemed to be the place at which the alcohol is sold.[5]

4.3.6   Prizes of bottles or cans of alcohol in a lottery, raffle or tombola are deemed not to constitute a licensable activity[6] provided that:

–   the lottery is promoted as an incident of an exempt entertainment;
–   (excluding legitimate expenses) the whole proceeds of the entertainment are applied for purposes other than private gain;
–   the alcohol is in a sealed container;
–   no prize in the lottery is a money prize;
–   tickets or chances in the lottery are sold or issued and the result declared only at the premises where the entertainment takes place during the entertainment; and
–   the opportunity to take part in the lottery is not the only or main inducement to attend the entertainment.

4.3.7   The former disqualification of service areas and garages has been retained. The ban on alcohol sales at service areas on motorways is absolute. With regard to garages, the test remains the same – whether the premises are used primarily as a garage or form part of premises which are primarily so used.

4.3.8   There is a complete ban on the sale of alcohol on a moving vehicle.[7] (Trains and vessels are not 'vehicles'. 'Vehicle' means a vehicle intended or adopted for use on roads.[8])

4.4   REGULATED ENTERTAINMENTS

4.4.1   Schedule 1 deals with regulated entertainments and defines what constitutes an entertainment for the purposes of the LA 2003. Schedule 1, Part 3 contains definitions of the terms used to describe the different entertainments. The forms of entertainment are:

(a)   a performance of a play – being the performance of any dramatic piece whether involving improvisation or not which is given

---

[4]   LA 2003, s 70.

[5]   Ibid, s 190.

[6]   Ibid, s 175.

[7]   Ibid, s 156.

[8]   Ibid, s 193.

wholly or in part by one or more persons actually present and performing and which, whether by speech, singing or action, involves the playing of a role. 'Performance' includes a rehearsal;[9]

(b) an exhibition of a film – meaning any exhibition of moving pictures;[10]

(c) an indoor sporting event – which is a sporting event which takes place wholly inside a building and at which the spectators present are also wholly inside that building. 'Building' means a roofed structure (other than a roof which can be opened and closed) and includes vessels and moveable structures. 'Sporting event' means any contest, exhibition or display of any sport. 'Sport' includes any game in which physical skill is the predominant factor and any form of physical recreation which is also engaged in for the purposes of competition or display;[11]

(d) a boxing or wrestling entertainment – which is any contest, exhibition or display of boxing or wrestling;[12]

(e) a performance of live music;

(f) any playing of recorded music – 'music' includes vocal or instrumental music or any combination of the two;[13]

(g) a performance of dance;

(h) entertainment of a similar character to the performance of live music, the playing of recorded music or the performance of dance if it takes place in the presence of an audience and is provided (at least in part) for the purpose of entertaining that audience.

4.4.2   Also caught by the LA 2003 is the provision of 'entertainment facilities' which are separately defined and regulated. 'Entertainment facilities' are defined as 'facilities for enabling persons to take part in entertainment which involves making music, dancing or similar activity for the purpose of or for purposes which involve the purpose of being entertained'.[14]

4.4.3   Poetry readings and performances by stand-up comedians (which do not involve music) are not regulated by the LA 2003.[15]

---

[9]   LA 2003, Sch 1, Part 3, para 14.

[10]   Ibid, para 15.

[11]   Ibid, para 16.

[12]   Ibid, para 17.

[13]   Ibid, para 18.

[14]   Ibid, Sch 1, Part 1, para 3.

[15]   Dr Kim Howells – *Hansard*, HC Standing Committee D, 1 April 2003, col 62.

4.5 EXEMPTIONS RELATING TO REGULATED ENTERTAINMENTS

4.5.1   In relation to the provision of regulated entertainment there are a number of exemptions[16] which come within the overall aims of the Government to reduce red tape or over-regulation. They are as follows.

Films – advertising and educational or information activities

4.5.2   The showing of films is not to be regarded as the provision of a regulated entertainment if the sole or main purpose is to demonstrate a product, advertise goods or services or provide information, education or instruction.[17] A similar exemption applies to films shown in museums or art galleries.[18]

Incidental music

4.5.3   Live or recorded music is exempt provided that it is incidental to some other activity that is not itself an entertainment or the provision of an entertainment facility regulated by the LA 2003. So, for example, the playing of background music (musak) in a hotel or the playing of a pianist in a restaurant for the benefit of the diners would not be regulated.[19]

4.5.4   The term 'incidental' is not defined in the LA 2003. In debate Dr Kim Howells described it thus:[20]

> 'Incidental live music is music that does not form part of the main attraction for visitors to a premises. Examples might include a piano played in the background in a restaurant, or carol singers in a shopping centre. However, if a band in a pub was advertised to draw in customers, or live music was played so loud that it could not possibly be regarded as incidental to another activity, it would be unlikely to benefit from the exemption. To clarify the matter further, we would expect the licensing authority to exercise this discretion as it currently does in regard to public entertainment licensing.'

Television and radio

4.5.5   The facility to watch or listen to live broadcasts is not regulated by the LA 2003 as the provision of a regulated entertainment.[21]

---

[16] LA 2003, Sch 1, Part 2.

[17] Ibid, para 5.

[18] Ibid, para 6.

[19] Ibid, para 7.

[20] *Hansard*, HC Standing Committee D, 1 April 2003, cols 67–68.

[21] LA 2003, Sch 1, Part 2, para 8.

Regulation was resisted by the Government who sought not to regulate in areas where, either there were existing statutory provisions such as the Hypnotism Act 1952, or where there was no provision at all:[22]

> 'We are not in the business of adding new layers of regulation. We are trying to deregulate and to streamline the regulation that it is necessary to maintain.'

Religious services and places of worship

4.5.6 Entertainments provided at a place of public religious worship, or for the purpose of, or incidental to, a religious meeting or service are exempt.[23] This means that all churches, for example, are excluded from the provisions of the LA 2003. Baroness Blackstone, on tabling the amendment to allow this exemption, made it clear that the exemption would cover instances when the entertainment provided was secular and went on to say: [24]

> 'I can say that all forms of entertainment in places of public worship will be exempted ... The trigger is "a place of public religious worship". That is the right wording, because it is an understood term and was agreed with the various religious groups. Case law tells us that not only must the place be available to the public for religious worship but it must be apparent that it is so available.'

Garden fêtes etc

4.5.7 A garden fête or similar function or event is also exempt.[25] The exemption does not apply, however, if the fête or similar event is promoted for private gain as defined in s 22 of the Lotteries and Amusements Act 1976:

> **'Meaning of "private gain" in relation to proceeds of entertainments, lotteries and gaming promoted on behalf of certain societies**
>
> (1) For the purpose of this Act proceeds of any entertainment, lottery or gaming promoted on behalf of a society to which this subsection extends which are applied for any purpose calculated to benefit the society as a whole shall not be held to be applied for purposes of private gain by reason only that their application for that purpose results in benefit to any person as an individual.
>
> (2) Subsection (1) above extends to any society which is established and conducted either—
>
> (a) wholly for purposes other than purposes of any commercial undertaking, or

---

[22] Dr Kim Howells – *Hansard*, HC Standing Committee D, 1 April 2003, col 62.

[23] LA 2003, Sch 1, Part 2, para 9.

[24] *Hansard*, HL Deb, vol 645, col 37 (24 February 2003).

[25] LA 2003, Sch 1, Part 2, para 10.

(b) wholly or mainly for the purpose of participation in or support of athletic sports or athletic games.'

Morris dancing

4.5.8   Morris dancing, the unamplified music which accompanies it and the facilities provided for morris dancing to take place are exempted.[26]

Vehicles in motion

4.5.9   The provision of entertainment or entertainment facilities on vehicles, which are not permanently or temporarily parked at the time, is also exempt.[27] Vehicles which are not permanently situated but which are to be used for one or more licensable activity whilst parked at a particular place, are treated as premises at that place for the purposes of the LA 2003.[28] Each different parking location is treated as a separate place.

Vessels

4.5.10   Vessels which are not permanently moored are treated as being premises at the place at which they are usually moored or berthed for the purposes of the LA 2003.[29] There is no exemption for vessels involved in local or national (as opposed to international) journeys.

General point

4.5.11   It is important to realise that whilst the above forms of entertainment may carry exemption from the need to obtain a premises licence, club premises certificate, or give notice of a temporary event, if combined with the sale or supply of alcohol, as may be quite common with a garden fête, for example, then appropriate authorisation will be required.

4.6   LATE NIGHT REFRESHMENTS

4.6.1   LA 2003, Sch 2 deals with late night refreshments. Late night refreshment is the provision, between the hours of 11 pm and 5 am, of hot food or hot drink to members of the public on or from any premises whether for consumption on or off the premises.[30]

---

[26] LA 2003, Sch 1, Part 2, para 11.

[27] Ibid, Sch 1, Part 2, para 12.

[28] Ibid, s 189(2).

[29] Ibid, s 189(1).

[30] Ibid, Sch 2, para 1(1)(a).

4.6.2 A person is deemed to provide late night refreshment if he holds himself out as willing to supply hot food or drink to any person on premises between the hours of 11 pm and 5 am if members of the public have been admitted to those premises.[31]

4.6.3 Food and drink is deemed to be hot if, before it is supplied, it is heated on the premises or elsewhere for the purpose of being consumed at a temperature above the ambient air temperature and is above that temperature at the time of supply. Food that is sold on premises where there are facilities for heating the food on the premises after the supply, is also caught.[32]

4.6.4 This will mean, for example, that service stations with microwave or grill facilities for the heating of pies, pasties and sausage rolls will need a premises licence if they are to operate between the hours of 11 pm and 5 am.

4.7 EXEMPTIONS RELATING TO LATE NIGHT REFRESHMENTS

Hotels, clubs and other places providing overnight accommodation

4.7.1 Hotels, clubs and other places providing overnight accommodation are exempt from the late night refreshment controls provided that the provision of hot food and drink is limited to:

– a member of a recognised club[33] (being a club which satisfies the qualifying conditions 1–3 of LA 2003, s 62) – if a club is not a qualifying club those attending are treated as members of the public);
– a person staying at the hotel or similar premises overnight[34] (to include guest houses, lodging houses, caravan sites and hostels);
– a guest of any of the above.[35]

Employees

4.7.2 Similarly employees and other workers fall into the exemptions provided. The exemptions relate to:

– an employee of a particular employer[36] (thus avoiding the need to license a staff canteen);

---

[31] LA 2003, Sch 2, para 1(1)(b).

[32] Ibid, para 2.

[33] Ibid, para 3(2)(a).

[34] Ibid, para 3(2)(b).

[35] Ibid, para 3(2)(e).

[36] Ibid, para 3(2)(c).

  –   a person engaged in a particular trade, a member of a particular
      profession or a follower of a particular vocation[37] (thus avoiding
      the need to license late night facilities for particular categories of
      night workers such as taxi drivers); or
  –   a guest of any of the above.[38]

Exhibition halls and 'near beer' premises in London

4.7.3   There are savings for the current system of licensing
exhibition halls and 'near beer' premises in London under the
Greater London Council (General Powers) Act 1966 and the London
Local Authorities Act 1995.[39]

Certain types of food and drink

4.7.4   Certain types of food and drink are also exempt.[40] They
include:

(a) hot drinks which consist of or contain alcohol (for which a
    premises licence, a club premises certificate or a temporary event
    notice would be needed in any event);
(b) hot drinks supplied by a vending machine, provided that
    payment is made to the machine and the supply made by the
    machine to a member of the public);
(c) hot food and drink supplied free of charge (the food or drink is
    not free if in order to obtain the food or drink a charge has been
    made for admission to the premises or for some other item);
(d) hot food or drink supplied by, or a person authorised by, a
    registered charity;
(e) hot food or drink supplied on a vehicle at a time when the vehicle
    is not permanently or temporarily parked.

General point

4.7.5   As with the exemptions for regulated entertainments so in
relation to late night refreshments it must be appreciated that if the
provision of the refreshments is combined with the sale or supply of
alcohol, a premises licence or club premises certificate will still be
required.

---

[37] LA 2003, Sch 2, para 3(2)(d).

[38] Ibid, Sch 2, para 3(2)(e).

[39] Ibid, Sch 2, para 4.

[40] Ibid, Sch 2, para 5.

Chapter 5

THE NEW LICENSING AUTHORITIES

*'We have the highest authority for believing that the meek shall inherit
the Earth; though I have never found any particular corroboration of
the aphorism in the records of Somerset House.'*

FE Smith (Lord Birkenhead)

5.1 INTRODUCTION

5.1.1   For all the licensable activities (as set out in Chapter 4) there is
to be in each local authority area a single licensing body referred to in
the LA 2003 as a 'licensing authority'. In fact that authority is the
council. Outside London it will normally be the district council.
Where in a county there is no district council it will be the county
council. In Wales it will be the county or county borough council, and
in London the London borough council or the Common Council of
the City of London.[1]

5.1.2   In two of the Inns of Court, Inner Temple and Middle Temple,
the Sub-Treasurer and Under-Treasurer somewhat surprisingly
retained their regulatory functions,[2] whereas the University of
Cambridge and the Vintners of the City of London[3] lost their
privileges and exemptions, as did the Board of the Green Cloth, which
was a committee of the Royal Household that licensed public houses
within the former area of the Royal Palaces.[4] Licensable activities
within the royal palaces are exempt from the provisions of the LA
2003.[5]

5.1.3   A licensing authority is responsible for the same geographical
area as that covered by the council.

---

[1]   LA 2003, s 3(1).

[2]   Ibid, s 3(1)(f) and (g).

[3]   Ibid, s 196.

[4]   This is the effect of LA 2003, s 195, which brought Crown lands within the scope
of the Act.

[5]   LA 2003, s 173(1)(e).

5.2 DUTIES OF LICENSING AUTHORITIES

5.2.1   Each licensing authority must carry out its functions under the LA 2003 with a view to promoting the licensing objectives[6] (see Chapter 3). Section 4 of the LA 2003 sets out those objectives, namely:

– the prevention of crime and disorder;
– public safety;
– the prevention of public nuisance; and
– the protection of children from harm.

5.2.2   The functions are referred to throughout the LA 2003 as the 'licensing functions'. In carrying out those functions, the licensing authority must have regard to its licensing statement published under s 5 (see Chapter 6) and the Guidance issued by the Secretary of State in accordance with s 182 of the LA 2003.[7]

5.2.3   There is, therefore a 'hierarchy of responsibilities' as expressed by Lord MacIntosh of Haringey:[8]

'Clause [section] 4 states:

"A licensing authority must carry out its functions ... with a view to promoting the licensing objectives."

That means it has no choice. It is not a weak provision; it is a strong requirement. Clause [section] 5 relates to the statement of licensing policy which is enormously important. However, it is produced by the individual licensing authority. It sets out over a three-year period ... the way in which the licensing authority interprets the four licensing objectives in the context of its own area. It has to do so with a degree of transparency that is set out in detail in the [section]; it has to publish; it has to argue; and it has to be prepared to listen to representations. Generally speaking this is, if you like, the local responsibility element of the way in which licensing policy is delivered.

Finally there is [s 182] which deals with guidance. I should remind the committee that guidance is not legislation; it is a document produced by the Secretary of State that is designed to secure that no unnecessary conflicts exist between the licensing policies set out by different licensing authorities. It also sets out the kind of issues that licensing authorities must consider when they are producing such a policy. The phrase for that is quite deliberately "have regard to"; in other words, when we are talking about guidance, which is neither legislation nor an instruction, the words "have regard to" are appropriate because an authority retains the ultimate discretion to depart from the guidance.

If an authority departs from the guidance, it has a public duty to show that it has had regard to the guidance – that is to say, that it has taken it seriously and used it in the process of formulating its objectives. Those

---

[6]   LA 2003, s 4(1).

[7]   Ibid, s 4(3).

[8]   *Hansard*, HL Deb, vol 642, cols 629–630 (17 December 2002).

are the three levels, as it were, through which we arrive at the basis upon which licensing authorities take individual decisions.'

5.3 LICENSING COMMITTEES

5.3.1 Each licensing authority, save for the Sub- or Under-Treasurers of the Inner and Middle Temples, must establish a licensing committee comprising at least 10 but not more than 15 members of the authority.[9]

5.3.2 Other than the formulation and revision of a statement of licensing policy, all licensing matters are automatically delegated to the licensing committee.[10]

5.3.3 Sometimes licensing matters overlap with other functions of a local authority, such as planning control. In those circumstances the local authority may either delegate that other function to the licensing committee, or delegate the licensing function to the committee dealing with the other function.[11] Alternatively the licensing authority may determine to retain the decision-making power relating to the other function.[12] Whichever decision route is chosen, unless the matter is urgent, the decision-making committee or the licensing authority itself must receive and consider a report from the licensing committee or the other committee (as appropriate) before making a determination.[13] The licensing authority should not refer another function to the licensing committee without first consulting the licensing committee.[14]

5.3.4 If a licensing committee is unable to perform a delegated function, say, for example, because of disqualification of a number of its members, the committee has to refer the matter back to the licensing authority.[15] Care must be taken, therefore with regard to the selection of licensing committee members in the first place. Those councillors who are likely to find themselves unable to sit in regard to a number of matters should not be members of a licensing committee.

5.3.5 The possibility of conflict between the roles of a ward councillor on the one hand, and being a member of the licensing committee on the other, was recognised during Parliamentary debate. Lord McIntosh of Haringey said of the proposed licensing authority:[16]

---

[9] LA 2003, s 6(1).

[10] Ibid, s 7(1).

[11] Ibid, s 7(3) and (5).

[12] Ibid, s 7(4).

[13] Ibid, s 7(4), (5) and (6).

[14] Ibid, s 7(7).

[15] Ibid, s 7(9).

[16] *Hansard,* HL Deb, vol 641, col 735 (26 November 2002).

'It is important that the body should be responsible to the local community, but we should take steps to ensure that it is not subordinate to any particular pressure group within the local community. We expect that the local authority panel undertaking licensing will not contain the councillors from the ward in question.'

5.3.6 Regrettably the LA 2003 did not contain any such provision.

5.4 DELEGATED POWERS

5.4.1 A licensing committee may delegate its functions to one or more sub-committees established by it or, in a limited number of circumstances, to an officer of the authority.[17] A sub-committee must comprise three members.[18] A number of sub-committees or officers with delegated powers could operate at the same time.[19] Directions can be given by the licensing committee with regard to delegated functions.[20]

5.4.2 The LA 2003 prohibits delegation by a licensing committee to an officer in relation to cases where representations have been made or police objections have been lodged.[21]

5.4.3 Likewise officers are not allowed to deal with reviews of premises licences or club premises certificates and reviews following closure orders.[22] The prohibition on delegation to officers in this latter category is stipulated to be on the basis that relevant representations have been made. Representations will not be relevant if they are vexatious or frivolous.[23] The LA 2003 is unclear as to who may make the determination that a representation is vexatious or frivolous.

5.4.4 In the Guidance it is recommended that the determination of relevance be delegated to an officer of the authority thereby avoiding political difficulties for ward councillors[24]. In view of the wording of s 10(4), that 'advice' must be questionable. The licence or certificate holder may wish to make representations as to relevance, as may the interested party. Such representations could be made in writing but to allow the parties to answer points made by each other would lead to a convoluted process. A better view might be that the decision as to whether or not a representation is relevant is also a matter to be

---

[17] LA 2003, s 10(1).

[18] Ibid, s 9(1).

[19] Ibid, s 10(3).

[20] Ibid, s 10(5).

[21] Ibid, s 10(4).

[22] Ibid, s 10(4)(b), (c) and (d).

[23] Ibid, s 52(7) and (8).

[24] Paragraphs 3.49 and 5.57 of the Guidance.

determined by members rather than an officer. It would undoubtedly be good practice and sensible for members to seek the advice of a legal officer in such matters.

5.5 RECORDS

5.5.1 Licensing authorities are required to keep and maintain a register containing details of:

(a) a record of each premises licence, club premises certificate and personal licence issued by it;
(b) a record of each temporary event notice received by it;
(c) all associated matters, for example applications and notices received by the authority, as set out in Sch 3 to the LA 2003;
(d) and such information as may be prescribed by regulations.[25]

5.5.2 Regulations may also be made to prescribe the form of the register and the manner in which it is kept.[26]

5.5.3 The register has to be made available to a member of the public during office hours for free inspection. A charge can be made for a copy of any entry, which must, however, be supplied, on request.[27]

5.5.4 When a premises licence or club premises certificate is issued by a licensing authority, that authority must also issue to the holder a summary[28] of that licence or certificate.

5.5.5 All licences or certificates must also be updated and reissued if necessary following, for example, the lapse of a premises licence or withdrawal of a club premises certificate or other determination.[29] If necessary, new summaries must be issued. This situation is most likely to arise following the determination of an appeal by a magistrates' court. If the licensing authority is not in possession of the licence or certificate it can require the holder to produce it within 14 days. Failure to produce, without a reasonable excuse, is an offence.

5.5.6 At one stage of the Licensing Bill's progress, the House of Lords imposed upon the Government the establishment of a central licensing authority to deal with the issue of personal licences. The Government overcame that move by promising to establish a central register of data supplied by local authorities to which licensing authorities and the police would have access. The powers for the establishment of such a central register are contained in LA 2003,

---

[25] LA 2003, s 8(1).

[26] Ibid, s 8(2).

[27] Ibid, s 8(3), (4) and (5).

[28] Ibid, ss 23 and 77.

[29] Ibid, ss 56, 93 and 134.

s 8(6) and (7). Local authorities will probably have to fund it. It is unlikely that the central register will be in place at the time when the majority of the Act's provisions come into force.

5.5.7   In Standing Committee, Dr Kim Howells said:[30]

> 'It is important to recognise that we live in a world of practical considerations and none of us should be under any misapprehension about the complexity or magnitude of the work involved, especially considering that measures would need to join up the licensing functions of around 410 authorities. There is still no extant example of a joined-up system of any significance covering every local authority in England and Wales ... Work has started, however, on the central database ...
>
> It is true that the national database will not be up and running before the beginning of the transition period, which is why we have identified a separate project on data standards that we will be driving forward in the run-up to the first appointed day. The aim of that project will be to ensure that all licensing authorities record the same information in the same way to facilitate the migration of data to the new system when it has been put in place ...
>
> What will happen before the national database has been set up? We have drafted the Bill to allow for a simple system based upon the effective communication between licensing authorities, which can be up and running from the date of Royal Assent, and for a central register to be developed in due course when the experience and technology is in place. I am confident that the local system will work well up to that point. The administrative burden on the licensing authority will be small. The licence holder will be given a duty to notify the licensing authority of a change in his or her address, as well as other relevant details such as convictions for relevant or foreign offences. It will not be a case of the licensing authority having to track down the licence holder.'

5.6   PROCEEDINGS BEFORE LICENSING COMMITTEES

5.6.1   There is a power to make regulations with regard to proceedings before a licensing authority, both with regard to the conduct of hearings and matters such as the quorum, access to the public and publicity.[31]

5.6.2   Subject to such regulations, a licensing committee may regulate its own procedures and those of its sub-committees.[32]

5.6.3   A commentary on hearings before licensing committees may be found in Chapter 13.

---

[30] *Hansard*, HC Standing Committee D, 8 April 2003, col 131.

[31] LA 2003, ss 9 and 183.

[32] Ibid, s 9(3).

Chapter 6

LICENSING POLICIES AND GUIDANCE ISSUED BY THE SECRETARY OF STATE

'If you open that Pandora's Box you never know what Trojan 'orses will jump out.'

Ernest Bevin
(*Foreign Secretary in the 1945 Labour Government, on the Council of Europe*)

6.1 INTRODUCTION

6.1.1 As mentioned in Chapter 5, in carrying out its functions, each licensing authority must have regard to both its licensing statement, published in accordance with the provisions of s 5 of the LA 2003, and the Guidance issued by the Secretary of State in accordance with s 182. The licensing statement is a statement of licensing policy of the licensing authority.[1]

6.1.2 Both the policy statement and the Guidance will be very important documents and will have to bear careful scrutiny. It is likely that they will have an impact on all determinations made under the LA 2003 and on appeals in respect of those determinations.

6.2 LICENSING STATEMENT

6.2.1 Each 3-year period – beginning with a date fixed by the Secretary of State – the licensing authority has to determine its policy and publish a statement of that policy before the beginning of that period.[2]

6.3 CONSULTATION

6.3.1 In the preparation of its policies, and before publication of the licensing statement, the licensing authority must consult:

(a) the chief officer of police;

---

[1] LA 2003, s 5(1).

[2] Ibid, s 5(1) and (2).

(b) the fire authority for the area;

and such persons as the licensing authority considers to be:

(c) representatives of the holders of premises licences;
(d) representatives of the holders of club premises certificates;
(e) representatives of the holders of personal licences; and
(f) representatives of businesses and residents in the area.[3]

6.3.2 Such consultation has to take place before any revision of the statement and before each three-yearly review.

6.3.3 No guidance is given in the LA 2003 as to how the licensing authority is to determine who is, or is not, a representative of businesses or residents and what is meant by 'in the area', save that before the publication of the first licensing policy statement the licensing authority must consult representative bodies for current licence holders.[4]

6.3.4 The guidance given by the Secretary of State is that:[5]

> 'Beyond the statutory requirements, it is for each licensing authority to decide the full extent of its consultation and for it to decide whether any particular body is representative of the group described in the statute. For example, personal licence holders may be represented locally by trade unions, professional bodies and by trade associations. When undertaking consultation exercises, licensing authorities should also have regard to cost and time. Licensing authorities should note that the Secretary of State will establish fee levels to include full cost recovery of all licensing functions including the preparation and publication of a statement of licensing policy, but this will be based on the statutory requirements. Where licensing authorities exceed these requirements, they should note that they would have to absorb those costs themselves. It is important that the transitional period is completed smoothly and efficiently, and the exercise of licensing functions, including the consideration of applications, cannot proceed without a statement of policy being in place.'

6.3.5 How should the consultation be conducted? In this context reference to what have become known as the 'Sedley Rules', formulated by Lord Justice Sedley when he was still in practice at the Bar, is most helpful. For consultation to be meaningful, the consultees must:

– be provided with material upon which a decision is likely to be made;
– be given time for intelligent consideration of that material and to respond to it;
– be given the opportunity to make considered representations, with supporting evidence where appropriate; and

---

[3] LA 2003, s 5(3).

[4] Ibid, Sch 8, Part 4, para 29.

[5] Paragraph 3.7 of the Guidance.

– have their representations conscientiously considered.

6.3.6 In areas such as cities where there are different neighbourhoods it may well be that licensing authorities have to carry out a number of consultation exercises. Failure to consult bodies who have a legitimate expectation of being consulted or who should reasonably be consulted will lead to claims for judicial review and arguments that decisions were based upon an unlawful policy statement in appeals to magistrates' courts.

6.3.7 With regard to appeals, the advice given by the Secretary of State is:[6]

> 'In hearing an appeal against any decision by a licensing authority, the magistrates' court concerned will have regard to that licensing authority's statement of licensing policy and the Guidance. However, the court would be entitled to depart from either the statement of licensing policy or this Guidance if it considered it appropriate to do so because of the particular circumstances of any individual case. In addition the court would disregard any part of a licensing policy statement or this Guidance it held to be ultra vires the 2003 Act.'

6.3.8 The 'Sedley Rules' were adapted by counsel, successfully, with regard to the right to make representations in *R (Chattington) v Chief Constable of South Wales and Others.*[7] If, for example, local residents were being given the opportunity to make representations after the police had sought a review of a premises licence then the provision of all relevant material and the time to consider it and make considered representations would be an important part of that process.

6.4 REVISION

6.4.1 When the licensing authority makes a revision to its policy, a statement as to that revision or the revised policy must be published.[8]

6.5 REGULATIONS

6.5.1 The Secretary of State has the power to make regulations with regard to the determination and review of licensing policies and also the preparation and publication of licensing statements.[9]

---

[6] Paragraph 10.8 of the Guidance.

[7] [2001] EWHC Admin 887, [2003] LLR 298.

[8] LA 2003, s 5(6).

[9] Ibid, s 5(7).

6.6   LICENSING GUIDANCE

6.6.1   The Secretary of State has a duty to give guidance to licensing authorities as to their functions. A draft of that guidance has to be laid before both Houses of Parliament and approved by resolution of each House. The Guidance must be published.[10]

6.6.2   There are powers enabling the Secretary of State to revise that Guidance[11] and for the parliamentary procedures to be followed in any revision. It was anticipated during parliamentary debate that the Guidance would be reviewed from time to time.[12]

6.6.3   The rule as to ultra vires delegated legislation will apply should the Minister misuse those powers and may apply should there be a failure to follow the proper procedures. Bennion states:[13]

> '**Section 58. Ultra vires delegated legislation.**
>
> (1)   Any provision of an instrument constituting delegated legislation is ineffective if the provision goes beyond the totality of the legislative power which (expressly or by implication) is conferred on the delegate by the enabling Act. The provision is then said to be ultra vires (beyond the powers). This applies even where the instrument has been sanctioned by a confirming authority. However the instrument is not to be treated as ineffective in any respect on the ground of ultra vires unless and until declared to be so by a court of competent jurisdiction.
>
> (2)   Except where to do so would produce an instrument the effect of which the delegate would not, or might not, have approved, such a court has the power to modify the terms of the instrument so as to remove its ultra vires quality provided the effect of the modified instrument would not be different in substance from the proposed effect of the original.'

6.6.4   The burden is upon the party asserting invalidity to establish it on a balance of probabilities.[14] This possibility has been recognised by the Secretary of State in the Guidance issued:[15]

> 'In hearing an appeal against any decision by a licensing authority, the magistrates' court concerned will have regard to that licensing authority's statement of licensing policy and the Guidance. However, the court would be entitled to depart from either the statement of licensing policy or this Guidance if it considered it appropriate to do so because of the particular circumstances of any individual case. In

---

[10] LA 2003, s 182.

[11] Ibid, s 182(3).

[12] Baroness Blackstone – *Hansard*, HL Deb, vol 642, col 639 (17 December 2002).

[13] Bennion, *Statutory Interpretation* (Butterworths, 3rd edn), at p 183.

[14] *Boddington v British Transport Police* [1998] 2 All ER 203.

[15] Paragraph 10.8 of the Guidance.

addition the court would disregard any part of a licensing policy statement or this Guidance it held to be ultra vires the 2003 Act.'

6.6.5 Towards the end of the Licensing Bill's passage through Parliament, when difficulties were being experienced with regard to small premises and the 'two-in-a-bar rule', the Government promised a review of the existing descriptions of regulated entertainment in the LA 2003 some 6 to 12 months after the end of the transition period. The Minister for Sport, Richard Caborn, promised that the powers in the LA 2003 to modify the position through secondary legislation would be used, if necessary.[16]

6.7 THE LAW RELATING TO LICENSING POLICIES

6.7.1 The law relating to licensing policies can be traced through a series of cases from *R v Torquay Licensing Justices ex parte Brockman*,[17] *R v Chester Crown Court ex parte Pascoe and Jones*,[18] and *R v Sheffield Crown Court ex parte Consterdine*[19] to *R (Westminster City Council) v Middlesex Crown Court and Chorion plc*.[20]

6.7.2 The law may be summed up as follows.

–   A licensing authority is entitled to have a policy – indeed, under the LA 2003 it is bound to publish a statement of its licensing policy.
–   That policy must not act as a fetter so as to exclude the exercise of the authority's discretion in every case.
–   Each application must be treated on its merits.
–   The licensing authority must be prepared to allow exceptions.
–   The reasons for the policy must be made clear.
–   It is for the party seeking to persuade the committee to depart from its policy to show that it can be done without imperilling it or the reasons which underlie it – or, to put it another way, the committee must consider whether, if it was to grant what is sought by way of exception, those reasons would still be met.
–   An appeal court should adopt the policy as its own and consider the application in the same way as the committee should have done.
–   A challenge to the policy can only be made through a claim for judicial review.

---

[16] *Hansard*, HC Deb, vol 408, cols 1116–1117 (8 July 2003).
[17] [1951] 2 KB 784, [1951] 2 All ER 656.
[18] 151 JP 752.
[19] (1998) 34 *Licensing Review* 19, [2002] LLR 712.
[20] [2002] EWHC Admin 1104, [2002] LLR 538.

6.7.3   Those last points about the appellate court adopting the policy and not dealing with an appeal as if it were a challenge by way of judicial review were the view of Scott Baker J in the *Chorion* case.[21] In view of the terms of the LA 2003, however, the situation as to an appeal to a magistrates' court may now be different. Section 181 gives the magistrates' court the powers to:

(a) dismiss the appeal;
(b) substitute for the decision appealed against any other decision which could have been made by the licensing authority; or
(c) remit the case to the licensing authority to dispose of it in accordance with the direction of the court.

6.7.4   The Guidance issued by the Secretary of State is that:[22]

> 'An appeal may therefore review the merits of the decision on the facts and consider points of law or address both.'

That comment, when read with the guidance given to magistrates' courts[23] (see **6.3.7**) seems to suggest that it will be possible, therefore, to challenge a decision of a licensing authority on the ground that the policy upon which it was based was unlawful.

---

[21] [2002] EWHC Admin 1104, [2002] LLR 538.

[22] Paragraph 10.7 of the Guidance.

[23] Paragraph 10.8 of the Guidance.

Chapter 7

PREMISES LICENCES

'And malt does more than Milton can to justify God's ways to man
Ale, man, ale's the stuff to drink for fellows whom it hurts to think.'

AE Housman
(*A Shropshire Lad*)

7.1 INTRODUCTION

7.1.1 One of the most fundamental changes to licensing laws is introduced in the new concept of the premises licence. It brings all 'licensable activities', which covers the sale of alcohol, entertainment, some sporting activities, late night refreshment licences, and theatres and cinemas into one licence, in any venue.

7.1.2 The Government's intention, as described by Baroness Blackstone in her introduction of the Bill to the House of Lords,[1] is to:

> '... introduce major benefits for business by sweeping away unnecessary red tape. It will amalgamate six existing licensing regimes covering the sale of alcohol, provision of public entertainment and late night refreshment and replace them with a single system of premises licence. Businesses will be able to apply for a single premises licence to cover all the licensable activities that they wish to provide.'

7.1.3 It is the premises that are licensed. The licence is linked to the licence holder but, whilst the holder remains legally capable of holding a licence, the licence is permanent. There is no need to renew and, unless surrendered or revoked after a review, the premises licence can run indefinitely. This gives continuity; the licence stays with the premises regardless of any change in ownership.

7.1.4 A 'premises licence' is defined as a licence granted in respect of any premises which authorises the premises to be used for one or more licensable activities.[2]

---

[1] *Hansard*, HL Deb, vol 641, col 643 (26 November 2002).

[2] LA 2003, s 11.

7.2   THE RELEVANT LICENSING AUTHORITY

7.2.1   The licensing authority responsible for the issue and control of premises licences is the local authority (licensing authority) for the area in which the premises are situated. If the premises straddle the boundary between two authorities, the applicant must apply to the authority in whose area the greater part of the premises lies. If that cannot be determined he can nominate which authority is to be the relevant authority for licensing purposes.[3]

7.3   DEFINITION OF 'PREMISES'

7.3.1   'Premises', as defined in the LA 2003, is 'any place and includes a vehicle, vessel or moveable structure'.[4] This very wide definition means that, for example:

– a vessel is treated as if it were premises situated at the place where it is usually moored;
– if a vehicle or structure is not permanently sited at one place and is intended to be used for one or more licensable activity, then it is treated as if it were premises situated wherever the licensable activity is to take place. So the big top of a travelling circus, or a beer tent that moves from one agricultural show to another, would have to apply for a premises licence for every site on the tour;
– a hot-dog stand regularly parked outside a nightclub will need a premises licence.

7.4   WHO CAN APPLY

7.4.1   The applicant for a premises licence can be any one of the following:[5]

– an individual over the age of 18 who runs, or intends to run, a business providing any one of the licensable activities from a particular premises;
– a person charged with a statutory function (such as a local authority) or acting by virtue of the Royal Prerogative (under a royal charter, for example);
– a recognised club;
– a charity;
– a school or educational institution;
– a hospital or health service body;

---

[3]   LA 2003, s 12.

[4]   Ibid, s 193.

[5]   Ibid, s 16.

- armed services personnel in relation to services premises;
- a police force;
- others as prescribed.

7.4.2 The terms 'charity', 'educational institution', 'health service body', 'independent hospital', 'proprietor' of an educational institution in relation to a school and 'statutory function' are all defined in LA 2003, s 16.

7.5 APPLICATION FOR A PREMISES LICENCE

7.5.1 The Guidance given by the Secretary of State contains the following passage:[6]

'Four fundamental principles underpin the 2003 Act. The first is that applicants for premises licences or for major variations of such licences are expected to conduct a thorough risk assessment with regard to the licensing objectives when preparing their applications. The second is that operating schedules should be reviewed by professional bodies expert in the areas concerned. The third is that local residents are free to raise reasonable and relevant representations about the proposals. The fourth is that the role of the licensing authority is primarily to regulate the carrying on of the licensable activity when specific interests in those activities conflict. When considering applications, it is expected that licensing authorities will seek to uphold these principles.'

7.5.2 Apart from the third (ease of comment by local residents), none of these guiding principles is embodied in the LA 2003 and it is not easy to see exactly how they will work in practice. If applicants are expected to demonstrate that they have abided by the Guidance, that will involve a considerable amount of additional effort and expense, quite the reverse of the much-vaunted 'light touch' reduction in bureaucracy that the Government intended.

7.5.3 It is, of course, only in circumstances where representations have been made that the licensing authority will have cause to consider the operating schedule and any risk assessment. By virtue of LA 2003, s 18, if the applicant has completed the forms properly and paid the fee and if no representation has been received by the licensing authority, then subject to the mandatory conditions and conditions consistent with the operating schedule the licence must be granted.

7.5.4 The application has to be made in the prescribed form[7] to the relevant licensing authority[8] and must be accompanied by:

- an operating schedule;

---

[6] Paragraph 5.50 of the Guidance.

[7] LA 2003, s 17.

[8] Ibid, s 12.

–   a plan of the premises;
–   the consent of the designated premises supervisor;
–   the fee.

7.5.5 Regulations will set out the notice and advertising requirements. It is likely that these will include the posting of an A3 sized notice outside the premises for a set period and the provision of information as to where the detailed contents of the application can be viewed. Local authorities will be encouraged to put applications onto their websites.

7.5.6   The application must be served on the responsible authorities. 'Responsible authorities' mean any of the police, fire authority, Health and Safety Executive, local planning authority, environmental health department and a body recognised by the licensing authority as responsible for the protection of children from harm. Other 'responsible bodies' are involved in relation to vessels, and more may be prescribed by regulation.[9]

7.6   THE OPERATING SCHEDULE

7.6.1   This is a crucial document. It will set out the basis for operations of the whole licensed business and should be the subject of discussions with the police, fire authority and environmental health officers. The intention is that, as far as possible, all contentious matters will be ironed out before the application comes before the local authority licensing committee. If there is no representation from any interested party or responsible authority, the application will be granted. So it is in the interests of the applicant to try to resolve any potential problems in advance to avoid a hearing.

7.6.2   Once the application has been granted the details of the operating schedule will be incorporated in the licence as conditions. Breach of those conditions could result in prosecution, review and revocation. It is in everyone's interest that the conditions should be accurate and clearly stated.

7.6.3   In the Guidance it is anticipated that:[10]

> 'The conditions that are necessary for the promotion of the licensing objectives should emerge initially from a prospective licence or certificate holder's risk assessment.'

7.6.4   The local authority must impose relevant mandatory conditions and, following a hearing or the receipt of representations, can impose additional conditions provided that they are necessary to promote one or more of the licensing objectives. Such additional conditions should be kept to a minimum and not repeat existing legislation.

---

[9]   LA 2003, s 13(4).

[10]   Paragraph 7.4 of the Guidance.

7.6.5   In the Guidance the Secretary of State expressed the view that ideally the operating schedule should include:[11]

–   a general description of the style and character of the business to be conducted on the premises (for example, a supermarket, or a cinema with six screens and a bar, or a restaurant, or a public house with two bars, a dining area and a garden open to customers);
–   an indication of the type of entertainment available on the premises, whether or not licensable under the LA 2003 so that the responsible authorities and interested parties can form a proper view as to what may be necessary at such premises for the protection of children from harm.

7.6.6   The operating schedule must include the following:[12]

(a) the relevant licensable activities;
(b) the times during which it is proposed that the relevant licensable activities are to take place;
(c) any other times during which it is proposed that the premises are to be open to the public;
(d) where the applicant wishes the licence to have effect for a limited period, that period;
(e) where alcohol is to be supplied, details of the designated supervisor;
(f) whether that alcohol is to be supplied for consumption on or off the premises or both;
(g) the steps which are proposed to promote the licensing objectives; and
(h) such other matters as may be prescribed in regulations.

The relevant licensable activities

7.6.7   This could include the retail sale of alcohol, 2 nights a week of live music and a regular darts championship, or ballet in a marquee and a bar, in fact whatever the applicant wishes to provide by way of licensable entertainment or supply of alcohol.

The intended times when the licensable activities will take place

7.6.8   This will probably be the most contentious issue. The LA 2003 does away with permitted hours and allows for theoretical 24-hour opening, depending upon the premises and the merits of each case. The intention is that for every application the local authority should look at the specific circumstances of each premises and, using their local expertise, decide upon opening hours suitable to the location and the type of business that is to be run. In an urban location, the applicant may wish to cater for office workers during the day and early

---

[11] Paragraph 5.32 of the Guidance.
[12] LA 2003, s 17(4).

evening and then to a very late night dance crowd, and the application would therefore be for 11 am to 6 am for the sale of alcohol, and from, say, 10 pm to 6 am for dancing and live music. If representations are received, the licensing authority will have to look at the potential nuisance to residents within the vicinity, to think of any steps that could reduce the possibility of nuisance and to resort to restrictions of licensed hours only when all other avenues have been exhausted.

7.6.9 In the Guidance, licensing authorities are specifically dissuaded from 'zoning', which was unsuccessfully tried in Edinburgh some years ago but abandoned when it was found that customers simply migrated from one early closing zone to the adjacent streets where later opening was permitted.[13] Likewise 'staggered closing times', that is when pubs close 15 or 30 minutes after one another, to try and disperse customers gradually, are not recommended. The thinking here is that it would merely encourage drinkers to stagger from one premises to another, refining the drinking-to-closing-time culture that the Government is so keen to see changed.

7.6.10 Instead it will be up to each licensing committee to be flexible to ensure that people leave city centres over a gradual period; it is believed that longer opening hours will enable this to happen naturally. Public transport will have a vital role to play in ensuring that late night crowds can disperse easily.

7.6.11 Separate hours can be requested for different licensable activities. In the case of a supermarket it would be expected that the application for hours should be for all hours that the shop will be open. It is not open to the authority to take into account any extraneous matters, for example employees' rights, those rights being protected by other legislation.

7.6.12 The Guidance is clear that: 'Above all, licensing authorities should not fix pre-determined closing times for particular areas'.[14]

Any other times that the premises will be open to the public

7.6.13 Any other times that the premises will be open to the public (or, in the case of a club, club members) while not providing any licensable activity also need to be set out. This will be important, for example for public houses which open early just to serve coffee, or for the café which also intends to operate after 11 pm as a late night takeaway.

If the licence is for a limited period only

7.6.14 If the licence is for a limited period only, the exact period for which it is required should be set out. In the case of a village fête this could be a couple of days, or for a major music festival over a week or

---

[13] Paragraph 7.7 of the Guidance.

[14] Paragraph 7.9 of the Guidance.

more, specifying the different licensable activities that will take place at different times.

Information as to the proposed designated premises supervisor

7.6.15   This should include the licence number of the personal licence held by the proposed supervisor and the issuing authority.

The supply of alcohol

7.6.16   The operating schedule must state whether alcohol is to be served and if so whether it will be for consumption on or off the premises or both. A simple statement should be sufficient, the broader details being covered in the initial paragraph of the operating schedule.

The steps that will be taken by the applicant to promote the licensing objectives

7.6.17   The steps taken will depend upon the type of premises. An obvious example would be the employment of door staff at, or the exclusion of children from, a nightclub. The licensing objectives are the light by which the whole LA 2003 is to be viewed. This requirement is not a superficial gloss on the management of the premises but a crucial part of the licence application. Unworkable conditions flowing from a poorly drawn operating schedule, or imposed because foreseeable problems had not been addressed, could result in a review and revocation.

7.7   THE PLAN

7.7.1   An application must be accompanied by a plan of the premises, in the prescribed form, to show the full layout of the premises with a particular eye to its suitability as licensed premises. The plan will remain as the document of record for the local authority and, if alterations are to be made, an application for variation will be needed.

7.8   CONSENT OF THE DESIGNATED PREMISES SUPERVISOR

7.8.1   This is needed where the licence is to include the sale of alcohol.

7.9   FEES

7.9.1   The fees are to be set centrally with the intention that the level of fee will enable the local authority to cover adequately all the new functions required by the LA 2003 whilst ensuring that the fees are kept within a reasonable limit. The requisite fee will have to be sent with each application. There is also a power to order the payment of an annual fee by a premises licence holder.[15] The current fees estimate[16] shows a fee range of £100–£500 for permanent sites depending on the site, and an annual charge of £50–£150 to cover the authorities' year-to-year costs and ensure a revenue stream.

7.10   DETERMINATION OF APPLICATION FOR PREMISES LICENCE

7.10.1   The licensing authority must grant the premises licence, subject to any conditions consequent to the operating schedule and the compulsory conditions imposed in accordance with LA 2003, ss 19, 20 and 21, if applicable, provided that:

–   the application has been correctly advertised;
–   all responsible authorities have been served with a copy of the application; and
–   no relevant representation has been received.[17]

7.10.2   If 'relevant representations' are made, the licensing authority must hold a hearing unless it is agreed with the applicant and those who made representations that a hearing is not required.[18]

7.10.3   Having regard to the representations made at the hearing (or in writing if it has been agreed that there is no need for a hearing) the licensing authority must consider the application in the light of the licensing objectives and take whatever steps it thinks necessary to promote them.

7.10.4   The steps are:[19]

(a)   to grant the licence as requested, subject to the conditions suggested in the operating schedule (amended or varied as required to meet the licensing objectives) and the mandatory conditions; or
(b)   to grant the application but exclude from it any of the licensable activities on the original application; or
(c)   to refuse to specify the proposed premises supervisor; or
(d)   to reject the application.

---

[15]   LA 2003, s 55(2).

[16]   Taken from the Department of Culture, Media and Sport Regulatory Impact Assessment (15 November 2002).

[17]   LA 2003, s 18(1) and (2).

[18]   Ibid, s 18(3).

[19]   Ibid, s 18(4).

7.11   RELEVANT REPRESENTATIONS

7.11.1   Within LA 2003, s 18, representations to the licensing authority are considered 'relevant' if they:[20]

(a) concern the impact of the potential grant of the licence on the promotion of the licensing objectives;
(b) were made by an interested party or responsible authority within the period prescribed in the regulations, have not been withdrawn and, in the case of an interested party, are not vexatious or frivolous;
(c) were made by the police and relate to the person identified as the designated premises supervisor; and
(d) are not excluded representations by virtue of the provisions governing provisional statements.

7.11.2   Interested parties are defined as meaning any of:[21]

(a) a person living in the vicinity of the premises;
(b) a body representing persons who live in that vicinity;
(c) a person involved in a business in that vicinity;
(d) a body representing persons involved in such businesses.

7.11.3   Whether the representation is frivolous or vexatious is a matter for the licensing authority to determine. Clearly, if the representation does not relate to the impact that the grant of a licence might have on the promotion of at least one of the licensing objectives, it will be held to be irrelevant. Otherwise each representation will have to be considered on its merits. Is it serious or trivial? Is the representation made for ulterior purposes? Additional considerations will apply when considering representations made in the course of a review of an existing licence.

7.11.4   If the licensing authority decides that representations made by an interested party are frivolous or vexatious it must inform the interested party of the decision and its reasons.[22]

7.11.5   The term 'vicinity' has not been defined in the LA 2003. The Explanatory Notes are also silent. In the Commons, the then Minister for Tourism, Film and Broadcasting, Dr Kim Howells, said: [23]

> 'The word "vicinity" can mean an area and a neighbourhood. We have chosen not to define that in the Bill to allow for flexibility and responsiveness to circumstances.'

7.11.6   Where the police express concerns about the proposed premises supervisor, the representation must include a statement that 'due to the exceptional circumstances of the case . . . the designation

---

[20] LA 2003, s 18(6) and (7).

[21] Ibid, s 13(3).

[22] Ibid, s 18(8).

[23] *Hansard*, HC Standing Committee D, 10 April 2003, col 222.

of the person concerned ... would undermine the crime prevention objective'.[24]

7.12 CONDITIONS

7.12.1 Conditions can be imposed on the licence only if they can be justified with reference to the licensing objectives. The premises licence can be granted with different conditions that apply to either the differing areas of the premises or to different qualifying activities, giving the authority maximum flexibility.[25]

7.12.2 If alcohol is sold there are two compulsory conditions:[26]

(1) no alcohol may be supplied unless there is a designated premises supervisor in respect of the premises licence or if the designated premises supervisor does not hold a licence or has had his personal licence suspended; and
(2) every supply of alcohol must be made or authorised by someone who holds a personal licence.

This does not mean that either the designated supervisor or a personal licence holder has to be present whenever alcohol is sold. Conditions to that effect could only be imposed if necessary for the promotion of one of the licensing objectives.[27]

7.12.3 Where a premises licence authorises the exhibition of films, the licence must include a condition requiring the admission of children to be restricted in accordance with any recommendation of the film classification body specified in the licence or by the licensing authority.[28] A film classification body is defined by reference to the Video Recordings Act 1984 and the only body designated under that Act is the British Board of Film Classification.

7.12.4 Where a premises licence includes a condition requiring the presence of security staff at any time, the licence must include a condition that each such individual must be licensed by the Security Industry Authority.[29] However, this does not apply to the door staff at cinemas or theatres.[30]

7.12.5 Very firm advice with regard to the imposition of conditions is given to licensing authorities in the Guidance issued by the Secretary of State:[31]

---

[24] LA 2003, s 18(9)(b).

[25] Ibid, s 18(10).

[26] Ibid, s 19.

[27] Paragraph 7.57 of the Guidance.

[28] LA 2003, s 20.

[29] Ibid, s 21.

[30] Ibid, s 21(2).

[31] Paragraph 7.5 of the Guidance.

'The licensing authority may not therefore impose any conditions unless its discretion has been engaged following the making of relevant representations and it has been satisfied at a hearing of the validity of the concerns raised. It may then only impose such conditions as are necessary to promote the licensing objectives. However, in order to minimise disputes and the necessity for hearings it would be sensible for applicants to consult with all responsible authorities when operating schedules are being prepared. This would allow for proper liaison before representations prove necessary.'

7.12.6 Conditions which relate to people with disabilities, which enter into workplace disputes, which duplicate other statutory provisions, or which involve moral judgements about standards of decency, are all strongly discouraged.[32] In relation to each of the licensing objectives, the Guidance contains a pool of suggested conditions which might be applicable in a particular case.[33]

7.12.7 Conditions which seek to impose censorship on plays are forbidden.[34]

7.13 PROVISIONAL STATEMENT

7.13.1 To avoid difficulties facing those who wish to invest in a new venture but do not have the security of knowing that a premises licence will be granted, LA 2003, s 29 provides for the making of an application for a 'provisional statement'.

7.13.2 The basis of the application is that premises are being, or are about to be, constructed for the purpose of being used for one or more licensable activities, or are being, or are about to be altered or extended for the same purposes (whether or not they are being used for a licensing purpose already).

7.13.3 The application has to be made on the prescribed form and must be accompanied by the requisite fee and a schedule of works.[35] The schedule of works comprises a statement as to the proposed use of the premises, plans of work and such other information as prescribed in the regulations. An application for a provisional statement proceeds on the basis that the premises will be constructed, substantially, in accordance with the schedule of works.

7.13.4 The advantage of obtaining a provisional statement is that, save for exceptional circumstances, it prevents any representations which could have been made at the provisional statement stage being raised when the premises licence is sought. Any such representation

---

[32] Part 7 of the Guidance.

[33] Annexes D–H of the Guidance.

[34] LA 2003, s 22.

[35] Ibid, s 29.

must be regarded as irrelevant unless there has been a material change in either the premises or the environs since the provisional statement was granted, or the interested party who wishes to make a representation has a reasonable excuse for not having made it at the provisional statement stage.[36]

7.13.5   A provisional statement will be to the effect that either the applicant has complied with the statutory provisions and no relevant representation has been made or, following the receipt of representations and a hearing, the authority has determined that if the premises had been constructed in accordance with the schedule of works, the authority would have taken one of the steps available to it when determining a full premises licence application.[37]

7.13.6   The procedures for the making of an application for a provisional statement can be found in LA 2003, ss 29–32. For the most part they replicate the procedures relating to an application for a premises licence.

7.14   DETERMINATION OF APPLICATIONS

7.14.1   Once determined, whether granted, granted with conditions, or rejected, the licensing authority must give notice of the outcome of the application to:

(a) the applicant;
(b) any person who made relevant representations in respect of the application; and
(c) the police.

7.14.2   If representations were made but the application has been granted, the licensing authority must state its reasons for the decision as to any steps taken in accordance with LA 2003, s 18(3)(b) and those reasons must be set out in the notice.[38]

7.14.3   If the application is rejected, again reasons must be given and set out in a notice to all the persons involved.[39]

7.14.4   If granted, the licence must be issued and a summary provided to the applicant.

7.14.5   The applicant, any interested party who made a relevant representation and the police, if they are aggrieved by the decision of the licensing authority, have a right of appeal to the magistrates' court.[40]

---

[36] LA 2003, s 32.

[37] Those are the steps set out in LA 2003, s 18(3)(b) (see **7.10.4**).

[38] LA 2003, s 23(2).

[39] Ibid, s 23(3).

[40] For appeals, see Chapter 14.

7.15 FORM OF PREMISES LICENCE

7.15.1 The exact form of the licence and the separate summary will be set out in the regulations, but will include:[41]

– the name and address of the licence holder;
– a plan of the premises;
– the licensable activities permitted;
– if these include the supply of alcohol, the name and address of the designated premises supervisor;
– any conditions to which the licence is subject;
– if the licence is not permanent, then the dates for which it is to have effect.

7.15.2 If a premises licence is lost, damaged, or destroyed, the licensing authority must provide a copy upon payment of a fee, once it has been established that:

(a) the licence has been lost, stolen, damaged, or destroyed; and
(b) if lost or stolen that this has been reported to the police.

7.15.3 There is a duty to notify changes to the licence. The holder of a premises licence must notify the licensing authority[42] as soon as possible of any change in:

(a) the licence holder's name and address;
(b) the name and address of the designated premises supervisor (unless that person has already done so, in which case the supervisor should give the licence holder a copy of the notice served on the licensing authority),

in each case sending the licence to be altered and the requisite fee. If the licence cannot be forwarded, a statement of the reasons for the failure to produce it must be sent to the licensing authority.

7.15.4 There is also a duty to keep and produce the licence.[43] If the licence authorises any licensable activities then the holder of the premises licence must ensure that the licence (or a properly certified copy) is kept at the premises and that a nominated person is responsible for it. The nominated person must be either:

(a) the holder of the licence; or
(b) someone working at the premises whom the holder of the licence has nominated in writing.

7.15.5 However, it is up to the holder of the licence to ensure that the summary of the licence (or a certified copy) and a notice setting out the position of the nominated person are prominently displayed

---

[41] LA 2003, s 24.
[42] Ibid, s 33.
[43] Ibid, s 57.

at the premises. Failure to display or produce the licence for inspection upon demand is an offence.[44]

7.16   DURATION OF LICENCE

7.16.1   A premises licence runs until:

– it is surrendered;
– it is revoked; or
– it expires (if granted only for a limited period).

7.16.2   A premises licence will lapse upon:

– the death, incapacity or insolvency of the licence holder;[45]or
– if it is a company, it becomes insolvent or is dissolved; or
– if it is a club, it ceases to be a recognised club.

7.16.3   In addition, a premises licence is of no effect whilst suspended under review.

7.16.4   Surrender is effected by the licence holder simply notifying the licensing authority in writing and enclosing the licence.[46] The licence lapses once received by the authority.

7.16.5   The licence may be reinstated if an application for transfer is made within the 7 days after surrender or lapse through death, incapacity, insolvency or company dissolution. This application must be made in accordance with the provisions of LA 2003, ss 42 and 43 (see **7.20**), in which case the premises licence is reinstated immediately the transfer application is received by the licensing authority. This provision cannot be used more than once.[47]

7.16.6   Similarly, following the death or other incapacity of the premises licence holder, an application can be made for an interim authority to continue the business.[48] The applicant must be either the personal representative, in the case of the death of the former licence holder, or have an enduring power of attorney, or be an insolvency practitioner, or have a prescribed interest in the premises.[49] Only one application for an interim authority can be made. An interim authority lasts for 2 months unless cancelled. During that period the holder of the interim authority can make an application for a transfer of the licence.

---

[44] LA 2003, s 57(4).

[45] Ibid, s 27.

[46] Ibid, s 28.

[47] Ibid, s 50.

[48] Ibid, s 47.

[49] This will apparently include 'pub operating companies and owners of premises': Dr Kim Howells – HC Standing Committee D, 8 April 2003, col 197.

7.16.7   An application for an interim authority must be made within the 7 days after the lapse of the licence. Once received by the licensing authority it takes immediate effect, but the premises licence lapses again if a copy of the application is not given to the police within that same 7-day period. The licensing authority has to provide to the applicant a copy of the premises licence and the summary. If the applicant is not the designated premises supervisor, he must notify the supervisor immediately.[50]

7.16.8   The police may object to an interim authority if satisfied that the exceptional circumstances of the case are such that a failure to cancel the interim authority would undermine the crime prevention objective.[51] Notice to that effect must be given to the licensing authority within 48 hours. The licensing authority must then hold a hearing and cancel the interim authority if it considers it necessary for the promotion of the crime prevention objective. The interim authority lapses when notice of its cancellation is given to the holder of the interim authority. Both the holder of the interim authority and the police have a right of appeal.

7.16.9   The practical effect of the interim authority provisions can be demonstrated as follows. If Fred Bloggs, a public house tenant for his local brewery, dies on 1 May it would be open to either Mrs Bloggs, as his personal representative, or the brewery to apply for an interim authority to the local licensing authority; the notice and fee must be served no later than 8 May; and the police must be given a copy of the notice by 8 May. If it were served on 3 May the interim authority would run until 8 July, by which time an application for transfer must have been lodged. If this procedure were not followed, a new licence would need to be applied for.

7.17   VARIATION OF A PREMISES LICENCE

7.17.1   It is open to the holder of the premises licence to apply for a variation of the premises licence at any time, subject to the procedural requirements set out in the regulations.[52] A fee will be payable. The licence holder must send the licence (or an explanation of why it cannot be sent) with the application, unless the only matter for variation is a change of the designated premises supervisor (in which case different provisions apply).

7.17.2   If the licensing authority receives any relevant representations, a hearing must be held (unless all parties agree that

---

[50]   LA 2003, s 49.

[51]   Ibid, s 48(1).

[52]   Ibid, s 34.

this is not necessary). Otherwise the application for variation must be granted.[53]

7.17.3 A representation will be relevant only if:

- it is concerned with the impact of the variation upon the promotion of the licensing objectives; and
- it is made by an interested party or responsible authority within the specified time and not withdrawn prior to the hearing; and
- if made by an interested party, it is neither frivolous nor vexatious.

7.17.4 Following a hearing (if necessary) the licensing authority must either modify the conditions of the licence or reject the whole or any part of the application.[54] The guiding principle, as elsewhere in the LA 2003, is the promotion of the licensing objectives.

7.17.5 When the application (or any part) has been determined, whether granted or rejected, the licensing authority must notify the applicant, the makers of any relevant representations and the police. If the variation has been allowed the notice must state when the variation will take effect, normally as set out in the application. The authority must give reasons for any decisions reached upon relevant representations, with regard to the steps to be taken to promote the licensing objectives or the rejection of the application. Aggrieved parties have a right of appeal to the magistrates' court.

7.17.6 As in other cases, if the licensing authority rejects a representation as frivolous or vexatious it must explain why it made that decision.[55] There is no appeal against the rejection of representations on the grounds of frivolity or vexation. The disappointed interested party can apply for judicial review of the licensing authority's decision.

7.17.7 It is not possible to change the premises to which the licence relates nor to extend the period of the licence in a variation,[56] but it is open to the authority to apply different conditions to different parts of the premises or differing licensable activities.[57]

7.18 VARIATION OF DESIGNATED PREMISES SUPERVISOR

7.18.1 Only the holder of the premise licence can apply to vary the designated premises supervisor. The application, in the prescribed form and with a fee, must be sent to the current designated supervisor, the licensing authority and the police, accompanied by:

---

[53] LA 2003, s 35(1) and (2).

[54] Ibid, s 35(4).

[55] Ibid, s 36(5).

[56] Ibid, s 36(6).

[57] Ibid, s 36(7).

- the consent of the intended new supervisor; and
- the licence (or a statement of the reasons why the licence is not available).

7.18.2 The police can object to the proposed designated supervisor if they believe that the exceptional circumstances of the case are such that granting the application would undermine the crime prevention objective.[58] If the police object, the licensing authority must hold a hearing (unless all involved agree that this is not necessary) at which the application must be considered and a decision reached either to grant the variation or to reject it on the basis that it is necessary for the promotion of the crime prevention objective. The decision, once reached, must be notified to the applicant licence holder, the proposed new supervisor and the police, stating the time when the variation will take effect and, giving reasons for the decision.[59]

7.18.3 If an application for the variation of a designated premises supervisor includes a request that it should take immediate effect (which will be necessary to enable the supply of alcohol to continue in circumstances where a previous supervisor has left unexpectedly, for example), it will take effect when the application is received by the licensing authority. The variation of supervisor then remains effective until either the application is granted, withdrawn or rejected.[60]

7.18.4 When an application for variation of the designated premises supervisor has been granted or rejected, the holder of the premises licence must notify the existing designated supervisor either that he has been replaced or that the application has been rejected; failure to do so is an offence.[61]

7.19 REQUEST TO BE REMOVED AS DESIGNATED PREMISES SUPERVISOR

7.19.1 A designated premises supervisor can give notice to the licensing authority that he wishes to cease being the designated supervisor for particular premises.[62]

7.19.2 If the supervisor is also the holder of the premises licence he must send the licence with the notice of cessation. If he is not the premises licence holder he must notify the premises licence holder within 48 hours. He must also tell the premises licence holder that the premises licence (or a statement of the reasons for failure to produce the licence) must be sent to the licensing authority within 14 days.

---

[58] LA 2003, s 37(5).

[59] Ibid, s 39.

[60] Ibid, s 38.

[61] Ibid, s 40.

[62] Ibid, s 41.

7.19.3 The effect of giving notice to the licensing authority and complying with the provisions regarding the premises licence is that from the time the notice is received by the licence authority, or a later time if so specified in the notice, the person concerned is no longer treated as the designated premises supervisor.

7.20   TRANSFER OF PREMISES LICENCE

7.20.1   Anyone who could apply for a premises licence (see **7.4**) can apply for the transfer of a licence into his name. The application must be served on the licensing authority and the local police, in the form prescribed and with the fee as per the regulations. The premises licence (or a statement as to why it is not practicable to send it) must be sent with the application.[63]

7.20.2   The police can object if satisfied that the exceptional circumstances of the case are such that granting the transfer would undermine the crime prevention objective. Notice of any police objection must be given within 14 days.[64]

7.20.3   Unusually for the LA 2003 the conditions upon which the transfer can be granted are all expressed in the negative.[65] The transfer must be rejected unless either:

(a) it contains an application to take immediate effect in the interim; or
(b) the holder of the premises licence consents to the transfer; or
(c) the applicant has been excused from obtaining the holder's consent because he has taken all reasonable steps to obtain it and, once the application is granted, the applicant will be able to trade from the premises as permitted by the licence.

Otherwise, unless the police have objected, the transfer must be granted.

7.20.4   If the police decide to object to the transfer then the licensing authority must hold a hearing (unless all parties agree that this is not necessary), and the licensing authority must grant the transfer unless refusal would be a better way of promoting the crime prevention objective.[66]

7.20.5   Once the transfer application has been determined the licensing authority must notify:

–   the applicant;
–   the local police; and

---

[63] LA 2003, s 42.

[64] Ibid, s 42(6) and (7).

[65] Ibid, s 44.

[66] Ibid, s 44(5).

– the previous holder of the premises certificate.

If the application is granted against police objections, or rejected, the licensing authority must give its reasons for the decision.

7.20.6 It is the applicant's duty to notify the designated premises supervisor of the transfer; failure to do so is an offence.[67]

7.20.7 An applicant must be exempted from the requirement to obtain the consent of the existing premises licence holder if he can show to the licensing authority's satisfaction that he has taken all reasonable steps to obtain that consent and that if the application for transfer was to be granted he would be in a position to use the premises for the authorised licensed activities. This provision protects the owners of licensed premises in the case of defaulting tenants.

7.20.8 The owners of property and others with an interest in property such as mortgagees and occupiers can protect their interests by, in effect, registering those interests with the licensing authority. This is done by giving notice to the licensing authority using the prescribed form and paying a fee. The effect of such a notice lasts for 12 months and so must be repeated annually.[68]

7.20.9 The effect of an owner giving notice is that the licensing authority must notify the owner immediately of an application to make any change relating to the licensed premises and of the right to request a copy of the information contained in any entry in the licensing register.

7.20.10 It is likely that those with a property interest in licensed premises will be able to make applications for an interim authority under LA 2003, s 47 in the event of a licence lapsing through surrender, for example, or on the death, incapacity or insolvency of the holder of the premises licence.[69] Such persons will also be able to apply for a transfer, thereby effecting a reinstatement of the licence.[70]

7.21 REVIEWS OF PREMISES LICENCES

7.21.1 Whilst trying to make things easier for businesses and to encourage flexibility, the Government also promised to clamp down on crime and anti-social behaviour that can blight local communities. The balance was struck by providing for a review of a premises licence where problems had arisen after the initial grant.

7.21.2 When introducing the Bill to the House of Lords, Baroness Blackstone said:[71]

---

[67] LA 2003, s 46.

[68] Ibid, s 178.

[69] Dr Kim Howells – *Hansard,* HC Standing Committee D, 8 April 2003, col 197.

[70] LA 2003, s 50.

[71] *Hansard,* HL Deb, vol 641, col 642 (26 November 2002).

'Our plans to enable local residents to make representations about any applications for new or varied licences will give them a greater say than ever before in licensing decisions. We have gone further still. Local residents and businesses, as well as expert bodies, will have the power to request that the licensing authority review existing licences where problems arise. Such a review could result in the modification of the licence, its suspension, or, ultimately, revocation.'

7.21.3   As elsewhere in the LA 2003, however, the Government have been keen to stress that '[f]irst and foremost the grounds for an application for review must be relevant to one or more of the licensing objectives'.[72]

7.21.4   The review of a premises licence[73] can be requested at any time by an interested party or a responsible authority.

7.21.5   The form of the review notice will be laid out in regulations which will also stipulate upon whom it must be served, where it must be advertised and the time frame for others concerned to make representations.

7.21.6   At any time the licensing authority can reject any ground for review if it is satisfied:

(a)   that the ground is not relevant to one or more of the licensing objectives; or
(b)   in the case of an application made by an interested party, that the ground is frivolous, vexatious or is a repetition.[74]

7.21.7   A ground will be deemed to be a repetition if it is identical or substantially similar to:

–   a ground for review specified in an earlier application for review made in respect of the same premises licence and determined by the authority; or
–   representations considered by the licensing authority when determining whether or not to grant the original application for a premises licence; or
–   representations which would have been considered at the time of the original grant but were excluded because a provisional statement had been made earlier; *and*

a reasonable interval has not elapsed since the earlier application for review or grant of the licence.[75]

7.21.8   A 'reasonable interval' is not defined in the LA 2003. The Explanatory Notes do not explain what is meant by a reasonable period. In the Guidance, the Secretary of State recommends that

---

[72] Dr Kim Howells – *Hansard*, HC Standing Committee D, col 306 (29 April 2003).

[73] LA 2003, s 51.

[74] Ibid, s 51(4).

[75] Ibid, s 51(5).

licensing authorities should not permit more than one review originating from interested parties within a period of 12 months.[76]

7.21.9 The licensing authority must hold a hearing[77] to consider an application to review made in accordance with the regulations and any relevant representations that have been made in response to it, although this cannot be done until after the application has been correctly advertised.

7.21.10 Keeping always the promotion of the licensing objectives as the only goal, the authority can take one or more of the following six steps:

(1) modify any of the conditions of the licence, either permanently or temporarily for a period of up to 3 months; or
(2) remove one of the qualifying activities from the licence, again either permanently or temporarily for up to 3 months; or
(3) remove the designated premises supervisor; or
(4) suspend the licence altogether for up to 3 months; or
(5) revoke the licence completely; or
(6) leave the premises licence in its existing state.

7.21.11 When the application (or any part) has been determined, whether granted or rejected, the licensing authority must notify:

(a) the holder of the premises licence;
(b) the applicant;
(c) the makers of any relevant representations; and
(d) the police.

The authority must give reasons for any decisions reached upon relevant representations, with regard to the steps to be taken to promote the licensing objectives.[78]

7.21.12 Any aggrieved party to the hearing has a right of appeal to the magistrates' court. If, however, a ground set out in an application for review made by an interested party has been rejected, as being irrelevant, vexatious, frivolous or repetitious, that may not be challenged on appeal but would be subject to a claim for judicial review.

7.21.13 If an appeal is lodged, any decision about a review, whether resulting in modification or removal of a qualifying activity, suspension, or withdrawal of the licence will not take effect until either the end of the appeal period or the appeal, once lodged, has been determined. (See Chapter 14.)

7.21.14 As a clarification of the position where the local authority could be both applicant (for example, the environmental health

---

[76] Paragraph 5.82 of the Guidance.

[77] LA 2003, s 52.

[78] Ibid, s 52(10).

department) and judge and jury (as licensing authority), LA 2003, s 53 states that for the purposes of review the authority is included as a responsible authority, and can apply for the review of a premises licence.

7.22 POWERS OF ENTRY

7.22.1 Unlike clubs, which have the benefit of being private premises and are therefore subject to a comparatively restricted inspection procedure, other premises are open to entry and inspection by virtue of the powers provided in the LA 2003. In this category will fall those clubs which, for commercial reasons, decide to apply for a premises licence.

7.22.2 A constable or authorised person may at any reasonable time before the determination of an application relating to a premises licence (which includes a grant, provisional statement, variation and review) enter the premises in order to assess either the likely effect of granting the application on the licensing objectives or, in the case of a review, the existing effect of licensed activities on those objectives.[79] An authorised person exercising this power must be able to produce the authorisation. Reasonable force can be used. To obstruct an authorised person in the exercise of this power is an offence. It is already an offence to obstruct a constable in the exercise of his duty.[80]

7.22.3 An 'authorised person' is defined in LA 2003, s 13 as any of:

(a) an officer of the licensing authority duly authorised by that authority;
(b) a fire officer;
(c) a health and safety officer;
(d) an officer of the local authority, authorised by that authority to carry out one or more of its statutory functions in relation to minimising or preventing the risk of pollution of the environment or harm to human health;
(e) a navigational or shipping inspector; and
(f) any other person prescribed by the regulations.

7.23 EXCLUDED PREMISES

7.23.1 Section 176 of the LA 2003 continues the disqualification of certain premises from selling by retail or supplying alcohol. Those premises are service areas on motorways and garages. The Secretary of State is given power to amend the definition of excluded premises and to add or remove types of premises by order.[81]

---

[79] LA 2003, s 59.
[80] Police Act 1996.
[81] LA 2003, s 176(2).

7.23.2 In relation to garages, the express words of the defining subsection are:[82]

'(b) premises used primarily as a garage or which form part of premises which are primarily so used.'

Premises are 'used as a garage' if they are used for one or more of the following:[83]

- the retailing of petrol;
- the retailing of derv;
- the sale of motor vehicles;
- the maintenance of motor vehicles.

7.23.3 The transfer of these provisions from the old legislation[84] to the LA 2003 brings into play the authorities relating to that legislation and in particular *Green v Inner London Licensing Justices*[85] and *R v Liverpool Crown Court, ex parte Goodwin*.[86] In *Green* the justices had made a false comparison by comparing the gross income from the sale of fuel (including taxes and duties) with the net turnover derived from the sales of other goods. In *Goodwin* the Crown Court had wrongly taken into account the appearance of the premises and how those premises were known locally. The proper question is: 'What is the intensity of use by customers at the premises?'.

7.23.4 The phrase 'intensity of use by customers' was used by the Minister in the House of Lords, when explaining the Government's retention of the prohibition.[87]

7.24 SMALL PREMISES

7.24.1 In the death throes of the Bill's passage through Parliament, the Government suffered two defeats in the House of Lords with regard to its stance over the abolition of what had come to be known as the 'two-in-a-bar rule'. This was a reference to s 182 of the Licensing Act 1964 which gave exemption from the need to obtain a public entertainments licence (music and dancing licence) in relation to wireless and television broadcasts or public entertainment by way of music and singing only which is provided solely by the reproduction of recorded sound, or by not more than two performers, or sometimes in one of those ways and sometimes in the other.

---

[82] LA 2003, s 176(2).

[83] Ibid, s 176(4).

[84] Licensing Act 1964, s 9(3), (4), (4A) and (4B).

[85] (1994) *Licensing Review* (October).

[86] [2002] LLR 698.

[87] Baroness Blackstone – *Hansard*, HL Deb, vol 643, col 457 (20 January 2003).

7.24.2   The Government's original stance had been quite firm. Lord McIntosh stated:[88]

> 'I turn to what is clearly a passionate concern – of mine as well as of others – and that is the subject of music. I believe that there has been a profound misunderstanding of what the Bill seeks to achieve. It was suggested that by abolishing the two-in-a-bar rule, which we all agree was completely anachronistic, somehow we are damaging the possibilities of live music. That could not be further from the truth.
>
> The truth of the matter is that considerations that we must take into account in licensing music are two-fold; one is noise and the other is safety. It does not matter whether the music is live or canned from a noise or safety point of view. In the past, canned music has been allowed and live music discouraged by the two-in-a-bar rule. If we make adequate provision for noise [and] safety ... then we are meeting the requirements of licensing. But there will be no additional imposition on licensed premises because, as I said, the licence for live music will be an integral part of the premises licence. It will cost no more than obtaining the alcohol licence in the first place.'

7.24.3   The argument moved on, however, from the cost of the original application putting off those who might otherwise provide facilities for live music to the cost of compliance with conditions imposed by licensing authorities putting them off. A compromise was reached at the last minute by the insertion into the Bill of s 177 – dancing and live music at certain small premises.

7.24.4   This complicated provision means that where premises:

– have a premises licence which allows for both the supply of alcohol and music entertainment; but
– are used primarily for the supply of alcohol; and
– cannot have more than 200 persons in them,

then any conditions relating to the provision of music entertainment:

– do not have effect at all in relation to live, unamplified music between the hours of 8 am and midnight (provided that no other form of regulated entertainment is taking place at the same time); and
– otherwise do not have effect save that they relate to the prevention of crime and disorder or public safety,

unless, in either case, they have been imposed, or brought into effect, following a review.

7.24.5   So a small public house with a capacity,[89] which must include customers and those living or working on the premises, of not more

---

[88] *Hansard*, HL Deb, vol 641, col 736 (26 November 2002).

[89] The 'capacity' is that imposed by way of either a fire certificate imposed under the Fire Precautions Act 1971 or a limit imposed by the licensing authority in accordance with recommendations made by the fire authority: LA 2003, s 177(8).

than 200 and which has the provision of music entertainment as one of its licensable activities has the freedom to provide unamplified live music between 8 am and 12 midnight without interference from the licensing authority.

7.24.6   If the music to be provided after midnight is amplified or recorded, and is not incidental music which is exempt from the provisions of the LA 2003, then the only 'music entertainment' conditions that apply are those relating to crime and disorder or public safety and not to public nuisance.

7.24.7   Despite the comments made by the Minister for Sport in the closing speech in the House of Commons when he said: 'Conditions that relate to public nuisance will be in place from midnight onwards'[90] it will be only after the neighbours, as interested parties, have complained about the noise and a review has been held that conditions relating to public nuisance and the protection of children from harm can be attached, or brought into effect, to apply to music entertainment at any time.

---

[90] Richard Caborn – *Hansard*, HC Deb, vol 408, col 1129 (8 July 2003).

Chapter 8

CLUBS

*'Mankind is not a tribe of animals to which we owe compassion.
Mankind is a club to which we owe our subscription.'*

GK Chesterton

8.1 INTRODUCTION

8.1.1   Clubs, be they political, sporting or working men's clubs, have always been treated differently from other licensed premises. The members' clubs to which this section applies are 'not-for-profit' organisations, as distinct from proprietary clubs which are owned by an individual or company and run as a business

8.1.2   This legal difference has an historical basis in that the premises of members' clubs are private; they belong to the members and are used for the members, not the general public. The members of each club are free to run the club as they wish; to create their own rules and set out the criteria for the use of the premises by guests and associates. Because the members together own the club they also jointly own the alcohol purchased by the club for their convenience. As a result there is no 'sale' of alcohol to club members, only a 'supply', and a charge is made in each case simply to maintain equality between members.

8.1.3   In introducing the Bill to the House of Lords, Baroness Blackstone summarised the Government's special approach to clubs. She said:[1]

> 'We recognise the value to the community of registered members clubs such as working men's or political clubs. We recognise that such clubs are private premises to which access is restricted and where alcohol is not supplied for profit. We intend to protect the special position of such clubs. Although they will have to promote the licensing objectives in the same way as other licensed premises, they will not require the full premises licence. The Bill will, however, bring clubs into line with other premises in relation to sales to and consumption by children.'

8.1.4   Until now, clubs have needed only to register with the courts, and not to obtain a licence in the usual way. The Government has been anxious to retain the unique character of clubs in general and to

---

[1]   *Hansard*, HL Deb, vol 641, col 645 (26 November 2002).

ensure that they keep their sometimes quirky nature, whilst at the same time bringing them into the new regime with sufficient regulation to ensure that their special nature is not abused. To this end, simple criteria in the LA 2003 will enable 'qualifying clubs' to be 'licensed' by means of a club premises certificate. Much has been made in both Houses of Parliament of the 'light touch' provisions that will regulate clubs in future.

8.1.5   The different status of qualifying clubs is reflected in the new Act. Unlike other licensed premises, clubs with the benefit of a club premises certificate have the following advantages, under Part 4:

–   there is no requirement to specify a designated premises supervisor on the licence;
–   there is no requirement for a member or employee of the club to hold a personal licence;
–   there are no police powers of immediate closure, or court powers to close all premises in a certain area; and
–   they enjoy more limited rights of entry for the police and authorised officers as a result of the private nature of the premises.

8.1.6   A club premises certificate is a certificate granted under Part 4 of the LA 2003 in respect of premises occupied by, and habitually used for the purposes of, a club.[2] The certificate is granted by the licensing authority and certifies that the club premises may be used for the licensable activities set out in the certificate and that the club is a 'qualifying club'.

8.2   APPLICATION FOR A CLUB PREMISES CERTIFICATE

8.2.1   An application for a club premises certificate may be made by any qualifying club (see **8.3**) for 'any premises which are occupied by and habitually used for the purposes of the club'.[3] The application is made to the licensing authority in whose area the club premises are situated (or, if it straddles two licensing authorities, the authority in whose area the greater part of the premises is situated).[4] In the unlikely event that the boundary line between the two authorities is exactly in the middle of the club premises, the applicant club can choose to which licensing authority to apply.

8.2.2   As with other licences, the licensing authority will be the local authority and the application itself will be very similar to that for a premises licence. It will include:

–   an operating schedule (see **8.2.4**);

---

[2]   LA 2003, s 60.

[3]   Ibid, s 71(1).

[4]   Ibid, s 68.

- a plan of the premises;
- a copy of the club rules;
- a fee (the Government is intending to set fees in bands based on the size and location of the venue);[5]
- a plan, in the prescribed form; and
- such other matters as may be prescribed.

8.2.3   Regulations will require the application to be advertised to enable any interested parties to make representations to the licensing authority, and the application will also need to be served upon each responsible authority, ie the police, fire and environmental health departments for each area. This list may be added to by the regulations, which will also set out the time frames for advertising and for any 'relevant representations' to be made.

8.2.4   Although the exact requirements of the club operating schedule will be set out in the regulations, it will include details of the following:

- how the licensing objectives will be promoted, to include any conditions that the applicant club would be willing to have on the club premises certificate;
- the qualifying club activities (see **8.4**) referred to as the 'relevant club activities';
- the hours during which the relevant club activities are to occur;
- any other times when the club premises will be open to members and their guests; and
- any other matters as prescribed.

Inspection

8.2.5   Prior to the determination of the application it is open to any authorised person or police officer to inspect the premises upon giving 48 hours' notice. Tight time limits apply to the inspection period, which runs for 14 days from the date of the application. It can only be extended by up to 7 days if the licensing authority believes that reasonable steps have been taken to arrange the viewing but that it has not been possible. The onus is very much on the authorities, fire, environmental health or police, to arrange the inspection in good time.[6]

8.3   QUALIFYING CLUBS

8.3.1   There are five general conditions, which must be fulfilled, to enable a club to qualify for a club premises certificate.[7] They are:

---

[5]   Dr Kim Howells – *Hansard*, HC Standing Committee D, 29 April 2003, col 323.

[6]   LA 2003, s 96.

[7]   Ibid, s 62.

(1) under the rules of the club no one may be admitted to membership or admitted for any of the privileges of membership until 2 days have elapsed between their application and membership itself – this replicates the existing '48 hour rule';

(2) the club rules must prevent anyone who becomes a member without initial application or nomination from enjoying the privileges of membership until two days after their becoming members, again repeating the 48 hour rule;

(3) the club must be established and conducted in good faith (see **8.5**);

(4) the club must have at least 25 members – should club membership drop below this magic number, a period of 3 months' grace is allowed for the club to try and recruit new members, otherwise it would lose its club premises certificate;[8]

(5) alcohol can only be supplied on the premises to members by or on behalf of the club.

8.3.2   If a club intends to sell alcohol there are three additional conditions:[9]

(6) that the purchase and supply of alcohol on behalf of a club must be managed by an elected committee of adult club members;

(7) that no one involved in the purchase of the alcohol should receive any commission at the expense of the club;

(8) that nobody involved in the supply of alcohol should receive any monetary benefit from the supply of alcohol by the club to its members and guests. Nothing in this prevents the bar steward of a club from receiving a bonus for overall performance if his contract so allows, although this would not be possible if the steward was also a member of the club.

8.3.3   There is no need for a designated premises supervisor, unless the club decides to widen its activities by, for example, allowing the general public to hire the club hall for wedding receptions, in which case a standard premises licence would be needed and a designated premises supervisor specified.

8.4   QUALIFYING CLUB ACTIVITIES

8.4.1   Section 1(2) of the LA 2003 sets out the qualifying club activities:

(a) the supply of alcohol to a member (off sales and on sales);

(b) sale to the guest of a member (on sales only);

(c) the provision of regulated entertainment to club members and their guests.

---

[8]   LA 2003, s 90(2).

[9]   Ibid, s 64.

8.4.2 The supply of alcohol to members is, as described above, not technically a sale at all, merely the provision to the member of a stock of alcohol which he already owns through membership of the club. Members are expected to pay for drinks merely in order to ensure fair distribution of the club's assets between 'Joe, who drinks six pints a week, and Harry, who drinks 10. No profit is made by anyone involved in the supply'.[10]

8.4.3 However, a club premises certificate cannot authorise the supply of alcohol to be consumed off the premises (allowing members to take beer or other drinks home with them) unless it is also allows consumption on the premises.[11]

8.4.4 A club premises certificate which allows off sales must be subject to three conditions:

(1) that the takeaway drinks can only be supplied when the club is open to members for consumption on the premises (the hours set out in the club premises certificate);
(2) any alcohol supplied for consumption off the premises must be in a sealed container (this would include a screw-top bottle); and
(3) supplies for consumption off the club premises can only be to a member, not to a guest.[12]

Sales to a guest

8.4.5 Members' guests are allowed to purchase alcohol from the club; this is defined to include associate members of the club and guests of associate members. A person is an 'associate member' for the purposes of the LA 2003 if he is admitted to the club in accordance with the rules of the club as a member of another club and that other club is a recognised club.[13]

8.4.6 Should a club wish to widen its activities, for example to allow members of the public to hire the club premises for events such as fundraising concerts, it is quite open to it to apply for a premises licence in the usual way. In this case, a designated premises supervisor would be required.

8.4.7 The provision of regulated entertainment includes entertainment provided on behalf of the club for the benefit of the members and their guests. It covers anything for which a charge is made, or which is intended to raise money for charity. Regulated entertainment would include plays, films, and publicly performed dance or live or recorded music.

---

[10] Dr Kim Howells – *Hansard*, HC Standing Committee D, 29 April 2003, col 338.

[11] LA 2003, s 73.

[12] Ibid, s 73.

[13] Ibid, s 68. A 'recognised club' is defined in s 193 as being a club which satisfies conditions 1–3 of the general conditions in s 62.

8.4.8   If the licensing authority considers that a club with a club premises certificate no longer fulfils the criteria of a qualifying club in relation to a qualifying club activity it may notify the club that the certificate is to be withdrawn, or that it is withdrawn in relation to a particular activity.[14] If the problem relates to the number of members having fallen below 25, the licensing authority has to give the club 3 months' notice of the intended withdrawal of the certificate.[15]

8.5   TEST OF 'GOOD FAITH'

8.5.1   Section 63 of the LA 2003 sets out the factors to be taken into account in deciding whether a club is in fact established and conducted in good faith. These matters include:

(a) any arrangements restricting the club's free purchase of alcohol;
(b) how money or property belonging to the club is used; permitted uses include charitable, political or benevolent purposes, or for the general benefit of the club. It would not be acceptable for the club to use any of its revenue for private gain;
(c) the way in which members obtain information about the club's finances;
(d) the account books and other records of the club's finances;
(e) the nature of the club premises.

8.5.2   If the licensing authority decides that the club is not a qualifying club because it is not established or conducted in good faith, then it must inform the club of that decision and set out its reasons.[16]

8.6   DETERMINATION OF APPLICATION

8.6.1   The licensing authority must grant the club premises certificate if the applicant club has complied with the regulations (as to notice, advertising and fees) and no relevant representation has been received. The mandatory conditions and conditions consistent with the club operating schedule must be imposed – but only those conditions.[17]

8.6.2   If relevant representations are made, the licensing authority must hold a hearing unless it is agrees with the applicant and all others who have made relevant representations that a hearing is not required. Having considered the representations and their evidential base, together with any representations made on behalf of the club, the licensing authority must consider the application in the light of

---

[14] LA 2003, s 90.

[15] Ibid, s 90(2).

[16] Ibid, s 63(3).

[17] Ibid, s 72(1) and (2).

the licensing objectives and take whatever steps it thinks necessary to promote them.[18]

8.6.3 Relevant representations must relate to one or more of the licensing objectives; and must be made within the prescribed time limits by either a responsible authority or an interested party. If made by an interested party, the representations must be neither frivolous nor vexatious. As in the case of an application for a premises licence, if the licensing authority consider a representation by an interested party to be frivolous or vexatious, the reasons of the authority must be given to that person.[19]

8.6.4 The steps which the licensing committee can take are:

(a) to grant the certificate as requested; or
(b) to grant the certificate with conditions, being those initially included in the operating schedule and/or additional conditions that the licensing authority deems necessary for the promotion of the licensing objectives; or
(c) to grant the certificate without the inclusion of one or more of the qualifying club activities on the original application; or
(d) to reject the application.[20]

Conditions

8.6.5 Conditions can be imposed on the certificate only if they can be justified with reference to the licensing objectives. The club premises certificate can be granted with different conditions that apply to either differing areas of the club premises or to different qualifying club activities, giving the authority maximum flexibility.[21] Conditions that seek to limit the sale of alcohol or provision of entertainment to members' guests or associate members where the club rules would otherwise permit it are prohibited, as are conditions to censor the content of plays.[22]

8.6.6 The licensing authority must give notice of the outcome of the application to the applicant club, anyone who made a relevant representation and the police. The notice must include reasons for any decisions made subsequent to representations.[23] This would apply whether or not the determination of the application was made after a hearing or by agreement between the applicant club, the authority and any interested parties.

---

[18] LA 2003, s 72(3).

[19] Ibid, s 72(8) and (9).

[20] Ibid, s 72(4).

[21] Ibid, s 72(10).

[22] Ibid, ss 75 and 76.

[23] Ibid, s 77.

8.7 FORM OF CLUB PREMISES CERTIFICATE

8.7.1 Although the exact form will be prescribed in regulations,[24] the certificate will include:

(a) the name and registered address of the club;
(b) the address to which the certificate relates;
(c) a plan of the premises;
(d) the qualifying club activities for which the premises may be used; and
(e) any conditions to which the certificate is subject.

It is intended that in addition to the certificate itself there will be a summary of the certificate, which must be displayed at the club premises.

8.7.2 If the club premises certificate is lost, stolen, damaged or destroyed, the licensing authority must provide a copy, upon payment of a fee, once it has been established that the certificate or summary has been lost, stolen, damaged or destroyed and, if lost or stolen, that the loss or theft has been reported to the police.

8.7.3 This second point has been included because, since the LA 2003 makes it an offence to fail to produce the certificate without reasonable excuse, it was argued by the Government that it would therefore be in the club's interest to report such loss to the police at the first opportunity. The secretary of the club would be the person responsible for safe keeping of the certificate.

8.7.4 The club secretary must notify the licensing authority[25] upon:

– a change of name; or
– a change of club rules; or
– a change in the club's registered address,

in each case sending the club premises certificate to be altered and a fee (probably about £10).[26] This procedure will not enable the club to change the premises to which the certificate relates. These notifications must be made within 28 days of the changes or an offence will be committed by the secretary.

Duty to keep and produce certificate

8.7.5 If the certificate authorises a qualifying club activity then the club secretary must ensure that the certificate (or a properly certified copy) is kept at the premises to which it relates and that a nominated person is responsible for it. The person must be nominated by the secretary, and must be either:

– the secretary;

---

[24] LA 2003, s 78.

[25] Ibid, ss 82 and 83.

[26] Dr Kim Howells – *Hansard*, HC Standing Committee D, 6 May 2003, col 389.

– any member of the club; or
– someone working at and employed by the club.

The licensing authority must be notified of the identity of the nominated person.[27]

8.7.6   The nominated person must ensure that both:

– the summary of the certificate (or a certified copy); and
– a notice stating the position that the nominated person holds at the club,

are clearly displayed at the club. Failure to display or produce the certificate for inspection upon demand is an offence.[28]

8.8   DURATION

8.8.1   A club premises certificate will remain in force until it is either surrendered or withdrawn by the licensing authority following the failure of the club to continue as a qualifying club or after a review. A club premises certificate is of no effect whilst suspended upon review.[29]

8.8.2   Surrender is effected by the club simply notifying the licensing authority in writing, and enclosing the certificate. The certificate lapses once received by the authority.[30]

8.9   VARIATION

8.9.1   It is open to a club to apply for a variation[31] of the club premises certificate at any time, subject to requirements to advertise and notify various authorities, which will be set out in regulations. The club will also be open to inspection by the police, fire authority or environmental health department. A fee will be payable.

8.9.2   The club must send to the licensing authority its club certificate, or an explanation of why the certificate is not available.

8.9.3   If the licensing authority receives any relevant representations, a hearing must be held, unless all parties agree that this is not necessary. As in the case of a grant, a representation will be relevant if it:

– is concerned with the impact of the variation upon the promotion of the licensing objectives; and

---

[27] LA 2003, s 94.

[28] Ibid.

[29] Ibid, s 80.

[30] Ibid, s 81.

[31] Ibid, s 84.

–   is made by an interested party or responsible authority (see **8.10.2**) within the specified time and not withdrawn prior to the hearing; and

–   if made by an interested party, is not frivolous or vexatious.[32]

8.9.4   If no relevant representation is received, the licensing authority must grant the variation sought.[33] If relevant representations have been received and considered, the licensing authority must either modify the conditions of the certificate, or reject the whole or any part of the application. The guiding principle, as elsewhere in the LA 2003, is the promotion of the licensing objectives.[34]

8.9.5   When the application (or any part) has been determined following the receipt of relevant representations, whether granted or rejected, the licensing authority must notify the applicant, the makers of any relevant representations and the police.[35] The notice must state when the variation will take effect, normally as set out in the application. The authority must give reasons for any decisions reached upon relevant representations, with regard to the steps to be taken to promote the licensing objectives.[36]

8.9.6   If the authority has decided that a representation was frivolous or vexatious it must explain why it made that decision.

8.9.7   It is not possible to change the premises to which the certificate relates in a variation, but it is open to the authority to apply different conditions to different parts of the premises or differing club activities.

8.10   REVIEW OF THE CLUB PREMISES CERTIFICATE

8.10.1   As elsewhere in the LA 2003, the Government has been keen to stress that 'first and foremost the grounds for an application for review must be relevant to one or more of the licensing objectives'.[37]

8.10.2   The review of a club premises certificate[38] can be requested at any time by:

---

[32] LA 2003, s 85(6).

[33] Ibid, s 85(2).

[34] Ibid, s 85.

[35] Ibid, s 86.

[36] Ibid, s 86(2).

[37] Dr Kim Howells – *Hansard*, HC Standing Committee D, 29 April 2003, col 306.

[38] LA 2003, s 87.

- an interested party – which includes someone living or working, or representing people living or working, 'in the vicinity' of the premises;[39]
- a responsible authority – which includes the police, fire authority, health and safety at work officers, planning officers, the licensing authority itself, as represented by the environmental health department, and navigational authorities;[40]
- a member of the club.

8.10.3 The form of the review notice will be laid out in regulations. It must be served on the club and all responsible authorities, and must state the time in which representations should be made. The authority must then advertise the application and invite representations; the advertisement must state the time period for making representations, as in the notice.

8.10.4 The authority can reject an application for review, or any ground in the application, at any time if it is felt to be irrelevant to the licensing objectives, frivolous or vexatious (but only if made by an interested party) or the repetition of a ground used before. This would include a ground for review essentially the same as an earlier ground, unless a 'reasonable interval' had elapsed. This is again left deliberately vague and will be up to the authority to determine depending upon the circumstances of each case, although the Guidance issued by the Secretary of State suggests a 12-month interval to be reasonable.

8.10.5 The licensing authority must hold a hearing[41] to consider the application and any relevant representations that have been made in response to it, although this cannot be done until after the application has been correctly advertised.

8.10.6 As with consideration of a review of a premises licence, a representation will be relevant if it:

- relates to one or more of the licensing objectives; and
- was made by the club, an interested party or responsible authority within the specified time and not withdrawn prior to the hearing; and
- if made by an interested party (not a responsible authority), is neither frivolous nor vexatious.[42]

8.10.7 Having considered the representations and supporting evidence and keeping always the promotion of the licensing objectives as the only relevant purpose, the steps the authority can take are:

---

[39] LA 2003, s 13(3). This has been left deliberately vague, but according to Dr Kim Howells: 'The word vicinity can mean an area and a neighbourhood' – *Hansard*, HC Standing Committee D, 10 April 2003, col 222.

[40] LA 2003, s 13(4).

[41] Ibid, s 88.

[42] Ibid, s 88(7) and (8).

(a) to modify any of the conditions of the certificate, either permanently or temporarily for a period of up to 3 months;

(b) to remove one of the qualifying club activities from the certificate, again either permanently or temporarily for up to 3 months;

(c) to suspend the certificate altogether for up to 3 months;

(d) to withdraw the certificate completely;

(e) to leave the certificate in its existing state.[43]

8.10.8 When the application (or any part) has been determined, whether granted or rejected, the licensing authority must notify the club, the applicant, the makers of any relevant representations and the police. The authority must give reasons for any decisions reached upon relevant representations, with regard to the steps to be taken to promote the licensing objectives.[44]

8.10.9 Any decision about review, whether resulting in modification or removal of a qualifying activity, suspension, or withdrawal of the certificate, will not take effect until either the end of the appeal period or the appeal, once lodged, has been determined.[45]

8.10.10 As a clarification of the position where the local authority could be both applicant (eg an environmental health department), and judge and jury (as licensing authority), LA 2003, s 89 states that for the purposes of review the authority is included as a responsible authority, and can apply for the review of a club premises certificate.

8.11 POWERS OF ENTRY

8.11.1 Clubs are private premises, owned and run by the members. One of the privileges of this position is that the police have far more limited rights of entry and inspection than is the case for licensed premises which are open to the general public. A club with a club premises certificate can be searched by the police if a constable has reasonable cause to believe that any offence related to the supply of drugs has been or is likely to be committed, or that there is likely to be a breach of the peace. Reasonable force may be used to gain entry in these circumstances.[46]

8.11.2 In any other case, the only right of entry is for inspection prior to an application for a new club premises certificate or for variation or review of an existing certificate.[47] In these circumstances an 'authorised person', being a fire officer, health and safety officer, local authority (eg environmental health) officer or a navigational or shipping inspector as well as a police constable authorised by the chief

---

[43] LA 2003, s 88(3), (4) and (6).

[44] Ibid, s 88(10).

[45] Ibid, s 88(11).

[46] Ibid, s 97.

[47] Ibid, s 96(1).

officer of police, may enter the premises to inspect, but then only at a reasonable time within 14 days of the application being made and after giving the club 48 hours' written notice of the inspection. This very tight timetable can be extended by 7 days upon application by the authorised person to the local authority, but only then if the licensing authority deems that the authorised person had acted promptly in attempting to inspect but that the inspection was not possible.[48]

8.12   INDUSTRIAL AND PROVIDENT SOCIETIES, MINERS' WELFARE INSTITUTES AND FRIENDLY SOCIETIES

8.12.1   These organisations are afforded their own sections in the LA 2003 to enable them to qualify as clubs despite their being formed in different ways from most clubs. The intention is that both incorporated and unincorporated associations, formed for whatever purpose, will be able to apply for club certificates.[49] It enables bodies managed in part by employers and in part by members or employees or their representatives to apply. Any registered industrial and provident society, or registered and incorporated friendly society or miners' welfare institute will be treated as satisfying the conditions for being a qualifying club, and thereby be able to apply for a club premises certificate if they can be shown to meet the requirements concerning their management and constitution.[50]

---

[48] LA 2003, s 96.

[49] Dr Kim Howells – *Hansard*, HC Standing Committee D, 29 April 2003, col 344.

[50] LA 2003, ss 65 and 66.

Chapter 9

TEMPORARY EVENTS

'If all be true that I do think
There are five reasons we should drink
Good wine – a friend – or being dry –
Or lest we should be by and by –
Or any other reason why.'

Dean Aldrich

9.1 INTRODUCTION

9.1.1 Under the old laws, a licence was always required for the sale of alcohol by retail no matter what the aims or purposes of the seller. So, for a charity garden fête where beer and wine were served as refreshments or bottles were available as prizes in the tombola or lucky dip, a licence was needed. In reality many such unlicensed events took place and the authorities tended to turn a blind eye. The need for a licence for such minor sales has been obviated by the provisions of LA 2003, s 175, which exempt raffles and tombolas which are incidental to exempt entertainments as defined by s 3(1) of the Lotteries and Amusements Act 1976:

> 'In this Act "exempt entertainment" means a bazaar, sale of work, fete, dinner dance, sporting or athletic event or other entertainment of a similar character, whether limited to one day or extending over two or more days.'

9.1.2 Of greater concern to the authorities, for reasons of public safety and the prevention of disorder and nuisance were parties, social events, festivals and the like attended, in some cases, by very large numbers of people. In order to sell alcohol at such events either an existing licensee had to apply for permission to use his justices' licence at the premises where the event was taking place (an occasional licence), or, in the case of non-profit-making functions, one of the organisers had to apply for a temporary licence (an occasional permission).

9.1.3 If the event involved the provision of musical entertainment and dancing for the public, for example, an application would have to be made to the local authority for a (temporary) public entertainments licence. There were similar provisions for temporary cinematograph and theatre licences.

9.1.4   For relatively small-scale affairs all these forms of temporary licence have been replaced by the concept of a 'temporary event' which can involve any of the varieties of licensable activities. Such events will be lawful and will not require applications for a premises licence provided that there is compliance with the provisions of Part 5 of the LA 2003.

9.1.5   The purpose of providing for temporary events was set out by Lord McIntosh of Haringey:[1]

> 'Let me repeat our aim as regards temporary event notices. We are trying to identify those applicants and events that are so rare or modest as not to be licensable activities. Many events will benefit because they are licensable activities already, and therefore the requirement to provide a temporary notice is a good deal lighter than what happens now. That is the intention of the Bill. The "light touch" system is to benefit those who do not generally engage in the business of carrying on licensable activities – that is to say, those who do not have a personal licence – by allowing them, for example, to hold a fundraising event in a hall without a premises licence.'

9.2   PERMITTED TEMPORARY ACTIVITIES

9.2.1   A permitted temporary activity is a licensable activity carried on in accordance with a temporary event notice given under LA 2003, s 100 and in compliance with the provisions of Part 5.[2] In effect anyone wishing to organise a small-scale temporary event, which will not go on longer than 96 hours and at which alcohol will be sold or other licensable activities will take place, can do so provided that he gives notice to the local authority for the area in which the event is to take place and to the police and no action is taken by the police to prevent that notice coming into effect.[3]

9.2.2   If the event or the premises used, stretches across the boundary of two local authorities, notice must be given to both of them.

9.3   TEMPORARY EVENT NOTICE

9.3.1   Where it is proposed to hold an event which will last not longer than 96 hours and which will involve one or more licensable activities, the holding of that event can be made lawful by the giving of a temporary event notice.[4]

---

[1]   *Hansard*, HL Deb, vol 643, col 385 (16 January 2003).

[2]   LA 2003, s 98.

[3]   Ibid, s 100.

[4]   Ibid, s 100(1).

9.3.2 The individual who gives the notice becomes the 'premises user' for the purposes of the event.[5] He must be 18 years or older.[6] The use of the term 'individual' means that it is not open to a body corporate to give notice of a proposed temporary event.

9.3.3 The notice must be in the prescribed form and set out the following information (and any other information prescribed in the regulations):[7]

(a) the relevant licensable activities;
(b) the period during which it is proposed to use the premises concerned (not to exceed 96 hours);
(c) the times during the event period when it is proposed that the licensable activities shall take place;
(d) the maximum number of persons to be allowed on the premises at the same time (not to exceed 500);
(e) if alcohol is to be sold or supplied, whether it will be for consumption on or off the premises or both.

9.3.4 If the sale or supply of alcohol is to be one of the licensable activities then the temporary event notice must make it a condition of using the premises concerned that all those sales or supplies are made by or under the authority of the premises user.[8]

9.3.5 Two copies of the notice must be given to the local authority in the prescribed form not later than 10 working days before the day on which the event begins. Thus, if the event is to take place on a Saturday, for example, for the avoidance of doubt the notice would have to be with the local authority by the Friday just over 2 weeks earlier. (It could be argued that giving the notice by delivering it to the local authority's offices on, say, the Sunday would comply with the provisions of the LA 2003. Posting it on the Friday would not.) The notice must be sent or delivered to the principal office of the local authority or such other office as it has specified for the receipt of such notices.[9]

9.3.6 The notice must be accompanied by the prescribed fee.[10]

9.3.7 A copy of the notice must also be given to the chief officer of police for the area not later than 10 working days before the day on which the event begins. If the premises concerned fall within two police areas, both chief officers of police must be given a copy of the temporary event notice.[11]

---

[5] LA 2003, s 100(2).

[6] Ibid, s 100(3).

[7] Ibid, s 100(4) and (5).

[8] Ibid, s 100(6).

[9] Ibid, s 184.

[10] Ibid, s 100(7). The fee is likely to be in the region of £20: per Lord McIntosh – *Hansard*, HL Deb, vol 643, col 386 (16 January 2003).

[11] Ibid, s 104.

9.3.8   A temporary event notice may be withdrawn by the premises user by giving notice to that effect no later than 24 hours before the beginning of the event.[12]

9.4 RESTRICTIONS ON THE USE OF PREMISES FOR TEMPORARY EVENTS

9.4.1   There has to be a gap of at least 24 hours between temporary events held at the same premises by the same premises user. Should that gap not exist the notice will be void.[13]

9.4.2   The premises will be treated as the same premises if any part of the premises to be used forms part of the premises in use for the earlier or later event.[14]

9.4.3   The premises user will be treated as being the same individual if the earlier or later notice has been given by an associate or a business colleague.[15] An associate is defined as being the spouse of the premises user, child, grandchild, grandparent, brother or sister or employee or agent of the premises user or any of their spouses. A spouse is a person living with another as that person's husband or wife. An individual is treated as a business colleague of the premises user if the business in which he is involved relates to one or more licensable activities and either of the overlapping events relates to one of those business activities.[16]

9.4.4   No more than 12 temporary events can be held in any one calendar year at particular premises,[17] and the premises themselves can be used for no more than 15 days in a calendar year.[18]

9.4.5   Premises users who hold a personal licence can give notice of no more than 50 temporary events to be held in any one calendar year.[19]

9.4.6   Premises users who do not hold a personal licence can give no more than five notices in any one calendar year.[20]

9.4.7   If the event period specified in the notice straddles 2 years the restrictions apply separately in relation to each of those years. In other

---

[12] LA 2003, s 103.

[13] Ibid, s 101(1).

[14] Ibid, s 101(2)(d).

[15] Ibid, s 101(2)(b).

[16] Ibid, s 101(3) and (4).

[17] Ibid, s 107(4).

[18] Ibid, s 107(5).

[19] Ibid, s 107(2).

[20] Ibid, s 107(3).

words the event is counted twice – once in year one and once in year two.[21]

9.4.8   Whenever the limits on the number of events held in a particular year would be exceeded, the licensing authority must give the premises user a counter notice, which will have the effect of making the proposed event an unlawful event in relation to any licensable activities conducted during the event.[22] Such a counter notice must be given not later than 24 hours before the beginning of the event period specified in the original notice.[23] A copy of any counter notice must be sent to the police immediately.

9.4.9   Again, notices given by associates or business colleagues of a premises user are treated as having been given by the premises user.

9.5   OBJECTIONS TO TEMPORARY EVENT NOTICES

9.5.1   A licensing authority which receives a temporary event notice must acknowledge receipt by sending or delivering one of the copies back to the premises user before the end of the next working day (2 days if the notice was received on a non-working day). The duty to acknowledge does not apply in the case of the notice being withdrawn or a counter notice served because the proposed event would be in excess of the permitted numbers for the user or the premises.[24]

9.5.2   Within 48 hours of receipt of a copy of the temporary event notice, the police must decide whether or not allowing the premises to be used in accordance with the notice would undermine the crime prevention objective. If the chief officer of police is satisfied that the crime prevention objective would be undermined, he must give a notice of objection to the licensing authority and the premises user within that 48-hour period. The 'objection notice' must state the reasons for the police being satisfied that the crime prevention objective would be undermined. The police do not have to consider the proposed use of the premises if the licensing authority has served a counter notice because the limits for such events have been exceeded.[25]

9.5.3   In the event of an objection notice having been given by the police, the licensing authority must hold a hearing (unless all concerned agree that a hearing is unnecessary). If, having regard to the objection notice, the licensing authority is satisfied that it is

---

[21] LA 2003, s 107(6).

[22] Ibid, s 107(1).

[23] Ibid, s 107(8).

[24] Ibid, s 102.

[25] Ibid, s 104.

necessary for the promotion of the crime prevention objective it must give a counter notice to the premises user.[26]

9.5.4   If the licensing authority determines not to give a counter notice it must give notice to the premises user and the police of its decision. If, however, the licensing authority determines to give a counter notice it must give two notices to the premises user – a notice of its decision and a notice of the reasons for its decision. Both notices must be copied to the police. The decision must be made and the notices given at least 24 hours before the event is due to begin.[27]

9.5.5   If two licensing authorities are involved because the proposed event would take place in both licensing areas, the authorities must act jointly in the decision-making process.[28]

9.5.6   There is also a compromise provision which comes into play after a notice of objection has been given by the police. At any time before the hearing, the police may, with the agreement of the premises user, modify the temporary event notice by making changes to it. For example, the hours during which licensable activities are proposed to take place may be reduced, or the numbers of people attending may be changed. If such a compromise is reached, the objection notice is treated as having been withdrawn. A copy of the modified notice must be sent to the licensing authority before a hearing is held.[29]

9.5.7   As with two licensing authorities, if two police force areas are involved, an event notice could be modified only with the consent of the other chief officer of police.[30]

9.5.8   There is a right of appeal against the giving of a counter notice following objection by the police. Similarly the police have a right of appeal if the licensing authority refuses to give a counter notice following the lodging of a police objection. The appeal lies to the magistrates' court. The usual 21 days for lodging an appeal are available but no appeal may be brought later than 5 working days before the day upon which the event was due to begin.[31]

9.5.9   There is no right of appeal against a counter notice served on the basis that the limits on the numbers of temporary event notices given by the premises user or in relation to particular premises have been exceeded. The giving of such a counter notice could only be challenged by way of judicial review.

---

[26] LA 2003, s 105(2).

[27] Ibid, s 105(3).

[28] Ibid, s 105(5).

[29] Ibid, s 106.

[30] Ibid, s 106(5).

[31] Ibid, Sch 5, para 16.

9.6 CONTROL OF TEMPORARY EVENTS

9.6.1 A constable or authorised officer of the licensing authority has a right of entry to premises identified in a temporary event notice at any reasonable time in order to assess the likely effect on the promotion of the crime prevention objective. Clearly this right can be exercised before the event in question. An authorised officer must produce his authority if asked to do so.[32]

9.6.2 It is an offence intentionally to obstruct an authorised officer exercising his powers of entry. The LA 2003 does not create an offence of obstructing a police constable engaged upon such activities but such behaviour would no doubt constitute an offence under the Police Act 1996.

9.6.3 The premises user must ensure that a copy of the temporary event notice is displayed prominently at the premises or that a notice to the effect that the temporary event notice is in the custody of a nominated person working at the premises is so displayed. Curiously, if the premises user is present, the LA 2003 simply requires that the temporary event notice be in his custody without any need for its display.[33]

9.6.4 A constable or authorised officer can require production of the temporary event notice if it is not displayed. Failure to display the notice or produce it upon request is an offence.[34]

9.6.5 If the temporary event notice returned to the premises user by the licensing authority is lost, stolen, damaged or destroyed, the premises user may apply to the licensing authority for a copy. The application for a copy must be accompanied by a fee and must not be made more than one month after the end of the temporary event. The licensing authority must issue a certified copy of the notice if satisfied that it has been lost, stolen, damaged or destroyed, save that in the case of a lost or stolen notice, the authority must also be satisfied that the loss or theft was reported to the police.[35]

9.6.6 The powers, under LA 2003, Part 8, of the police or magistrates' courts to make closure orders apply equally to premises in which temporary events are being held.

---

[32] LA 2003, s 108.

[33] Ibid, s 109.

[34] Ibid, s 109(8).

[35] Ibid, s 110.

Chapter 10

PERSONAL LICENCES

*'The leader writer of a great northern daily said on the morning after
King Edward died that if he had not been a king he would have been
the best type of sporting publican.'*

James Agate

10.1 INTRODUCTION

10.1.1 One of the principal features of the new scheme is the
creation of a personal licence which, as the name suggests, applies
only to the individual licence holder. Save for the purposes of certain
temporary events, it is illegal for a person without a personal licence
(or authorisation given by a personal licence holder) to sell alcohol by
retail. Personal licences are not required for the supply of alcohol to
members of a club with a club premises certificate or for the other
licensable activities within the LA 2003.

10.1.2 For the sale or supply of alcohol in licensed premises there
must be a nominated personal licence holder. Not all employees need
to be licence holders but they must be authorised to sell or supply
alcohol by a personal licence holder.[1]

10.1.3

'The argument for licensing people, as well as premises, is that there
needs to be a reasonable assurance that anyone responsible for the sale
of alcohol is aware of his or her obligations and is capable of fulfilling
them. In addition, a great many public houses are these days managed by
people on behalf of large pub operating companies and the normal
transfer of managers from one set of premises to another is
unnecessarily inhibited by the current law which ties the licence holder
and the venue together. A split licensing system therefore offers much
greater flexibility to the industry in terms of human resources. The
licence would be held by the person running the premises on a day to
day basis where alcohol is sold; it is unnecessary to licence all staff doing
the serving or selling. However, personal licence holders should, as a
matter of good management practice, ensure that their staff receive
adequate training and guidance. The greater flexibility offered by the
proposed system must be balanced with tough powers allowing the

---

[1] LA 2003, s 19. Mandatory conditions where licence authorises supply of alcohol.

police or the licensing authority to deal effectively with errant personal licence holders.'[2]

10.1.4 Save for the protection of existing holders of justices' licences who will be entitled to a personal licence if they make an application during the relevant stage of the transitional period (see Chapter 15) all prospective personal licence holders must possess a licensing qualification. The accredited qualifications will be prescribed by regulation. However, the Government has already issued a syllabus for the new qualification. The syllabus contains a framework of subjects that courses must cover in order for the resulting qualification to gain accreditation.[3]

10.1.5 The authority responsible for the issue and control of a personal licence is the local authority (licensing authority) for the area in which the applicant for a personal licence is ordinarily resident.[4] If an applicant for a personal licence is not 'ordinarily resident' in England and Wales, for example someone living in Scotland or mainland Europe, he may apply to any English or Welsh licensing authority. Thereafter the initial issuing authority remains responsible for control of the licence, which might include endorsing relevant convictions, suspensions, revocation, renewals and surrender.

10.1.6 In the White Paper, the Government proposed a national database to enable the licensing authorities and the police to check the validity of licences and the licensee's history.[5] During the Bill's passage through the House of Lords, an additional clause was inserted creating a central licensing authority to deal with personal licences. The main areas of concern were the fragmented basis of having 400 plus local authorities dealing with personal licences and holders who may have moved a considerable distance from the issuing area and the inability of the police or local authorities to keep track of licence holders. In Standing Committee in the House of Commons, the Government restored the original draft clause whilst undertaking to work with the police and local authorities to establish a national database run by local authorities and to which the police and local authorities would have access. It is unlikely that the national database will have been established during the transitional period of the new legislation but the forms and records will be designed in such a way that each authority keeps data in the same way thereby allowing for easy transition to the national database.

---

[2] Extract from the White Paper, *Time For Reform: Proposals for the modernisation of our licensing laws*, Cm 4696 (The Stationery Office, 2000), p 22.

[3] Department of Culture, Media and Sport Press Notice 091/03 (31 July 2003).

[4] LA 2003, s 117.

[5] *Time for Reform*, Cm 4696 (The Stationery Office, 2000), p 23.

10.1.7   Personal licences will have the character of a driving licence and contain details of the holder's name and address as well as any relevant convictions or court orders.

10.2   APPLICATION FOR A PERSONAL LICENCE

10.2.1   Any person, that is any individual (not a company), aged 18 or over may apply for a personal licence.[6] The form of the application, the procedures for making an application (information and documents to be supplied) and the appropriate band of fees will be set out in the regulations.[7]

10.2.2   A 'personal licence' is defined[8] as a licence which 'is granted by a licensing authority to an individual, and authorises that individual to supply alcohol or authorise the supply of alcohol, in accordance with a premises licence'.

10.2.3   'Supplying alcohol' means selling alcohol by retail or supplying alcohol by or on behalf of a club to the order of a member of that club.[9]

10.2.4   The application must be made to the licensing authority in whose area the applicant is ordinarily resident if the applicant lives in England or Wales. Otherwise the application may be made to any licensing authority.[10]

10.2.5   An individual is allowed to hold only one personal licence at any one time. Any second or subsequent licence held at the same time is declared void.[11]

10.3   DETERMINATION OF APPLICATION

10.3.1   The licensing authority must grant the personal licence if the applicant:

(a) is 18 years or older;
(b) possesses an appropriate licensing qualification (or is exempt by virtue of the regulations);

---

[6] LA 2003, s 117.

[7] Ibid, s 133.

[8] Ibid, s 111.

[9] Ibid, s 111(2). It is not necessary for a club with the benefit of a club premises certificate to engage the services of a personal licence holder but it is expected that, for commercial reasons, some qualifying clubs will prefer to apply for a premises licence.

[10] Ibid, s 117(2).

[11] Ibid, s 118.

(c) has not had a personal licence forfeited within the period of 5 years leading up to the date of the application; and

(d) has not been convicted of one of the offences set out in LA 2003, Sch 4 or a foreign offence (unless the conviction is a spent conviction).[12]

10.3.2 If the only failure by the applicant to meet the statutory criteria relates to a conviction for a relevant offence (or foreign offence) which is not a spent conviction, the licensing authority must refer the matter to the police for the area.[13] If the applicant fails to meet one of the other criteria, the licence cannot be granted.[14]

10.3.3 A 'relevant offence' is an offence listed in LA 2003, Sch 4. A 'foreign offence' means an offence (other than a relevant offence) under the law of any place outside England and Wales. The Secretary of State may amend or add to the list of relevant offences by order.[15]

10.3.4 A conviction for a relevant offence or a foreign offence must be disregarded if it is spent for the purposes of the Rehabilitation of Offenders Act 1974.[16] This clears up the uncertainty with regard to 'spent' convictions under the existing law.[17]

10.3.5 If, following the making of an application for a personal licence, the applicant is convicted of a relevant offence or a foreign offence, he must, as soon as reasonably practicable, notify the licensing authority. To fail to do so is to commit an offence.[18] There is a power to revoke should a relevant conviction come to light after the grant of a personal licence.[19]

10.3.6 If the chief officer of police is satisfied that the granting of a personal licence to the applicant would undermine the crime prevention objective, he must give notice to that effect, with reasons, to the licensing authority within 14 days of receipt of the reference. If no such notice is given the licence must be granted. If notice is given the licensing authority must hold a hearing to consider the objection unless it is agreed that no hearing is necessary whereupon the matter can be dealt with on paper.[20]

---

[12] LA 2003, s 120.

[13] Ibid, s 120(4).

[14] Ibid, s 120(3).

[15] Ibid, s 113.

[16] Ibid, s 114.

[17] *R v Hastings Magistrates' Court ex parte McSpirit* (1994) *The Times*, June 23, in which it was held that licensing justices could exercise the powers of a judicial authority and therefore bring into account spent convictions and the circumstances relating to them.

[18] LA 2003, s 123.

[19] Ibid, s 124.

[20] Ibid, s 120(4), (5) and (6).

10.3.7 If the licensing authority considers it necessary, for the promotion of the crime prevention objective, to reject the application it must do so. Otherwise the licensing authority must grant the licence.[21] There is no other ground for refusing an application for a personal licence made by a qualified individual.

10.3.8 The licensing authority must give notice to the applicant and the chief officer of police when it grants a personal licence and, if the police objected, it must set out its reasons for granting the application.[22] The licence must be issued immediately ('forthwith').[23] If the application is rejected, the licensing authority must give a notice to the applicant and the police which, again, contains a statement of the reasons for the rejection.[24]

10.4 QUALIFICATIONS

10.4.1 'Licensing qualifications' are defined[25] as:

(a) a qualification accredited (by the Secretary of State) at the time of its award and awarded by a body accredited at that time;
(b) a qualification awarded before the coming into force of LA 2003, s 120 and certified by the Secretary of State; or
(c) a qualification obtained in Scotland, Northern Ireland or in an EEA State which is equivalent to one of the above qualifications.

10.5 FORM OF PERSONAL LICENCE

10.5.1 The licence must be in a form prescribed by the regulations[26] and must specify:

– the holder's name and address;
– the licensing authority which granted the licence;
– the relevant offences for which the licence holder has been convicted, dates of conviction and sentences.

10.5.2 If the personal licence is lost or stolen, damaged, or destroyed, the holder may apply to the original licensing authority for a copy. Any theft or loss must be reported to the police. If it is satisfied that the original licence has been lost, stolen, destroyed, or damaged, the licensing authority must issue a certified copy which is in identical

---

[21] LA 2003, s 120(7).

[22] Ibid, s 122(1).

[23] Ibid, s 125.

[24] Ibid, s 122(2).

[25] Ibid, s 120(8).

[26] Ibid, s 125(4).

form to the licence at the time of its loss etc. The certified copy has the same validity as the original licence.[27]

10.5.3   If a licence holder changes his name and/or address, he must notify the issuing authority of that change as soon as is reasonably practicable. The personal licence, or a statement of reasons for failure to provide the licence, must accompany the notice of the change. It is an offence to fail to notify a change of name or address without a reasonable excuse.[28]

10.5.4   When a personal licence holder is working on premises which have a premises licence or the benefit of a temporary event notice authorising the supply of alcohol, upon request by a constable or an officer authorised by the licensing authority, he must produce the personal licence. Failure to do so, without reasonable excuse, is an offence.[29]

10.6   DURATION

10.6.1   A personal licence is valid for 10 years and may be renewed for further periods of 10 years.[30]

10.6.2   That validity is subject to surrender, forfeiture, revocation, or suspension.[31]

10.6.3   A personal licence which is due to expire will continue in existence pending any determination of a renewal application.[32]

10.7   RENEWAL

10.7.1   An application for the renewal of a personal licence must be made to the 'relevant authority', that is, the licensing authority which first issued the licence.[33]

10.7.2   The personal licence, or a statement of reasons for the failure to provide the licence, must accompany the application.[34]

10.7.3   An application for renewal can be made only during a strict time slot. The duration of the period for making the application for renewal is set at just 2 months which begins 3 months before the date

---

[27] LA 2003, s 126.

[28] Ibid, s 127.

[29] Ibid, s 135.

[30] Ibid, s 115(1).

[31] Ibid, s 115(2).

[32] Ibid, s 119.

[33] Ibid, s 117(3).

[34] Ibid, s 117(4).

upon which the licence is due to expire.[35] There is no 'slip' provision so that failure to make the application for renewal during the appropriate time slot will mean that an application for a new personal licence must be made. Since any second or subsequent personal licence is void if granted when an existing personal licence is in force, any new grant could be validly made only after the expiry of the old licence.

10.7.4 If the application for renewal is made during the appropriate time slot then the old licence will continue in force until such time as the application for renewal is determined or withdrawn.[36]

10.8 DETERMINATION OF APPLICATION FOR RENEWAL

10.8.1 There is only one issue relevant to the determination of an application for renewal and that is the promotion of the crime prevention objective.

10.8.2 If it appears to the licensing authority that the applicant has been convicted of any the offences set out in LA 2003, Sch 4 (other than a spent conviction), or a foreign offence, since the date of the grant or last renewal, as with an application for a new licence, the licensing authority must give notice to the police.[37] The police then have 14 days to decide whether or not to object and to give notice of that objection.

10.8.3 As far as the police objection is concerned, it is irrelevant whether or not the conviction occurred before or after the grant or last renewal.[38] Presumably this provision is intended to catch those circumstances where the licensing authority was not aware of a relevant conviction at the time of the previous renewal or grant. Unfortunately the provision does not sit easily with LA 2003, s 121(2) – the duty of the licensing authority to give notice to the police – because it is only upon receipt of such notice that the police have the right to object. There is, however, a power to revoke in the circumstances of convictions coming to light after the grant or renewal of a personal licence.[39]

10.8.4 When judging foreign offences, the police will have to form a view as to whether the offence is comparable with any of the offences set out in LA 2003, Sch 4. If the police do not object within 14 days of the receipt of a notice under s 121(2), then the renewal must be

---

[35] LA 2003, s 117(6).

[36] Ibid, s 119.

[37] Ibid, s 121(2).

[38] Ibid, s 121(4).

[39] Ibid, s 124.

granted.[40] If objection is made, and not withdrawn, then there must be a hearing unless it is agreed by the applicant, police and licensing authority to be unnecessary.[41]

10.8.5   Again, as with the grant of a personal licence, the licensing authority must give its reasons for granting against a police objection or for rejecting an application for renewal.[42]

10.8.6   Rejection can only be on the basis that renewal would undermine the crime prevention objective.

10.8.7   The appeal provisions relating to personal licences can be found in LA 2003, Sch 5, para 17. They contain a power in both the licensing authority and the magistrates' court to order that a personal licence is to continue in force or be reinstated, subject to conditions imposed by the court or the licensing authority, pending the outcome of the appeal.

10.9 CONVICTIONS

10.9.1   If the holder of a personal licence is charged with a relevant offence he must inform the magistrates' court dealing with the allegation no later than his first appearance before that court. In addition the personal licence must be produced to the court or, if that is not practicable, the existence of the personal licence and the name of the issuing licensing authority must be revealed and reasons given why the licence cannot be produced.[43]

10.9.2   Similar provisions apply if a person is granted a personal licence after having been charged with a relevant offence. At the next court appearance, there is a duty to inform the court and produce the licence.[44]

10.9.3   If the personal licence is surrendered or revoked, or an application is made for such a licence or its renewal then, again, the criminal court must be notified.[45]

10.9.4   Failure to comply with the provisions of LA 2003, s 128 is a criminal offence.[46]

---

[40] LA 2003, s 121(5).

[41] Ibid, s 121(6).

[42] Ibid, s 122.

[43] Ibid, s 128.

[44] Ibid, s 128(2).

[45] Ibid, s 128(4) and (5).

[46] Ibid, s 128(6).

10.10 POWERS OF THE CRIMINAL COURTS UPON CONVICTION

10.10.1 If a personal licence holder is convicted by a magistrates' court or the Crown Court of a relevant offence, that court may order the forfeiture of the personal licence or its suspension for a period of up to 6 months.[47] In exercising its discretion the court may take into account any previous conviction of the licence holder for a relevant offence.[48]

10.10.2 The sentencing court may suspend the operation of its order pending appeal, on such terms as it thinks fit, and the various appellate courts have the same discretionary power. Otherwise the order for forfeiture or suspension takes immediate effect.[49]

10.10.3 The criminal court before which a personal licence holder is convicted of a relevant offence must notify the licensing authority that issued the licence of the details of the conviction and any sentence passed (including any s 129 order – forfeiture or suspension of a personal licence). A copy of the notice must be sent to the licence holder. Similar provisions apply to appellate courts with regard to their decisions.[50]

10.10.4 If the licence holder has not informed the criminal court of the fact that he is the holder of, or has applied for, a personal licence, then he is under a duty to notify the licensing authority, giving full details of the conviction and sentence as soon as is reasonably practicable.[51] The personal licence must be sent with the notification.

10.11 DUTIES OF THE LICENSING AUTHORITY

10.11.1 The licensing authority has a duty to amend a personal licence to ensure that it contains an accurate record[52] of:

– a renewal (s 121);
– any change of name or address (s 127);
– a revocation following the coming to light of the conviction of the licence holder for a relevant offence (s 124(4));
– a conviction and sentence notified by the licence holder (s 123(1));
– a conviction and sentence notified by the court (s 131);

---

[47] LA 2003, s 129.

[48] Ibid, s 129(3).

[49] Ibid, ss 129(4) and (5) and 130.

[50] Ibid, s 131.

[51] Ibid, s 132.

[52] Ibid, s 134.

- a decision in criminal proceedings notified by an appellate court (s 132); and
- any appeal against a decision of the licensing authority with regard to the renewal or revocation of the licence.

10.11.2   In order to enable it to carry out its duties, a licensing authority may require the production of a personal licence within 14 days of receipt of a notice to that effect.[53] It is an offence to fail to comply with such a requirement.

10.11.3   It is difficult to understand why the criminal court to which a personal licence has to be produced should not have been placed under a duty to send the licence, together with the notification of the conviction and sentence, to the licensing authority.

10.12   SURRENDER OF A PERSONAL LICENCE

10.12.1   Where the holder of a personal licence wishes to surrender it, he may do so by giving notice to that effect to the issuing licensing authority. The notice must be accompanied by the personal licence, or if that is not practicable a statement of the reasons for the failure to return the licence.[54]

10.12.2   Where notice of surrender is given it takes effect upon receipt by the licensing authority.[55]

---

[53] LA 2003, s 134(4).

[54] Ibid, s 116.

[55] Ibid, s 116(3).

Chapter 11

OFFENCES

'Wagner has such lovely moments but awful quarters of an hour.'

Gioacchino Rossini

11.1 INTRODUCTION

11.1.1 LA 2003, Part 7 deals with offences but does not contain every offence created by the Act. In various different parts of the LA 2003, offences such as failure to comply with statutory requirements or an order of a court are made criminal acts. The main bulk of offences created by the LA 2003 are to be found, however, in Part 7.

11.1.2 As might be anticipated, different penalties are imposed for different offences. In some cases, reference is made to the standard scale of penalties imposable for summary offences. In other cases, specific levels of fines or terms of imprisonment are set out in the LA 2003. There is no power for the amendment of any penalty or level of penalty by statutory instrument. Any such amendment would, therefore, require primary legislation.

11.1.3 Rights of entry to investigate licensable activities are given in LA 2003, s 179. Both constables and authorised persons, being officers of the licensing authority or others such as fire officers and environmental health officers,[1] have the right of entry if they have reason to believe that the premises are either being used or about to be used for a licensable activity. Reasonable force can be used. An authorised person has to provide evidence of the authority to exercise the power of entry. Obstruction of a constable or authorised officer is an offence. It is important to note that clubs with the benefit of just a club premises certificate and no other form of authority (eg a temporary event notice) are not subject to these rights of entry.

11.1.4 A constable has the right to enter any premises, whether or not licensed, if he has reason to believe that an offence under the LA 2003 has been, is being or is about to be committed.[2]

11.1.5 Proceedings for an offence under the LA 2003 may be instituted by a licensing authority, by the police through the Crown Prosecution Service (Director of Public Prosecutions) and, in the case

---

[1] See LA 2003, s 13(2) for a full list of authorised persons.

[2] LA 2003, s 180.

of the sale or supply of alcohol to children, by the local weights and measures authority. Instead of the normal 6-month time limit for the laying of an information (to commence criminal proceedings) a period of 12 months is allowed under the LA 2003.[3]

11.1.6　For the avoidance of doubt, when in relation to a sale of alcohol, the place where the contract is made is a place different from that where the alcohol is appropriated, the sale is to be treated as taking place at the place where the alcohol is appropriated to the contract.[4] So that, for example in the case of an order for a case of wine being made to the vendor's office, by post, e-mail or in person but then being despatched from the warehouse and delivered to the buyer, the sale will be deemed to take place at the warehouse when the case of wine is handed over to the delivery van driver.

11.1.7　Many of the offences created by the LA 2003 can be described properly as regulatory offences and as such are offences of strict liability. A statutory due diligence defence is provided in the case of the offences of carrying on an unauthorised licensable activity (LA 2003, s 136(1)(a)); exposing alcohol for unauthorised sale (LA 2003, s 137); or having alcohol on premises for unauthorised sale (LA 2003, s 138).[5]

11.1.8　LA 2003, s 139(1) reads:

> 'In proceedings against a person for an offence to which subsection (2) applies it is a defence that—
>
> (a)　his act was due to mistake, or to reliance on information given to him or to an act or omission by another person, or to some other cause beyond his control, and
> (b)　he took all reasonable precautions and exercised all due diligence to avoid committing the offence.'

11.1.9　It is likely that the burden of proving such a defence will be seen by the courts as a legal burden (rather than an evidential burden) but that such a burden in the context of licensing offences is both necessary and proportionate and therefore compatible with the European Convention for the Protection of Human Rights and Fundamental Freedoms so that there is no need to 'read down' the legislation under s 3(1) of the Human Rights Act 1998.

11.1.10　For a careful study of the effect of strict liability in the context of licensing cases, a leading authority is *R (Grundy & Co) v Halton Magistrates' Court*[6] which should be read in conjunction with *Sheldrake v DPP*.[7]

[3]　LA 2003, s 186.
[4]　Ibid, s 190.
[5]　Ibid, s 139.
[6]　[2003] EWHC 272 (Admin), [2003] LLR 335.
[7]　[2003] EWHC 273 (Admin).

11.2 BODIES CORPORATE AND ASSOCIATIONS

11.2.1   Provision is made to catch officers or managing members of a body corporate so that they may be prosecuted if it can be shown that the offence was committed with the consent or connivance of the officer/member or to have been attributable to any neglect on his part.[8] The body corporate can also be prosecuted.

11.2.2   Similarly, if a partner can be shown to have consented to or connived in the commission of an offence or that it was attributable to neglect, he can be prosecuted as well as the partnership.[9]

11.2.3   In the case of an unincorporated association other than a partnership, the same rules apply to officers of the association and members of the governing body.[10] Regulations may be made to catch a body corporate or unincorporated body formed or recognised under law outside the territory of the United Kingdom.[11]

11.2.4   If a fine is imposed on an unincorporated association it is to be paid out of association funds.[12] Proceedings are to be brought in the name of the association (not in those of its members). This is in marked contrast to the civil liability of such associations, a good example of which is the case of *Collins v Lane, Cornish and Worcester Norton Sports Club Ltd.*[13] In that case Mr Collins brought proceedings against the chairman and secretary of Worcester Norton Shooting Club which was affiliated to Worcester Norton Sports Club Ltd following his unfair expulsion from the shooting club. The Court of Appeal upheld his claim for breach of contract following the unfair disciplinary proceedings and awarded damages against the chairman and secretary whilst dismissing the claim against the club.

11.2.5   Rules of court as to the service of documents, for example, and general procedures are to apply to unincorporated associations as they do to a body corporate. Proceedings may be commenced against a body corporate or unincorporated association at any place at which it has a place of business.[14]

11.3 UNAUTHORISED LICENSABLE ACTIVITIES

11.3.1   It is an offence for a person to carry on (or to attempt to carry on) a licensable activity on or from any premises otherwise than in accordance with a premises licence, a club premises certificate, or a

---

[8]   LA 2003, s 187(1).

[9]   Ibid, s 187(4).

[10]   Ibid, s 187(6).

[11]   Ibid, s 187(7).

[12]   Ibid, s 188(1).

[13]   [2003] LLR 19.

[14]   LA 2003, s 188.

temporary event notice. This offence would appear to be a strict liability offence.[15] A statutory defence of due diligence is provided.[16]

11.3.2   There are exemptions[17] in the case of the unauthorised activity being the provision of regulated entertainment for the performer in a play, the sporting participant (in an indoor sporting event), the boxer or wrestler, the musician, disc jockey, dancer or other entertainer. Presumably the descriptions of the various artists in LA 2003, s 136(2) would also cover the strip-tease artist or lap dancer.

11.3.3   A person who knowingly allows a licensable activity to be carried on otherwise than in accordance with a premises licence, a club premises certificate, or a temporary event notice is also guilty of an offence.[18] Note the use of the word 'knowingly' to differentiate the person allowing the premises to be used from the person who carries on an unauthorised activity.

11.3.4   The use of the term 'knowingly' has been the subject of much litigation in the field of licensing law. Of particular importance are the authorities dealing with responsibility for action under delegated authority. Generally the courts have accepted the principle of imputed knowledge resulting from delegation.[19] More recently the doctrine of delegation was considered in *Southwark Borough Council v Allied Domecq Leisure Ltd*[20] in which it was held that knowledge of the commission of an offence under Local Government Act 1963, Sch 12, para 10(1)(a) could be imputed to an area manager.

11.3.5   The penalty for the summary offence of carrying on an unauthorised licensable activity (in its various forms) is 6 months' imprisonment or a fine of £20,000 or both.

11.4   UNAUTHORISED SALE OF ALCOHOL

11.4.1   It is an offence if a person exposes alcohol for sale by retail on any premises where a sale would be an unauthorised licensable activity.[21] The maximum penalty, on summary conviction, is 6 months' imprisonment, or £20,000, or both. In addition the court may order the forfeiture and destruction of the alcohol and any container for it. Alternatively the court can order that the alcohol be dealt with in such other manner as the court thinks appropriate.

11.4.2   The term 'exposes' is not defined in the LA 2003.

---

[15] LA 2003, s 136(1)(a).

[16] Ibid, s 139.

[17] Ibid, s 136(2).

[18] Ibid, s 136(1)(b).

[19] See *R v Winson* [1969] 1 QB 371, [1968] 3 All ER 197; *Howker v Robinson* [1973] QB 178, [1972] 2 All ER 786.

[20] [1998] 162 JP 1010.

[21] LA 2003, s 137.

11.4.3 It is also an offence to have possession of, or to be in control of, alcohol for the purpose of sale by retail or supply in circumstances where that activity would be an unauthorised licensable activity.[22] The term 'supply' relates specifically to supply to, or to the order of, members of a club. The heading used in the LA 2003 for this offence reads 'Keeping alcohol on premises for unauthorised sale', but no mention of the word 'premises' is made in the section itself. A street trader, for example, could be guilty of the offence of possessing alcohol for sale by retail. The maximum penalty for the offence is a fine not exceeding level 2 on the standard scale. The court can also make an order with regard to the forfeiture and disposal of the alcohol.

11.5 DRUNKENNESS AND DISORDERLY CONDUCT

11.5.1 All the old offences relating to drunkenness on the part of an individual have been left in place. The Act concentrates upon the responsibility of the supplier of the alcohol but also creates a new offence of failing to leave licensed premises when asked by the licence holder or his agent or a constable.[23]

11.5.2 It is an offence *knowingly* to allow disorderly conduct on premises that have the benefit of a premises licence, a club premises certificate or a temporary event notice.[24] The people who are liable for prosecution for such an offence are:

–   any person working at the premises in a capacity to prevent the conduct (it matters not whether the person working is being paid for that work);
–   the holder of the premises licence;
–   a member or officer of a club who is present in a capacity to prevent the disorderly conduct;
–   a premises user in relation to premises used for a permitted temporary event activity.

The penalty for these offences is a fine at level 3 on the standard scale.

11.5.3 Any of the same group of people commits an offence if they knowingly sell or attempt to sell alcohol to a person who is drunk or allows alcohol to be sold to that person.[25] In the case of a club, the offence is one of supplying or attempting to supply alcohol to a person who is drunk.[26] The capacity to supply the alcohol is the qualifying factor. Again the maximum fine is at level 3 on the standard scale.

---

[22] LA 2003, s 138.

[23] Ibid, s 143.

[24] Ibid, s 140.

[25] Ibid, s 141.

[26] Ibid, s 141(3).

11.5.4   It is also an offence knowingly to obtain or to attempt to obtain alcohol for a person who is drunk to consume on the premises where the alcohol is obtained.[27] This offence would not apply to the purchaser of alcohol from, say, an off-licence to be consumed by a drunk in the street. (The maximum penalty is a fine at level 3 on the standard scale.)

11.5.5   A person who is either drunk or disorderly must leave licensed premises, club premises or premises in which a temporary event is being held, if asked to do so by a person in authority at the premises or a constable. Failure to comply with such a request is an offence.[28] It is also an offence for that person to re-enter or attempt to re-enter the premises having been asked to leave. The people in authority are the same group as at **11.5.2**, which will include, for example, someone working on the door (whether paid or unpaid). The maximum penalty is a fine at level 1 on the standard scale. The only defence is that the person who is drunk or disorderly had a reasonable excuse for failing to leave or for going back in or attempting to go back in. What is or is not a reasonable excuse will be for the courts to determine.

11.5.6   A constable is under a statutory duty to help expel a drunk or disorderly person or prevent his re-entry.[29]

11.6 SMUGGLED GOODS

11.6.1   In order to deal with the increasing problem of tax or duty evasion by the sale of smuggled alcohol or cigarettes on licensed premises, the LA 2003 creates the offence of knowingly keeping or allowing to be kept on licensed premises, club premises or temporary event premises, goods which have been imported without payment of duty (or otherwise unlawfully imported).[30]

11.6.2   Anyone who has the capacity to permit such keeping on the relevant premises is guilty of the offence if he knowingly keeps or allows to be kept the smuggled goods on the premises. The maximum penalty is at level 3 on the standard scale. The smuggled goods can be forfeited and destroyed or dealt with in such other way as the court may order.

---

[27] LA 2003, s 142.

[28] Ibid, s 143.

[29] Ibid, s 143(4).

[30] Ibid, s 144.

11.7 CHILDREN AND ALCOHOL

11.7.1 It is an offence to sell alcohol to an individual under 18 years old.[31]

11.7.2 It is a defence for the person charged with the unlawful sale by reason of his own conduct that he believed the individual was aged 18 or over and either he had taken all reasonable steps to establish the individual's age, or nobody could have reasonably suspected from the individual's appearance that he was aged under 18.[32]

11.7.3 'All reasonable steps to establish an individual's age' are deemed to have been taken if the person selling the alcohol has asked the individual for evidence of age and that evidence would have convinced a reasonable person.[33]

11.7.4 It is a defence for the person charged with the offence by reason of some other person's act or default that he exercised all due diligence to avoid committing the offence.[34]

11.7.5 Exactly the same offences are committed in relation to clubs when alcohol is supplied to an individual member under the age of 18 or, to the order of a member of the club, to an individual who is aged under 18. Both the club and the person supplying the alcohol are guilty.[35]

11.7.6 It is also an offence to allow the sale or supply of alcohol to individuals under the age of 18.[36] The people who are treated as being able to allow such sales or supplies are those who work (whether paid or not) at the premises in a capacity which authorises them to prevent such sales or supplies or, additionally in the case of a club, a member or officer of the club who is present in a capacity to prevent the supply.

11.7.7 The maximum penalty is a fine at level 5 on the standard scale.

11.7.8 Almost identical provisions prohibit the sale or supply of liqueur confectionery to children under 16.[37] For that offence, the maximum penalty is set at level 3 on the standard scale.

11.7.9 An individual under the age of 18 commits an offence if he buys or attempts to buy alcohol (or if in a club alcohol is supplied or an attempt is made to have alcohol supplied).[38] (The maximum penalty is at level 3 on the standard scale.)

---

[31] LA 2003, s 146(1).

[32] Ibid, s 146(4).

[33] Ibid, s 146(5).

[34] Ibid, s 146(6).

[35] Ibid, s 146(2).

[36] Ibid, s 147.

[37] Ibid, s 148.

[38] Ibid, s 149(1).

11.7.10   It is also an offence to buy or attempt to buy alcohol on behalf of an individual aged under 18 (or in relation to a club to make or to attempt to make arrangements whereby alcohol is supplied to an individual under the age of 18).[39]

11.7.11   It is a separate offence to buy or attempt to buy (or in a club to arrange or attempt to arrange for the supply of) alcohol for an individual under the age of 18 for consumption on the premises.[40] There are exemptions for this separate offence in relation to 16- and 17-year-olds accompanied by and bought or supplied with alcohol by a person over the age of 18 when the alcohol is beer, cider, or wine and is for consumption at a table meal.[41] In these cases the maximum penalty is a fine at level 5 on the standard scale.

11.7.12   It is a defence to the offences of purchasing for or supplying alcohol that the purchaser/club member had no reason to suspect that the individual was aged under 18.[42]

11.7.13   Local weights and measures authorities have a statutory duty to enforce the provisions relating to the sale of alcohol to children, and statutory authority to authorise any person to make test purchases.[43] There is a specific saving for the use of children by constables or weights and measures inspectors for test purchases.[44]

11.7.14   It is an offence for an individual under the age of 18 knowingly to consume alcohol on premises with a premises licence or club premises certificate, or with the benefit of a temporary event notice.[45] (The maximum penalty is at level 3.) It is also an offence knowingly to allow an individual under the age of 18 to consume alcohol on such premises.[46] (The maximum penalty is at level 5.) Again there is the exemption for accompanied 16- and 17-year-olds relating to beer, cider or wine with a table meal.

11.7.15   There is a series of provisions dealing with the employment of children in licensed or club premises and premises used for a temporary event (referred to as 'relevant premises') and using children to obtain alcohol (LA 2003, ss 151–153).

11.7.16   It is an offence for a person who works in relevant premises knowingly to deliver alcohol sold or supplied on the premises or to allow such alcohol to be delivered to an individual under the age of

---

[39] LA 2003, s 149(3).

[40] Ibid, s 149(4).

[41] Ibid, s 149(5).

[42] Ibid, s 149(6).

[43] Ibid, s 154.

[44] Ibid, s 154(2).

[45] Ibid, s 150(1).

[46] Ibid, s 150(2).

18.[47] The offence is not committed if the alcohol is delivered at a place where the purchaser of the alcohol or the person supplied lives or works; where the individual under the age of 18 works on the premises and the job involves the delivery of alcohol; or where the alcohol is sold or supplied for consumption on the relevant premises. In the latter case, the sale or supply would be caught by other prohibitions.

11.7.17 It is an offence to send an individual under the age of 18 to obtain alcohol from relevant premises for consumption off those premises.[48] Sending a child (individual aged under 18) to intermediate premises is also caught. Those under 18 who work in relevant premises and whose jobs include the delivery of alcohol are exempt. There is the usual saving for test purchases made by children sent by constables or weights and measures inspectors.

11.7.18 Unsupervised sales or supplies of alcohol by those aged under 18 are also made illegal.[49] There is an important exemption where the alcohol is sold or supplied for consumption with a table meal in premises used (or used in part) for the provision of table meals and not used (or not in that part used) for the sale or supply of alcohol to persons not having table meals. The people liable for the offence are the holder of the premises licence, the designated supervisor, an officer of a club or member present in the capacity to prevent such supplies, the premises user or, in relation to licensed premises or a temporary event, an individual aged 18 or over specifically authorised for the purposes of LA 2003, s 153 to supervise sales by those aged under 18.

11.7.19 'Table meal' is defined as 'a meal eaten by a person seated at a table, or at a counter or other structure which serves the purpose of a table and is not used for the service of refreshments for consumption by persons not seated at a table or structure serving the purpose of a table'.[50]

11.8 UNACCOMPANIED CHILDREN PROHIBITED FROM CERTAIN PREMISES

11.8.1 Late in the Licensing Bill's passage through Parliament a further offence was added to deal with concerns about the access of children to licensed premises. *Unaccompanied children* under the age of 16 are prohibited from premises that are exclusively or primarily used for the supply and consumption of alcohol.[51] Those premises might be a premises with a premises licence, a club with a club

---

[47] LA 2003, s 151.

[48] Ibid, s 152.

[49] Ibid, s 153.

[50] Ibid, s 159.

[51] Ibid, s 145.

premises certificate or premises being used for a temporary event. A child is deemed to be 'unaccompanied' if not in the company of someone who is aged 18 years or over.

11.8.2   Generally speaking those in a position to prevent unaccompanied children from being present in such premises commit an offence if they allow an unaccompanied child to be on the premises knowing that the premises are exclusively or primarily used for the sale or supply of alcohol or, in any event, between the hours of 12 midnight and 5 am.

11.8.3   The people in a position of responsibility are:[52]

(a) any person who works at the premises (whether paid or unpaid) who is in a capacity which allows him to request that the unaccompanied child leave the premises;
(b) the holder of the premises licence;
(c) the designated premises supervisor;
(d) a member or officer of a club there in a capacity which allows him to request that an unaccompanied child leave the premises; and
(e) the premises user in relation to a temporary event.

11.8.4   An offence is not committed if the child is simply passing through the premises and there is no other convenient means of access or egress.[53]

11.8.5   Where a person is charged with an offence under this provision by reason of his own conduct, it is a defence that he believed that the unaccompanied child was aged 16 or over, or that the person accompanying the child was aged 18 or over, and either that he had taken all reasonable steps to establish the age of the child or person accompanying the child, or nobody could reasonably have suspected from the appearance of the child or person accompanying the child that they were under the ages of 16 and 18 respectively.[54]

11.8.6   Reasonable steps are deemed to have been taken if the child or person accompanying the child was asked for evidence of age and that evidence would have convinced a reasonable person.[55]

11.8.7   The penalty for this offence is a fine not exceeding level 3 on the standard scale.

11.9   CONFISCATION OF ALCOHOL BY CONSTABLES

11.9.1   The Confiscation of Alcohol (Young Persons) Act 1997 gave the right to a constable to require the surrender of alcohol by a young

---

[52] LA 2003, s 145(3).

[53] Ibid, s 145(5).

[54] Ibid, s 145(6).

[55] Ibid, s 145(7).

person under the age of 18 but not if the alcohol was in a sealed container. That restriction has now been removed if the constable reasonably believes that the young person is or has been consuming or intends to consume the alcohol in the places described in that Act.[56]

11.10 VEHICLES AND TRAINS

11.10.1 The sale by retail of alcohol on or from a vehicle not temporarily or permanently parked is unlawful. The maximum penalty is 3 months' imprisonment, or a fine of £20,000, or both. It is a defence that the act was due to mistake or reliance upon information given by another person or to some other cause beyond the person's control and that all reasonable precautions were taken and due diligence exercised.[57]

11.10.2 A vehicle is defined as 'a vehicle intended or adapted for use on roads'.[58]

11.10.3 A magistrates' court may make an order prohibiting the sale of alcohol on a train which travels to or from a station in its area or at stations in its area. The application for such an order has to be made by a senior police officer of the rank of inspector or above. The order must be necessary to prevent disorder. It must be served on the necessary train operators immediately. It is then an offence, punishable with 3 months' imprisonment, or a £20,000 fine, or both, to sell, attempt to sell or allow the sale of alcohol in contravention of an order.[59]

11.11 FALSE STATEMENTS

11.11.1 A person who knowingly or recklessly makes a false statement in connection with a licensing application to a licensing authority commits an offence punishable with a fine at level 5 of the standard scale. Making a false statement includes producing, furnishing, signing or otherwise making use of a document that contains a false statement.[60]

---

[56] LA 2003, s 155.

[57] Ibid, s 156.

[58] Ibid, s 193.

[59] Ibid, s 157.

[60] Ibid, s 158.

Chapter 12

CLOSURE OF PREMISES

'I am only a beer teetotaller not a champagne teetotaller.'

George Bernard Shaw

12.1 INTRODUCTION

12.1.1   Both the police and the courts have the power to order the temporary closure of licensed premises in specified circumstances. The existing powers afforded to the police, courts and local authorities under the Public Entertainments Licences (Drug Misuse) Act 1997, Licensing Act 1964, ss 179A–179K and 188, and the Criminal Justice and Police Act 2001 will be repealed. Thus the code for closure orders set out in LA 2003, Part 8 is now the only source of police, local authority or judicial powers.

12.1.2   The same applies to premises in respect of which a temporary event notice has effect, but the closure powers do not apply to clubs with a club premises certificate.

12.1.3   For licence holders, the new provisions are a considerable improvement on the provisions of the Public Entertainments Licences (Drug Misuse) Act 1997 whereby closure orders could be made without any notice to the licence holder, and reviews were sometimes conducted without the licence holder having access to the information put before the local authority by the police.

12.2 GENERAL CLOSURE ORDERS

12.2.1   The power to make a temporary closure order relating to all licensed premises, or premises with the benefit of a temporary event notice, in a particular area, whether licensed for the supply of alcohol or not, lies only with the magistrates' court. The power can be exercised only on the application of a senior police officer of the rank of superintendent or above.[1]

12.2.2   The only ground for making a general closure order is that the court is satisfied that it is necessary to prevent disorder.[2]

---

[1]   LA 2003, s 160(1) and (2).

[2]   Ibid, s 160(3).

12.2.3   Where there is or is expected to be disorder, for example by rival fans of football clubs or opposing protesters, the magistrates' court for the area concerned may make an order that all licensed premises which are situated at or near the place of the disorder or expected disorder be closed for a period not exceeding 24 hours. In a city centre, such an order could feasibly apply to premises such as theatres, cinemas, large hotels and department stores or supermarkets, as well as public houses and off-licences. When debated in Parliament, the Government was confident that since the court had to be satisfied that a closure order was necessary to prevent disorder it was unlikely that premises such as large hotels or department stores would be affected.

12.2.4   Dr Kim Howells did say, however:[3]

> 'In this respect we are talking about supermarkets and other premises that sell alcohol ... It is possible that a crowd that was inclined to disorder would be more of a threat if it were allowed to remain together but prevented from buying alcohol or would normally expect to be able to do so. I understand the concerns raised about large supermarkets. However, what if football fans were running through an area and causing trouble, for example? ... If the football fans were causing trouble, would supermarkets be happy if they could come into the shops but were not allowed to buy alcohol? Does anyone really believe that the fans would be deterred by some sort of cordoning off of the alcohol section, or by a supermarket security guard? ... If the circumstances are serious enough to require the issuing of a closure notice for an area, the answer must be to close all of the licensed premises, or premises where a temporary event notice has effect, for the limited period mentioned in the order, and not simply to stop premises from selling alcohol and carrying on other licensable activities.'

12.2.5   It is an offence knowingly to keep open premises to which a general closure order relates. The use of the word 'knowingly' means that the offence is not a strict liability offence and that proof of knowledge of the existence of the closure order will be required. This is important because there is no provision in this part of the LA 2003 as to the service of a general closure order. The offence can be committed by either a manager of the premises kept open, the holder of the premises licence, the designated supervisor, or, in the case of a temporary event, the premises user.[4]

12.2.6   A constable may use such force as is necessary in order to close premises affected by a general closure order.

---

[3]   *Hansard*, HC Standing Committee D, 15 May 2003, cols 621–622.

[4]   LA 2003, s 160(4) and (5).

12.3 SPECIFIC CLOSURE ORDERS

12.3.1   A different procedural regime applies to orders to close specified premises on a temporary basis. In short the decision to close may be taken by a police officer of the rank of Inspector or above. The magistrates' court must be notified of the decision and as soon as practicable must set up a hearing to review the order. The decision of the magistrates' court must be reported to the licensing authority, which must then conduct a review of the licence in question.

Decision making by the police

12.3.2   To make a specified closure order in relation to particular licensed premises or premises in respect of which a temporary event notice is in effect the senior police officer must have a reasonable belief that:

(a) there is, or is likely imminently to be, disorder on, or in the vicinity of or related to, the premises and that the closure is necessary in the interests of public safety; or

(b) a public nuisance is being caused by noise coming from the premises and the closure of the premises is necessary to prevent that nuisance.[5]

12.3.3   'Imminent' is defined in the Collins and Oxford English dictionaries as meaning 'likely to happen soon'. 'Public nuisance' has a common law meaning upon which the Government was content to rely without the need for definition of that term in the LA 2003.

12.3.4   In the decision-making process, the same senior police officer has to have regard to the conduct of the manager of the premises, the premises licence holder, the designated supervisor, or the premises user (in the case of a temporary event) – all referred to as 'the appropriate person' – in relation to the disorder or nuisance.[6]

12.3.5   The specified closure order must specify the premises to which it relates, the period for which the premises are to be closed (not to exceed 24 hours in the first instance), the grounds upon which the order is made and the effect of the statutory provisions relating to such orders (as set out in LA 2003, ss 162–168).[7]

12.3.6   The closure order comes into effect at the time a constable gives notice of it to the appropriate person. The LA 2003 uses unusual wording in this case – 'to an appropriate person who is connected with any of the activities to which the disorder or nuisance relates'. 'Appropriate person' is defined, in relation to any premises, as meaning:

---

[5]   LA 2003, s 161(1).

[6]   Ibid, s 161(3).

[7]   Ibid, s 161(4).

(a) any person who holds a premises licence in respect of the premises;
(b) any designated supervisor of the premises;
(c) the premises user in relation to a temporary event notice; or
(d) a manager of the premises.[8]

12.3.7 A premises licence holder might have no knowledge of the disorder but if the notice was served upon him he would be expected to take immediate action to comply with it. The reality will surely be that these emergency orders will be made and served at the time of actual disorder or noise nuisance upon the person in charge of the premises at the time.

12.3.8 It is an offence to permit, without reasonable excuse, premises to be open in contravention of a closure order. Whether or not premises are kept open is a matter of fact for the courts to determine. Nevertheless the LA 2003 contains a definition to assist with the determination of the facts:[9]

> 'Relevant premises are open if a person other than [an appropriate person, a person who usually lives at the premises or a member of the family of either of those people] enters the premises and—
>
> (a) buys or is otherwise supplied with food, drink or anything usually sold on the premises, or
> (b) while he is on the premises, they are used for the provision of regulated entertainment.'

12.3.9 Use of premises where there is no premises licence for non-licensable activities outside the period given in a temporary event notice are to be disregarded, as are qualifying club activities and certain supplies of hot food and drink which are exempt from the late night refreshment provisions of LA 2003, Sch 2.[10] (Examples are the supply of hot food and drink to hotel guests and members of recognised clubs.)

12.3.10 The penalty is a maximum of 3 months' imprisonment, or a fine of £20,000, or both. Again a police constable may use such force as is necessary to ensure compliance with a specified closure order.[11]

12.4 EXTENSION OF CLOSURE ORDERS

12.4.1 The same senior police officer who made the specified closure order can extend that order beyond its original, or latest, expiry time.[12]

---

[8] LA 2003, s 171(5).

[9] Ibid, s 171(2) and (4).

[10] Ibid, s 171(3).

[11] Ibid, s 169.

[12] Ibid, s 162.

12.4.2   The senior police officer can order an extension if he has a reasonable belief that the magistrates' court will not have made a decision on the order, or any extension to it, before the end of the closure period.

12.4.3   The grounds for granting the extension of a closure order are either continuing necessity, in the interests of public safety, because of disorder or likely disorder, or continuing nuisance or likely nuisance caused by noise coming from the premises.

12.4.4   The extension comes into force when notice of it is given to the appropriate person connected with the premises. The extension cannot exceed 24 hours from the end of the previous closure order or extension and will not be effective at all unless served before the end of the previous closure order or extension.[13]

12.5   CANCELLATION OF A CLOSURE ORDER

12.5.1   The same senior police officer who made the specified closure order, or ordered its extension, may cancel it at any time before the magistrates' court determines whether to exercise any of its powers.[14]

12.5.2   The same senior police officer must cancel a closure order if he does not have a reasonable belief that continued closure of the premises is necessary in the interests of public safety or that it is necessary to ensure that no public nuisance is caused by noise coming from the premises.[15] An example of such a situation might be where the maker of the noise or disturbance has left the premises and is unlikely to return within the period of the closure order or its current extension.

12.5.3   Notice of cancellation must be given to an appropriate person connected with the activities related to the disorder or nuisance which caused the closure order to be made in the first place.[16]

12.6   POWERS OF THE MAGISTRATES' COURT

12.6.1   Whenever a specified closure order is made the police must, as soon as is reasonably practicable, apply to the magistrates' court for the area for it to consider the order. If the premises concerned are

---

[13] LA 2003, s 162(4).

[14] Ibid, s 163(1).

[15] Ibid, s 163(2).

[16] Ibid, s 163(3).

licensed premises then the senior police officer must also notify the licensing authority.[17]

12.6.2 The magistrates' court must hold a hearing as soon as is reasonably practicable after receiving an application from the police. The court must then consider whether it is appropriate to exercise any of its powers and then determine whether or not to do so. This two-stage process means that even if it is appropriate for the court to exercise its powers under the LA 2003 the court still has a discretion as to whether or not to exercise those powers.[18]

12.6.3 The powers available to the court are:

(a) revocation of the closure order;
(b) ordering the premises to remain closed or to be closed until the licensing authority has reviewed the situation;
(c) ordering the premises to remain closed until the review but with certain exceptions;
(d) ordering the premises to remain closed until the review unless certain conditions are satisfied.[19]

It is significant to note that the magistrates' court hearing still comes into play even though a closure order has expired and not been extended, or has been cancelled.

12.6.4 The grounds upon which the magistrates' court may exercise its powers are exactly the same upon which the senior police officer had to consider in the first place or in the case of any extension.[20]

12.6.5 The magistrates' court can be properly constituted with only one justice sitting. All evidence must be given on oath. Any decision of the magistrates' court must be notified to the licensing authority.

12.6.6 Only if the premises concerned cease to be licensed premises, as defined in LA 2003, s 161(8) – that is, they no longer have the benefit of a premises licence (say, for example, because the licence has been surrendered), or a temporary event notice – can a magistrates' court hearing be avoided.[21]

12.6.7 Nowhere in the LA 2003 is provision made for procedural rules governing the hearing of applications for consideration of closure orders. The power to make rules or to give guidance relates only to hearings and proceedings before licensing authorities. There is a reference in LA 2003, s 165(9) to the exercise of the magistrates' court's powers being in the place required for a hearing of a complaint but the procedures are not said to be by way of complaint so that the Magistrates' Courts Rules 1981 relating to complaints do not

---

[17] LA 2003, s 164.
[18] Ibid, s 165(1).
[19] Ibid, s 165(2).
[20] Ibid, s 165(3).
[21] Ibid, s 165(5).

apply. Presumably the Magistrates' Courts Rules will be amended to incorporate provisions for dealing with the hearing of these applications.

12.6.8 In any event, the European Convention for the Protection of Human Rights and Fundamental Freedoms will apply entitling holders of premises licences to a fair hearing. A licence is a possession for the purposes of Art 1 of the First Protocol to the Convention[22] and so the holder is not to be deprived of it except in the public interest and subject to the conditions provided for by law and by the general principles of international law. This should mean that the holder of a premises licence and the designated supervisor or manager (and probably a temporary event promoter) know of the date of the hearing, have adequate time to prepare for it and have prior knowledge of the evidence upon which the police will rely.

12.6.9 Whilst adequate time to prepare will be required, it is unlikely to be in the interests of the premises licence holder whose premises are still closed to delay the hearing unnecessarily.

12.6.10 A person aggrieved by the decision of the magistrates' court – a term which has a meaning understood by licensing lawyers to include the owner of the premises, a mortgagee, and any other person 'immediately' aggrieved and not merely 'consequently' aggrieved[23] – has 21 days in which to lodge an appeal. The appeal will be heard by the Crown Court.

12.7 REVIEW BY THE LICENSING AUTHORITY

12.7.1 As has been seen, the making of a closure order in respect of licensed premises automatically triggers both a hearing before the magistrates' court and a review by the relevant licensing authority.

12.7.2 When a closure order has been made and the licensing authority has received a notice of the determination of the magistrates' court, the licensing authority must review the premises licence. A determination on that review must be made no later than 28 days after receipt of the notice from the magistrates' court.[24]

12.7.3 Regulations will deal with the giving of notice of the review, closure order and magistrates' courts' determination, to the holder of a premises licence and each responsible authority and the advertising of the review inviting representations from those responsible authorities and interested parties.[25]

[22] *Tre Traktorer AB v Sweden* (1991) 13 EHRR 309. See also *Sporrong and Lonnroth v Sweden* (1983) 5 EHRR 35.
[23] *R v Andover Justices* (1886) 16 QBD 71 and *Garrett v Middlesex Justices* (1884) 12 QBD 620.
[24] LA 2003, s 167(1).
[25] Ibid, s 167(4).

12.7.4   The licensing authority has to hold a hearing to consider the original order, the magistrates' court's determination and any relevant representations. Regulations will be made and guidance given as to the conduct of the review hearing.

12.7.5   At the end of the hearing the licensing authority must take such steps as it considers necessary for the promotion of the licensing objectives.[26] The steps it can take are:

(a) to modify the conditions of the premises licence;
(b) to exclude a licensable activity from the scope of the licence (for example a form of entertainment);
(c) to remove the designated premises supervisor from the licence;
(d) to suspend the licence for a period not exceeding 3 months;
(e) to revoke the licence.[27]

To modify the conditions means altering, omitting or adding any condition save that the statutory conditions (LA 2003, ss 19 and 20) cannot be modified. Modifications or exclusions can be for a limited period, which must be specified and may not exceed 3 months.[28]

12.7.6   Any representation has to be relevant – that means relevant to one or more of the licensing objectives – and made by the holder of the premises licence, a responsible authority, or an interested party. As in all other matters raised by an interested party, the representation will not be relevant if it is frivolous or vexatious.[29]

12.7.7   A note of the licensing authority's determination upon review, and the reasons for making the determination, must be given to the holder of the premises licence, any person who made relevant representations and to the chief officer of police for the area.[30]

12.7.8   A determination upon review to revoke the licence does not come into effect until the end of the period allowed for appealing – and if an appeal is lodged until the disposal of that appeal. If, however, the premises has been closed pending the outcome of the review the premises must remain closed (although the licence will technically remain in force).[31]

12.7.9   If the premises has been closed pending the review by reason of a magistrates' court order and if the licensing authority on review decides to make an order other than revocation, for example to modify the conditions, that determination comes into effect at the time the licence holder is notified of it. The licensing authority may, however, suspend the operation of its determination in whole or in part until the determination of any appeal.

---

[26] LA 2003, s 167(6).
[27] Ibid, s 167(6).
[28] Ibid, s 167(8).
[29] Ibid, s 167(9) and (10).
[30] Ibid, s 167(12).
[31] Ibid, s 168(5) and (7).

12.7.10   The magistrates' court also has the power to suspend a determination of a licensing authority pending an appeal.[32]

12.7.11   A person who, without reasonable excuse, allows premises to be open in contravention of a determination of a licensing authority to revoke the licence (those premises having been closed at the time of the review) commits an offence punishable with a maximum penalty of 3 months' imprisonment, or a fine of £20,000, or both.[33]

12.8   EXEMPTION OF THE POLICE FROM LIABILITY FOR DAMAGES

12.8.1   Both police constables and chief officers of police are granted immunity from awards of damages in respect of anything done in relation to closure orders.[34]

12.8.2   The immunity does not apply if the act or omission of the police is shown to have been in bad faith.

12.8.3   Also the immunity does not apply to an award of damages in respect of a claim under s 6(1) of the Human Rights Act 1998 for breach of rights under the European Convention for the Protection of Human Rights and Fundamental Freedoms.

---

[32] LA 2003, Sch 5, para 18(3) and (4).

[33] Ibid, s 168(8) and (9).

[34] Ibid, s 170.

Chapter 13

HEARINGS

'This is a British murder enquiry and some degree of justice must be seen to be more or less done.'

Tom Stoppard
(*Jumpers*)

13.1 INTRODUCTION

13.1.1 Local authorities have held 'licensing' hearings for many years. Sadly the experiences of those attending such hearings has been very mixed. They have varied from the well-organised court-like hearings conducted in an atmosphere of professional calm, to late night bear gardens with objectors screaming at applicants from the public gallery and no semblance of order or control on the part of the licensing committee.

13.1.2 In some areas, detailed procedures have been adopted ensuring that adequate notice is given to all parties and that each party has the chance to question the evidence and submissions made by the other(s). In other places little detail is given about objections, applicants are not allowed to call evidence or to ask questions of those opposed to the application and local authority officers are permitted to give unchallenged advice.

13.1.3 It is doubtful whether in those areas where carefully drafted procedures have not been devised the local authority concerned, as a public authority, provides for the parties a fair hearing in accordance with Art 6 of the European Convention for the Protection of Human Rights and Fundamental Freedoms.

13.1.4 The LA 2003 provides little guidance as to the nature and form of hearings before the new licensing authorities. Section 183 provides the power to make regulations with regard to hearings before licensing authorities. Section 9 provides the power to make regulations governing procedures before licensing committees (dealing with matters such as the quorum, publicity and public access). Otherwise, licensing authorities are at liberty to devise their own procedures.[1]

---

[1] LA 2003, s 9(3).

13.1.5   Much of the decision making will be undertaken either by
sub-committees or officers of the authority (see Chapter 5). In
whichever case it is suggested that the 'common law' rules as to natural
justice and the right to a fair hearing will continue to apply. Certainly
wherever a decision of, say, a sub-committee has to be confirmed by
the licensing authority, the final decision maker must be informed of
the nature and effect of any representations made to the sub-
committee and, in summary, the evidence put before the sub-
committee.[2]

13.2   RULES AND REGULATIONS

13.2.1   The LA 2003 provides[3] that regulations may prescribe the
procedure to be followed in relation to a hearing held by a licensing
authority under the LA 2003 and in particular may make provision
for:

–   the giving of notice of hearings;
–   expedited hearings;
–   rules of evidence;
–   legal representation; and
–   time limits.

13.2.2   The LA 2003 does, however, prevent the licensing authority
making orders as to costs.[4] The intention of the Government was to
limit the cost of making an application, thus reducing the burden on
legitimate businesses, and also not to deter local residents from
making appropriate representations.

13.2.3   If not provided for in the regulations, rules as to debate,
quorum, voting and other procedural matters relating to the
functions of local authorities and local authority committees will be
found in the local authority's standing orders. A copy of the standing
orders is normally available for inspection by members of the public.
It is normal practice for decisions to be taken by majority voting, with
the chair having a second or casting vote.

13.2.4   The local authority will also have a code of conduct for its
members, which may prevent members taking part in certain
decisions. If, for example, a ward councillor made representations on
behalf of his electors who were people living in the vicinity of premises
in respect of which an application had been made for a premises
licence, that councillor could not take part in the making of the
decision even if he was a member of the licensing committee. Some

---

[2]   *R v Chester City Council and Others ex parte Quietlynn Ltd* (1983) *The Times*, October
       19, per Woolf J.

[3]   LA 2003, s 183(1).

[4]   Ibid, s 183(2).

codes of conduct even go so far as to prevent that councillor taking part in the preceding discussion about the application.

13.3 BIAS

13.3.1 If a member of the licensing authority has a pecuniary interest, whether direct or indirect in any matter relating to a licensing application he must disclose that fact as soon as practicable and not take part in either the discussion or the making of the decision.[5] The pecuniary interest arises if a member, or any nominee of his, is a member of a company or other body, or he is a partner of or employed by a person or body, which has a direct pecuniary interest in the matter to be determined.[6]

13.3.2 If a councillor is married to a person who has a direct or indirect pecuniary interest of which the councillor is aware, then that too is deemed to be an interest of the councillor.[7]

13.3.3 Shares or securities held which do not exceed £1,000 or one-hundredth of the value of the issued share capital, whichever is the less, must be disclosed but do not preclude the member from taking part in the decision making.[8] A councillor is not treated as having a pecuniary interest merely by being a ratepayer or local resident benefiting from the council's services.[9] Also an interest so remote or small that it could not reasonably be regarded as likely to influence a councillor can be properly disregarded.[10]

13.3.4 In 1994 the Department of Environment gave advice[11] to councillors on the issue of bias in the following terms:

> 'The law makes specific provision requiring you to disclose pecuniary interests, direct and indirect. But interests which are not pecuniary can be just as important. Kinship, friendship, membership of an association, society or trade union, trusteeship and many other kinds of relationship can sometimes influence your judgment and give the impression that you might be acting for personal motives. A good test is to ask yourself whether others would think that the interest is of a kind to make this possible. If you think they would, or if you are in doubt, disclose the interest and withdraw from the meeting unless under Standing Orders you are specifically invited to stay.'

---

[5] Local Government Act 1972, s 94(1).

[6] Ibid, s 95(1).

[7] Ibid, s 95(3).

[8] Ibid, s 97(6).

[9] Ibid, s 97(4).

[10] Ibid, s 97(5).

[11] Department of Environment, *National Code of Local Government Conduct* (Circular 94/75).

13.3.5   Should a licensing decision be taken by a committee which included a member with a pecuniary interest, the decision is likely to be void for being contrary to natural justice.[12]

13.4   RIGHT TO A FAIR HEARING

13.4.1   Despite the comparative informality with which some hearings before local authority committees have been conducted, it has long been held that the judicial principles embodied in the expression 'natural justice' should be applied. In a leading case in 1892 the decision of the House of Lords in *Sharp v Wakefield*[13] was applied to a licensing decision made by a county council in respect of a music and dancing licence. In *R v London County Council ex parte Akkersdyk, ex parte Fermenia,*[14] AL Smith J said:

> 'It is true that [the county council] are authorised to grant or refuse a licence as they in their discretion shall think proper, but the discretion is to be exercised, as Lord Halsbury put it in *Sharp v Wakefield* [1891] AC 173, "according to the rules of reason and justice" ... In our judgment, when so acting, they are not emancipated from the ordinary principles upon which justice is administered in this kingdom.'

13.4.2   The principles embodied in Art 6 of the European Convention for the Protection of Human Rights and Fundamental Freedoms have been part of the legal tradition in the United Kingdom for a long time. Proceedings with regard to licensing come within Art 6(1) of the Convention:

> 'Article 6 – Right to a Fair Trial
>
> (1)   In the determination of his civil rights and obligations, or of any criminal charge against him, everyone is entitled to a fair and public hearing within a reasonable time by an independent and impartial tribunal established by law. Judgment shall be pronounced publicly but the press and public may be excluded from all or part of the trial in the interests of morals, public order or national security in a democratic society, where the interests of juveniles or the protection of the private lives of the parties so require, or to the extent strictly necessary in the opinion of the court in special circumstances where publicity would prejudice the interests of justice.'

13.4.3   It could be argued that, despite the statutory sanctioning of the procedure in LA 2003, s 53 whereby one arm or department of a local authority might apply for a review of a premises licence to another arm of the same authority, the licensing committee, Art 6

---

[12] *R v London County Council ex parte Akkersdyk, ex parte Fermenia* [1892] 1 QB 190.

[13] [1891] AC 173.

[14] [1892] 1 QB 190.

would be breached because the licensing committee was not an 'independent and impartial tribunal'. The approach of the courts has been to follow the European jurisprudence to the effect that decisions taken by a tribunal not deemed to be independent and impartial are not incompatible with Art 6(1) provided that they are subject to review by an independent and impartial tribunal such as a superior court.[15] Licensing authority decisions will be subject to review by both the magistrates' court and the High Court and, therefore, the process will be deemed to be compatible with Art 6.

13.4.4 In general terms it was always thought that if there was a contested application then there should be a hearing even though that might not have been required by statute.[16] However, in *The Queen on the Application of Spearing v London Borough of Hammersmith and Fulham and Ablethird Ltd*,[17] where the only objection was a 'trade' objection, it was held lawful for a decision to grant to have been taken at officer level under delegated powers without a hearing.

13.4.5 Where a person has a right or an interest or a legitimate expectation then an authority cannot act to deprive him of that right, interest or expectation without a hearing and the giving of reasons for its decision.[18]

13.4.6 Recognising those principles, there is a major change made by the LA 2003 in that a hearing must be held where there are objections to an application or where a licence is subject to review, unless the authority and all the parties agree that a hearing is not necessary.

13.4.7 Similarly, a person is not to be deprived of the ability to earn his living 'except for just cause and in accordance with natural justice'.[19] The same applies to any refusal to renew or determination to revoke a licence.[20] A licence is recognised as property in the European Human Rights jurisprudence and therefore, in accordance with Art 1 of the First Protocol, not to be removed unless in accordance with law, necessary in the interests of society, and proportionate with the purpose of the removal.[21] That approach has

---

[15] See *R (Alconbury Developments Ltd and Others) v Secretary of State for the Environment, Transport and the Regions* [2001] UKHL 23, [2002] 2 WLR 1389.

[16] See *R v Huntingdon District Council ex parte Cowan* [1984] 1 All ER 58.

[17] [2001] EWHC Admin 1109, [2002] LLR 401.

[18] *Breen v Amalgamated Engineering Union* [1971] 2 QB 175.

[19] Per Lord Denning MR in *R v Barnsley Metropolitan Borough Council ex parte Hook* [1976] 1 WLR 534 (where the council removed a market stall holder's licence, having heard evidence from the markets manager in the absence of the stall holder).

[20] *McInnes v Onslow-Fane* [1978] 3 All ER 211; *R v Windsor Licensing Justices ex parte Hodes* [1983] 1 WLR 685, [1983] 2 All ER 551.

[21] *Tre Traktorer AB v Sweden* (1991) 13 EHRR 309; *Sporrong and Lonnroth v Sweden* (1983) 5 EHRR 35.

been followed in the courts of both England and Wales and Scotland.[22]

13.4.8   There have been different opinions as to whether or not an applicant for a new licence or a variation of an existing licence is protected by Art 1 of the First Protocol to the European Convention for the Protection of Human Rights and Fundamental Freedoms. In *Catscratch Ltd and Lettuce Holdings Ltd v City of Glasgow Licensing Board*,[23] the Court of Session held that a failure to grant an extension to a licence did amount to an interference with property, whereas in *Di Ciacca v Scottish Ministers* the same court held that a refusal to vary planning conditions to allow longer opening hours did not bring Art 1 of the First Protocol into play.[24]

13.4.9   At common law it may not be only those directly affected by a decision who should be consulted and have the right to make representations.[25] Whether the same test can be applied in relation to hearings under the LA 2003 remains to be seen. The difference may lie in the designation of those who can 'appear' or make representations to the licensing authority as set out in and defined in the LA 2003. In the Guidance issued by the Secretary of State, the statutory definition of interested parties[26] is expected to be given 'its widest possible interpretation' so that it includes residents' associations, charities, churches and medical practices.[27]

13.4.10   A failure to give a notice prescribed by the LA 2003 or regulations so that a party was unaware of a hearing would constitute a breach of the rules of natural justice.[28] Similarly a failure to provide an applicant with details of representations made against him[29] or to raise matters at the hearing of which he had not had prior notice would amount to a breach of natural justice.[30] If an application is made for an adjournment, because information has not been provided until the last minute for example, then the committee should grant an

---

[22] See, for example, *Crompton (T/A David Crompton Haulage) v Department of Transport North Western Area* [2003] EWCA Civ 64, [2003] LLR 237 and *Adams v Licensing Division No 3 of the South Lanarkshire Council* [2002] LLR 271.

[23] [2001] LLR 610.

[24] [2003] LLR 426. It was held that Art 1 of the First Protocol to the Convention protects existing rights (and certain legitimate expectations) but does not guarantee a right to acquire what one does not have. The decision to refuse to remove a condition attached to an existing grant of planning permission did not encroach upon any existing right.

[25] See *R v Liverpool Corporation ex parte Liverpool Taxi Fleet Operators' Association* [1975] 2 QB 299.

[26] LA 2003, s 13.

[27] Paragraph 5.23 of the Guidance.

[28] *R v Diggines ex parte Rahmani* [1985] 2 WLR 611.

[29] *R v Huntingdon District Council ex parte Cowan* [1984] 1 All ER 58.

[30] *Tudor v Ellesmere Port and Neston Borough Council* (1987) *The Times*, May 8.

adjournment if to refuse it would deny one of the parties a fair hearing.[31]

13.4.11   Where, however, the decision to be taken by the licensing authority is to be of general effect, for example the fixing of fees within the scale provided by the Secretary of State, the principle that persons affected must be allowed a hearing has been held not to apply.[32]

13.5   DISCRETION

13.5.1   Today most local authorities are statutory corporations. Most licensing authorities will be statutory bodies and subject, therefore, to judicial supervision. The circumstances in which the courts might intervene were expressed by Lord Reid in *Anisminic*:[33]

> '... there are many cases where, although the tribunal had jurisdiction to enter on the enquiry, it has done or failed to do something which is of such a nature that its decision is a nullity. It may have given its decision in bad faith. It may have made a decision which it had no power to make. It may have failed in the course of the enquiry to comply with the requirements of natural justice. It may in perfect good faith have misconstrued the provisions giving it power to act so that it failed to deal with a question remitted to it. It may have refused to take into account something it was required to take into account. Or it may have based its decision on some matter which, under the provisions setting it up, it had no right to take into account. I do not intend this list to be exhaustive. But if it decides a question remitted to it for decision without committing any of these errors it is as much entitled to decide that question wrongly as it is to decide it rightly.'[34]

13.5.2   With regard to whether or not a licensing authority has exercised its discretion properly, the classic test remains the *Wednesbury* test. In *Associated Provincial Picture Houses Ltd v Wednesbury Corporation*[35] Lord Greene MR stated:

> 'The exercise of such discretion must be a real exercise of the discretion. If, in the statute conferring the discretion, there is to be found expressly or by implication matters which the authority exercising the discretion ought to have regard to, then in exercising the discretion, it must have regard to those matters. Conversely, if the nature of the subject matter and the general interpretation of the Act makes it clear that certain matters would not be germane to the matter in question, the authority

---

[31]   *R v Birmingham City Council and Others ex parte Quietlynn Ltd* [1985] 83 LGR 461.

[32]   *R v Greater London Council ex parte The Rank Organisation* (1982) *The Times*, February 18.

[33]   *Anisminic v Foreign Compensation Commission* [1969] 2 AC 147.

[34]   [1969] 2 AC 147 at p 171.

[35]   [1948] 1 KB 223.

must disregard those irrelevant collateral matters ... It is true to say that
if a decision on a competent matter is so unreasonable that no
reasonable authority could ever have come to it, then the courts can
interfere ... but to prove a case of that kind would require something
quite overwhelming.'

13.5.3 Contrary to Lord Greene's expectation, instances of local
authorities making decisions which 'no authority could ever have
come to' proved not to be so rare. Other terms such as 'irrational'
came to be used. In 1977 in *Secretary of State for Education and Science v
Tameside Metropolitan Borough Council*,[36] Lord Diplock said:

'In public law "unreasonable" as descriptive of the way in which a public
authority has purported to exercise a discretion vested in it by statute has
become a term of legal art. To fall within this expression it must be
conduct which no sensible authority acting with due appreciation of its
responsibilities would have decided to adopt.'

13.5.4 Political influences would be unacceptable in licensing
decisions. Resolutions passed on moral grounds, as opposed to
statutory or administrative grounds have been held to be unlawful.[37] A
licensing authority's policy statement which was not based upon the
legislative objectives of the LA 2003 would be open to challenge
generally and specifically if applied in relation to a particular licensing
decision.

13.5.5 In general, licensing authorities are entitled to have policies.
They are useful to achieve consistency. However, polices must not be
allowed to fetter the discretion of the authority.[38] If the authority so
fetters its discretion that no application could succeed against that
policy, it will have failed to exercise its discretion at all.[39]

13.5.6 The difference between the new law and past circumstances
is that licensing authorities will have to comply with the guidance
given by the Secretary of State under LA 2003, s 182 or give their
reasons for failure to comply.

13.6 GUIDANCE

13.6.1 LA 2003, s 182 requires the Secretary of State to issue
guidance ('the licensing Guidance') to licensing authorities on the
discharge of their functions under the LA 2003. A draft of the
Licensing Guidance must be laid before both Houses of Parliament
and approved by resolution of each House. The Secretary of State may

---

[36] [1977] AC 1014.

[37] *R v Somerset County Council ex parte Fewings* [1995] 1 WLR 1037.

[38] *R (Westminster City Council) v Middlesex Crown Court and Chorion plc* [2002] EWHC
Admin 1104, [2002] LLR 538; *R v Chester Crown Court ex parte Pascoe and Jones* 151
JP 752.

[39] *Sagnata Investments Ltd v Norwich Corporation* [1971] 2 QB 614.

revise the Guidance from time to time but again the revised version must be laid before Parliament. The Guidance and any revision must be published.

13.6.2 In carrying out its licensing functions, a licensing authority must have regard to any guidance issued by the Secretary of State under LA 2003, s 182.[40] It must also have regard to its own licensing statement of policy made under s 5 of the LA 2003. Since, however, the making of the licensing statement is itself a licensing function, the authority must have regard to the guidance when making that statement. In the Guidance, the Secretary of State has recognised that she cannot anticipate every possible scenario or set of circumstances that may arise and 'so long as the guidance has been properly and carefully considered, licensing authorities may depart from it'.[41] Authorities are cautioned, however, that if they do depart from the Guidance they will need to give good and full reasons for their actions.

13.6.3 With regard to hearings before a licensing authority, the guidance given is:[42]

> 'As a matter of practice, licensing authorities should seek to focus the hearing on the steps needed to promote the particular licensing objective which has given rise to the specific conflict and avoid straying into disputed areas. In determining the application the licensing authority must give appropriate weight to:
>
> – the argument and evidence presented by all parties;
> – this Guidance;
> – its own statement of policy;
> – steps that are necessary to promote the licensing objectives.'

13.6.4 Advice is given with regard to the imposition of conditions making it clear that conditions may only be imposed if necessary for the promotion of the licensing objectives.[43] Conditions relating to aspects covered by other legislation are deemed unnecessary and, therefore, could not be justified.[44]

13.6.5 With regard to review hearings, the Guidance makes clear that licensing authorities may not initiate their own reviews.[45] Those parts of the local authority identified as responsible authorities may, of course, initiate review proceedings but their representations must be treated in the same way as any other representations received by the licensing authority.[46] The Secretary of State anticipates that responsible authorities and authorised persons will work together

---

[40] LA 2003, s 4(3).

[41] Paragraph 2.3 of the Guidance.

[42] Paragraph 5.52 of the Guidance.

[43] Paragraph 5.53 of the Guidance.

[44] See Part 7 of the Guidance.

[45] Paragraph 5.78 of the Guidance.

[46] Paragraph 5.79 of the Guidance.

with licence holders and interested parties to meet the licensing objectives. Good practice will involve early warnings and advice when problems are identified.[47]

13.6.6   Of particular interest is the Guidance given with regard to the commission of criminal offences relating to licensed premises. The Secretary of State is of the view that licensing authorities cannot assume the role of the criminal courts and that reviews should not be allowed as a means of avoiding the more stringent tests associated with criminal prosecutions. The Guidance also states:

> 'Similarly, licensing authorities are expected to be conscious of attempts to bring issues before them when criminal prosecutions have failed. ... Where a review follows convictions or the failure of a prosecution in the criminal courts, it is not for the licensing authority to attempt to go behind the finding of the courts, which should be treated as a matter of undisputed evidence.'

13.6.7   It is difficult to find the basis for this guidance in the LA 2003. It certainly is contrary to the existing state of the law.[48]

13.6.8   It has to be accepted that the regulation of licensed premises and personal licence holders, following convictions for criminal offences, forms an important part of the scheme of the legislation justifying the hope that criminal activities will first be the subject of criminal proceedings. If, however, a group of residents were to be dissatisfied with the failure of the police to take criminal proceedings with regard to activities in local premises, or even to mount a half-hearted prosecution, it is difficult to imagine a licensing authority being able to refuse to conduct a review hearing or, during such a hearing, to ignore the evidence presented by those residents of such criminal activities. In that regard, it is likely that the lower standard of proof, the balance of probabilities, would still apply.

13.7   REPRESENTATIONS BY INTERESTED PARTIES

13.7.1   Interested parties are defined as any of the following:

–   a person living in the vicinity of the premises;
–   a body representing persons who live in that vicinity;
–   a person involved in a business in that vicinity;
–   a body representing persons involved in such businesses.[49]

13.7.2   Whenever interested parties oppose an application or seek a review of a premises licence or club premises certificate, there is first a

---

[47] Paragraph 5.80 of the Guidance.

[48] *The Queen on the Application of Crew (Chief Constable of the West Midlands Police) v Birmingham Licensing Justices* [2001] EWHC Admin 1113, [2002] LLR 293; *McCool v Rushcliffe Borough Council* [1998] 3 All ER 889.

[49] LA 2003, s 13(3).

filtering process involving a judgment as to whether or not the representation is relevant, that is, it is neither vexatious or frivolous. The Guidance given by the Secretary of State is that it is a matter for the licensing authority to determine. The test is an objective one – whether an ordinary and reasonable person would consider the issues raised to be vexatious or frivolous.[50]

13.7.3 Both terms have been the subject of judicial consideration, and Parliament will be deemed to have had those interpretations in mind when passing the LA 2003.

13.7.4 In the context of vexatious litigants, 'vexatious', a familiar term in legal parlance, has been described by Lord Bingham CJ as follows:[51]

> 'The hallmark of a vexatious proceeding is in my judgment that it has little or no basis in law (or at least no discernible basis); that whatever the intention of the proceeding may be, its effect is to subject the defendant to inconvenience, harassment and expense out of all proportion to any gain likely to accrue to the claimant; and that it involves an abuse of the process of the court, meaning by that a use of the court process for a purpose or in a way which is significantly different from the ordinary and proper use of the court process.'

13.7.5 'Frivolous' has been defined as meaning 'futile, misconceived, hopeless or of academic interest only' in the context of an application to a court to state a case for the opinion of the High Court.[52]

13.7.6 The Guidance recognises the difficulties facing ward councillors seeking to represent their voters. Decisions as to whether or not representations are relevant must not be made on the basis of a political judgment. To overcome such problems, the Secretary of State recommends that advice from an official should always be sought and positively recommends delegation of this part of the decision making process to officials.[53]

13.8 ADMISSION OF THE PUBLIC AND PROVISION OF INFORMATION

13.8.1 Regulations will be made to govern the proceedings before a licensing authority.[54] It is probable that such regulations will deal with:

[50] Paragraphs 5.55–5.57 of the Guidance.
[51] *A-G v Barker* [2000] 1 FLR 759 at 764.
[52] *R v Mildenhall Magistrates ex parte Forest Heath District Council* (1997) *The Times*, May 17.
[53] Paragraph 5.57 of the Guidance.
[54] LA 2003, s 9(2).

–   proceedings before licensing committees and sub-committees (including such matters as the quorum for meetings);
–   public access to meetings and the ability of a licensing authority to exclude members of the public from a hearing or part of a hearing;
–   publicity to be given to meetings;
–   agendas and records; and
–   public access to agendas and records and reports.

13.8.2   Under the current law, access by the public to meetings is guaranteed by a combination of the Public Bodies (Admissions to Meetings) Act 1960, Local Government Act 1972, s 100 and Local Government (Access to Information) Act 1985, s 1. The public may be excluded on two grounds. The first is with regard to an item of business which involves 'confidential information'. The second relates to 'exempt information'. Schedule 12A to the Local Government Act 1972 contains a list of such 'exempt information' which for the most part concerns information relating to the financial or business affairs of any particular person.

13.8.3   The LA 2003 provides that information provided to the licensing authority or a responsible authority for the purpose of facilitating the exercise of that authority's functions under the Act must not be further disclosed except to a licensing authority or responsible authority for licensing purposes.[55]

---

[55] LA 2003, s 185.

Chapter 14

APPEALS

'New opinions are always suspected, and usually opposed without any other reason but because they are not already common.'

John Locke

(*An Essay Concerning Human Understanding*)

14.1 INTRODUCTION

14.1.1 The various statutes which governed licensed activities before their repeal by the LA 2003 afforded a right of appeal in a variety of circumstances and sometimes, without explanation, denied that right. Appeals from decisions of local authorities sometimes went to the local magistrates' court and sometimes to the Crown Court. Almost all magistrates' court decisions could be appealed, by any of the parties, to the Crown Court.

14.1.2 Magistrates' courts are creatures of statute and their powers and procedures are governed by statute law. Such courts have no power to do anything that is not set out in either primary or secondary legislation. Similarly, there is no right of appeal from a magistrates' court unless that right is given in the relevant legislation.

14.1.3 Under the LA 2003, appeals lie from certain decisions of the licensing authority to the local magistrates' court. In most circumstances the former right of appeal from the magistrates' court to the Crown Court has been removed. There is an exception in relation to a magistrates' court's decision on consideration of a closure order made by a senior police officer.[1] In that case, an appeal lies to the Crown Court by virtue of the provisions of s 166. The distinction for this provision is that the magistrates' court is not acting as an appellate court in relation to a decision of the licensing authority but as a court of first instance.

14.1.4 The supervisory role of the High Court through judicial review remains unaffected. The High Court, however, will continue to be reluctant to exercise its discretion where an alternative remedy exists. This means that, in most cases, a party aggrieved by a decision of a licensing authority in a particular case will be expected to seek a remedy in an appeal under the provisions of the LA 2003 rather than challenge the authority through a claim for judicial review.

---

[1] LA 2003, s 165.

14.1.5   Under previous legislation, many appeal decisions were said to be 'final'. For example, a judgment of the Crown Court on an appeal under s 21 of the Licensing Act 1964 was 'final'.[2] The effect of 'finality' was to preclude an appeal by case stated.[3] There remains in such cases the availability of a challenge by way of a claim for judicial review.[4] A decision of the High Court upon an appeal by case stated in civil proceedings is also 'final' and cannot be appealed to the Court of Appeal.[5]

14.1.6   The LA 2003 does not make appeal decisions made by magistrates' courts 'final'. Whilst no appeal will lie to the Crown Court, the provisions relating to appeal by case stated will apply. The relevant statutory provisions are contained in ss 111–114 of the Magistrates' Courts Act 1980 and rr 76–81 of the Magistrates' Courts Rules 1981. In addition, in relation to the proceedings before the High Court, CPR Part 52 (Appeals) and the associated Practice Direction come into play. It is important to note that the time limit for making an application to the magistrates' court to state a case is inflexible. There is no power to extend the initial period of 21 days.[6]

14.1.7   The provisions relating to and, by omission, restricting rights of appeal from a decision of the licensing authority are to be found in LA 2003, s 181 and Sch 5.

14.2   POWERS OF MAGISTRATES' COURTS

14.2.1   On an appeal against a decision of a licensing authority, a magistrates' court has a wide discretion. It may:

–   dismiss the appeal;
–   substitute for the decision appealed any other decision which could have been made by the licensing authority; or
–   remit the case to the licensing authority to dispose of it in accordance with the direction of the court.[7]

14.2.2   The power to remit and give directions places the magistrates' court in a quasi-review situation. There has been a long-running dispute between those advising local authorities and those advising appellants in relation to the role of the magistrates' courts upon appeals from local authorities, for example in cases involving appeals against decisions relating to public entertainments

---

[2]   Licensing Act 1964, s 23.

[3]   Supreme Court Act 1981, s 28 and *Westminster City Council v Lunepalm* (1985) *The Times,* December 10.

[4]   *Tehrani v Rostron* [1972] 1 QB 182 per Lord Denning MR at 187–188.

[5]   Supreme Court Act 1981, s 18(1)(c) and *Fleury and Others v Westminster City Council* [2003] EWCA Civ 1007, [2003] LLR 456.

[6]   *Michael v Gowland* [1977] 1 WLR 296, [1977] 2 All ER 328.

[7]   LA 2003, s 181(2).

licences. Whilst, at present, it is clear that an appeal to the magistrates' court cannot be used to challenge a policy decision of the local authority,[8] there remains confusion as to the degree to which the appellate court should be asked to review the decision making process of the local authority in considering an appeal.

14.2.3 Local authorities have argued that appeals should be heard de novo (as new – from a fresh start), whilst appellants have argued that consideration should also be given to the behaviour of the local authority on the part of its officials and those members involved in the decision making process. There are cases which support, in part, both arguments.[9] If the appellate court must take into account the decision of the licensing authority and 'hesitate long before reaching a different conclusion' from that of the licensing authority, it must follow that the appellate court can consider the decision making process. In a recent case with regard to the constitution of the Crown Court when hearing an appeal from licensing justices, Laws LJ expressed the view (obiter) that an appeal by way of rehearing should be a rehearing 'in the full and proper sense' and seemed to consign the old quarter sessions cases to the past.[10]

14.2.4 The Guidance issued by the Secretary of State is that:

> 'In hearing an appeal against any decision by a licensing authority, the magistrates' court concerned will have regard to that licensing authority's statement of licensing policy and the Guidance. However, the court would be entitled to depart from either the statement of licensing policy or this Guidance if it considered it appropriate to do so because of the particular circumstances of any individual case. In addition the court would disregard any part of a licensing policy statement or this Guidance, it held to be ultra vires the 2003 Act.'[11]

and:

> 'An appeal may therefore review the merits of the decision on the facts and consider points of law or address both.'[12]

14.2.5 It would appear, therefore, that what was contemplated by the Government was that magistrates' courts would be able to review

---

[8] *R (Westminster City Council) v Middlesex Crown Court and Chorion plc* [2002] EWHC 1104 (Admin), [2002] LLR 538.

[9] *Stepney Borough Council v Joffe* [1949] 1 KB 599 (per Lord Goddard CJ at pp 602–603) and *R v Essex Quarter Sessions ex parte Thomas* [1966] 1 WLR 359 (per Lord Parker CJ at pp 362H–363B), both judgments being approved by the Court of Appeal in *Sagnata Investments Ltd v Norwich Corporation* [1971] 2 QB 614. See also *R v Knightsbridge Crown Court ex parte Aspinall Curzon Ltd* (1982) *The Times*, December 16, in which Woolf J adopted the words of Lord Parker CJ in *ex parte Thomas* (above).

[10] *The Queen on the application of the Chief Constable of Lancashire v Preston Crown Court and Gosling* [2001] EWHC Admin 928, [2002] LLR 14.

[11] Paragraph 10.8 of the Guidance.

[12] Paragraph 10.7 of the Guidance.

the decisions of licensing authorities and the policies upon which they were based.

14.2.6 If magistrates' courts are not to be allowed to venture into the area of review then there will be a compelling case for the exercise by the High Court of its powers on judicial review despite the availability of an appeal to the magistrates' court.[13]

14.2.7 An appeal to the magistrates' court will be by way of a rehearing. This means that different evidence may be presented and different submissions made. In particular, evidence of events occurring since the decision of the licensing authority was made will be admissible.[14]

14.2.8 The magistrates' court will be expected to give reasons for its decisions. This is now an expectation of all courts following the enactment of the Human Rights Act 1998.[15] In particular, where in an appeal there are no objections and no evidence led against the appellant's case, cogent reasons would have to be given for reaching a conclusion adverse to the appellant.[16] The reasons must be adequate.[17] It is not sufficient to regurgitate the terms of the LA 2003 or to say that all the evidence and the submissions made have been considered. The parties should be able to ascertain from the statement of reasons why an application has been granted or refused.[18]

14.2.9 On hearing an appeal, the magistrates' court also has a wide discretion as to costs. It may make such order as to costs as it thinks fit.[19] The court must give its reasons for its decision as to costs.[20] That discretion has been severely circumscribed by a line of authorities, which were reported in the first volume of *Licensing Law Reports*.[21] Of

[13] *R v Hereford Magistrates' Court ex parte Rowlands and Ingram* [1998] QB 110, [1997] 2 WLR 854.

[14] *Westminster City Council v Zestfair* (1989) 153 JP 613 and *Rushmoor Borough Council v Richards* (1996) 160 LG Rev 460.

[15] *English v Emery Reimbold & Strick Ltd* [2002] EWCA Civ 605, [2002] 1 WLR 2409, [2002] 3 All ER 385.

[16] *R v Teeside Crown Court ex parte Ellwood* (1990) 154 JP 496.

[17] *R v Gloucester Crown Court ex parte Warner*, sub nom *R v Licensing Justices for Gloucester ex parte Warner* [2001] LLR 687.

[18] Good examples of this are the persuasive decisions in *Camec (Scotland) Ltd v City of Glasgow Licensing Board and Others* [2003] LLR 389 and *William Hill (Caledonia) Ltd v City of Glasgow Licensing Board and Ladbrokes Ltd* [2003] LLR 549.

[19] LA 2003, s 181(2).

[20] *R (Cunningham) v Exeter Crown Court* [2003] EWHC 184 (Admin), [2003] LLR 325.

[21] Published by Jordan Publishing Limited in 2001.

particular importance are the decisions relating to the award of costs against local authorities and the police.[22]

14.2.10   The conclusions to be drawn from those cases are:

– in licensing cases, costs do not simply follow the event;
– the provision to order such costs as the court thinks fit applies both to the quantum of the costs, if any, and as to which party should pay them;
– what the court will think just and reasonable will depend on all the relevant facts and circumstances of the case before the court;
– no order can be made against the police simply on the basis that costs follow the event. The court can only make such an order if it can be shown that the police's position has been unreasonable or prompted by some improper motive. If the police act responsibly in accordance with their duty under the LA 2003, no adverse order for costs can be made against them. It must be clear that the police have acted otherwise than in good faith or have acted unreasonably before they are exposed to an order for costs;
– where an appellant has successfully challenged an administrative decision made by the police or a regulatory authority acting honestly, reasonably, properly and on grounds that reasonably appeared to be sound, in the exercise of its public duty, the court should consider, in addition to any other relevant fact or circumstances, both:
    – the financial prejudice to the particular appellant in the particular circumstances if an order for costs is not made in his favour; and
    – the need to encourage public authorities to make and stand by honest, reasonable and apparently sound administrative decisions made in the public interest without fear of exposure to undue financial prejudice if the decision is successfully challenged.

14.3   PREMISES LICENCE

14.3.1   Part 1 of Sch 5 to the LA 2003 provides a right of appeal in the following circumstances:

---

[22] *City of Bradford Metropolitan District Council v Booth* [2001] LLR 151; *R v Merthyr Tydfil Crown Court ex parte Chief Constable of Dyfed Powys Police* [2001] LLR 133; *Chief Constable of Derbyshire v Goodman and Newton* [2001] LLR 127; *R v Totnes Licensing Justices ex parte Chief Constable of Devon and Cornwall* (1990) 156 JP 587; *Chief Constable of West Midlands Police v Coventry Crown Court and Tubman* [2001] LLR 144 and *R v Stafford Crown Court ex parte Wilf Gilbert (Staffs) Ltd* [2001] LLR 138.

- following the rejection of an application in relation to a premises licence;[23]
- following the grant of a premises licence, either by the applicant against the imposition of conditions or by a person who opposed the granting of the licence or contended that conditions ought to have been imposed (having made relevant representations);[24]
- against the issue of a provisional statement;[25]
- against the variation of a premises licence;[26]
- by the police against the variation of a premises licence in relation to the specification of the premises supervisor;[27]
- by the police against the transfer of a premises licence;[28]
- against a decision to cancel or not to cancel an interim authority;[29]
- against a decision made upon a review of a premises licence.[30]

14.3.2 An appeal under LA 2003, Part 1 lies to the magistrates' court for the petty sessions area in which the premises are situated.[31] The appeal is commenced by giving notice of appeal to the justices' chief executive for the magistrates' court. Notice must be given within 21 days. The period of 21 days begins on the day on which the appellant was notified of the decision by the licensing authority.[32]

14.3.3 If the police or an objector – that is a person who made relevant representations – is the appellant, then the holder of the premises licence becomes a respondent as well as the licensing authority.[33] The same applies in relation to an interim authority notice when the giver of the notice becomes an additional respondent to the appeal.[34]

14.3.4 Whereas when the applicant in relation to a premises licence is the appellant (in an appeal against a refusal to grant a premises licence, for example), those who opposed the grant (the police or local residents) are not made respondents. In those cases, the licensing authority has to bear the burden of presenting the case against grant to the magistrates' court.

---

[23] LA 2003, Sch 5, para 1.
[24] Ibid, para 2.
[25] Ibid, para 3.
[26] Ibid, para 4.
[27] Ibid, para 5.
[28] Ibid, para 6.
[29] Ibid, para 7.
[30] Ibid, para 8.
[31] Ibid, para 9(1).
[32] Ibid, para 9(2).
[33] Ibid, para 9(3).
[34] Ibid, para 9(4).

14.4   CLUB PREMISES CERTIFICATE

14.4.1   Part 2 of Sch 5 to the LA 2003 provides a right of appeal where:

–   a licensing authority rejects an application for a club premises certificate or an application to vary the certificate;[35]
–   a club certificate is granted, by the club against the imposition of conditions, or by an objector, who made relevant representations, against the grant or failure to impose appropriate conditions;[36]
–   an application to vary the conditions of a club premises certificate is granted;[37]
–   a decision has been made on an application for a review of a club premises certificate;[38]
–   a club premises certificate is withdrawn by the licensing authority.[39]

14.4.2   An appeal under LA 2003, Part 2 must be made to the magistrates' court for the petty sessions area in which the premises concerned are situated. A notice of appeal must be given within 21 days to the justices' chief executive. The period of 21 days starts with the day on which the appellant was notified of the decision appealed against by the licensing authority.[40]

14.4.3   Where the appeal is brought by an objector (a person who made relevant representations) then the club that holds or held the club premises certificate is made a respondent in addition to the licensing authority.[41]

14.5   TEMPORARY EVENT NOTICE

14.5.1   LA 2003, Sch 5, Part 3, para 16 provides a right of appeal to the giver of a temporary event notice when a counter notice is served by the licensing authority following the lodging of a police objection. A similar right of appeal against a refusal to serve a counter notice is given to the police.

14.5.2   The provisions relating to the procedures and timetable are the same as with premises licences and club premises certificates save that no appeal may be brought later than 5 working days before the

---

[35]   LA 2003, Sch 5, para 10.

[36]   Ibid, para 11.

[37]   Ibid, para 12.

[38]   Ibid, para 13.

[39]   Ibid, para 14.

[40]   Ibid, para 15.

[41]   Ibid, para 15(3).

day upon which the temporary event is due to start.[42] Such a time limit is needed in order to give the magistrates' court time to arrange for the hearing of the appeal before the temporary event is due to take place.

14.5.3   There is no right of appeal against the service of a counter notice because the number of events promoted by the individual or in relation to the particular premises exceeds the statutory limits.

14.6   PERSONAL LICENCE

14.6.1   LA 2003, Sch 5, Part 3, para 18 provides a right of appeal to an individual in the following circumstances relating to personal licences:

–   where a licensing authority rejects an application for a personal licence;
–   where a licensing authority refuses to renew a personal licence; or
–   it revokes a personal licence.

14.6.2   A right of appeal is also provided to a chief officer of police who has served an objection notice to the grant or renewal of a personal licence. Similarly, where convictions come to light after the grant or renewal of a personal licence and the police have given notice seeking the revocation of that licence, they have a right of appeal should the licensing authority refuse to revoke.[43]

14.6.3   The time limits and procedures are the same as for appeals relating to premises licences. Should a personal licence be due to expire or have expired before the date when an appeal against a refusal to renew or revoke is heard, both the licensing authority and the magistrates' court have the power to order that the licence shall continue in effect until the determination of the appeal subject to such conditions as the court or authority thinks fit.[44]

14.6.4   Provisions relating to appeals against forfeiture or suspension of a personal licence are not found in Sch 5 but in Part 6 of the LA 2003 itself. Such orders form part of the sentence of the court concerned, a magistrates' court or the Crown Court. The rights of appeal which apply are those which apply in any criminal case. Sections 129 and 130 give powers to the sentencing court or the appellate court to suspend the order of forfeiture or suspension pending an appeal.

---

[42] LA 2003, Sch 5, para 16(6).

[43] Ibid, para 17(2), (3) and (5).

[44] Ibid, para 17(10).

14.7 REVIEW FOLLOWING CLOSURE ORDER

14.7.1 LA 2003, Sch 5, Part 3, para 18 deals with appeals where a licensing authority makes a decision on a review of a premises licence following the making of a closure order. Both the holder of the premises licence and any person who made relevant representations may appeal.

14.7.2 The magistrates' court dealing with any appeal against a review decision has the same powers as the licensing authority had to suspend the operation of the decision in whole or in part and to determine whether premises which were closed at the time of the review remain closed or not, pending the appeal.[45]

14.7.3 The procedures and timetable are the same as with an appeal relating to a premises licence. If the appellant is not the holder of the premises licence then that person becomes a respondent to the appeal in addition to the licensing authority.[46]

---

[45] LA 2003, Sch 5, para 18(3).

[46] Ibid, para 18(6).

Chapter 15

TRANSITIONAL PROVISIONS

'It is a fact of history that in every age of transition men are never so firmly bound to one way of life as when they are about to abandon it, so that fanaticism and intolerance reach their most intense forms just before tolerance and mutual acceptance come to be the natural order.'

Bernard Levin

15.1 INTRODUCTION

15.1.1 Section 200 of the LA 2003 brings into effect Sch 8, which contains transitional provisions dealing with the change from the old administrative regime, with its various authorities and licences, to the new order. In respect of premises with the various types of licence or certificate, and clubs with club registration certificates, there will be a set period of 6 months within which existing licence or certificate holders can apply for new or replacement licences or certificates. The period in which holders of justices' licences can apply for a personal licence will be fixed by the Secretary of State but will be not less than 6 months.

15.1.2 Part 1 of Sch 8 to the LA 2003 contains a comprehensive code for applications to be made to convert existing licences for the sale of alcohol and the provision of various entertainments into new premises licences. With each of the transitional provisions (for premises, clubs and personal licences) there is a deeming provision whereby if the relevant licensing authority does not determine the application for conversion within a set period the application is deemed to have been granted.

15.1.3 It will not be open to a licensing authority to defer consideration of applications for conversion whilst determining its licensing policy. The deeming provisions are unavoidable and cannot be displaced.[1] Such provisions have proved effective in Scotland as in the Civic Government Scotland Act 1982.

15.1.4 Part 2 of Sch 8 contains the provisions for converting a club registration certificate into a new club premises certificate issued in accordance with LA 2003, s 60.

---

[1] For an example of the effect of a deeming provision, see *Barclay v Renfrewshire Council* [2002] LLR 603.

15.1.5   Part 3 sets out the procedures for the transitional grant of a new personal licence to existing holders of a justices' licence issued under the Licensing Act 1964, Part 1.

15.1.6   There are protective provisions in each part whereby the relevant licensing authority must grant any transitional application unless there is a police objection. A police objection can be based only upon an undermining of the crime prevention objective, which is defined as meaning the licensing objective to prevent crime and disorder.[2] Similarly, with regard to existing justices' licences, existing permitted hours are protected and licensing authorities have to have regard to existing children's certificates.

15.1.7   In certain instances, local authorities have not adopted legislation governing, for example, late night refreshment or private places of entertainment. The transitional provisions do not cater for such circumstances. When the main parts of the LA 2003 come into force, applications will have to be made for new premises licences under the new LA 2003. Similarly, current wholesalers who sell alcohol to members of the public (in cases of not less than 12 bottles) and who do not have a justices' licence will have to apply for a new premises licence should they wish to continue to sell to members of the public.

15.1.8   The consequence for an existing licence or certificate holder who fails to apply for a converted licence or certificate is that when the main parts of new LA 2003 come into force, the existing licence will no longer be valid and an application will have to be made for a new licence or certificate using the new procedures.

15.2 CONVERSION OF EXISTING LICENCES

15.2.1   The terms 'existing licence' and 'new licence' are defined in LA 2003, Sch 8, Part 1, para 1(1). An 'existing licence' means:

(a) a justices' licence;
(b) a canteen licence;
(c) a licence under London Government Act 1963, Sch 12 (public entertainments licence in London);
(d) a licence under the Private Places of Entertainment (Licensing) Act 1967;
(e) a licence under the Theatres Act 1968 (including any notice in force under s 199(c) of the Licensing Act 1964 (relating to the sale of alcohol));
(f) a licence under the Late Night Refreshment Houses Act 1969;
(g) a licence under Local Government (Miscellaneous Provisions) Act 1982, Sch 1 (public entertainments licence outside London);
(h) a licence under the Cinemas Act 1985; or

---

[2] LA 2003, s 193.

(i)   a licence under London Local Authorities Act 1990, Part 2 (night cafes in London).

15.2.2   A 'new licence' is defined as a licence issued by the licensing authority to replace the existing licence.

15.2.3   Conversion is not automatic. The holder of an existing licence or licences will have to apply to the licensing authority for the area in which the premises are situated for a new licence to replace the existing licences.[3]

15.2.4   An application for conversion has to be made within 6 months of a date to be appointed by the Secretary of State referred to in the LA 2003 as the 'first appointed day'. A new (replacement) licence comes into effect on the 'second appointed day'. Any existing licence continues in force until the second appointed day, which, presumably, will be the day when the main provisions of the LA 2003 are brought into force.

15.2.5   The application for conversion must be made either by the holder of an existing licence or licences, or with the holder's consent. There will be a specified form for the application. Relevant documents, such as the existing licence(s), a plan of the premises and other documents specified in the regulations, must be sent with the application together with the specified fee.[4] An obvious example of another document would be an existing children's certificate. Where the application is made with the consent of the existing licence holder, that consent must also be filed with the application.

15.2.6   The application must set out which licensable activities are authorised by the existing licences and certificates and, if the supply of alcohol is one of those activities, a premises supervisor must be designated. Appropriate information about the proposed premises supervisor must be given. If the original licence or certificates are not available, certified copies must be provided.

15.2.7   A copy of the application must be served on the chief officer of police for the area within 48 hours of making the application.[5] The police will then have to decide whether or not to object to the conversion of the existing licence into a new one. An objection is made by giving notice to the licensing authority and the applicant. It must be done within 28 days of the date of the receipt of the copy application.[6]

15.2.8   The right to object is carefully circumscribed. It applies only where, either the licence has been revoked or renewal has been

---

[3]   LA 2003, Sch 8, para 2.

[4]   Ibid, para 2(5) and (6).

[5]   Ibid, para 3.

[6]   Ibid, para 3(5). The day of receipt of the copy of the application counts as the first of the 28 days.

refused and there is an appeal pending, or there has been a material change of circumstances since the grant or last renewal of the licence in question. Even then an objection, in the form of a notice, can only be made if the chief officer of police is satisfied that to convert the existing licence(s) (or one of them) would undermine the crime prevention objective.[7]

15.2.9 It would appear, therefore, that if, for example, a licence has been revoked because of complaints by local residents about noise nuisance and an appeal is pending, the police will be powerless to object to a conversion. Nor does anyone else have that power because LA 2003, Sch 8 provides for no other party to be involved in an application for the conversion of an existing licence into a new one. The saving provision in those circumstances can be found in para 8 whereby if an existing licence is revoked, or if an appeal against revocation is pending immediately before the second appointed day (when the new licence comes into force) and that appeal is later dismissed or abandoned, then the new licence or the relevant part of it lapses.

15.2.10 The same saving provision does not apply in the case of a refusal to renew. If the grounds for refusing to renew did not involve matters which could be said to undermine the crime prevention objective, neither the police nor anyone else will have any right to object to the conversion of the existing licence to a new licence. Providing that an appeal against a refusal to renew has not been dismissed or abandoned by the time the licensing authority comes to make its determination, or sufficient time has elapsed whereby a grant of the new license is deemed, the conversion must take place. If the appeal against refusal to renew or revocation is dismissed or abandoned before the licensing authority comes to make its determination, the application for conversion to a new licence cannot be granted.[8]

15.2.11 If the police objection based upon an undermining of the crime prevention objective is maintained, the licensing authority must hold a hearing. The hearing cannot be delegated to an officer but can be avoided if the licensing authority, the applicant and the chief officer of police agree. The licensing authority must determine whether to grant or reject the application for a new licence. If, for example, it is only one of the licensable activities to which objection is taken then the authority must make a determination on that part of the application. Reasons for rejection must be given to the applicant and the police.[9]

---

[7] LA 2003, Sch 8, para 3(2) and (3).

[8] Ibid, para 4(5).

[9] Ibid, paras 4 and 5. There appears to be no requirement to give reasons if the application is granted despite police objections.

15.2.12 If there is no police objection, the application must be granted.[10] A failure to determine the application within 2 months of the date of receipt of the application by the licensing authority results in a deemed grant.[11] The period of 2 months starts on the day that the application is received by the licensing authority. Upon granting the application, the licensing authority must give to the applicant a notice to that effect and issue both the new licence and a summary of that licence.[12]

15.2.13 The new licence takes effect as a s 11 premises licence (subject to the mandatory conditions imposed by LA 2003, ss 19, 20 and 21). It must authorise the premises to be used for the existing licensable activities and with such conditions or restrictions as reproduce the effect of any existing conditions or restrictions.[13] Where premises have the benefit of a special hours certificate, the statutory conditions relating to that certificate, for example, that the sale of alcohol must be ancillary to the provision of music, dancing and substantial refreshment, will have to be incorporated into the new (corrected) licence. When the supply of alcohol is involved, a premises supervisor must be designated.[14] The licensing authority has to have regard to an existing children's certificate when framing any restriction.[15] There is no power to grant a new licence for a limited period unless the applicant has specifically asked for that.

15.2.14 When the application is made for conversion, the licence holder may apply for a variation at the same time.[16] The variation may relate to the designation of the premises supervisor or any other kind of variation. Once such an application is received the new provisions for dealing with variation applications (LA 2003, ss 34–39) come into play. Those provisions include the regulations as to advertisement and the ability of interested parties such as local residents to make representations. A licensing authority must not deal with a variation application until after a new (replacement) licence has been granted.[17] If, however, the licensing authority fails to determine the application for variation within 2 months of the date of receipt of the application for conversion and variation, the application for variation is treated as having been rejected, thereby bringing the appeal provisions into play.[18]

---

[10] LA 2003, Sch 8, para 4(2).

[11] Ibid, para 4(4).

[12] Ibid, para 5(1).

[13] Ibid, para 6(5) and (6).

[14] Ibid, para 6(7).

[15] Ibid, para 6(9).

[16] Ibid, para 7.

[17] Ibid, para 7(2).

[18] Ibid, para 7(3).

[19] Ibid, para 9.

15.2.15   A licence holder who has an application for conversion rejected in whole or in part may appeal.[20] So may the police, if they have objected and the new licence has been granted. Strangely, so may an applicant for a new licence who has had his new licence amended following the dismissal of his appeal against revocation of an existing licence or certificate that has been converted into part of the new licence.[21]

Permitted hours

15.2.16   An existing licence holder may prefer to apply for a fresh premises licence rather than a new (replacement) licence. When a public house has had the benefit of entertainment in the form of music performed by not more than two musicians, the licensee may wish to continue to provide that entertainment which would not be allowed under the converted licence. Provided that the existing licence holder makes his application for a premises licence within a period to be determined by the Secretary of State (which must be not less than 6 months), his existing permitted hours will be protected.[22]

15.2.17   The only circumstance where the existing permitted hours will not be protected is when the police have objected (ie made relevant representations) based upon a material change in circumstances since the licence was granted or last renewed and the ground that the crime prevention objective will be undermined.[23] An application for a premises licence made by an existing licence holder who wishes to add, for example, other licensable activities, if made within the time limits set by the Secretary of State, would not give an opportunity for local residents to make representations about existing opening or permitted hours.

Provisional grants

15.2.18   Where a provisional grant of a justices' licence (Licensing Act 1964, s 6) has been made before the main parts of the LA 2003 come into force, but has not been declared final, the successful applicant can apply for a premises licence. If that application is made within the time limits set by the Secretary of State and provided that the premises have been completed substantially in accordance with the deposited plans, the licensing authority must have regard to the provisional grant when determining the application for a premises licence.[24]

---

[20] LA 2003, Sch 8, para 9.

[21] Ibid, para 9(3).

[22] Ibid, para 11(1) and (2).

[23] Ibid, para 11(3).

[24] Ibid, para 12.

15.3 CLUB CERTIFICATES

15.3.1 LA 2003, Sch 8, Part 2 contains the code for the conversion of existing club registration certificates into club premises certificates. An 'existing club certificate' is defined as a certificate held by a club under Part 2 of the Licensing Act 1964.[25] A club premises certificate is a certificate issued in accordance with LA 2003, s 60.

15.3.2 If a club registration certificate is in force on the first appointed day, the club may within a period of 6 months from that date apply for a club premises certificate to replace the existing club registrations certificate.[26]

15.3.3 The application must be in the specified form and be accompanied by the existing certificate, a plan of the premises and other documents to be specified in the regulations, together with the specified fee. The existing qualifying club activities must also be set out in the application form. If the existing registration certificate is missing, a certified copy may be used.[27]

15.3.4 Notice must be given by the club to the police within 48 hours of the application being made. As with an existing justices' licence, if there is an outstanding appeal against revocation or refusal to renew the existing certificate, or if there has been a material change in circumstances since the registration or last renewal of registration of the club, the police may object. The objection can only be based upon an undermining of the crime prevention objective.[28]

15.3.5 In the event of a police objection being maintained, a hearing is required unless the licensing authority, the club and the police agree to dispense with a hearing. The licensing authority's decision must be based only upon whether or not the grant of the club premises certificate would undermine the prevention of crime objective.[29] If the application is rejected, reasons must be given to the club and the police.[30] Both the club and the police have a right of appeal.[31]

15.3.6 In the absence of a police objection (which has to be made within 28 days of receipt of the notice of application) the licensing authority must grant the application.[32] If 2 months elapse from the date of the receipt of the application by the licensing authority

---

[25] LA 2003, Sch 8, para 13(1).

[26] Ibid, para 14(1) and (2).

[27] Ibid, para 14.

[28] Ibid, para 15.

[29] Ibid, Sch 8, para 16.

[30] Ibid, para 17. There is no requirement to give reasons if the application is granted despite police objections.

[31] Ibid, para 21.

[32] Ibid, para 16(2).

without that authority having determined the application, the club premises certificate is deemed to have been granted.[33]

15.3.7 If, however, the old club registration certificate is revoked before the second appointed day, or an appeal against revocation is outstanding and, following the second appointed day, is either dismissed or abandoned, then the new club premises certificate will lapse automatically.[34]

15.3.8 A determination to grant or a deemed grant must be followed, immediately, by a notice to that effect, together with the issue of a club premises certificate and a summary of that certificate.[35] The new certificate takes effect upon the second appointed day. It must authorise the premises to be used for the existing qualifying club activities and, with the exception of the statutory conditions set out in LA 2003, ss 73, 74 and 75, must be subject to the same conditions and restrictions as apply to the existing club registration certificate.[36]

15.3.9 Again, as with a conversion of an existing justices' licence, an application for conversion of an existing club registration certificate may be accompanied by an application to vary. The application to vary is subject to the same statutory regime as any future application to vary (see LA 2003, ss 84–86). Such an application to vary cannot be determined until the application to convert has been dealt with. If the application to vary is not determined within a period of 2 months from the date of receipt by the licensing authority of the application to convert and vary, the application to vary is treated as having been rejected.[37] Such a deemed rejection would bring into play the appeal provisions.

15.3.10 A club may appeal against a rejected application for conversion, and the police may appeal against a grant of a converted club premises certificate if they have objected.[38]

15.4 PERSONAL LICENCES

15.4.1 LA 2003, Sch 8, Part 3 contains the provisions whereby the holder of a justices' licence – that is a licence under the Licensing Act 1964, Part I – can apply during the transitional period for a personal licence. The duration of the transitional period will be fixed by the Secretary of State but cannot be less than 6 months.[39]

---

[33] LA 2003, Sch 8, para 16(4).

[34] Ibid, para 20.

[35] Ibid, para 17.

[36] Ibid, para 18.

[37] Ibid, para 19.

[38] Ibid, para 21.

[39] Ibid, para 23.

15.4.2 The application must be made to the licensing authority for the area in which the holder of the justices' licence is ordinarily resident (or to which an application would be made if the applicant were applying for the first time in accordance with the provisions of LA 2003, s 117). With the application must be sent the justices' licence, or a certified copy of it, an endorsed photograph verifying the likeness of the applicant (size to be specified in the regulations) and, where the applicant has been convicted of a Sch 4 offence or foreign offence since the grant, transfer or last renewal of the justices' licence, details of that offence.[40]

15.4.3 A copy of the application must be given to the police within 48 hours.[41] If the applicant has been convicted of a Sch 4 offence or a foreign offence in the relevant period and the police consider that the grant to him of a personal licence would undermine the crime prevention objective, the police must give notice to that effect to the applicant and the licensing authority not later than 28 days after receipt of the copy of the application.[42] There is no other ground for objection. Only where the licensee has been convicted of a relevant offence since the grant or last renewal of his licence can the police object. LA 2003, s 120, which deals with the determination of applications for the grant of a personal licence, is specifically disapplied in relation to application for conversion.[43]

15.4.4 In making a determination on an application for a personal licence by a holder of a justices' licence during the transitional period, the licensing authority must consider only two issues:

(a) whether the applicant holds a justices' licence; and
(b) whether there has been a police objection and, if so, it is satisfied that it is necessary for the promotion of the prevention of crime objective to reject the application.[44]

15.4.5 If the applicant does hold a justices' licence and there has been no police objection, the new personal licence must be granted.[45]

15.4.6 If the licensing authority has not determined the application within 3 months of the date of its receipt by the authority, the new personal licence is deemed to have been granted.[46]

15.4.7 If there has been a police objection the licensing authority must determine whether or not it is necessary, in order to promote the crime prevention objective, to reject the application. There has to be a

---

[40] LA 2003, Sch 8, para 23(3).

[41] Ibid, para 23(1)(c).

[42] Ibid, para 25.

[43] Ibid, para 24.

[44] Ibid, para 26.

[45] Ibid, para 26(1).

[46] Ibid, para 26(4).

hearing if the objection has not been withdrawn. The hearing cannot be delegated to an officer of the authority.[47] There is no specific requirement in the transitional provisions for the giving of reasons but there is a cross-reference to LA 2003, s 122, which deals with the notification of determinations and does require the giving of reasons for either a rejection of an application or a grant in the face of a police objection.[48] In any event, it is a matter of good practice to give reasons and necessary in order to comply with Art 6 of the European Convention for the Protection of Human Rights and Fundamental Freedoms.[49]

15.4.8   Both the applicant and the police have a right of appeal and the relevant provisions of Sch 5 (appeals) apply.[50]

15.5 MISCELLANEOUS PROVISIONS

15.5.1   Since licensing authorities will have to start work on drawing up their policies before current licensing laws are repealed, there are also transitional provisions dealing with consultation and representations. This means that representatives of holders of existing justices' licences and existing club registration certificates have to be consulted.[51]

15.5.2   Since the Finance Act 1995, there have been provisions to replace references to 'methylated spirits' with 'denatured alcohol'. Those provisions have not yet been brought into force but have been incorporated within the new LA 2003 in the definition of alcohol. There is, therefore, a saving provision relating to references to 'methylated spirits' until such time as the 1995 provisions are brought into force.[52]

15.5.3   There are at present certain special provisions which apply only in London in relation to public exhibitions, entertainment booking offices and sex encounter establishments. LA 2003, Sch 8, paras 31 and 32 contain saving provisions to maintain those special provisions.

15.5.4   Similarly, despite the repeal of the Cinemas Act 1985 the provisions of that Act which relate to the definitions of a sex cinema and apply to the supply of R18 video recordings are retained in relevant regulatory legislation.[53]

---

[47] LA 2003, Sch 8, para 26.

[48] Ibid, para 26(6).

[49] *English v Emery Reimbold & Strick Ltd* [2002] EWCA Civ 605, [2002] 1 WLR 2409, [2002] 3 All ER 385.

[50] LA 2003, Sch 8, para 27.

[51] Ibid, Sch 8, para 29.

[52] Ibid, Sch 8, para 30.

[53] Ibid, para 33.

APPENDIX

LICENSING ACT 2003

CONTENTS

PART 1

LICENSABLE ACTIVITIES

Section
1   Licensable activities and qualifying club activities
2   Authorisation for licensable activities and qualifying club activities

PART 2

LICENSING AUTHORITIES

The authorities

3   Licensing authorities

Functions of licensing authorities etc

4   General duties of licensing authorities
5   Statement of licensing policy
6   Licensing committees
7   Exercise and delegation of functions
8   Requirement to keep a register

Licensing committees

9   Proceedings of licensing committee
10   Sub-delegation of functions by licensing committee etc

PART 3

PREMISES LICENCES

Introductory

11   Premises licence
12   The relevant licensing authority
13   Authorised persons, interested parties and responsible authorities
14   Meaning of 'supply of alcohol'
15   Meaning of 'designated premises supervisor'

Grant of premises licence

16   Applicant for premises licence
17   Application for premises licence
18   Determination of application for premises licence
19   Mandatory conditions where licence authorises supply of alcohol
20   Mandatory condition: exhibition of films
21   Mandatory condition: door supervision
22   Prohibited conditions: plays
23   Grant or rejection of application
24   Form of licence and summary
25   Theft, loss, etc of premises licence or summary

Duration of licence

26   Period of validity of premises licence
27   Death, incapacity, insolvency etc of licence holder
28   Surrender of premises licence

Provisional statement

29   Application for a provisional statement where premises being built, etc
30   Advertisement of application for provisional statement
31   Determination of application for provisional statement
32   Restriction on representations following provisional statement

Duty to notify certain changes

33   Notification of change of name or address

Variation of licences

34   Application to vary premises licence
35   Determination of application under section 34
36   Supplementary provision about determinations under section 35
37   Application to vary licence to specify individual as premises supervisor
38   Circumstances in which section 37 application given interim effect
39   Determination of section 37 application
40   Duty of applicant following determination under section 39
41   Request to be removed as designated premises supervisor

Transfer of premises licence

42   Application for transfer of premises licence
43   Circumstances in which transfer application given interim effect
44   Determination of transfer application
45   Notification of determination under section 44
46   Duty to notify designated premises supervisor of transfer

Interim authority notices

47   Interim authority notice following death etc of licence holder
48   Cancellation of interim authority notice following police objections

49   Supplementary provision about interim authority notices

Transfer following death etc of licence holder

50   Reinstatement of licence on transfer following death etc of holder

Review of licences

51   Application for review of premises licence
52   Determination of application for review
53   Supplementary provision about review

General provision

54   Form etc of applications and notices under Part 3
55   Fees

Production of licence, rights of entry, etc

56   Licensing authority's duty to update licence document
57   Duty to keep and produce licence
58   Provision supplementary to section 57
59   Inspection of premises before grant of licence etc

PART 4

CLUBS

Introductory

60   Club premises certificate

Qualifying clubs

61   Qualifying clubs
62   The general conditions
63   Determining whether a club is established and conducted in good faith
64   The additional conditions for the supply of alcohol
65   Industrial and provident societies, friendly societies etc
66   Miners' welfare institutes

Interpretation

67   Associate members and their guests
68   The relevant licensing authority
69   Authorised persons, interested parties and responsible authorities
70   Other definitions relating to clubs

Grant of club premises certificate

71   Application for club premises certificate
72   Determination of application for club premises certificate
73   Certificate authorising supply of alcohol for consumption off the premises

74 Mandatory condition: exhibition of films
75 Prohibited conditions: associate members and their guests
76 Prohibited conditions: plays
77 Grant or rejection of application for club premises certificate
78 Form of certificate and summary
79 Theft, loss, etc of certificate or summary

Duration of certificate

80 Period of validity of club premises certificate
81 Surrender of club premises certificate

Duty to notify certain changes

82 Notification of change of name or alteration of rules of club
83 Change of relevant registered address of club

Variation of certificates

84 Application to vary club premises certificate
85 Determination of application under section 84
86 Supplementary provision about applications under section 84

Review of certificates

87 Application for review of club premises certificate
88 Determination of application for review
89 Supplementary provision about review

Withdrawal of certificates

90 Club ceasing to be a qualifying club

General provision

91 Form etc of applications and notices under Part 4
92 Fees

Production of certificate, rights of entry, etc

93 Licensing authority's duty to update club premises certificate
94 Duty to keep and produce certificate
95 Provision supplementary to section 94
96 Inspection of premises before grant of certificate etc
97 Other powers of entry and search

PART 5

PERMITTED TEMPORARY ACTIVITIES

Introductory

98 Meaning of 'permitted temporary activity'

99 The relevant licensing authority

Temporary event notices

100 Temporary event notice
101 Minimum of 24 hours between event periods
102 Acknowledgement of notice
103 Withdrawal of notice

Police objections

104 Objection to notice by the police
105 Counter notice following police objection
106 Modification of notice following police objection

Limits on temporary event notices

107 Counter notice where permitted limits exceeded

Rights of entry, production of notice, etc

108 Right of entry where temporary event notice given
109 Duty to keep and produce temporary event notice

Miscellaneous

110 Theft, loss, etc of temporary event notice

PART 6

PERSONAL LICENCES

Introductory

111 Personal licence
112 The relevant licensing authority
113 Meaning of 'relevant offence' and 'foreign offence'
114 Spent convictions
115 Period of validity of personal licence
116 Surrender of personal licence

Grant and renewal of licences

117 Application for grant or renewal of personal licence
118 Individual permitted to hold only one personal licence
119 Licence continued pending renewal
120 Determination of application for grant
121 Determination of application for renewal
122 Notification of determinations
123 Duty to notify licensing authority of convictions during application period
124 Convictions coming to light after grant or renewal
125 Form of personal licence

126 Theft, loss, etc of personal licence

Duty to notify certain changes

127 Duty to notify change of name or address

Conviction of licence holder for relevant offence

128 Duty to notify court of personal licence
129 Forfeiture or suspension of licence on conviction for relevant offence
130 Powers of appellate court to suspend order under section 129
131 Court's duty to notify licensing authority of convictions
132 Licence holder's duty to notify licensing authority of convictions

General provision

133 Form etc of applications and notices under Part 6
134 Licensing authority's duty to update licence document

Production of licence

135 Licence holder's duty to produce licence

PART 7

OFFENCES

Unauthorised licensable activities

136 Unauthorised licensable activities
137 Exposing alcohol for unauthorised sale
138 Keeping alcohol on premises for unauthorised sale etc
139 Defence of due diligence

Drunkenness and disorderly conduct

140 Allowing disorderly conduct on licensed premises etc
141 Sale of alcohol to a person who is drunk
142 Obtaining alcohol for a person who is drunk
143 Failure to leave licensed premises etc

Smuggled goods

144 Keeping of smuggled goods

Children and alcohol

145 Unaccompanied children prohibited from certain premises
146 Sale of alcohol to children
147 Allowing the sale of alcohol to children
148 Sale of liqueur confectionery to children under 16
149 Purchase of alcohol by or on behalf of children
150 Consumption of alcohol by children
151 Delivering alcohol to children
152 Sending a child to obtain alcohol

153 Prohibition of unsupervised sales by children
154 Enforcement role for weights and measures authorities

Confiscation of alcohol

155 Confiscation of sealed containers of alcohol

Vehicles and trains

156 Prohibition on sale of alcohol on moving vehicles
157 Power to prohibit sale of alcohol on trains

False statement relating to licensing etc

158 False statements made for the purposes of this Act

Interpretation

159 Interpretation of Part 7

PART 8

CLOSURE OF PREMISES

Closure of premises in an identified area

160 Orders to close premises in area experiencing disorder

Closure of identified premises

161 Closure orders for identified premises
162 Extension of closure order
163 Cancellation of closure order
164 Application to magistrates' court by police
165 Consideration of closure order by magistrates' court
166 Appeal from decision of magistrates' court
167 Review of premises licence following closure order
168 Provision about decisions under section 167
169 Enforcement of closure order
170 Exemption of police from liability for damages

Interpretation

171 Interpretation of Part 8

PART 9

MISCELLANEOUS AND SUPPLEMENTARY

Special occasions

172 Relaxation of opening hours for special occasions

Exemptions etc

173 Activities in certain locations not licensable
174 Certifying of premises on grounds of national security

175 Exemption for raffle, tombola, etc

Service areas and garages etc

176 Prohibition of alcohol sales at service areas, garages etc

Small premises

177 Dancing and live music in certain small premises

Rights of freeholders etc

178 Right of freeholder etc to be notified of licensing matters

Rights of entry

179 Rights of entry to investigate licensable activities
180 Right of entry to investigate offences

Appeals

181 Appeals against decisions of licensing authorities

Guidance, hearings etc

182 Guidance
183 Hearings
184 Giving of notices, etc
185 Provision of information

General provisions about offences

186 Proceedings for offences
187 Offences by bodies corporate etc
188 Jurisdiction and procedure in respect of offences

Vessels, vehicles and moveable structures

189 Vessels, vehicles and moveable structures

Interpretation

190 Location of sales
191 Meaning of 'alcohol'
192 Meaning of 'sale by retail'
193 Other definitions
194 Index of defined expressions

Supplementary and general

195 Crown application
196 Removal of privileges and exemptions
197 Regulations and orders
198 Minor and consequential amendments
199 Repeals

200 Transitional provision etc
201 Short title, commencement and extent

    Schedule 1 – Provision of regulated entertainment
        Part 1 – General definitions
        Part 2 – Exemptions
        Part 3 – Interpretation
    Schedule 2 – Provision of late night refreshment
    Schedule 3 – Matters to be entered in licensing register
    Schedule 4 – Personal licence: relevant offences
    Schedule 5 – Appeals
        Part 1 – Premises licences
        Part 2 – Club premises certificates
        Part 3 – Other appeals
    Schedule 6 – Minor and consequential amendments
    Schedule 7 – Repeals
    Schedule 8 – Transitional provision etc
        Part 1 – Premises licences
        Part 2 – Club premises certificates
        Part 3 – Personal licences
        Part 4 – Miscellaneous and general

PART 1

LICENSABLE ACTIVITIES

1 Licensable activities and qualifying club activities

(1) For the purposes of this Act the following are licensable activities –

  (a) the sale by retail of alcohol,
  (b) the supply of alcohol by or on behalf of a club to, or to the order of, a member of the club,
  (c) the provision of regulated entertainment, and
  (d) the provision of late night refreshment.

(2) For those purposes the following licensable activities are also qualifying club activities –

  (a) the supply of alcohol by or on behalf of a club to, or to the order of, a member of the club,
  (b) the sale by retail of alcohol by or on behalf of a club to a guest of a member of the club for consumption on the premises where the sale takes place, and
  (c) the provision of regulated entertainment where that provision is by or on behalf of a club for members of the club or members of the club and their guests.

(3) In this Act references to the supply of alcohol by or on behalf of a club to, or to the order of, a member of the club do not include a reference to any supply which is a sale by retail of alcohol.

(4) Schedule 1 makes provision about what constitutes the provision of regulated entertainment for the purposes of this Act.

(5) Schedule 2 makes provision about what constitutes the provision of late night refreshment for those purposes (including provision that certain activities carried on in relation to certain clubs or hotels etc, or certain employees, do not constitute provision of late night refreshment and are, accordingly, not licensable activities).

(6) For the purposes of this Act premises are 'used' for a licensable activity if that activity is carried on on or from the premises.

(7) This section is subject to sections 173 to 175 (which exclude activities from the definition of licensable activity in certain circumstances).

2 Authorisation for licensable activities and qualifying club activities

(1) A licensable activity may be carried on –

- (a)   under and in accordance with a premises licence (see Part 3), or
- (b)   in circumstances where the activity is a permitted temporary activity by virtue of Part 5.

(2) A qualifying club activity may be carried on under and in accordance with a club premises certificate (see Part 4).

(3) Nothing in this Act prevents two or more authorisations having effect concurrently in respect of the whole or a part of the same premises or in respect of the same person.

(4) For the purposes of subsection (3) 'authorisation' means –

- (a)   a premises licence;
- (b)   a club premises certificate;
- (c)   a temporary event notice.

PART 2

LICENSING AUTHORITIES

The authorities

3 Licensing authorities

(1) In this Act 'licensing authority' means –

- (a)   the council of a district in England,
- (b)   the council of a county in England in which there are no district councils,
- (c)   the council of a county or county borough in Wales,
- (d)   the council of a London borough,
- (e)   the Common Council of the City of London,
- (f)   the Sub-Treasurer of the Inner Temple,
- (g)   the Under-Treasurer of the Middle Temple, or
- (h)   the Council of the Isles of Scilly.

(2) For the purposes of this Act, a licensing authority's area is the area for which the authority acts.

Functions of licensing authorities etc

4 General duties of licensing authorities

(1) A licensing authority must carry out its functions under this Act ('licensing functions') with a view to promoting the licensing objectives.

(2) The licensing objectives are –

  (a) the prevention of crime and disorder;
  (b) public safety;
  (c) the prevention of public nuisance; and
  (d) the protection of children from harm.

(3) In carrying out its licensing functions, a licensing authority must also have regard to –

  (a) its licensing statement published under section 5, and
  (b) any guidance issued by the Secretary of State under section 182.

5 Statement of licensing policy

(1) Each licensing authority must in respect of each three year period –

  (a) determine its policy with respect to the exercise of its licensing functions, and
  (b) publish a statement of that policy (a 'licensing statement') before the beginning of the period.

(2) In this section 'three year period' means –

  (a) the period of three years beginning with such day as the Secretary of State may by order appoint, and
  (b) each subsequent period of three years.

(3) Before determining its policy for a three year period, a licensing authority must consult –

  (a) the chief officer of police for the licensing authority's area,
  (b) the fire authority for that area,
  (c) such persons as the licensing authority considers to be representative of holders of premises licences issued by that authority,
  (d) such persons as the licensing authority considers to be representative of holders of club premises certificates issued by that authority,
  (e) such persons as the licensing authority considers to be representative of holders of personal licences issued by that authority, and
  (f) such other persons as the licensing authority considers to be representative of businesses and residents in its area.

(4) During each three year period, a licensing authority must keep its policy under review and make such revisions to it, at such times, as it considers appropriate.

(5) Subsection (3) applies in relation to any revision of an authority's policy as it applies in relation to the original determination of that policy.

(6) Where revisions are made, the licensing authority must publish a statement of the revisions or the revised licensing statement.

(7) Regulations may make provision about the determination and revision of policies, and the preparation and publication of licensing statements, under this section.

6 Licensing committees

(1) Each licensing authority must establish a licensing committee consisting of at least ten, but not more than fifteen, members of the authority.

(2) This section does not apply in relation to the Sub-Treasurer of the Inner Temple or the Under-Treasurer of the Middle Temple.

7 Exercise and delegation of functions

(1) All matters relating to the discharge by a licensing authority of its licensing functions are, by virtue of this subsection, referred to its licensing committee and, accordingly, that committee must discharge those functions on behalf of the authority.

(2) Subsection (1) does not apply to –

(a)   any function conferred on the licensing authority by section 5 (statement of licensing policy), or
(b)   any function discharged under subsection (5)(a) below by a committee (other than a licensing committee),

or any matter relating to the discharge of any such function.

(3) A licensing authority may arrange for the discharge by its licensing committee of any function of the authority which –

(a)   relates to a matter referred to that committee by virtue of subsection (1), but
(b)   is not a licensing function.

(4) Where the licensing authority does not make arrangements under subsection (3) in respect of any such function, it must (unless the matter is urgent) consider a report of its licensing committee with respect to the matter before discharging the function.

(5) Where a matter relates to a licensing function of a licensing authority and to a function of the authority which is not a licensing function ('the other function'), the authority may –

(a)   refer the matter to another of its committees and arrange for the discharge of the licensing function by that committee, or
(b)   refer the matter to its licensing committee (to the extent it is not already so referred under subsection (1)) and arrange for the discharge of the other function by the licensing committee.

(6) In a case where an authority exercises its power under subsection (5)(a), the committee to which the matter is referred must (unless the matter is urgent) consider a report of the authority's licensing committee with respect to the matter before discharging the function concerned.

(7) Before exercising its power under subsection (5)(b), an authority must consult its licensing committee.

(8) In a case where an authority exercises its power under subsection (5)(b), its licensing committee must (unless the matter is urgent) consider any report of any of the authority's other committees with respect to the matter before discharging the function concerned.

(9) Where a licensing committee is unable to discharge any function delegated to it in accordance with this section because of the number of its members who are unable to take part in the consideration or discussion of any matter or vote on any question with respect to it, the committee must refer the matter back to the licensing authority and the authority must discharge that function.

(10) This section does not apply in relation to the Sub-Treasurer of the Inner Temple or the Under-Treasurer of the Middle Temple.

8 Requirement to keep a register

(1) Each licensing authority must keep a register containing –

    (a)   a record of each premises licence, club premises certificate and personal licence issued by it,

    (b)   a record of each temporary event notice received by it,

    (c)   the matters mentioned in Schedule 3, and

    (d)   such other information as may be prescribed.

(2) Regulations may require a register kept under this section to be in a prescribed form and kept in a prescribed manner.

(3) Each licensing authority must provide facilities for making the information contained in the entries in its register available for inspection (in a legible form) by any person during office hours and without payment.

(4) If requested to do so by any person, a licensing authority must supply him with a copy of the information contained in any entry in its register in legible form.

(5) A licensing authority may charge such reasonable fee as it may determine in respect of any copy supplied under subsection (4).

(6) The Secretary of State may arrange for the duties conferred on licensing authorities by this section to be discharged by means of one or more central registers kept by a person appointed pursuant to the arrangements.

(7) The Secretary of State may require licensing authorities to participate in and contribute towards the cost of any arrangements made under subsection (6).

Licensing committees

9 Proceedings of licensing committee

(1) A licensing committee may establish one or more sub-committees consisting of three members of the committee.

(2) Regulations may make provision about –

   (a)   the proceedings of licensing committees and their sub-committees (including provision about the validity of proceedings and the quorum for meetings),

   (b)   public access to the meetings of those committees and sub-committees,

   (c)   the publicity to be given to those meetings,

   (d)   the agendas and records to be produced in respect of those meetings, and

   (e)   public access to such agendas and records and other information about those meetings.

(3) Subject to any such regulations, each licensing committee may regulate its own procedure and that of its sub-committees.

10 Sub-delegation of functions by licensing committee etc

(1) A licensing committee may arrange for the discharge of any functions exercisable by it –

   (a)   by a sub-committee established by it, or

   (b)   subject to subsection (4), by an officer of the licensing authority.

(2) Where arrangements are made under subsection (1)(a), then, subject to subsections (4) and (5), the sub-committee may in turn arrange for the discharge of the function concerned by an officer of the licensing authority.

(3) Arrangements under subsection (1) or (2) may provide for more than one sub-committee or officer to discharge the same function concurrently.

(4) Arrangements may not be made under subsection (1) or (2) for the discharge by an officer of –

   (a)   any function under –

       (i)   section 18(3) (determination of application for premises licence where representations have been made),

       (ii)   section 31(3) (determination of application for provisional statement where representations have been made),

       (iii)   section 35(3) (determination of application for variation of premises licence where representations have been made),

       (iv)   section 39(3) (determination of application to vary designated premises supervisor following police objection),

       (v)   section 44(5) (determination of application for transfer of premises licence following police objection),

       (vi)   section 48(3) (consideration of police objection made to interim authority notice),

       (vii)   section 72(3) (determination of application for club premises certificate where representations have been made),

       (viii)   section 85(3) (determination of application to vary club premises certificate where representations have been made),

       (ix)   section 105(2) (decision to give counter notice following police objection to temporary event notice),

(x)   section 120(7) (determination of application for grant of personal licence following police objection),

(xi)   section 121(6) (determination of application for renewal of personal licence following police objection), or

(xii) section 124(4) (revocation of licence where convictions come to light after grant etc),

(b) any function under section 52(2) or (3) (determination of application for review of premises licence) in a case where relevant representations (within the meaning of section 52(7)) have been made,

(c) any function under section 88(2) or (3) (determination of application for review of club premises certificate) in a case where relevant representations (within the meaning of section 88(7)) have been made, or

(d) any function under section 167(5) (review following closure order), in a case where relevant representations (within the meaning of section 167(9)) have been made.

(5) The power exercisable under subsection (2) by a sub-committee established by a licensing committee is also subject to any direction given by that committee to the sub-committee.

PART 3

PREMISES LICENCES

Introductory

11 Premises licence

In this Act 'premises licence' means a licence granted under this Part, in respect of any premises, which authorises the premises to be used for one or more licensable activities.

12 The relevant licensing authority

(1) For the purposes of this Part the 'relevant licensing authority' in relation to any premises is determined in accordance with this section.

(2) Subject to subsection (3), the relevant licensing authority is the authority in whose area the premises are situated.

(3) Where the premises are situated in the areas of two or more licensing authorities, the relevant licensing authority is –

(a) the licensing authority in whose area the greater or greatest part of the premises is situated, or

(b) if there is no authority to which paragraph (a) applies, such one of those authorities as is nominated in accordance with subsection (4).

(4) In a case within subsection (3)(b) –

(a) an applicant for a premises licence must nominate one of the licensing authorities as the relevant licensing authority in relation to the application and any licence granted as a result of it, and

(b)   an applicant for a statement under section 29 (provisional statement) in respect of the premises must nominate one of the licensing authorities as the relevant licensing authority in relation to the statement.

13 Authorised persons, interested parties and responsible authorities

(1) In this Part in relation to any premises each of the following expressions has the meaning given to it by this section –

    'authorised person',
    'interested party',
    'responsible authority'.

(2) 'Authorised person' means any of the following –

(a)   an officer of a licensing authority in whose area the premises are situated who is authorised by that authority for the purposes of this Act,

(b)   an inspector appointed under section 18 of the Fire Precautions Act 1971 (c 40),

(c)   an inspector appointed under section 19 of the Health and Safety at Work etc Act 1974 (c 37),

(d)   an officer of a local authority, in whose area the premises are situated, who is authorised by that authority for the purposes of exercising one or more of its statutory functions in relation to minimising or preventing the risk of pollution of the environment or of harm to human health,

(e)   in relation to a vessel, an inspector, or a surveyor of ships, appointed under section 256 of the Merchant Shipping Act 1995 (c 21),

(f)   a person prescribed for the purposes of this subsection.

(3) 'Interested party' means any of the following –

(a)   a person living in the vicinity of the premises,
(b)   a body representing persons who live in that vicinity,
(c)   a person involved in a business in that vicinity,
(d)   a body representing persons involved in such businesses.

(4) 'Responsible authority' means any of the following –

(a)   the chief officer of police for any police area in which the premises are situated,

(b)   the fire authority for any area in which the premises are situated,

(c)   the enforcing authority within the meaning given by section 18 of the Health and Safety at Work etc Act 1974 for any area in which the premises are situated,

(d)   the local planning authority within the meaning given by the Town and Country Planning Act 1990 (c 8) for any area in which the premises are situated,

(e)   the local authority by which statutory functions are exercisable in any area in which the premises are situated in relation to minimising or preventing the risk of pollution of the environment or of harm to human health,

(f) a body which –
  (i)   represents those who, in relation to any such area, are responsible for, or interested in, matters relating to the protection of children from harm, and
  (ii) is recognised by the licensing authority for that area for the purposes of this section as being competent to advise it on such matters,
(g) any licensing authority (other than the relevant licensing authority) in whose area part of the premises is situated,
(h) in relation to a vessel –
  (i)   a navigation authority (within the meaning of section 221(1) of the Water Resources Act 1991 (c 57)) having functions in relation to the waters where the vessel is usually moored or berthed or any waters where it is, or is proposed to be, navigated at a time when it is used for licensable activities,
  (ii) the Environment Agency,
  (iii) the British Waterways Board, or
  (iv) the Secretary of State,
(i) a person prescribed for the purposes of this subsection.

(5) For the purposes of this section, 'statutory function' means a function conferred by or under any enactment.

14 Meaning of 'supply of alcohol'

For the purposes of this Part the 'supply of alcohol' means –

(a) the sale by retail of alcohol, or
(b) the supply of alcohol by or on behalf of a club to, or to the order of, a member of the club.

15 Meaning of 'designated premises supervisor'

(1) In this Act references to the 'designated premises supervisor', in relation to a premises licence, are to the individual for the time being specified in that licence as the premises supervisor.

(2) Nothing in this Act prevents an individual who holds a premises licence from also being specified in the licence as the premises supervisor.

Grant of premises licence

16 Applicant for premises licence

(1) The following persons may apply for a premises licence –

(a) a person who carries on, or proposes to carry on, a business which involves the use of the premises for the licensable activities to which the application relates,
(b) a person who makes the application pursuant to –
  (i)   any statutory function discharged by that person which relates to those licensable activities, or
  (ii) any function discharged by that person by virtue of Her Majesty's prerogative,

(c)   a recognised club,

(d)   a charity,

(e)   the proprietor of an educational institution,

(f)   a health service body,

(g)   a person who is registered under Part 2 of the Care Standards Act 2000 (c 14) in respect of an independent hospital,

(h)   the chief officer of police of a police force in England and Wales,

(i)   a person of such other description as may be prescribed.

(2) But an individual may not apply for a premises licence unless he is aged 18 or over.

(3) In this section –

'charity' has the same meaning as in section 96(1) of the Charities Act 1993 (c 10);

'educational institution' means –

(a)   a school, or an institution within the further or higher education sector, within the meaning of section 4 of the Education Act 1996 (c 56), or

(b)   a college (including any institution in the nature of a college), school, hall or other institution of a university, in circumstances where the university receives financial support under section 65 of the Further and Higher Education Act 1992 (c 13);

'health service body' means –

(a)   an NHS trust established by virtue of section 5 of the National Health Service and Community Care Act 1990 (c 19),

(b)   a Primary Care Trust established by virtue of section 16A of the National Health Service Act 1977 (c 49), or

(c)   a Local Health Board established by virtue of section 16BA of that Act;

'independent hospital' has the same meaning as in section 2(2) of the Care Standards Act 2000 (c 14);

'proprietor' –

(a)   in relation to a school within the meaning of section 4 of the Education Act 1996, has the same meaning as in section 579(1) of that Act, and

(b)   in relation to an educational institution other than such a school, means the governing body of that institution within the meaning of section 90(1) of the Further and Higher Education Act 1992; and

'statutory function' means a function conferred by or under any enactment.

17 Application for premises licence

(1) An application for a premises licence must be made to the relevant licensing authority.

(2) Subsection (1) is subject to regulations under –

(a)   section 54 (form etc of applications etc);

(b)   section 55 (fees to accompany applications etc).

(3) An application under this section must also be accompanied –

(a) by an operating schedule,

(b) by a plan of the premises to which the application relates, in the prescribed form, and

(c) if the licensable activities to which the application relates ('the relevant licensable activities') include the supply of alcohol, by a form of consent in the prescribed form given by the individual whom the applicant wishes to have specified in the premises licence as the premises supervisor.

(4) An 'operating schedule' is a document which is in the prescribed form and includes a statement of the following matters –

(a) the relevant licensable activities,

(b) the times during which it is proposed that the relevant licensable activities are to take place,

(c) any other times during which it is proposed that the premises are to be open to the public,

(d) where the applicant wishes the licence to have effect for a limited period, that period,

(e) where the relevant licensable activities include the supply of alcohol, prescribed information in respect of the individual whom the applicant wishes to have specified in the premises licence as the premises supervisor,

(f) where the relevant licensable activities include the supply of alcohol, whether the supplies are proposed to be for consumption on the premises or off the premises, or both,

(g) the steps which it is proposed to take to promote the licensing objectives,

(h) such other matters as may be prescribed.

(5) The Secretary of State must by regulations –

(a) require an applicant to advertise his application within the prescribed period –
  (i)   in the prescribed form, and
  (ii) in a manner which is prescribed and is likely to bring the application to the attention of the interested parties likely to be affected by it;

(b) require an applicant to give notice of his application to each responsible authority, and such other persons as may be prescribed, within the prescribed period;

(c) prescribe the period during which interested parties and responsible authorities may make representations to the relevant licensing authority about the application.

18 Determination of application for premises licence

(1) This section applies where the relevant licensing authority –

(a) receives an application for a premises licence made in accordance with section 17, and

(b) is satisfied that the applicant has complied with any requirement imposed on him under subsection (5) of that section.

(2) Subject to subsection (3), the authority must grant the licence in accordance with the application subject only to –

(a) such conditions as are consistent with the operating schedule accompanying the application, and
(b) any conditions which must under section 19, 20 or 21 be included in the licence.

(3) Where relevant representations are made, the authority must –

(a) hold a hearing to consider them, unless the authority, the applicant and each person who has made such representations agree that a hearing is unnecessary, and
(b) having regard to the representations, take such of the steps mentioned in subsection (4) (if any) as it considers necessary for the promotion of the licensing objectives.

(4) The steps are –

(a) to grant the licence subject to –
  (i)   the conditions mentioned in subsection (2)(a) modified to such extent as the authority considers necessary for the promotion of the licensing objectives, and
  (ii) any condition which must under section 19, 20 or 21 be included in the licence;
(b) to exclude from the scope of the licence any of the licensable activities to which the application relates;
(c) to refuse to specify a person in the licence as the premises supervisor;
(d) to reject the application.

(5) For the purposes of subsection (4)(a)(i) the conditions mentioned in subsection (2)(a) are modified if any of them is altered or omitted or any new condition is added.

(6) For the purposes of this section, 'relevant representations' means representations which –

(a) are about the likely effect of the grant of the premises licence on the promotion of the licensing objectives,
(b) meet the requirements of subsection (7),
(c) if they relate to the identity of the person named in the application as the proposed premises supervisor, meet the requirements of subsection (9), and
(d) are not excluded representations by virtue of section 32 (restriction on making representations following issue of provisional statement).

(7) The requirements of this subsection are –

(a) that the representations were made by an interested party or responsible authority within the period prescribed under section 17(5)(c),

(b)   that they have not been withdrawn, and

(c)   in the case of representations made by an interested party (who is not also a responsible authority), that they are not, in the opinion of the relevant licensing authority, frivolous or vexatious.

(8) Where the authority determines for the purposes of subsection (7)(c) that any representations are frivolous or vexatious, it must notify the person who made them of the reasons for its determination.

(9) The requirements of this subsection are that the representations –

(a)   were made by a chief officer of police for a police area in which the premises are situated, and

(b)   include a statement that, due to the exceptional circumstances of the case, he is satisfied that the designation of the person concerned as the premises supervisor under the premises licence would undermine the crime prevention objective.

(10) In discharging its duty under subsection (2) or (3)(b), a licensing authority may grant a licence under this section subject to different conditions in respect of –

(a)   different parts of the premises concerned;

(b)   different licensable activities.

19 Mandatory conditions where licence authorises supply of alcohol

(1) Where a premises licence authorises the supply of alcohol, the licence must include the following conditions.

(2) The first condition is that no supply of alcohol may be made under the premises licence –

(a)   at a time when there is no designated premises supervisor in respect of the premises licence, or

(b)   at a time when the designated premises supervisor does not hold a personal licence or his personal licence is suspended.

(3) The second condition is that every supply of alcohol under the premises licence must be made or authorised by a person who holds a personal licence.

20 Mandatory condition: exhibition of films

(1) Where a premises licence authorises the exhibition of films, the licence must include a condition requiring the admission of children to the exhibition of any film to be restricted in accordance with this section.

(2) Where the film classification body is specified in the licence, unless subsection (3)(b) applies, admission of children must be restricted in accordance with any recommendation made by that body.

(3) Where –

(a)   the film classification body is not specified in the licence, or

(b)   the relevant licensing authority has notified the holder of the licence that this subsection applies to the film in question, admission of children must be restricted in accordance with any recommendation made by that licensing authority.

(4) In this section –

> 'children' means persons aged under 18; and
> 'film classification body' means the person or persons designated as the authority under section 4 of the Video Recordings Act 1984 (c 39) (authority to determine suitability of video works for classification).

21 Mandatory condition: door supervision

(1) Where a premises licence includes a condition that at specified times one or more individuals must be at the premises to carry out a security activity, the licence must include a condition that each such individual must be licensed by the Security Industry Authority.

(2) But nothing in subsection (1) requires such a condition to be imposed –

    (a)   in respect of premises within paragraph 8(3)(a) of Schedule 2 to the Private Security Industry Act 2001 (c 12) (premises with premises licences authorising plays or films), or

    (b)   in respect of premises in relation to –

        (i)   any occasion mentioned in paragraph 8(3)(b) or (c) of that Schedule (premises being used exclusively by club with club premises certificate, under a temporary event notice authorising plays or films or under a gaming licence), or

        (ii)   any occasion within paragraph 8(3)(d) of that Schedule (occasions prescribed by regulations under that Act).

(3) For the purposes of this section –

    (a)   'security activity' means an activity to which paragraph 2(1)(a) of that Schedule applies, and

    (b)   paragraph 8(5) of that Schedule (interpretation of references to an occasion) applies as it applies in relation to paragraph 8 of that Schedule.

22 Prohibited conditions: plays

(1) In relation to a premises licence which authorises the performance of plays, no condition may be attached to the licence as to the nature of the plays which may be performed, or the manner of performing plays, under the licence.

(2) But subsection (1) does not prevent a licensing authority imposing, in accordance with section 18(2)(a) or (3)(b), 35(3)(b) or 52(3), any condition which it considers necessary on the grounds of public safety.

23 Grant or rejection of application

(1) Where an application is granted under section 18, the relevant licensing authority must forthwith –

    (a)   give a notice to that effect to –

(i)   the applicant,
(ii)   any person who made relevant representations in respect of the application, and
(iii) the chief officer of police for the police area (or each police area) in which the premises are situated, and
(b)   issue the applicant with the licence and a summary of it.

(2) Where relevant representations were made in respect of the application, the notice under subsection (1)(a) must state the authority's reasons for its decision as to the steps (if any) to take under section 18(3)(b).

(3) Where an application is rejected under section 18, the relevant licensing authority must forthwith give a notice to that effect, stating its reasons for the decision, to –

(a)   the applicant,
(b)   any person who made relevant representations in respect of the application, and
(c)   the chief officer of police for the police area (or each police area) in which the premises are situated.

(4) In this section 'relevant representations' has the meaning given in section 18(6).

24 Form of licence and summary

(1) A premises licence and the summary of a premises licence must be in the prescribed form.

(2) Regulations under subsection (1) must, in particular, provide for the licence to –

(a)   specify the name and address of the holder;
(b)   include a plan of the premises to which the licence relates;
(c)   if the licence has effect for a limited period, specify that period;
(d)   specify the licensable activities for which the premises may be used;
(e)   if the licensable activities include the supply of alcohol, specify the name and address of the individual (if any) who is the premises supervisor in respect of the licence;
(f)   specify the conditions subject to which the licence has effect.

25 Theft, loss, etc of premises licence or summary

(1) Where a premises licence or summary is lost, stolen, damaged or destroyed, the holder of the licence may apply to the relevant licensing authority for a copy of the licence or summary.

(2) Subsection (1) is subject to regulations under section 55(1) (fee to accompany applications).

(3) Where an application is made in accordance with this section, the relevant licensing authority must issue the holder of the licence with a copy of the licence or summary (certified by the authority to be a true copy) if it is satisfied that –

(a)   the licence or summary has been lost, stolen, damaged or destroyed, and

(b)   where it has been lost or stolen, the holder has reported that loss or theft to the police.

(4) The copy issued under this section must be a copy of the premises licence or summary in the form in which it existed immediately before it was lost, stolen, damaged or destroyed.

(5) This Act applies in relation to a copy issued under this section as it applies in relation to an original licence or summary.

Duration of licence

26 Period of validity of premises licence

(1) Subject to sections 27 and 28, a premises licence has effect until such time as –

(a)   it is revoked under section 52, or

(b)   if it specifies that it has effect for a limited period, that period expires.

(2) But a premises licence does not have effect during any period when it is suspended under section 52.

27 Death, incapacity, insolvency etc of licence holder

(1) A premises licence lapses if the holder of the licence –

(a)   dies,

(b)   becomes mentally incapable (within the meaning of section 13(1) of the Enduring Powers of Attorney Act 1985 (c 29)),

(c)   becomes insolvent,

(d)   is dissolved, or

(e)   if it is a club, ceases to be a recognised club.

(2) This section is subject to sections 47 and 50 (which make provision for the reinstatement of the licence in certain circumstances).

(3) For the purposes of this section, an individual becomes insolvent on –

(a)   the approval of a voluntary arrangement proposed by him,

(b)   being adjudged bankrupt or having his estate sequestrated, or

(c)   entering into a deed of arrangement made for the benefit of his creditors or a trust deed for his creditors.

(4) For the purposes of this section, a company becomes insolvent on –

(a)   the approval of a voluntary arrangement proposed by its directors,

(b)   the appointment of an administrator in respect of the company,

(c)   the appointment of an administrative receiver in respect of the company, or

(d)   going into liquidation.

(5) An expression used in this section and in the Insolvency Act 1986 (c 45) has the same meaning in this section as in that Act.

28 Surrender of premises licence

(1) Where the holder of a premises licence wishes to surrender his licence he may give the relevant licensing authority a notice to that effect.

(2) The notice must be accompanied by the premises licence or, if that is not practicable, by a statement of the reasons for the failure to provide the licence.

(3) Where a notice of surrender is given in accordance with this section, the premises licence lapses on receipt of the notice by the authority.

(4) This section is subject to section 50 (which makes provision for the reinstatement in certain circumstances of a licence surrendered under this section).

Provisional statement

29 Application for a provisional statement where premises being built, etc

(1) This section applies to premises which –

   (a)   are being or are about to be constructed for the purpose of being used for one or more licensable activities, or
   (b)   are being or are about to be extended or otherwise altered for that purpose (whether or not they are already being used for that purpose).

(2) A person may apply to the relevant licensing authority for a provisional statement if –

   (a)   he is interested in the premises, and
   (b)   where he is an individual, he is aged 18 or over.

(3) In this Act 'provisional statement' means a statement issued under section 31(2) or (3)(c).

(4) Subsection (2) is subject to regulations under –

   (a)   section 54 (form etc of applications etc);
   (b)   section 55 (fees to accompany applications etc).

(5) An application under this section must also be accompanied by a schedule of works.

(6) A schedule of works is a document in the prescribed form which includes –

   (a)   a statement made by or on behalf of the applicant including particulars of the premises to which the application relates and of the licensable activities for which the premises are to be used,
   (b)   plans of the work being or about to be done at the premises, and
   (c)   such other information as may be prescribed.

(7) For the purposes of this Part, in relation to any premises in respect of which an application for a provisional statement has been made, references to the work being satisfactorily completed are to work at the premises being

completed in a manner which substantially complies with the schedule of works accompanying the application.

30 Advertisement of application for provisional statement

(1) This section applies where an application is made under section 29.

(2) The duty to make regulations imposed on the Secretary of State by section 17(5) (advertisement etc of application) applies in relation to an application under section 29 as it applies in relation to an application under section 17.

(3) Regulations made under section 17(5)(a) by virtue of subsection (2) may, in particular, require advertisements to contain a statement in the prescribed form describing the effect of section 32 (restriction on representations following issue of a provisional statement).

31 Determination of application for provisional statement

(1) This section applies where the relevant licensing authority –

   (a)   receives a provisional statement application, and
   (b)   is satisfied that the applicant has complied with any requirement imposed on him by virtue of section 30.

(2) Where no relevant representations are made, the authority must issue the applicant with a statement to that effect.

(3) Where relevant representations are made, the authority must –

   (a)   hold a hearing to consider them, unless the authority, the applicant and each person who has made such representations agree that a hearing is unnecessary,
   (b)   determine whether, on the basis of those representations and the provisional statement application, it would consider it necessary to take any steps under section 18(3)(b) if, on the work being satisfactorily completed, it had to decide whether to grant a premises licence in the form described in the provisional statement application, and
   (c)   issue the applicant with a statement which –
         (i)   gives details of that determination, and
         (ii)   states the authority's reasons for its decision as to the steps (if any) that it would be necessary to take under section 18(3)(b).

(4) The licensing authority must give a copy of the provisional statement to –

   (a)   each person who made relevant representations, and
   (b)   the chief officer of police for each police area in which the premises are situated.

(5) In this section 'relevant representations' means representations –

   (a)   which are about the likely effect on the licensing objectives of the grant of a premises licence in the form described in the provisional statement application, if the work at the premises was satisfactorily completed, and
   (b)   which meet the requirements of subsection (6).

(6) The requirements are –

    (a)   that the representations are made by an interested party or responsible authority within the period prescribed under section 17(5)(c) by virtue of section 30,

    (b)   that the representations have not been withdrawn, and

    (c)   in the case of representations made by an interested party (who is not also a responsible authority), that they are not, in the opinion of the relevant licensing authority, frivolous or vexatious.

(7) Where the authority determines for the purposes of subsection (6)(c) that any representations are frivolous or vexatious, it must notify the person who made them of the reasons for its determination.

(8) In this section 'provisional statement application' means an application made in accordance with section 29.

32 Restriction on representations following provisional statement

(1) This section applies where a provisional statement has been issued in respect of any premises ('the relevant premises') and a person subsequently applies for a premises licence in respect of –

    (a)   the relevant premises or a part of them, or

    (b)   premises that are substantially the same as the relevant premises or a part of them.

(2) Where –

    (a)   the application for the premises licence is an application for a licence in the same form as the licence described in the application for the provisional statement, and

    (b)   the work described in the schedule of works accompanying the application for that statement has been satisfactorily completed,

representations made by a person ('the relevant person') in respect of the application for the premises licence are excluded representations for the purposes of section 18(6)(d) if subsection (3) applies.

(3) This subsection applies if –

    (a)   given the information provided in the application for the provisional statement, the relevant person could have made the same, or substantially the same, representations about that application but failed to do so, without reasonable excuse, and

    (b)   there has been no material change in circumstances relating either to the relevant premises or to the area in the vicinity of those premises since the provisional statement was made.

Duty to notify certain changes

33 Notification of change of name or address

(1) The holder of a premises licence must, as soon as is reasonably practicable, notify the relevant licensing authority of any change in –

    (a)   his name or address,

(b) unless the designated premises supervisor has already notified the authority under subsection (4), the name or address of that supervisor.

(2) Subsection (1) is subject to regulations under section 55(1) (fee to accompany application).

(3) A notice under subsection (1) must also be accompanied by the premises licence (or the appropriate part of the licence) or, if that is not practicable, by a statement of the reasons for the failure to produce the licence (or part).

(4) Where the designated premises supervisor under a premises licence is not the holder of the licence, he may notify the relevant licensing authority under this subsection of any change in his name or address.

(5) Where the designated premises supervisor gives a notice under subsection (4), he must, as soon as is reasonably practicable, give the holder of the premises licence a copy of that notice.

(6) A person commits an offence if he fails, without reasonable excuse, to comply with this section.

(7) A person guilty of an offence under subsection (6) is liable on summary conviction to a fine not exceeding level 2 on the standard scale.

Variation of licences

34 Application to vary premises licence

(1) The holder of a premises licence may apply to the relevant licensing authority for variation of the licence.

(2) Subsection (1) is subject to regulations under –

(a) section 54 (form etc of applications etc);
(b) section 55 (fees to accompany applications etc).

(3) An application under this section must also be accompanied by the premises licence (or the appropriate part of that licence) or, if that is not practicable, by a statement of the reasons for the failure to provide the licence (or part).

(4) This section does not apply to an application within section 37(1) (application to vary licence to specify individual as premises supervisor).

(5) The duty to make regulations imposed on the Secretary of State by subsection (5) of section 17 (advertisement etc of application) applies in relation to applications under this section as it applies in relation to applications under that section.

35 Determination of application under section 34

(1) This section applies where the relevant licensing authority –

(a) receives an application, made in accordance with section 34, to vary a premises licence, and
(b) is satisfied that the applicant has complied with any requirement imposed on him by virtue of subsection (5) of that section.

(2) Subject to subsection (3) and section 36(6), the authority must grant the application.

(3) Where relevant representations are made, the authority must –

(a) hold a hearing to consider them, unless the authority, the applicant and each person who has made such representations agree that a hearing is unnecessary, and

(b) having regard to the representations, take such of the steps mentioned in subsection (4) (if any) as it considers necessary for the promotion of the licensing objectives.

(4) The steps are –

(a) to modify the conditions of the licence;
(b) to reject the whole or part of the application;

and for this purpose the conditions of the licence are modified if any of them is altered or omitted or any new condition is added.

(5) In this section 'relevant representations' means representations which –

(a) are about the likely effect of the grant of the application on the promotion of the licensing objectives, and
(b) meet the requirements of subsection (6).

(6) The requirements are –

(a) that the representations are made by an interested party or responsible authority within the period prescribed under section 17(5)(c) by virtue of section 34(5),
(b) that they have not been withdrawn, and
(c) in the case of representations made by an interested party (who is not also a responsible authority), that they are not, in the opinion of the relevant licensing authority, frivolous or vexatious.

(7) Subsections (2) and (3) are subject to sections 19, 20 and 21 (which require certain conditions to be included in premises licences).

36 Supplementary provision about determinations under section 35

(1) Where an application (or any part of an application) is granted under section 35, the relevant licensing authority must forthwith give a notice to that effect to –

(a) the applicant,
(b) any person who made relevant representations in respect of the application, and
(c) the chief officer of police for the police area (or each police area) in which the premises are situated.

(2) Where relevant representations were made in respect of the application, the notice under subsection (1) must state the authority's reasons for its decision as to the steps (if any) to take under section 35(3)(b).

(3) The notice under subsection (1) must specify the time when the variation in question takes effect.

That time is the time specified in the application or, if that time is before the applicant is given that notice, such later time as the relevant licensing authority specifies in the notice.

(4) Where an application (or any part of an application) is rejected under section 35, the relevant licensing authority must forthwith give a notice to that effect stating its reasons for rejecting the application to –

    (a)   the applicant,
    (b)   any person who made relevant representations in respect of the application, and
    (c)   the chief officer of police for the police area (or each police area) in which the premises are situated.

(5) Where the relevant licensing authority determines for the purposes of section 35(6)(c) that any representations are frivolous or vexatious, it must notify the person who made them of the reasons for that determination.

(6) A licence may not be varied under section 35 so as –

    (a)   to extend the period for which the licence has effect, or
    (b)   to vary substantially the premises to which it relates.

(7) In discharging its duty under subsection (2) or (3)(b) of that section, a licensing authority may vary a premises licence so that it has effect subject to different conditions in respect of –

    (a)   different parts of the premises concerned;
    (b)   different licensable activities.

(8) In this section 'relevant representations' has the meaning given in section 35(5).

37 Application to vary licence to specify individual as premises supervisor

(1) The holder of a premises licence may –

    (a)   if the licence authorises the supply of alcohol, or
    (b)   if he has applied under section 34 to vary the licence so that it authorises such supplies,

apply to vary the licence so as to specify the individual named in the application ('the proposed individual') as the premises supervisor.

(2) Subsection (1) is subject to regulations under –

    (a)   section 54 (form etc of applications etc);
    (b)   section 55 (fees to accompany applications etc).

(3) An application under this section must also be accompanied by –

    (a)   a form of consent in the prescribed form given by the proposed individual, and
    (b)   the premises licence (or the appropriate part of that licence) or, if that is not practicable, a statement of the reasons for the failure to provide the licence (or part).

(4) The holder of the premises licence must give notice of his application –

(a)   to the chief officer of police for the police area (or each police area) in which the premises are situated, and

(b)   to the designated premises supervisor (if there is one),

and that notice must state whether the application is one to which section 38 applies.

(5) Where a chief officer of police notified under subsection (4) is satisfied that the exceptional circumstances of the case are such that granting the application would undermine the crime prevention objective, he must give the relevant licensing authority a notice stating the reasons why he is so satisfied.

(6) The chief officer of police must give that notice within the period of 14 days beginning with the day on which he is notified of the application under subsection (4).

38 Circumstances in which section 37 application given interim effect

(1) This section applies where an application made in accordance with section 37, in respect of a premises licence which authorises the supply of alcohol, includes a request that the variation applied for should have immediate effect.

(2) By virtue of this section, the premises licence has effect during the application period as if it were varied in the manner set out in the application.

(3) For this purpose 'the application period' means the period which –

(a)   begins when the application is received by the relevant licensing authority, and

(b)   ends –

    (i)   if the application is granted, when the variation takes effect,

    (ii)   if the application is rejected, at the time the rejection is notified to the applicant, or

    (iii)   if the application is withdrawn before it is determined, at the time of the withdrawal.

39 Determination of section 37 application

(1) This section applies where an application is made, in accordance with section 37, to vary a premises licence so as to specify a new premises supervisor ('the proposed individual').

(2) Subject to subsection (3), the relevant licensing authority must grant the application.

(3) Where a notice is given under section 37(5) (and not withdrawn), the authority must –

(a)   hold a hearing to consider it, unless the authority, the applicant and the chief officer of police who gave the notice agree that a hearing is unnecessary, and

(b)   having regard to the notice, reject the application if it considers it necessary for the promotion of the crime prevention objective to do so.

(4) Where an application under section 37 is granted or rejected, the relevant licensing authority must give a notice to that effect to –

  (a)   the applicant,
  (b)   the proposed individual, and
  (c)   the chief officer of police for the police area (or each police area) in which the premises are situated.

(5) Where a chief officer of police gave a notice under subsection (5) of that section (and it was not withdrawn), the notice under subsection (4) of this section must state the authority's reasons for granting or rejecting the application.

(6) Where the application is granted, the notice under subsection (4) must specify the time when the variation takes effect.

That time is the time specified in the application or, if that time is before the applicant is given that notice, such later time as the relevant licensing authority specifies in the notice.

40 Duty of applicant following determination under section 39

(1) Where the holder of a premises licence is notified under section 39(4), he must forthwith –

  (a)   if his application has been granted, notify the person (if any) who has been replaced as the designated premises supervisor of the variation, and
  (b)   if his application has been rejected, give the designated premises supervisor (if any) notice to that effect.

(2) A person commits an offence if he fails, without reasonable excuse, to comply with subsection (1).

(3) A person guilty of an offence under subsection (2) is liable on summary conviction to a fine not exceeding level 3 on the standard scale.

41 Request to be removed as designated premises supervisor

(1) Where an individual wishes to cease being the designated premises supervisor in respect of a premises licence, he may give the relevant licensing authority a notice to that effect.

(2) Subsection (1) is subject to regulations under section 54 (form etc of notices etc).

(3) Where the individual is the holder of the premises licence, the notice under subsection (1) must also be accompanied by the premises licence (or the appropriate part of the licence) or, if that is not practicable, by a statement of the reasons for the failure to provide the licence (or part).

(4) In any other case, the individual must no later than 48 hours after giving the notice under subsection (1) give the holder of the premises licence –

  (a)   a copy of that notice, and
  (b)   a notice directing the holder to send to the relevant licensing authority within 14 days of receiving the notice –

(i)   the premises licence (or the appropriate part of the licence), or
(ii)   if that is not practicable, a statement of the reasons for the failure to provide the licence (or part).

(5) A person commits an offence if he fails, without reasonable excuse, to comply with a direction given to him under subsection (4)(b).

(6) A person guilty of an offence under subsection (5) is liable on summary conviction to a fine not exceeding level 3 on the standard scale.

(7) Where an individual –

(a)   gives the relevant licensing authority a notice in accordance with this section, and
(b)   satisfies the requirements of subsection (3) or (4),

he is to be treated for the purposes of this Act as if, from the relevant time, he were not the designated premises supervisor.

(8) For this purpose 'the relevant time' means –

(a)   the time the notice under subsection (1) is received by the relevant licensing authority, or
(b)   if later, the time specified in the notice.

Transfer of premises licence

42 Application for transfer of premises licence

(1) Subject to this section, any person mentioned in section 16(1) (applicant for premises licence) may apply to the relevant licensing authority for the transfer of a premises licence to him.

(2) Where the applicant is an individual he must be aged 18 or over.

(3) Subsection (1) is subject to regulations under –

(a)   section 54 (form etc of applications etc);
(b)   section 55 (fees to accompany applications etc).

(4) An application under this section must also be accompanied by the premises licence or, if that is not practicable, a statement of the reasons for the failure to provide the licence.

(5) The applicant must give notice of his application to the chief officer of police for the police area (or each police area) in which the premises are situated.

(6) Where a chief officer of police notified under subsection (5) is satisfied that the exceptional circumstances of the case are such that granting the application would undermine the crime prevention objective, he must give the relevant licensing authority a notice stating the reasons why he is so satisfied.

(7) The chief officer of police must give that notice within the period of 14 days beginning with the day on which he is notified of the application under subsection (5).

43 Circumstances in which transfer application given interim effect

(1) Where –

- (a) an application made in accordance with section 42 includes a request that the transfer have immediate effect, and
- (b) the requirements of this section are met,

then, by virtue of this section, the premises licence has effect during the application period as if the applicant were the holder of the licence.

(2) For this purpose 'the application period' means the period which –

- (a) begins when the application is received by the relevant licensing authority, and
- (b) ends –
  - (i)   when the licence is transferred following the grant of the application, or
  - (ii) if the application is rejected, when the applicant is notified of the rejection, or
  - (iii) when the application is withdrawn.

(3) Subject to subsections (4) and (5), an application within subsection (1)(a) may be made only with the consent of the holder of the premises licence.

(4) Where a person is the holder of the premises licence by virtue of an interim authority notice under section 47, such an application may also be made by that person.

(5) The relevant licensing authority must exempt the applicant from the requirement to obtain the holder's consent if the applicant shows to the authority's satisfaction –

- (a) that he has taken all reasonable steps to obtain that consent, and
- (b) that, if the application were one to which subsection (1) applied, he would be in a position to use the premises during the application period for the licensable activity or activities authorised by the premises licence.

(6) Where the relevant licensing authority refuses to exempt an applicant under subsection (5), it must notify the applicant of its reasons for that decision.

44 Determination of transfer application

(1) This section applies where an application for the transfer of a licence is made in accordance with section 42.

(2) Subject to subsections (3) and (5), the authority must transfer the licence in accordance with the application.

(3) The authority must reject the application if none of the conditions in subsection (4) applies.

(4) The conditions are –

(a) that section 43(1) (applications given interim effect) applies to the application,

(b) that the holder of the premises licence consents to the transfer,

(c) that the applicant is exempted under subsection (6) from the requirement to obtain the holder's consent to the transfer.

(5) Where a notice is given under section 42(6) (and not withdrawn), and subsection (3) above does not apply, the authority must –

(a) hold a hearing to consider it, unless the authority, the applicant and the chief officer of police who gave the notice agree that a hearing is unnecessary, and

(b) having regard to the notice, reject the application if it considers it necessary for the promotion of the crime prevention objective to do so.

(6) The relevant licensing authority must exempt the applicant from the requirement to obtain the holder's consent if the applicant shows to the authority's satisfaction –

(a) that he has taken all reasonable steps to obtain that consent, and

(b) that, if the application were granted, he would be in a position to use the premises for the licensable activity or activities authorised by the premises licence.

(7) Where the relevant licensing authority refuses to exempt an applicant under subsection (6), it must notify the applicant of its reasons for that decision.

45 Notification of determination under section 44

(1) Where an application under section 42 is granted or rejected, the relevant licensing authority must give a notice to that effect to –

(a) the applicant, and

(b) the chief officer of police for the police area (or each police area) in which the premises are situated.

(2) Where a chief officer of police gave a notice under subsection (6) of that section (and it was not withdrawn), the notice under subsection (1) of this section must state the licensing authority's reasons for granting or rejecting the application.

(3) Where the application is granted, the notice under subsection (1) must specify the time when the transfer takes effect.

That time is the time specified in the application or, if that time is before the applicant is given that notice, such later time as the relevant licensing authority specifies in the notice.

(4) The relevant licensing authority must also give a copy of the notice given under subsection (1) –

(a) where the application is granted –

    (i) to the holder of the licence immediately before the application was granted, or

(ii)   if the application was one to which section 43(1) applied, to the holder of the licence immediately before the application was made (if any),

(b)   where the application is rejected, to the holder of the premises licence (if any).

46 Duty to notify designated premises supervisor of transfer

(1) This section applies where –

(a)   an application is made in accordance with section 42 to transfer a premises licence in respect of which there is a designated premises supervisor, and

(b)   the applicant and that supervisor are not the same person.

(2) Where section 43(1) applies in relation to the application, the applicant must forthwith notify the designated premises supervisor of the application.

(3) If the application is granted, the applicant must forthwith notify the designated premises supervisor of the transfer.

(4) A person commits an offence if he fails, without reasonable excuse, to comply with this section.

(5) A person guilty of an offence under subsection (4) is liable on summary conviction to a fine not exceeding level 3 on the standard scale.

Interim authority notices

47 Interim authority notice following death etc of licence holder

(1) This section applies where –

(a)   a premises licence lapses under section 27 in a case within subsection (1)(a), (b) or (c) of that section (death, incapacity or insolvency of the holder), but

(b)   no application for transfer of the licence has been made by virtue of section 50 (reinstatement of licence on transfer following death etc).

(2) A person who –

(a)   has a prescribed interest in the premises concerned, or

(b)   is connected to the person who held the premises licence immediately before it lapsed ('the former holder'),

may, during the initial seven day period, give to the relevant licensing authority a notice (an 'interim authority notice') in respect of the licence.

(3) Subsection (2) is subject to regulations under –

(a)   section 54 (form etc of notices etc);

(b)   section 55 (fees to accompany applications etc).

(4) Only one interim authority notice may be given under subsection (2).

(5) For the purposes of subsection (2) a person is connected to the former holder of the premises licence if, and only if –

(a) the former holder has died and that person is his personal representative,

(b) the former holder has become mentally incapable and that person acts for him under a power of attorney created by an instrument registered under section 6 of the Enduring Powers of Attorney Act 1985 (c 29), or

(c) the former holder has become insolvent and that person is his insolvency practitioner.

(6) Where an interim authority notice is given in accordance with this section –

(a) the premises licence is reinstated from the time the notice is received by the relevant licensing authority, and

(b) the person who gave the notice is from that time the holder of the licence.

(7) But the premises licence lapses again –

(a) at the end of the initial seven day period unless before that time the person who gave the interim authority notice has given a copy of the notice to the chief officer of police for the police area (or each police area) in which the premises are situated;

(b) at the end of the interim authority period, unless before that time a relevant transfer application is made to the relevant licensing authority.

(8) Nothing in this section prevents the person who gave the interim authority notice from making a relevant transfer application.

(9) If –

(a) a relevant transfer application is made during the interim authority period, and

(b) that application is rejected or withdrawn,

the licence lapses again at the time of the rejection or withdrawal.

(10) In this section –

'becomes insolvent' is to be construed in accordance with section 27;

'initial seven day period', in relation to a licence which lapses as mentioned in subsection (1), means the period of seven days beginning with the day after the day the licence lapses;

'insolvency practitioner', in relation to a person, means a person acting as an insolvency practitioner in relation to him (within the meaning of section 388 of the Insolvency Act 1986 (c 45));

'interim authority period' means the period beginning with the day on which the interim authority notice is received by the relevant licensing authority and ending –

(a) two months after that day, or

(b) if earlier, when it is terminated by the person who gave the interim authority notice notifying the relevant licensing authority to that effect;

'mentally incapable' has the same meaning as in section 27(1)(b); and 'relevant transfer application' in relation to the premises licence, is an application under section 42 which is given interim effect by virtue of section 43.

48 Cancellation of interim authority notice following police objections

(1) This section applies where –

(a)   an interim authority notice by a person ('the relevant person') is given in accordance with section 47,

(b)   the chief officer of police for the police area (or each police area) in which the premises are situated is given a copy of the interim authority notice before the end of the initial seven day period (within the meaning of that section), and

(c)   that chief officer (or any of those chief officers) is satisfied that the exceptional circumstances of the case are such that a failure to cancel the interim authority notice would undermine the crime prevention objective.

(2) The chief officer of police must no later than 48 hours after he receives the copy of the interim authority notice give the relevant licensing authority a notice stating why he is so satisfied.

(3) Where a notice is given by the chief officer of police (and not withdrawn), the authority must –

(a)   hold a hearing to consider it, unless the authority, the relevant person and the chief officer of police agree that a hearing is unnecessary, and

(b)   having regard to the notice given by the chief officer of police, cancel the interim authority notice if it considers it necessary for the promotion of the crime prevention objective to do so.

(4) An interim authority notice is cancelled under subsection (3)(b) by the licensing authority giving the relevant person a notice stating that it is cancelled and the authority's reasons for its decision.

(5) The licensing authority must give a copy of a notice under subsection (4) to the chief officer of police for the police area (or each police area) in which the premises are situated.

(6) The premises licence lapses if, and when, a notice is given under subsection (4).

This is subject to paragraph 7(5) of Schedule 5 (reinstatement of premises licence where appeal made against cancellation of interim authority notice).

(7) The relevant licensing authority must not cancel an interim authority notice after a relevant transfer application (within the meaning of section 47) is made in respect of the premises licence.

49 Supplementary provision about interim authority notices

(1) On receipt of an interim authority notice, the relevant licensing authority must issue to the person who gave the notice a copy of the licence and a copy of the summary (in each case certified by the authority to be a true copy).

(2) The copies issued under this section must be copies of the premises licence and summary in the form in which they existed immediately before the licence lapsed under section 27, except that they must specify the person who gave the interim authority notice as the person who is the holder.

(3) This Act applies in relation to a copy issued under this section as it applies in relation to an original licence or summary.

(4) Where a person becomes the holder of a premises licence by virtue of section 47, he must (unless he is the designated premises supervisor under the licence) forthwith notify the supervisor (if any) of the interim authority notice.

(5) A person commits an offence if he fails, without reasonable excuse, to comply with subsection (4).

(6) A person guilty of an offence under subsection (5) is liable on summary conviction to a fine not exceeding level 3 on the standard scale.

Transfer following death etc of licence holder

50 Reinstatement of licence on transfer following death etc of holder

(1) This section applies where –

- (a) a premises licence lapses by virtue of section 27 (death, incapacity or insolvency etc of the holder), but no interim authority notice has effect, or
- (b) a premises licence lapses by virtue of section 28 (surrender).

(2) For the purposes of subsection (1)(a) an interim authority notice ceases to have effect when it is cancelled under section 48 or withdrawn.

(3) Notwithstanding the lapsing of the licence, a person mentioned in section 16(1) (who, in the case of an individual, is aged 18 or over) may apply under section 42 for the transfer of the licence to him provided that the application –

- (a) is made no later than seven days after the day the licence lapsed, and
- (b) is one to which section 43(1)(a) applies.

(4) Where an application is made in accordance with subsection (3), section 43(1)(b) must be disregarded.

(5) Where such an application is made, the premises licence is reinstated from the time the application is received by the relevant licensing authority.

(6) But the licence lapses again if, and when –

- (a) the applicant is notified of the rejection of the application, or
- (b) the application is withdrawn.

(7) Only one application for transfer of the premises licence may be made in reliance on this section.

Review of licences

51 Application for review of premises licence

(1) Where a premises licence has effect, an interested party or a responsible authority may apply to the relevant licensing authority for a review of the licence.

(2) Subsection (1) is subject to regulations under section 54 (form etc of applications etc).

(3) The Secretary of State must by regulations under this section –

    (a)   require the applicant to give a notice containing details of the application to the holder of the premises licence and each responsible authority within such period as may be prescribed;

    (b)   require the authority to advertise the application and invite representations about it to be made to the authority by interested parties and responsible authorities;

    (c)   prescribe the period during which representations may be made by the holder of the premises licence, any responsible authority or any interested party;

    (d)   require any notice under paragraph (a) or advertisement under paragraph (b) to specify that period.

(4) The relevant licensing authority may, at any time, reject any ground for review specified in an application under this section if it is satisfied –

    (a)   that the ground is not relevant to one or more of the licensing objectives, or

    (b)   in the case of an application made by a person other than a responsible authority, that –

        (i)   the ground is frivolous or vexatious, or

        (ii)   the ground is a repetition.

(5) For this purpose a ground for review is a repetition if –

    (a)   it is identical or substantially similar to –

        (i)   a ground for review specified in an earlier application for review made in respect of the same premises licence and determined under section 52, or

        (ii)   representations considered by the relevant licensing authority in accordance with section 18, before it determined the application for the premises licence under that section, or

        (iii)   representations which would have been so considered but for the fact that they were excluded representations by virtue of section 32, and

    (b)   a reasonable interval has not elapsed since that earlier application for review or the grant of the licence (as the case may be).

(6) Where the authority rejects a ground for review under subsection (4)(b), it must notify the applicant of its decision and, if the ground was rejected because it was frivolous or vexatious, the authority must notify him of its reasons for making that decision.

(7) The application is to be treated as rejected to the extent that any of the grounds for review are rejected under subsection (4).

Accordingly the requirements imposed under subsection (3)(a) and (b) and by section 52 (so far as not already met) apply only to so much (if any) of the application as has not been rejected.

52 Determination of application for review

(1) This section applies where –

- (a) the relevant licensing authority receives an application made in accordance with section 51,
- (b) the applicant has complied with any requirement imposed on him under subsection (3)(a) or (d) of that section, and
- (c) the authority has complied with any requirement imposed on it under subsection (3)(b) or (d) of that section.

(2) Before determining the application, the authority must hold a hearing to consider it and any relevant representations.

(3) The authority must, having regard to the application and any relevant representations, take such of the steps mentioned in subsection (4) (if any) as it considers necessary for the promotion of the licensing objectives.

(4) The steps are –

- (a) to modify the conditions of the licence;
- (b) to exclude a licensable activity from the scope of the licence;
- (c) to remove the designated premises supervisor;
- (d) to suspend the licence for a period not exceeding three months;
- (e) to revoke the licence;

and for this purpose the conditions of the licence are modified if any of them is altered or omitted or any new condition is added.

(5) Subsection (3) is subject to sections 19, 20 and 21 (requirement to include certain conditions in premises licences).

(6) Where the authority takes a step mentioned in subsection (4)(a) or (b), it may provide that the modification or exclusion is to have effect for only such period (not exceeding three months) as it may specify.

(7) In this section 'relevant representations' means representations which –

- (a) are relevant to one or more of the licensing objectives, and
- (b) meet the requirements of subsection (8).

(8) The requirements are –

- (a) that the representations are made –
  - (i)   by the holder of the premises licence, a responsible authority or an interested party, and
  - (ii) within the period prescribed under section 51(3)(c),
- (b) that they have not been withdrawn, and

(c)   if they are made by an interested party (who is not also a responsible authority), that they are not, in the opinion of the relevant licensing authority, frivolous or vexatious.

(9) Where the relevant licensing authority determines that any representations are frivolous or vexatious, it must notify the person who made them of the reasons for that determination.

(10) Where a licensing authority determines an application for review under this section it must notify the determination and its reasons for making it to –

(a)   the holder of the licence,
(b)   the applicant,
(c)   any person who made relevant representations, and
(d)   the chief officer of police for the police area (or each police area) in which the premises are situated.

(11) A determination under this section does not have effect –

(a)   until the end of the period given for appealing against the decision, or
(b)   if the decision is appealed against, until the appeal is disposed of.

53 Supplementary provision about review

(1) This section applies where a local authority is both –

(a)   the relevant licensing authority, and
(b)   a responsible authority,

in respect of any premises.

(2) The authority may, in its capacity as a responsible authority, apply under section 51 for a review of any premises licence in respect of the premises.

(3) The authority may, in its capacity as licensing authority, determine that application.

General provision

54 Form etc of applications and notices under Part 3

In relation to any application or notice under this Part, regulations may prescribe –

(a)   its form;
(b)   the manner in which it is to be made or given;
(c)   information and documents that must accompany it.

55 Fees

(1) Regulations may –

(a)   require applications under any provision of this Part (other than section 51) or notices under section 47 to be accompanied by a fee, and
(b)   prescribe the amount of the fee.

(2) Regulations may also require the holder of a premises licence to pay the relevant licensing authority an annual fee.

(3) Regulations under subsection (2) may include provision prescribing –

    (a)   the amount of the fee, and

    (b)   the time at which any such fee is due.

(4) Any fee which is owed to a licensing authority under subsection (2) may be recovered as a debt due to the authority.

Production of licence, rights of entry, etc

56 Licensing authority's duty to update licence document

(1) Where –

    (a)   the relevant licensing authority, in relation to a premises licence, makes a determination or receives a notice under this Part,

    (b)   a premises licence lapses under this Part, or

    (c)   an appeal against a decision under this Part is disposed of,

the relevant licensing authority must make the appropriate amendments (if any) to the licence and, if necessary, issue a new summary of the licence.

(2) Where a licensing authority is not in possession of the licence (or the appropriate part of the licence) it may, for the purposes of discharging its obligations under subsection (1), require the holder of a premises licence to produce the licence (or the appropriate part) to the authority within 14 days from the date on which he is notified of the requirement.

(3) A person commits an offence if he fails, without reasonable excuse, to comply with a requirement under subsection (2).

(4) A person guilty of an offence under subsection (3) is liable on summary conviction to a fine not exceeding level 2 on the standard scale.

57 Duty to keep and produce licence

(1) This section applies whenever premises in respect of which a premises licence has effect are being used for one or more licensable activities authorised by the licence.

(2) The holder of the premises licence must secure that the licence or a certified copy of it is kept at the premises in the custody or under the control of –

    (a)   the holder of the licence, or

    (b)   a person who works at the premises and whom the holder of the licence has nominated in writing for the purposes of this subsection.

(3) The holder of the premises licence must secure that –

    (a)   the summary of the licence or a certified copy of that summary, and

    (b)   a notice specifying the position held at the premises by any person nominated for the purposes of subsection (2),

are prominently displayed at the premises.

(4) The holder of a premises licence commits an offence if he fails, without reasonable excuse, to comply with subsection (2) or (3).

(5) A constable or an authorised person may require the person who, by virtue of arrangements made for the purposes of subsection (2), is required to have the premises licence (or a certified copy of it) in his custody or under his control to produce the licence (or such a copy) for examination.

(6) An authorised person exercising the power conferred by subsection (5) must, if so requested, produce evidence of his authority to exercise the power.

(7) A person commits an offence if he fails, without reasonable excuse, to produce a premises licence or certified copy of a premises licence in accordance with a requirement under subsection (5).

(8) A person guilty of an offence under this section is liable on summary conviction to a fine not exceeding level 2 on the standard scale.

(9) In subsection (3) the reference to the summary of the licence is a reference to the summary issued under section 23 or, where one or more summaries have subsequently been issued under section 56, the most recent summary to have been so issued.

(10) Section 58 makes provision about certified copies of documents for the purposes of this section.

58 Provision supplementary to section 57

(1) Any reference in section 57 to a certified copy of any document is a reference to a copy of that document which is certified to be a true copy by –

  (a)   the relevant licensing authority,
  (b)   a solicitor or notary, or
  (c)   a person of a prescribed description.

(2) Any certified copy produced in accordance with a requirement under section 57(5) must be a copy of the document in the form in which it exists at the time.

(3) A document which purports to be a certified copy of a document is to be taken to be such a copy, and to comply with the requirements of subsection (2), unless the contrary is shown.

59 Inspection of premises before grant of licence etc

(1) In this section 'relevant application' means an application under –

  (a)   section 17 (grant of licence),
  (b)   section 29 (provisional statement),
  (c)   section 34 (variation of licence), or
  (d)   section 51 (review of licence).

(2) A constable or an authorised person may, at any reasonable time before the determination of a relevant application, enter the premises to which the application relates to assess –

(a) in a case within subsection (1)(a), (b) or (c), the likely effect of the grant of the application on the promotion of the licensing objectives, and

(b) in a case within subsection (1)(d), the effect of the activities authorised by the premises licence on the promotion of those objectives.

(3) An authorised person exercising the power conferred by this section must, if so requested, produce evidence of his authority to exercise the power.

(4) A constable or an authorised person exercising the power conferred by this section in relation to an application within subsection (1)(d) may, if necessary, use reasonable force.

(5) A person commits an offence if he intentionally obstructs an authorised person exercising a power conferred by this section.

(6) A person guilty of an offence under this section is liable on summary conviction to a fine not exceeding level 2 on the standard scale.

PART 4

CLUBS

Introductory

60 Club premises certificate

(1) In this Act 'club premises certificate' means a certificate granted under this Part –

(a) in respect of premises occupied by, and habitually used for the purposes of, a club,

(b) by the relevant licensing authority, and

(c) certifying the matters specified in subsection (2).

(2) Those matters are –

(a) that the premises may be used by the club for one or more qualifying club activities specified in the certificate, and

(b) that the club is a qualifying club in relation to each of those activities (see section 61).

Qualifying clubs

61 Qualifying clubs

(1) This section applies for determining for the purposes of this Part whether a club is a qualifying club in relation to a qualifying club activity.

(2) A club is a qualifying club in relation to the supply of alcohol to members or guests if it satisfies both –

(a) the general conditions in section 62, and

(b) the additional conditions in section 64.

(3) A club is a qualifying club in relation to the provision of regulated entertainment if it satisfies the general conditions in section 62.

62 The general conditions

(1) The general conditions which a club must satisfy if it is to be a qualifying club in relation to a qualifying club activity are the following.

(2) Condition 1 is that under the rules of the club persons may not –

(a)   be admitted to membership, or

(b)   be admitted, as candidates for membership, to any of the privileges of membership,

without an interval of at least two days between their nomination or application for membership and their admission.

(3) Condition 2 is that under the rules of the club persons becoming members without prior nomination or application may not be admitted to the privileges of membership without an interval of at least two days between their becoming members and their admission.

(4) Condition 3 is that the club is established and conducted in good faith as a club (see section 63).

(5) Condition 4 is that the club has at least 25 members.

(6) Condition 5 is that alcohol is not supplied, or intended to be supplied, to members on the premises otherwise than by or on behalf of the club.

63 Determining whether a club is established and conducted in good faith

(1) In determining for the purposes of condition 3 in subsection (4) of section 62 whether a club is established and conducted in good faith as a club, the matters to be taken into account are those specified in subsection (2).

(2) Those matters are –

(a)   any arrangements restricting the club's freedom of purchase of alcohol;

(b)   any provision in the rules, or arrangements, under which –

(i)   money or property of the club, or

(ii)   any gain arising from the carrying on of the club,

is or may be applied otherwise than for the benefit of the club as a whole or for charitable, benevolent or political purposes;

(c)   the arrangements for giving members information about the finances of the club;

(d)   the books of account and other records kept to ensure the accuracy of that information;

(e)   the nature of the premises occupied by the club.

(3) If a licensing authority decides for any purpose of this Act that a club does not satisfy condition 3 in subsection (4) of section 62, the authority must give the club notice of the decision and of the reasons for it.

64 The additional conditions for the supply of alcohol

(1) The additional conditions which a club must satisfy if it is to be a qualifying club in relation to the supply of alcohol to members or guests are the following.

(2) Additional condition 1 is that (so far as not managed by the club in general meeting or otherwise by the general body of members) the purchase of alcohol for the club, and the supply of alcohol by the club, are managed by a committee whose members –

    (a)   are members of the club;
    (b)   have attained the age of 18 years; and
    (c)   are elected by the members of the club.

This subsection is subject to section 65 (which makes special provision for industrial and provident societies, friendly societies etc).

(3) Additional condition 2 is that no arrangements are, or are intended to be, made for any person to receive at the expense of the club any commission, percentage or similar payment on, or with reference to, purchases of alcohol by the club.

(4) Additional condition 3 is that no arrangements are, or are intended to be, made for any person directly or indirectly to derive any pecuniary benefit from the supply of alcohol by or on behalf of the club to members or guests, apart from –

    (a)   any benefit accruing to the club as a whole, or
    (b)   any benefit which a person derives indirectly by reason of the supply giving rise or contributing to a general gain from the carrying on of the club.

65 Industrial and provident societies, friendly societies etc

(1) Subsection (2) applies in relation to any club which is –

    (a)   a registered society, within the meaning of the Industrial and Provident Societies Act 1965 (c 12) (see section 74(1) of that Act),
    (b)   a registered society, within the meaning of the Friendly Societies Act 1974 (c 46) (see section 111(1) of that Act), or
    (c)   a registered friendly society, within the meaning of the Friendly Societies Act 1992 (c 40) (see section 116 of that Act).

(2) Any such club is to be taken for the purposes of this Act to satisfy additional condition 1 in subsection (2) of section 64 if and to the extent that –

    (a)   the purchase of alcohol for the club, and
    (b)   the supply of alcohol by the club,

are under the control of the members or of a committee appointed by the members.

(3) References in this Act, other than this section, to –

    (a)   subsection (2) of section 64, or

(b)   additional condition 1 in that subsection,

are references to it as read with subsection (1) of this section.

(4) Subject to subsection (5), this Act applies in relation to an incorporated friendly society as it applies in relation to a club, and accordingly –

(a)   the premises of the society are to be treated as the premises of a club,
(b)   the members of the society are to be treated as the members of the club, and
(c)   anything done by or on behalf of the society is to be treated as done by or on behalf of the club.

(5) In determining for the purposes of section 61 whether an incorporated friendly society is a qualifying club in relation to a qualifying club activity, the society is to be taken to satisfy the following conditions –

(a)   condition 3 in subsection (4) of section 62,
(b)   condition 5 in subsection (6) of that section,
(c)   the additional conditions in section 64.

(6) In this section 'incorporated friendly society' has the same meaning as in the Friendly Societies Act 1992 (see section 116 of that Act).

66 Miners' welfare institutes

(1) Subject to subsection (2), this Act applies to a relevant miners' welfare institute as it applies to a club, and accordingly –

(a)   the premises of the institute are to be treated as the premises of a club,
(b)   the persons enrolled as members of the institute are to be treated as the members of the club, and
(c)   anything done by or on behalf of the trustees or managers in carrying on the institute is to be treated as done by or on behalf of the club.

(2) In determining for the purposes of section 61 whether a relevant miners' welfare institute is a qualifying club in relation to a qualifying club activity, the institute is to be taken to satisfy the following conditions –

(a)   condition 3 in subsection (4) of section 62,
(b)   condition 4 in subsection (5) of that section,
(c)   condition 5 in subsection (6) of that section,
(d)   the additional conditions in section 64.

(3) For the purposes of this section –

(a)   'miners' welfare institute' means an association organised for the social well-being and recreation of persons employed in or about coal mines (or of such persons in particular), and
(b)   a miners' welfare institute is 'relevant' if it satisfies one of the following conditions.

(4) The first condition is that –

(a)   the institute is managed by a committee or board, and
(b)   at least two thirds of the committee or board consists –

(i)   partly of persons appointed or nominated, or appointed or elected from among persons nominated, by one or more licensed operators within the meaning of the Coal Industry Act 1994 (c 21), and

(ii)   partly of persons appointed or nominated, or appointed or elected from among persons nominated, by one or more organisations representing persons employed in or about coal mines.

(5) The second condition is that –

(a)   the institute is managed by a committee or board, but

(b)   the making of –

    (i)   an appointment or nomination falling within subsection (4)(b)(i), or

    (ii)   an appointment or nomination falling within subsection (4)(b)(ii),

is not practicable or would not be appropriate, and

(c)   at least two thirds of the committee or board consists –

    (i)   partly of persons employed, or formerly employed, in or about coal mines, and

    (ii)   partly of persons appointed by the Coal Industry Social Welfare Organisation or a body or person to which the functions of that Organisation have been transferred under section 12(3) of the Miners' Welfare Act 1952 (c 23).

(6) The third condition is that the premises of the institute are held on trusts to which section 2 of the Recreational Charities Act 1958 (c 17) applies.

Interpretation

67 Associate members and their guests

(1) Any reference in this Act (other than this section) to a guest of a member of a club includes a reference to –

(a)   an associate member of the club, and

(b)   a guest of an associate member of the club.

(2) For the purposes of this Act a person is an 'associate member' of a club if –

(a)   in accordance with the rules of the club, he is admitted to its premises as being a member of another club, and

(b)   that other club is a recognised club (see section 193).

68 The relevant licensing authority

(1) For the purposes of this Part the 'relevant licensing authority' in relation to any premises is determined in accordance with this section.

(2) Subject to subsection (3), the relevant licensing authority is the authority in whose area the premises are situated.

(3) Where the premises are situated in the areas of two or more licensing authorities, the relevant licensing authority is –

(a) the licensing authority in whose area the greater or greatest part of the premises is situated, or

(b) if there is no authority to which paragraph (a) applies, such one of those authorities as is nominated in accordance with subsection (4).

(4) In a case within subsection (3)(b), an applicant for a club premises certificate must nominate one of the licensing authorities as the relevant licensing authority in relation to the application and any certificate granted as a result of it.

69 Authorised persons, interested parties and responsible authorities

(1) In this Part in relation to any premises each of the following expressions has the meaning given to it by this section –

　'authorised person',
　'interested party',
　'responsible authority'.

(2) 'Authorised person' means any of the following –

(a) an officer of a licensing authority in whose area the premises are situated who is authorised by that authority for the purposes of this Act,

(b) an inspector appointed under section 18 of the Fire Precautions Act 1971 (c 40),

(c) an inspector appointed under section 19 of the Health and Safety at Work etc Act 1974 (c 37),

(d) an officer of a local authority, in whose area the premises are situated, who is authorised by that authority for the purposes of exercising one or more of its statutory functions in relation to minimising or preventing the risk of pollution of the environment or of harm to human health,

(e) in relation to a vessel, an inspector, or a surveyor of ships, appointed under section 256 of the Merchant Shipping Act 1995 (c 21),

(f) a person prescribed for the purposes of this subsection.

(3) 'Interested party' means any of the following –

(a) a person living in the vicinity of the premises,

(b) a body representing persons who live in that vicinity,

(c) a person involved in a business in that vicinity,

(d) a body representing persons involved in such businesses.

(4) 'Responsible authority' means any of the following –

(a) the chief officer of police for any police area in which the premises are situated,

(b) the fire authority for any area in which the premises are situated,

(c) the enforcing authority within the meaning given by section 18 of the Health and Safety at Work etc Act 1974 (c 37) for any area in which the premises are situated,

(d) the local planning authority within the meaning given by the Town and Country Planning Act 1990 (c 8) for any area in which the premises are situated,

(e) the local authority by which statutory functions are exercisable in any area in which the premises are situated in relation to minimising or preventing the risk of pollution of the environment or of harm to human health,

(f) a body which –

(i) represents those who, in relation to any such area, are responsible for, or interested in, matters relating to the protection of children from harm, and

(ii) is recognised by the licensing authority for that area for the purposes of this section as being competent to advise it on such matters,

(g) any licensing authority (other than the relevant licensing authority) in whose area part of the premises is situated,

(h) in relation to a vessel –

(i) a navigation authority (within the meaning of section 221(1) of the Water Resources Act 1991 (c 57)) having functions in relation to the waters where the vessel is usually moored or berthed or any waters where it is, or is proposed to be, navigated at a time when it is used for qualifying club activities,

(ii) the Environment Agency,

(iii) the British Waterways Board, or

(iv) the Secretary of State,

(i) a person prescribed for the purposes of this subsection.

(5) For the purposes of this section, 'statutory function' means a function conferred by or under any enactment.

70 Other definitions relating to clubs

In this Part –

'secretary', in relation to a club, includes any person (whether or not an officer of the club) performing the duties of a secretary;

'supply of alcohol to members or guests' means, in the case of any club, –

(a) the supply of alcohol by or on behalf of the club to, or to the order of, a member of the club, or

(b) the sale by retail of alcohol by or on behalf of the club to a guest of a member of the club for consumption on the premises where the sale takes place,

and related expressions are to be construed accordingly.

Grant of club premises certificate

71 Application for club premises certificate

(1) A club may apply for a club premises certificate in respect of any premises which are occupied by, and habitually used for the purposes of, the club.

(2) Any application for a club premises certificate must be made to the relevant licensing authority.

(3) Subsection (2) is subject to regulations under –

(a) section 91 (form etc of applications and notices under this Part);

(b)   section 92 (fees to accompany applications and notices).

(4) An application under this section must also be accompanied by –

(a)   a club operating schedule,
(b)   a plan of the premises to which the application relates, in the prescribed form, and
(c)   a copy of the rules of the club.

(5) A 'club operating schedule' is a document which is in the prescribed form, and includes a statement of the following matters –

(a)   the qualifying club activities to which the application relates ('the relevant qualifying club activities'),
(b)   the times during which it is proposed that the relevant qualifying club activities are to take place,
(c)   any other times during which it is proposed that the premises are to be open to members and their guests,
(d)   where the relevant qualifying club activities include the supply of alcohol, whether the supplies are proposed to be for consumption on the premises or both on and off the premises,
(e)   the steps which it is proposed to take to promote the licensing objectives, and
(f)   such other matters as may be prescribed.

(6) The Secretary of State must by regulations –

(a)   require an applicant to advertise the application within the prescribed period –
    (i)   in the prescribed form, and
    (ii)   in a manner which is prescribed and is likely to bring the application to the attention of the interested parties likely to be affected by it;
(b)   require an applicant to give notice of the application to each responsible authority, and such other persons as may be prescribed within the prescribed period;
(c)   prescribe the period during which interested parties and responsible authorities may make representations to the relevant licensing authority about the application.

72 Determination of application for club premises certificate

(1) This section applies where the relevant licensing authority –

(a)   receives an application for a club premises certificate made in accordance with section 71, and
(b)   is satisfied that the applicant has complied with any requirement imposed on the applicant under subsection (6) of that section.

(2) Subject to subsection (3), the authority must grant the certificate in accordance with the application subject only to –

(a)   such conditions as are consistent with the club operating schedule accompanying the application, and

(b) any conditions which must under section 73(2) to (5) or 74 be included in the certificate.

(3) Where relevant representations are made, the authority must –

(a) hold a hearing to consider them, unless the authority, the applicant and each person who has made such representations agree that a hearing is unnecessary, and

(b) having regard to the representations, take such of the steps mentioned in subsection (4) (if any) as it considers necessary for the promotion of the licensing objectives.

(4) The steps are –

(a) to grant the certificate subject to –
  (i) the conditions mentioned in subsection (2)(a) modified to such extent as the authority considers necessary for the promotion of the licensing objectives, and
  (ii) any conditions which must under section 73(2) to (5) or 74 be included in the certificate;

(b) to exclude from the scope of the certificate any of the qualifying club activities to which the application relates;

(c) to reject the application.

(5) Subsections (2) and (3)(b) are subject to section 73(1) (certificate may authorise off-supplies only if it authorises on-supplies).

(6) For the purposes of subsection (4)(a)(4)(a) the conditions mentioned in subsection (2)(a) are modified if any of them is altered or omitted or any new condition is added.

(7) For the purposes of this section, 'relevant representations' means representations which –

(a) are about the likely effect of the grant of the certificate on the promotion of the licensing objectives, and

(b) meet the requirements of subsection (8).

(8) The requirements are –

(a) that the representations were made by an interested party or responsible authority within the period prescribed under section 71(6)(c),

(b) that they have not been withdrawn, and

(c) in the case of representations made by an interested party (who is not also a responsible authority), that they are not, in the opinion of the relevant licensing authority, frivolous or vexatious.

(9) Where the authority determines for the purposes of subsection (8)(c) that any representations are frivolous or vexatious, it must notify the person who made them of the reasons for its determination.

(10) In discharging its duty under subsection (2) or (3)(b) a licensing authority may grant a club premises certificate subject to different conditions in respect of –

(a) different parts of the premises concerned;

(b)   different qualifying club activities.

73 Certificate authorising supply of alcohol for consumption off the premises

(1) A club premises certificate may not authorise the supply of alcohol for consumption off the premises unless it also authorises the supply of alcohol to a member of the club for consumption on those premises.

(2) A club premises certificate which authorises the supply of alcohol for consumption off the premises must include the following conditions.

(3) The first condition is that the supply must be made at a time when the premises are open for the purposes of supplying alcohol, in accordance with the club premises certificate, to members of the club for consumption on the premises.

(4) The second condition is that any alcohol supplied for consumption off the premises must be in a sealed container.

(5) The third condition is that any supply of alcohol for consumption off the premises must be made to a member of the club in person.

74 Mandatory condition: exhibition of films

(1) Where a club premises certificate authorises the exhibition of films, the certificate must include a condition requiring the admission of children to the exhibition of any film to be restricted in accordance with this section.

(2) Where the film classification body is specified in the certificate, unless subsection (3)(b) applies, admission of children must be restricted in accordance with any recommendation made by that body.

(3) Where –

(a)   the film classification body is not specified in the certificate, or
(b)   the relevant licensing authority has notified the club which holds the certificate that this subsection applies to the film in question,

admission of children must be restricted in accordance with any recommendation made by that licensing authority.

(4) In this section –

'children' means persons aged under 18; and
'film classification body' means the person or persons designated as the authority under section 4 of the Video Recordings Act 1984 (c 39) (authority to determine suitability of video works for classification).

75 Prohibited conditions: associate members and their guests

(1) Where the rules of a club provide for the sale by retail of alcohol on any premises by or on behalf of the club to, or to a guest of, an associate member of the club, no condition may be attached to a club premises certificate in respect of the sale by retail of alcohol on those premises by or on behalf of the club so as to prevent the sale by retail of alcohol to any such associate member or guest.

(2) Where the rules of a club provide for the provision of any regulated entertainment on any premises by or on behalf of the club to, or to a guest of, an associate member of the club, no condition may be attached to a club premises certificate in respect of the provision of any such regulated entertainment on those premises by or on behalf of the club so as to prevent its provision to any such associate member or guest.

76 Prohibited conditions: plays

(1) In relation to a club premises certificate which authorises the performance of plays, no condition may be attached to the certificate as to the nature of the plays which may be performed, or the manner of performing plays, under the certificate.

(2) But subsection (1) does not prevent a licensing authority imposing, in accordance with section 72(2) or (3)(b), 85(3)(b) or 88(3), any condition which it considers necessary on the grounds of public safety.

77 Grant or rejection of application for club premises certificate

(1) Where an application is granted under section 72, the relevant licensing authority must forthwith –

    (a) give a notice to that effect to –
        (i)   the applicant,
        (ii)   any person who made relevant representations in respect of the application, and
        (iii) the chief officer of police for the police area (or each police area) in which the premises are situated, and
    (b) issue the club with the club premises certificate and a summary of it.

(2) Where relevant representations were made in respect of the application, the notice under subsection (1)(a) must specify the authority's reasons for its decision as to the steps (if any) to take under section 72(3)(b).

(3) Where an application is rejected under section 72, the relevant licensing authority must forthwith give a notice to that effect, stating its reasons for that decision, to –

    (a) the applicant,
    (b) any person who made relevant representations in respect of the application, and
    (c) the chief officer of police for the police area (or each police area) in which the premises are situated.

(4) In this section 'relevant representations' has the meaning given in section 72(6).

78 Form of certificate and summary

(1) A club premises certificate and the summary of such a certificate must be in the prescribed form.

(2) Regulations under subsection (1) must, in particular, provide for the certificate to –

(a)   specify the name of the club and the address which is to be its relevant registered address, as defined in section 184(7);

(b)   specify the address of the premises to which the certificate relates;

(c)   include a plan of those premises;

(d)   specify the qualifying club activities for which the premises may be used;

(e)   specify the conditions subject to which the certificate has effect.

79 Theft, loss, etc of certificate or summary

(1) Where a club premises certificate or summary is lost, stolen, damaged or destroyed, the club may apply to the relevant licensing authority for a copy of the certificate or summary.

(2) Subsection (1) is subject to regulations under section 92(1) (power to prescribe fee to accompany application).

(3) Where an application is made in accordance with this section, the relevant licensing authority must issue the club with a copy of the certificate or summary (certified by the authority to be a true copy) if it is satisfied that –

(a)   the certificate or summary has been lost, stolen, damaged or destroyed, and

(b)   where it has been lost or stolen, the club has reported the loss or theft to the police.

(4) The copy issued under this section must be a copy of the club premises certificate or summary in the form in which it existed immediately before it was lost, stolen, damaged or destroyed.

(5) This Act applies in relation to a copy issued under this section as it applies in relation to an original club premises certificate or summary.

Duration of certificate

80 Period of validity of club premises certificate

(1) A club premises certificate has effect until such time as –

(a)   it is withdrawn under section 88 or 90, or

(b)   it lapses by virtue of section 81(3) (surrender).

(2) But a club premises certificate does not have effect during any period when it is suspended under section 88.

81 Surrender of club premises certificate

(1) Where a club which holds a club premises certificate decides to surrender it, the club may give the relevant licensing authority a notice to that effect.

(2) The notice must be accompanied by the club premises certificate or, if that is not practicable, by a statement of the reasons for the failure to produce the certificate.

(3) Where a notice is given in accordance with this section, the certificate lapses on receipt of the notice by the authority.

Duty to notify certain changes

82 Notification of change of name or alteration of rules of club

(1) Where a club –

(a) holds a club premises certificate, or

(b) has made an application for a club premises certificate which has not been determined by the relevant licensing authority,

the secretary of the club must give the relevant licensing authority notice of any change in the name, or alteration made to the rules, of the club.

(2) Subsection (1) is subject to regulations under section 92(1) (power to prescribe fee to accompany application).

(3) A notice under subsection (1) by a club which holds a club premises certificate must be accompanied by the certificate or, if that is not practicable, by a statement of the reasons for the failure to produce the certificate.

(4) An authority notified under this section of a change in the name, or alteration to the rules, of a club must amend the club premises certificate accordingly.

(5) But nothing in subsection (4) requires or authorises the making of any amendment to a club premises certificate so as to change the premises to which the certificate relates (and no amendment made under that subsection to a club premises certificate has effect so as to change those premises).

(6) If a notice required by this section is not given within the 28 days following the day on which the change of name or alteration to the rules is made, the secretary of the club commits an offence.

(7) A person guilty of an offence under subsection (6) is liable on summary conviction to a fine not exceeding level 2 on the standard scale.

83 Change of relevant registered address of club

(1) A club which holds a club premises certificate may give the relevant licensing authority notice of any change desired to be made in the address which is to be the club's relevant registered address.

(2) If a club which holds a club premises certificate ceases to have any authority to make use of the address which is its relevant registered address, it must as soon as reasonably practicable give to the relevant licensing authority notice of the change to be made in the address which is to be the club's relevant registered address.

(3) Subsections (1) and (2) are subject to regulations under section 92(1) (power to prescribe fee to accompany application).

(4) A notice under subsection (1) or (2) must also be accompanied by the club premises certificate or, if that is not practicable, by a statement of the reasons for the failure to produce the certificate.

(5) An authority notified under subsection (1) or (2) of a change to be made in the relevant registered address of a club must amend the club premises certificate accordingly.

(6) If a club fails, without reasonable excuse, to comply with subsection (2) the secretary commits an offence.

(7) A person guilty of an offence under subsection (6) is liable on summary conviction to a fine not exceeding level 2 on the standard scale.

(8) In this section 'relevant registered address' has the meaning given in section 184(7).

Variation of certificates

84 Application to vary club premises certificate

(1) A club which holds a club premises certificate may apply to the relevant licensing authority for variation of the certificate.

(2) Subsection (1) is subject to regulations under –

  (a) section 91 (form etc of applications);
  (b) section 92 (fees to accompany applications).

(3) An application under this section must also be accompanied by the club premises certificate or, if that is not practicable, by a statement of the reasons for the failure to provide the certificate.

(4) The duty to make regulations imposed on the Secretary of State by subsection (6) of section 71 (advertisement etc of application) applies in relation to applications under this section as it applies in relation to applications under that section.

85 Determination of application under section 84

(1) This section applies where the relevant licensing authority –

  (a) receives an application, made in accordance with section 84, to vary a club premises certificate, and
  (b) is satisfied that the applicant has complied with any requirement imposed by virtue of subsection (4) of that section.

(2) Subject to subsection (3) and section 86(6), the authority must grant the application.

(3) Where relevant representations are made, the authority must –

  (a) hold a hearing to consider them, unless the authority, the applicant and each person who has made such representations agree that a hearing is unnecessary, and
  (b) having regard to the representations, take such of the steps mentioned in subsection (4) (if any) as it considers necessary for the promotion of the licensing objectives.

(4) The steps are –

  (a) to modify the conditions of the certificate;
  (b) to reject the whole or part of the application;

and for this purpose the conditions of the certificate are modified if any of them is altered or omitted or any new condition is added.

(5) In this section 'relevant representations' means representations which –

    (a)   are about the likely effect of the grant of the application on the promotion of the licensing objectives, and

    (b)   meet the requirements of subsection (6).

(6) The requirements are –

    (a)   that the representations are made by an interested party or responsible authority within the period prescribed under section 71(6)(c) by virtue of section 84(4),

    (b)   that they have not been withdrawn, and

    (c)   in the case of representations made by an interested party (who is not also a responsible authority), that they are not, in the opinion of the relevant licensing authority, frivolous or vexatious.

(7) Subsections (2) and (3) are subject to sections 73 and 74 (mandatory conditions relating to supply of alcohol for consumption off the premises and to exhibition of films).

86 Supplementary provision about applications under section 84

(1) Where an application (or any part of an application) is granted under section 85, the relevant licensing authority must forthwith give a notice to that effect to –

    (a)   the applicant,

    (b)   any person who made relevant representations in respect of the application, and

    (c)   the chief officer of police for the police area (or each police area) in which the premises are situated.

(2) Where relevant representations were made in respect of the application, the notice under subsection (1) must specify the authority's reasons for its decision as to the steps (if any) to take under section 85(3)(b).

(3) The notice under subsection (1) must specify the time when the variation in question takes effect.

That time is the time specified in the application or, if that time is before the applicant is given the notice, such later time as the relevant licensing authority specifies in the notice.

(4) Where an application (or any part of an application) is rejected under section 85, the relevant licensing authority must forthwith give a notice to that effect stating its reasons for rejecting the application to –

    (a)   the applicant,

    (b)   any person who made relevant representations, and

    (c)   the chief officer of police for the police area (or each police area) in which the premises are situated.

(5) Where the relevant licensing authority determines for the purposes of section 85(6)(c) that any representations are frivolous or vexatious, it must give the person who made them its reasons for that determination.

(6) A club premises certificate may not be varied under section 85 so as to vary substantially the premises to which it relates.

(7) In discharging its duty under subsection (2) or (3)(b) of that section, a licensing authority may vary a club premises certificate so that it has effect subject to different conditions in respect of –

> (a) different parts of the premises concerned;
> (b) different qualifying club activities.

(8) In this section 'relevant representations' has the meaning given in section 85(5).

Review of certificates

87 Application for review of club premises certificate

(1) Where a club holds a club premises certificate –

> (a) an interested party,
> (b) a responsible authority, or
> (c) a member of the club,

may apply to the relevant licensing authority for a review of the certificate.

(2) Subsection (1) is subject to regulations under section 91 (form etc of applications).

(3) The Secretary of State must by regulations under this section –

> (a) require the applicant to give a notice containing details of the application to the club and each responsible authority within such period as may be prescribed;
> (b) require the authority to advertise the application and invite representations relating to it to be made to the authority;
> (c) prescribe the period during which representations may be made by the club, any responsible authority and any interested party;
> (d) require any notice under paragraph (a) or advertisement under paragraph (b) to specify that period.

(4) The relevant licensing authority may, at any time, reject any ground for review specified in an application under this section if it is satisfied –

> (a) that the ground is not relevant to one or more of the licensing objectives, or
> (b) in the case of an application made by a person other than a responsible authority, that –
> > (i)   the ground is frivolous or vexatious, or
> > (ii) the ground is a repetition.

(5) For this purpose a ground for review is a repetition if –

> (a) it is identical or substantially similar to –
> > (i)   a ground for review specified in an earlier application for review made in respect of the same club premises certificate and determined under section 88, or

> > (ii) representations considered by the relevant licensing authority in accordance with section 72, before it determined the application for the club premises certificate under that section, and
>
> (b) a reasonable interval has not elapsed since that earlier application or that grant.

(6) Where the authority rejects a ground for review under subsection (4)(b), it must notify the applicant of its decision and, if the ground was rejected because it was frivolous or vexatious, the authority must notify him of its reasons for making that decision.

(7) The application is to be treated as rejected to the extent that any of the grounds for review are rejected under subsection (4).

Accordingly, the requirements imposed under subsection (3)(a) and (b) and by section 88 (so far as not already met) apply only to so much (if any) of the application as has not been rejected.

88 Determination of application for review

(1) This section applies where –

> (a) the relevant licensing authority receives an application made in accordance with section 87,
> (b) the applicant has complied with any requirement imposed by virtue of subsection (3)(a) or (d) of that section, and
> (c) the authority has complied with any requirement imposed on it under subsection (3)(b) or (d) of that section.

(2) Before determining the application, the authority must hold a hearing to consider it and any relevant representations.

(3) The authority must, having regard to the application and any relevant representations, take such of the steps mentioned in subsection (4) (if any) as it considers necessary for the promotion of the licensing objectives.

(4) The steps are –

> (a) to modify the conditions of the certificate;
> (b) to exclude a qualifying club activity from the scope of the certificate;
> (c) to suspend the certificate for a period not exceeding three months;
> (d) to withdraw the certificate;

and for this purpose the conditions of the certificate are modified if any of them is altered or omitted or any new condition is added.

(5) Subsection (3) is subject to sections 73 and 74 (mandatory conditions relating to supply of alcohol for consumption off the premises and to exhibition of films).

(6) Where the authority takes a step within subsection (4)(a) or (b), it may provide that the modification or exclusion is to have effect for only such period (not exceeding three months) as it may specify.

(7) In this section 'relevant representations' means representations which –

(a)   are relevant to one or more of the licensing objectives, and

(b)   meet the requirements of subsection (8).

(8) The requirements are –

(a)   that the representations are made by the club, a responsible authority or an interested party within the period prescribed under section 87(3)(c),

(b)   that they have not been withdrawn, and

(c)   if they are made by an interested party (who is not also a responsible authority), that they are not, in the opinion of the relevant licensing authority, frivolous or vexatious.

(9) Where the relevant licensing authority determines that any representations are frivolous or vexatious, it must give the person who made them its reasons for that determination.

(10) Where a licensing authority determines an application for review under this section it must notify the determination and its reasons for making it to –

(a)   the club,

(b)   the applicant,

(c)   any person who made relevant representations, and

(d)   the chief officer of police for the police area (or each police area) in which the premises are situated.

(11) A determination under this section does not have effect –

(a)   until the end of the period given for appealing against the decision, or

(b)   if the decision is appealed against, until the appeal is disposed of.

89 Supplementary provision about review

(1) This section applies where a local authority is both –

(a)   the relevant licensing authority, and

(b)   a responsible authority,

in respect of any premises.

(2) The authority may, in its capacity as responsible authority, apply under section 87 for a review of any club premises certificate in respect of the premises.

(3) The authority may in its capacity as licensing authority determine that application.

Withdrawal of certificates

90 Club ceasing to be a qualifying club

(1) Where –

(a)   a club holds a club premises certificate, and

(b)   it appears to the relevant licensing authority that the club does not satisfy the conditions for being a qualifying club in relation to a qualifying club activity to which the certificate relates (see section 61), the authority must give a notice to the club withdrawing the certificate, so far as relating to that activity.

(2) Where the only reason that the club does not satisfy the conditions for being a qualifying club in relation to the activity in question is that the club has fewer than the required number of members, the notice withdrawing the certificate must state that the withdrawal –

    (a)   does not take effect until immediately after the end of the period of three months following the date of the notice, and

    (b)   will not take effect if, at the end of that period, the club again has at least the required number of members.

(3) The references in subsection (2) to the required number of members are references to the minimum number of members required by condition 4 in section 62(5) (25 at the passing of this Act).

(4) Nothing in subsection (2) prevents the giving of a further notice of withdrawal under this section at any time.

(5) Where a justice of the peace is satisfied, on information on oath, that there are reasonable grounds for believing –

    (a)   that a club which holds a club premises certificate does not satisfy the conditions for being a qualifying club in relation to a qualifying club activity to which the certificate relates, and

    (b)   that evidence of that fact is to be obtained at the premises to which the certificate relates,

he may issue a warrant authorising a constable to enter the premises, if necessary by force, at any time within one month from the time of the issue of the warrant, and search them.

(6) A person who enters premises under the authority of a warrant under subsection (5) may seize and remove any documents relating to the business of the club in question.

General provision

91 Form etc of applications and notices under Part 4

In relation to any application or notice under this Part, regulations may prescribe –

    (a)   its form;

    (b)   the manner in which it is to be made or given;

    (c)   information and documents that must accompany it.

92 Fees

(1) Regulations may –

    (a)   require applications under any provision of this Part (other than section 87) to be accompanied by a fee, and

    (b)   prescribe the amount of the fee.

(2) Regulations may also require the payment of an annual fee to the relevant licensing authority by or on behalf of a club which holds a club premises certificate.

(3) Regulations under subsection (2) may include provision –

(a) imposing liability for the making of the payment on the secretary or such other officers or members of the club as may be prescribed,
(b) prescribing the amount of any such fee, and
(c) prescribing the time at which any such fee is due.

(4) Any fee which is owed to a licensing authority under subsection (2) may be recovered as a debt due to the authority from any person liable to make the payment by virtue of subsection (3)(a).

Production of certificate, rights of entry, etc

93 Licensing authority's duty to update club premises certificate

(1) Where –

(a) the relevant licensing authority, in relation to a club premises certificate, makes a determination or receives a notice under this Part, or
(b) an appeal against a decision under this Part is disposed of,

the relevant licensing authority must make the appropriate amendments (if any) to the certificate and, if necessary, issue a new summary of the certificate.

(2) Where a licensing authority is not in possession of the club premises certificate, it may, for the purpose of discharging its obligations under subsection (1), require the secretary of the club to produce the certificate to the authority within 14 days from the date on which the club is notified of the requirement.

(3) A person commits an offence if he fails, without reasonable excuse, to comply with a requirement under subsection (2).

(4) A person guilty of an offence under subsection (3) is liable on summary conviction to a fine not exceeding level 2 on the standard scale.

94 Duty to keep and produce certificate

(1) This section applies whenever premises in respect of which a club premises certificate has effect are being used for one or more qualifying club activities authorised by the certificate.

(2) The secretary of the club must secure that the certificate, or a certified copy of it, is kept at the premises in the custody or under the control of a person (the 'nominated person') who –

(a) falls within subsection (3),
(b) has been nominated for the purpose by the secretary in writing, and
(c) has been identified to the relevant licensing authority in a notice given by the secretary.

(3) The persons who fall within this subsection are –

    (a)   the secretary of the club,

    (b)   any member of the club,

    (c)   any person who works at the premises for the purposes of the club.

(4) The nominated person must secure that –

    (a)   the summary of the certificate or a certified copy of that summary, and

    (b)   a notice specifying the position which he holds at the premises,

are prominently displayed at the premises.

(5) The secretary commits an offence if he fails, without reasonable excuse, to comply with subsection (2).

(6) The nominated person commits an offence if he fails, without reasonable excuse, to comply with subsection (4).

(7) A constable or an authorised person may require the nominated person to produce the club premises certificate (or certified copy) for examination.

(8) An authorised person exercising the power conferred by subsection (7) must, if so requested, produce evidence of his authority to exercise the power.

(9) A person commits an offence if he fails, without reasonable excuse, to produce a club premises certificate or certified copy of a club premises certificate in accordance with a requirement under subsection (7).

(10) A person guilty of an offence under this section is liable on summary conviction to a fine not exceeding level 2 on the standard scale.

(11) In subsection (4) the reference to the summary of the certificate is a reference to the summary issued under section 77 or, where one or more summaries have subsequently been issued under section 93, the most recent summary to be so issued.

(12) Section 95 makes provision about certified copies of club premises certificates and of summaries of club premises certificates for the purposes of this section.

95 Provision supplementary to section 94

(1) Any reference in section 94 to a certified copy of a document is a reference to a copy of the document which is certified to be a true copy by –

    (a)   the relevant licensing authority,

    (b)   a solicitor or notary, or

    (c)   a person of a prescribed description.

(2) Any certified copy produced in accordance with a requirement under subsection 94(7) must be a copy of the document in the form in which it exists at the time.

(3) A document which purports to be a certified copy of a document is to be taken to be such a copy, and to comply with the requirements of subsection (2), unless the contrary is shown.

96 Inspection of premises before grant of certificate etc

(1) Subsection (2) applies where –

    (a)   a club applies for a club premises certificate in respect of any premises,

    (b)   a club applies under section 84 for the variation of a club premises certificate held by it, or

    (c)   an application is made under section 87 for review of a club premises certificate.

(2) On production of his authority –

    (a)   an authorised person, or

    (b)   a constable authorised by the chief officer of police,

may enter and inspect the premises.

(3) Any entry and inspection under this section must take place at a reasonable time on a day –

    (a)   which is not more than 14 days after the making of the application in question, and

    (b)   which is specified in the notice required by subsection (4).

(4) Before an authorised person or constable enters and inspects any premises under this section, at least 48 hours' notice must be given to the club.

(5) Any person obstructing an authorised person in the exercise of the power conferred by this section commits an offence.

(6) A person guilty of an offence under subsection (5) is liable on summary conviction to a fine not exceeding level 2 on the standard scale.

(7) The relevant licensing authority may, on the application of a responsible authority, extend by not more than 7 days the time allowed for carrying out an entry and inspection under this section.

(8) The relevant licensing authority may allow such an extension of time only if it appears to the authority that –

    (a)   reasonable steps had been taken for an authorised person or constable authorised by the applicant to inspect the premises in good time, but

    (b)   it was not possible for the inspection to take place within the time allowed.

97 Other powers of entry and search

(1) Where a club premises certificate has effect in respect of any premises, a constable may enter and search the premises if he has reasonable cause to believe –

    (a)   that an offence under section 4(3)(a), (b) or (c) of the Misuse of Drugs Act 1971 (c 38) (supplying or offering to supply, or being concerned in supplying or making an offer to supply, a controlled drug) has been, is being, or is about to be, committed there, or

(b) that there is likely to be a breach of the peace there.

(2) A constable exercising any power conferred by this section may, if necessary, use reasonable force.

PART 5

PERMITTED TEMPORARY ACTIVITIES

Introductory

98 Meaning of 'permitted temporary activity'

(1) A licensable activity is a permitted temporary activity by virtue of this Part if –

(a) it is carried on in accordance with a notice given in accordance with section 100, and

(b) the following conditions are satisfied.

(2) The first condition is that the requirements of sections 102 (acknowledgement of notice) and 104(1) (notification of police) are met in relation to the notice.

(3) The second condition is that the notice has not been withdrawn under this Part.

(4) The third condition is that no counter notice has been given under this Part in respect of the notice.

99 The relevant licensing authority

In this Part references to the 'relevant licensing authority', in relation to any premises, are references to –

(a) the licensing authority in whose area the premises are situated, or

(b) where the premises are situated in the areas of two or more licensing authorities, each of those authorities.

Temporary event notices

100 Temporary event notice

(1) Where it is proposed to use premises for one or more licensable activities during a period not exceeding 96 hours, an individual may give to the relevant licensing authority notice of that proposal (a 'temporary event notice').

(2) In this Act, the 'premises user', in relation to a temporary event notice, is the individual who gave the notice.

(3) An individual may not give a temporary event notice unless he is aged 18 or over.

(4) A temporary event notice must be in the prescribed form and contain –

(a) a statement of the matters mentioned in subsection (5),

(b) where subsection (6) applies, a statement of the condition mentioned in that subsection, and

(c)   such other information as may be prescribed.

(5) Those matters are –

(a)   the licensable activities to which the proposal mentioned in subsection (1) relates ('the relevant licensable activities'),

(b)   the period (not exceeding 96 hours) during which it is proposed to use the premises for those activities ('the event period'),

(c)   the times during the event period when the premises user proposes that those licensable activities shall take place,

(d)   the maximum number of persons (being a number less than 500) which the premises user proposes should, during those times, be allowed on the premises at the same time,

(e)   where the relevant licensable activities include the supply of alcohol, whether supplies are proposed to be for consumption on the premises or off the premises, or both, and

(f)   such other matters as may be prescribed.

(6) Where the relevant licensable activities include the supply of alcohol, the notice must make it a condition of using the premises for such supplies that all such supplies are made by or under the authority of the premises user.

(7) The temporary event notice –

(a)   must be given to the relevant licensing authority (in duplicate) no later than ten working days before the day on which the event period begins, and

(b)   must be accompanied by the prescribed fee.

(8) The Secretary of State may, by order –

(a)   amend subsections (1) and (5)(b) so as to substitute any period for the period for the time being specified there;

(b)   amend subsection (5)(d) so as to substitute any number for the number for the time being specified there.

(9) In this section 'supply of alcohol' means –

(a)   the sale by retail of alcohol, or

(b)   the supply of alcohol by or on behalf of a club to, or to the order of, a member of the club.

101 Minimum of 24 hours between event periods

(1) A temporary event notice ('notice A') given by an individual ('the relevant premises user') is void if the event period specified in it does not –

(a)   end at least 24 hours before the event period specified in any other temporary event notice given by the relevant premises user in respect of the same premises before or at the same time as notice A, or

(b)   begin at least 24 hours after the event period specified in any other such notice.

(2) For the purposes of subsection (1) –

(a) any temporary event notice in respect of which a counter notice has been given under this Part or which has been withdrawn under section 103 is to be disregarded;

(b) a temporary event notice given by an individual who is an associate of the relevant premises user is to be treated as a notice given by the relevant premises user;

(c) a temporary event notice ('notice B') given by an individual who is in business with the relevant premises user is to be treated as a notice given by the relevant premises user if –

(i) that business relates to one or more licensable activities, and

(ii) notice A and notice B relate to one or more licensable activities to which the business relates (although not necessarily the same activity or activities);

(d) two temporary event notices are in respect of the same premises if the whole or any part of the premises in respect of which one of the notices is given includes or forms part of the premises in respect of which the other notice is given.

(3) For the purposes of this section an individual is an associate of another person if that individual is –

(a) the spouse of that person,

(b) a child, parent, grandchild, grandparent, brother or sister of that person,

(c) an agent or employee of that person, or

(d) the spouse of a person within paragraph (b) or (c).

(4) For the purposes of subsection (3) a person living with another as that person's husband or wife is to be treated as that person's spouse.

102 Acknowledgement of notice

(1) Where a licensing authority receives a temporary event notice (in duplicate) in accordance with this Part, it must acknowledge receipt of the notice by sending or delivering one notice to the premises user –

(a) before the end of the first working day following the day on which it was received, or

(b) if the day on which it was received was not a working day, before the end of the second working day following that day.

(2) The authority must mark on the notice to be returned under subsection (1) an acknowledgement of the receipt in the prescribed form.

(3) Subsection (1) does not apply where, before the time by which the notice must be returned in accordance with that subsection, a counter notice has been sent or delivered to the premises user under section 107 in relation to the temporary event notice.

103 Withdrawal of notice

(1) A temporary event notice may be withdrawn by the premises user giving the relevant licensing authority a notice to that effect no later than 24 hours

before the beginning of the event period specified in the temporary event notice.

(2) Nothing in section 102 or sections 104 to 107 applies in relation to a notice withdrawn in accordance with this section.

Police objections

104 Objection to notice by the police

(1) The premises user must give a copy of any temporary event notice to the relevant chief officer of police no later than ten working days before the day on which the event period specified in the notice begins.

(2) Where a chief officer of police who receives a copy notice under subsection (1) is satisfied that allowing the premises to be used in accordance with the notice would undermine the crime prevention objective, he must give a notice stating the reasons why he is so satisfied (an 'objection notice') –

   (a)   to the relevant licensing authority, and
   (b)   to the premises user.

(3) The objection notice must be given no later than 48 hours after the chief officer of police is given a copy of the temporary event notice under subsection (1).

(4) Subsection (2) does not apply at any time after the relevant chief officer of police has received a copy of a counter notice under section 107 in respect of the temporary event notice.

(5) In this section 'relevant chief officer of police' means –

   (a)   where the premises are situated in one police area, the chief officer of police for that area, and
   (b)   where the premises are situated in two or more police areas, the chief officer of police for each of those areas.

105 Counter notice following police objection

(1) This section applies where an objection notice is given in respect of a temporary event notice.

(2) The relevant licensing authority must –

   (a)   hold a hearing to consider the objection notice, unless the premises user, the chief officer of police who gave the objection notice and the authority agree that a hearing is unnecessary, and
   (b)   having regard to the objection notice, give the premises user a counter notice under this section if it considers it necessary for the promotion of the crime prevention objective to do so.

(3) The relevant licensing authority must –

   (a)   in a case where it decides not to give a counter notice under this section, give the premises user and the relevant chief officer of police notice of the decision, and
   (b)   in any other case –

(i)   give the premises user the counter notice and a notice stating the reasons for its decision, and

(ii) give the relevant chief officer of police a copy of both of those notices.

(4) A decision must be made under subsection (2)(b), and the requirements of subsection (3) must be met, at least 24 hours before the beginning of the event period specified in the temporary event notice.

(5) Where the premises are situated in the area of more than one licensing authority, the functions conferred on the relevant licensing authority by this section must be exercised by those authorities jointly.

(6) This section does not apply –

(a) if the objection notice has been withdrawn (whether by virtue of section 106 or otherwise), or

(b) if the premises user has been given a counter notice under section 107.

(7) In this section 'objection notice' and 'relevant chief officer of police' have the same meaning as in section 104.

106 Modification of notice following police objection

(1) This section applies where a chief officer of police has given an objection notice in respect of a temporary event notice (and the objection notice has not been withdrawn).

(2) At any time before a hearing is held or dispensed with under section 105(2), the chief officer of police may, with the agreement of the premises user, modify the temporary event notice by making changes to the notice returned to the premises user under section 102.

(3) Where a temporary event notice is modified under subsection (2) –

(a) the objection notice is to be treated for the purposes of this Act as having been withdrawn from the time the temporary event notice is modified, and

(b) from that time –

(i)   this Act has effect as if the temporary event notice given under section 100 had been the notice as modified under that subsection, and

(ii) to the extent that the conditions of section 98 are satisfied in relation to the unmodified notice they are to be treated as satisfied in relation to the notice as modified under that subsection.

(4) A copy of the temporary event notice as modified under subsection (2) must be sent or delivered by the chief officer of police to the relevant licensing authority before a hearing is held or dispensed with under section 105(2).

(5) Where the premises are situated in more than one police area, the chief officer of police may modify the temporary event notice under this section

only with the consent of the chief officer of police for the other police area or each of the other police areas in which the premises are situated.

(6) This section does not apply if a counter notice has been given under section 107.

(7) In this section 'objection notice' has the same meaning as in section 104(2).

Limits on temporary event notices

107 Counter notice where permitted limits exceeded

(1) Where a licensing authority –

    (a)   receives a temporary event notice ('notice A') in respect of any premises ('the relevant premises'), and

    (b)   is satisfied that subsection (2), (3), (4) or (5) applies,

the authority must give the premises user ('the relevant premises user') a counter notice under this section.

(2) This subsection applies if the relevant premises user –

    (a)   holds a personal licence, and

    (b)   has already given at least 50 temporary event notices in respect of event periods wholly or partly within the same year as the event period specified in notice A.

(3) This subsection applies if the relevant premises user –

    (a)   does not hold a personal licence, and

    (b)   has already given at least five temporary event notices in respect of such event periods.

(4) This subsection applies if at least 12 temporary event notices have already been given which –

    (a)   are in respect of the same premises as notice A, and

    (b)   specify as the event period a period wholly or partly within the same year as the event period specified in notice A.

(5) This subsection applies if, in any year in which the event period specified in notice A (or any part of it) falls, more than 15 days are days on which one or more of the following fall –

    (a)   that event period or any part of it,

    (b)   an event period specified in a temporary event notice already given in respect of the same premises as notice A or any part of such a period.

(6) If the event period in notice A straddles two years, subsections (2), (3) and (4) apply separately in relation to each of those years.

(7) A counter notice under this section must be in the prescribed form and given to the premises user in the prescribed manner.

(8) No such counter notice may be given later than 24 hours before the beginning of the event period specified in notice A.

(9) In determining whether subsection (2), (3), (4) or (5) applies, any temporary event notice in respect of which a counter notice has been given under this section or section 105 is to be disregarded.

(10) In determining for the purposes of subsection (2) or (3) the number of temporary event notices given by the relevant premises user –

    (a)   a temporary event notice given by an individual who is an associate of the relevant premises user is to be treated as a notice given by the relevant premises user;

    (b)   a temporary event notice ('notice B') given by an individual who is in business with the relevant premises user is to be treated as a notice given by the relevant premises user if –

        (i)   that business relates to one or more licensable activities, and

        (ii)   notice A and notice B relate to one or more licensable activities to which the business relates (but not necessarily the same activity or activities).

(11) Where a licensing authority gives a counter notice under this section it must, forthwith, send a copy of that notice to the chief officer of police for the police area (or each of the police areas) in which the relevant premises are situated.

(12) The Secretary of State may, by order, amend subsection (2)(b), (3)(b), (4) or (5) so as to substitute any number for the number for the time being specified there.

(13) For the purposes of this section –

    (a)   a temporary event notice is in respect of the same premises as notice A if it is in respect of the whole or any part of the relevant premises or premises which include the whole or any part of those premises,

    (b)   'year' means calendar year,

    (c)   'day' means a period of 24 hours beginning at midnight, and

    (d)   subsections (3) and (4) of section 101 (meaning of 'associate') apply as they apply for the purposes of that section.

Rights of entry, production of notice, etc

108 Right of entry where temporary event notice given

(1) A constable or an authorised officer may, at any reasonable time, enter the premises to which a temporary event notice relates to assess the likely effect of the notice on the promotion of the crime prevention objective.

(2) An authorised officer exercising the power conferred by this section must, if so requested, produce evidence of his authority to exercise the power.

(3) A person commits an offence if he intentionally obstructs an authorised officer exercising a power conferred by this section.

(4) A person guilty of an offence under this section is liable on summary conviction to a fine not exceeding level 2 on the standard scale.

(5) In this section 'authorised officer' means –

(a) an officer of the licensing authority in whose area the premises are situated, or

(b) if the premises are situated in the area of more than one licensing authority, an officer of any of those authorities,

authorised for the purposes of this Act.

109 Duty to keep and produce temporary event notice

(1) This section applies whenever premises are being used for one or more licensable activities which are or are purported to be permitted temporary activities by virtue of this Part.

(2) The premises user must either –

(a) secure that a copy of the temporary event notice is prominently displayed at the premises, or

(b) meet the requirements of subsection (3).

(3) The requirements of this subsection are that the premises user must –

(a) secure that the temporary event notice is kept at the premises in –
  (i)   his custody, or
  (ii) in the custody of a person who is present and working at the premises and whom he has nominated for the purposes of this section, and

(b) where the temporary event notice is in the custody of a person so nominated, secure that a notice specifying that fact and the position held at the premises by that person is prominently displayed at the premises.

(4) The premises user commits an offence if he fails, without reasonable excuse, to comply with subsection (2).

(5) Where –

(a) the temporary event notice is not displayed as mentioned in subsection (2)(a), and

(b) no notice is displayed as mentioned in subsection (3)(b),

a constable or authorised officer may require the premises user to produce the temporary event notice for examination.

(6) Where a notice is displayed as mentioned in subsection (3)(b), a constable or authorised officer may require the person specified in that notice to produce the temporary event notice for examination.

(7) An authorised officer exercising the power conferred by subsection (5) or (6) must, if so requested, produce evidence of his authority to exercise the power.

(8) A person commits an offence if he fails, without reasonable excuse, to produce a temporary event notice in accordance with a requirement under subsection (5) or (6).

(9) A person guilty of an offence under this section is liable on summary conviction to a fine not exceeding level 2 on the standard scale.

(10) In this section 'authorised officer' has the meaning given in section 108(5).

Miscellaneous

110 Theft, loss, etc of temporary event notice

(1) Where a temporary event notice acknowledged under section 102 is lost, stolen, damaged or destroyed, the premises user may apply to the licensing authority which acknowledged the notice (or, if there is more than one such authority, any of them) for a copy of the notice.

(2) No application may be made under this section more than one month after the end of the event period specified in the notice.

(3) The application must be accompanied by the prescribed fee.

(4) Where a licensing authority receives an application under this section, it must issue the premises user with a copy of the notice (certified by the authority to be a true copy) if it is satisfied that –

  (a) the notice has been lost, stolen, damaged or destroyed, and
  (b) where it has been lost or stolen, the premises user has reported that loss or theft to the police.

(5) The copy issued under this section must be a copy of the notice in the form it existed immediately before it was lost, stolen, damaged or destroyed.

(6) This Act applies in relation to a copy issued under this section as it applies in relation to an original notice.

PART 6

PERSONAL LICENCES

Introductory

111 Personal licence

(1) In this Act 'personal licence' means a licence which –

  (a) is granted by a licensing authority to an individual, and
  (b) authorises that individual to supply alcohol, or authorise the supply of alcohol, in accordance with a premises licence.

(2) In subsection (1)(b) the reference to an individual supplying alcohol is to him –

  (a) selling alcohol by retail, or
  (b) supplying alcohol by or on behalf of a club to, or to the order of, a member of the club.

112 The relevant licensing authority

For the purposes of this Part the 'relevant licensing authority', in relation to a personal licence, is the licensing authority which granted the licence.

113 Meaning of 'relevant offence' and 'foreign offence'

(1) In this Part 'relevant offence' means an offence listed in Schedule 4.

(2) The Secretary of State may by order amend that list so as to add, modify or omit any entry.

(3) In this Part 'foreign offence' means an offence (other than a relevant offence) under the law of any place outside England and Wales.

114 Spent convictions

For the purposes of this Part a conviction for a relevant offence or a foreign offence must be disregarded if it is spent for the purposes of the Rehabilitation of Offenders Act 1974 (c 53).

115 Period of validity of personal licence

(1) A personal licence –

  (a) has effect for an initial period of ten years beginning with the date on which it is granted, and
  (b) may be renewed in accordance with this Part for further periods of ten years at a time.

(2) Subsection (1) is subject to subsections (3) and (4) and to –

  (a) section 116 (surrender),
  (b) section 119 (continuation of licence pending renewal), and
  (c) paragraph 17 of Schedule 5 (continuation of licence pending disposal of appeal).

(3) A personal licence ceases to have effect when it is revoked under section 124 or forfeited under section 129.

(4) And a personal licence does not have effect during any period when it is suspended under section 129.

(5) Subsections (3) and (4) are subject to any court order under sections 129(4) or 130.

116 Surrender of personal licence

(1) Where the holder of a personal licence wishes to surrender his licence he may give the relevant licensing authority a notice to that effect.

(2) The notice must be accompanied by the personal licence or, if that is not practicable, by a statement of the reasons for the failure to provide the licence.

(3) Where a notice of surrender is given in accordance with this section, the personal licence lapses on receipt of the notice by the authority.

Grant and renewal of licences

117 Application for grant or renewal of personal licence

(1) An individual may apply –

    (a)   for the grant of a personal licence, or

    (b)   for the renewal of a personal licence held by him.

(2) An application for the grant of a personal licence –

    (a)   must, if the applicant is ordinarily resident in the area of a licensing authority, be made to that authority, and

    (b)   may, in any other case, be made to any licensing authority.

(3) An application for the renewal of a personal licence must be made to the relevant licensing authority.

(4) Where the application is for renewal of a personal licence, the application must be accompanied by the personal licence or, if that is not practicable, by a statement of the reasons for the failure to provide the licence.

(5) Subsection (1) is subject to regulations under section 133 (form etc of applications and notices under this Part).

(6) An application for renewal may be made only during the period of two months beginning three months before the time the licence would expire in accordance with section 115(1) if no application for renewal were made.

118 Individual permitted to hold only one personal licence

(1) An individual who makes an application for the grant of a personal licence under section 117 ('the initial application') may not make another such application until the initial application has been determined by the licensing authority to which it was made or has been withdrawn.

(2) A personal licence is void if, at the time it is granted, the individual to whom it is granted already holds a personal licence.

119 Licence continued pending renewal

(1) Where –

    (a)   an application for renewal is made in accordance with section 117, and

    (b)   the application has not been determined before the time the licence would, in the absence of this section, expire,

then, by virtue of this section, the licence continues to have effect for the period beginning with that time and ending with the determination or withdrawal of the application.

(2) Subsection (1) is subject to section 115(3) and (4) (revocation, forfeiture and suspension) and section 116 (surrender).

120 Determination of application for grant

(1) This section applies where an application for the grant of a personal licence is made to a licensing authority in accordance with section 117.

(2) The authority must grant the licence if it appears to it that –

  (a) the applicant is aged 18 or over,
  (b) he possesses a licensing qualification or is a person of a prescribed description,
  (c) no personal licence held by him has been forfeited in the period of five years ending with the day the application was made, and
  (d) he has not been convicted of any relevant offence or any foreign offence.

(3) The authority must reject the application if it appears to it that the applicant fails to meet the condition in paragraph (a), (b) or (c) of subsection (2).

(4) If it appears to the authority that the applicant meets the conditions in paragraphs (a), (b) and (c) of that subsection but fails to meet the condition in paragraph (d) of that subsection, the authority must give the chief officer of police for its area a notice to that effect.

(5) Where, having regard to –

  (a) any conviction of the applicant for a relevant offence, and
  (b) any conviction of his for a foreign offence which the chief officer of police considers to be comparable to a relevant offence,

the chief officer of police is satisfied that granting the licence would undermine the crime prevention objective, he must, within the period of 14 days beginning with the day he received the notice under subsection (4), give the authority a notice stating the reasons why he is so satisfied (an 'objection notice').

(6) Where no objection notice is given within that period (or the notice is withdrawn), the authority must grant the application.

(7) In any other case, the authority –

  (a) must hold a hearing to consider the objection notice, unless the applicant, the chief officer of police and the authority agree that it is unnecessary, and
  (b) having regard to the notice, must –
    (i)   reject the application if it considers it necessary for the promotion of the crime prevention objective to do so, and
    (ii) grant the application in any other case.

(8) In this section 'licensing qualification' means –

  (a) a qualification –
    (i)   accredited at the time of its award, and
    (ii) awarded by a body accredited at that time,
  (b) a qualification awarded before the coming into force of this section which the Secretary of State certifies is to be treated for the purposes of this section as if it were a qualification within paragraph (a), or

(c)   a qualification obtained in Scotland or Northern Ireland or in an EEA State (other than the United Kingdom) which is equivalent to a qualification within paragraph (a) or (b).

(9) For this purpose –

'accredited' means accredited by the Secretary of State; and
'EEA State' means a state which is a contracting party to the Agreement on the European Economic Area signed at Oporto on 2nd May 1992, as adjusted by the Protocol signed at Brussels on 17th March 1993.

121 Determination of application for renewal

(1) This section applies where an application for the renewal of a personal licence is made to the relevant licensing authority in accordance with section 117.

(2) If it appears to the authority that the applicant has been convicted of any relevant offence or foreign offence since the relevant time, the relevant licensing authority must give notice to that effect to the chief officer of police for its area.

(3) Where, having regard to –

(a)   any conviction of the applicant for a relevant offence, and
(b)   any conviction of his for a foreign offence which the chief officer of police considers to be comparable to a relevant offence,

the chief officer of police is satisfied that renewing the licence would undermine the crime prevention objective, he must, within the period of 14 days beginning with the day he received the notice under subsection (2), give the authority a notice stating the reasons why he is so satisfied (an 'objection notice').

(4) For the purposes of subsection (3)(a) and (b) it is irrelevant whether the conviction occurred before or after the relevant time.

(5) Where no objection notice is given within that period (or any such notice is withdrawn), the authority must grant the application.

(6) In any other case, the authority –

(a)   must hold a hearing to consider the objection notice unless the applicant, the chief officer of police and the authority agree that it is unnecessary, and
(b)   having regard to the notice, must –
   (i)   reject the application if it considers it necessary for the promotion of the crime prevention objective to do so, and
   (ii) grant the application in any other case.

(7) In this section 'the relevant time' means –

(a)   if the personal licence has not been renewed since it was granted, the time it was granted, and
(b)   if it has been renewed, the last time it was renewed.

122 Notification of determinations

(1) Where a licensing authority grants an application –

    (a)   it must give the applicant and the chief officer of police for its area a notice to that effect, and

    (b)   if the chief officer of police gave an objection notice (which was not withdrawn), the notice under paragraph (a) must contain a statement of the licensing authority's reasons for granting the application.

(2) A licensing authority which rejects an application must give the applicant and the chief officer of police for its area a notice to that effect containing a statement of the authority's reasons for rejecting the application.

(3) In this section –

    'application' means an application for the grant or renewal of a personal licence; and

    'objection notice' has the meaning given in section 120 or 121, as the case may be.

123 Duty to notify licensing authority of convictions during application period

(1) Where an applicant for the grant or renewal of a personal licence is convicted of a relevant offence or a foreign offence during the application period, he must as soon as reasonably practicable notify the conviction to the authority to which the application is made.

(2) A person commits an offence if he fails, without reasonable excuse, to comply with subsection (1).

(3) A person guilty of an offence under this section is liable on summary conviction to a fine not exceeding level 4 on the standard scale.

(4) In this section 'the application period' means the period that –

    (a)   begins when the application for grant or renewal is made, and

    (b)   ends when the application is determined or withdrawn.

124 Convictions coming to light after grant or renewal

(1) This section applies where, after a licensing authority has granted or renewed a personal licence, it becomes aware (whether by virtue of section 123(1), 131 or 132 or otherwise) that the holder of a personal licence ('the offender') was convicted during the application period of any relevant offence or foreign offence.

(2) The licensing authority must give a notice to that effect to the chief officer of police for its area.

(3) Where, having regard to –

    (a)   any conviction of the applicant for a relevant offence, and

    (b)   any conviction of his for a foreign offence which the chief officer of police considers to be comparable to a relevant offence, which occurred before the end of the application period, the chief officer of police is satisfied that continuation of the licence would undermine the crime prevention objective, he must, within the period of 14 days beginning with the day he received the notice under subsection (2), give the authority a notice stating the reasons why he is so satisfied (an 'objection notice').

(4) Where an objection notice is given within that period (and not withdrawn), the authority –

    (a)   must hold a hearing to consider the objection notice, unless the holder of the licence, the chief officer of police and the authority agree it is unnecessary, and

    (b)   having regard to the notice, must revoke the licence if it considers it necessary for the promotion of the crime prevention objective to do so.

(5) Where the authority revokes or decides not to revoke a licence under subsection (4) it must notify the offender and the chief officer of police of the decision and its reasons for making it.

(6) A decision under this section does not have effect –

    (a)   until the end of the period given for appealing against the decision, or

    (b)   if the decision is appealed against, until the appeal is disposed of.

(7) In this section 'application period', in relation to the grant or renewal of a personal licence, means the period that –

    (a)   begins when the application for the grant or renewal is made, and

    (b)   ends at the time of the grant or renewal.

125 Form of personal licence

(1) Where a licensing authority grants a personal licence, it must forthwith issue the applicant with the licence.

(2) The licence must –

    (a)   specify the holder's name and address, and

    (b)   identify the licensing authority which granted it.

(3) It must also contain a record of each relevant offence and each foreign offence of which the holder has been convicted, the date of each conviction and the sentence imposed in respect of it.

(4) Subject to subsections (2) and (3), the licence must be in the prescribed form.

126 Theft, loss, etc of personal licence

(1) Where a personal licence is lost, stolen, damaged or destroyed, the holder of the licence may apply to the relevant licensing authority for a copy of the licence.

(2) Subsection (1) is subject to regulations under section 133(2) (power to prescribe fee to accompany application).

(3) Where the relevant licensing authority receives an application under this section, it must issue the licence holder with a copy of the licence (certified by the authority to be a true copy) if it is satisfied that –

(a)   the licence has been lost, stolen, damaged or destroyed, and
(b)   where it has been lost or stolen, the holder of the licence has reported the loss or theft to the police.

(4) The copy issued under this section must be a copy of the licence in the form in which it existed immediately before it was lost, stolen, damaged or destroyed.

(5) This Act applies in relation to a copy issued under this section as it applies in relation to an original licence.

Duty to notify certain changes

127 Duty to notify change of name or address

(1) The holder of a personal licence must, as soon as reasonably practicable, notify the relevant licensing authority of any change in his name or address as stated in the personal licence.

(2) Subsection (1) is subject to regulations under section 133(2) (power to prescribe fee to accompany notice).

(3) A notice under subsection (1) must also be accompanied by the personal licence or, if that is not practicable, by a statement of the reasons for the failure to provide the licence.

(4) A person commits an offence if he fails, without reasonable excuse, to comply with this section.

(5) A person guilty of an offence under subsection (4) is liable on summary conviction to a fine not exceeding level 2 on the standard scale.

Conviction of licence holder for relevant offence

128 Duty to notify court of personal licence

(1) Where the holder of a personal licence is charged with a relevant offence, he must, no later than the time he makes his first appearance in a magistrates' court in connection with that offence –

(a)   produce to the court the personal licence, or
(b)   if that is not practicable, notify the court of the existence of the personal licence and the identity of the relevant licensing authority and of the reasons why he cannot produce the licence.

(2) Subsection (3) applies where a person charged with a relevant offence is granted a personal licence –

(a)   after his first appearance in a magistrates' court in connection with that offence, but
(b)   before –

(i)   his conviction, and sentencing for the offence, or his acquittal, or,

(ii) where an appeal is brought against his conviction, sentence or acquittal, the disposal of that appeal.

(3) At his next appearance in court in connection with that offence, that person must –

(a) produce to the court the personal licence, or

(b) if that is not practicable, notify the court of the existence of the personal licence and the identity of the relevant licensing authority and of the reasons why he cannot produce the licence.

(4) Where –

(a) a person charged with a relevant offence has produced his licence to, or notified, a court under subsection (1) or (3), and

(b) before he is convicted of and sentenced for, or acquitted of, that offence, a notifiable event occurs in respect of the licence,

he must, at his next appearance in court in connection with that offence, notify the court of that event.

(5) For this purpose a 'notifiable event' in relation to a personal licence means any of the following –

(a) the making or withdrawal of an application for renewal of the licence;

(b) the surrender of the licence under section 116;

(c) the renewal of the licence under section 121;

(d) the revocation of the licence under section 124.

(6) A person commits an offence if he fails, without reasonable excuse, to comply with this section.

(7) A person guilty of an offence under subsection (6) is liable on summary conviction to a fine not exceeding level 2 on the standard scale.

129 Forfeiture or suspension of licence on conviction for relevant offence

(1) This section applies where the holder of a personal licence is convicted of a relevant offence by or before a court in England and Wales.

(2) The court may –

(a) order the forfeiture of the licence, or

(b) order its suspension for a period not exceeding six months.

(3) In determining whether to make an order under subsection (2), the court may take account of any previous conviction of the holder for a relevant offence.

(4) Where a court makes an order under this section it may suspend the order pending an appeal against it.

(5) Subject to subsection (4) and section 130, an order under this section takes effect immediately after it is made.

130 Powers of appellate court to suspend order under section 129

(1) This section applies where –

    (a)   a person ('the offender') is convicted of a relevant offence, and

    (b)   an order is made under section 129 in respect of that conviction ('the section 129 order').

(2) In this section any reference to the offender's sentence includes a reference to the section 129 order and to any other order made on his conviction and, accordingly, any reference to an appeal against his sentence includes a reference to an appeal against any order forming part of his sentence.

(3) Where the offender –

    (a)   appeals to the Crown Court, or

    (b)   appeals or applies for leave to appeal to the Court of Appeal,

against his conviction or his sentence, the Crown Court or, as the case may be, the Court of Appeal may suspend the section 129 order.

(4) Where the offender appeals or applies for leave to appeal to the House of Lords –

    (a)   under section 1 of the Administration of Justice Act 1960 (c 65) from any decision of the High Court which is material to his conviction or sentence, or

    (b)   under section 33 of the Criminal Appeal Act 1968 (c 19) from any decision of the Court of Appeal which is material to his conviction or sentence,

the High Court or, as the case may require, the Court of Appeal may suspend the section 129 order.

(5) Where the offender makes an application in respect of the decision of the court in question under section 111 of the Magistrates' Courts Act 1980 (c 43) (statement of case by magistrates' court) or section 28 of the Supreme Court Act 1981 (c 54) (statement of case by Crown Court) the High Court may suspend the section 129 order.

(6) Where the offender –

    (a)   applies to the High Court for a quashing order to remove into the High Court any proceedings of a magistrates' court or of the Crown Court, being proceedings in or in consequence of which he was convicted or his sentence was passed, or

    (b)   applies to the High Court for permission to make such an application,

the High Court may suspend the section 129 order.

(7) Any power of a court under this section to suspend the section 129 order is a power to do so on such terms as the court thinks fit.

(8) Where, by virtue of this section, a court suspends the section 129 order it must send notice of the suspension to the relevant licensing authority.

(9) Where the section 129 order is an order for forfeiture of the licence, an order under this section to suspend that order has effect to reinstate the licence for the period of the suspension.

131 Court's duty to notify licensing authority of convictions

(1) This section applies where a person who holds a personal licence ('the relevant person') is convicted, by or before a court in England and Wales, of a relevant offence in a case where –

    (a)   the relevant person has given notice under section 128 (notification of personal licence), or

    (b)   the court is, for any other reason, aware of the existence of that personal licence.

(2) The appropriate officer of the court must (as soon as reasonably practicable) –

    (a)   send to the relevant licensing authority a notice specifying –

        (i)   the name and address of the relevant person,

        (ii)   the nature and date of the conviction, and

        (iii) any sentence passed in respect of it, including any order made under section 129, and

    (b)   send a copy of the notice to the relevant person.

(3) Where, on an appeal against the relevant person's conviction for the relevant offence or against the sentence imposed on him for that offence, his conviction is quashed or a new sentence is substituted for that sentence, the court which determines the appeal must (as soon as reasonably practicable) arrange –

    (a)   for notice of the quashing of the conviction or the substituting of the sentence to be sent to the relevant licensing authority, and

    (b)   for a copy of the notice to be sent to the relevant person.

(4) Where the case is referred to the Court of Appeal under section 36 of the Criminal Justice Act 1988 (c 33) (review of lenient sentence), the court must cause –

    (a)   notice of any action it takes under subsection (1) of that section to be sent to the relevant licensing authority, and

    (b)   a copy of the notice to be sent to the relevant person.

(5) For the purposes of subsection (2) 'the appropriate officer' is –

    (a)   in the case of a magistrates' court, the clerk of the court, and

    (b)   in the case of the Crown Court, the appropriate officer;

and section 141 of the Magistrates' Courts Act 1980 (c 43) (meaning of 'clerk of a magistrates' court') applies in relation to this subsection as it applies in relation to that section.

132 Licence holder's duty to notify licensing authority of convictions

(1) Subsection (2) applies where the holder of a personal licence –

- (a) is convicted of a relevant offence, in a case where section 131(1) does not apply, or
- (b) is convicted of a foreign offence.

(2) The holder must –

- (a) as soon as reasonably practicable after the conviction, give the relevant licensing authority a notice containing details of the nature and date of the conviction, and any sentence imposed on him in respect of it, and
- (b) as soon as reasonably practicable after the determination of any appeal against the conviction or sentence, or of any reference under section 36 of the Criminal Justice Act 1988 (c 33) in respect of the case, give the relevant licensing authority a notice containing details of the determination.

(3) A notice under subsection (2) must be accompanied by the personal licence or, if that is not practicable, a statement of the reasons for the failure to provide the licence.

(4) A person commits an offence if he fails, without reasonable excuse, to comply with this section.

(5) A person guilty of an offence under subsection (4) is liable on summary conviction to a fine not exceeding level 2 on the standard scale.

General provision

133 Form etc of applications and notices under Part 6

(1) In relation to any application under section 117 or notice under this Part, regulations may prescribe –

- (a) its form,
- (b) the manner in which it is to be made or given, and
- (c) the information and documents that must accompany it.

(2) Regulations may also –

- (a) require applications under section 117 or 126 or notices under section 127 to be accompanied by a fee, and
- (b) prescribe the amount of the fee.

134 Licensing authority's duty to update licence document

(1) Where –

- (a) the relevant licensing authority makes a determination under section 121 or 124(4),
- (b) it receives a notice under section 123(1), 127, 131 or 132, or
- (c) an appeal against a decision under this Part is disposed of,

in relation to a personal licence, the authority must make the appropriate amendments (if any) to the licence.

(2) Where, under section 131, notice is given of the making of an order under section 129, the relevant licensing authority must make an endorsement on the licence stating the terms of the order.

(3) Where, under section 131, notice is given of the quashing of such an order, any endorsement previously made under subsection (2) in respect of it must be cancelled.

(4) Where a licensing authority is not in possession of a personal licence, it may, for the purposes of discharging its obligations under this section, require the holder of the licence to produce it to the authority within 14 days beginning with the day on which he is notified of the requirement.

(5) A person commits an offence if he fails, without reasonable excuse, to comply with a requirement under subsection (4).

(6) A person guilty of an offence under subsection (5) is liable on summary conviction to a fine not exceeding level 2 on the standard scale.

Production of licence

135 Licence holder's duty to produce licence

(1) This section applies where the holder of a personal licence is on premises to make or authorise the supply of alcohol, and such supplies –

   (a)   are authorised by a premises licence in respect of those premises, or

   (b)   are a permitted temporary activity on the premises by virtue of a temporary event notice given under Part 5 in respect of which he is the premises user.

(2) Any constable or authorised officer may require the holder of the personal licence to produce that licence for examination.

(3) An authorised officer exercising the power conferred by subsection (2) must, if so requested, produce evidence of his authority to exercise the power.

(4) A person who fails, without reasonable excuse, to comply with a requirement under subsection (2) is guilty of an offence.

(5) A person guilty of an offence under subsection (4) is liable on summary conviction to a fine not exceeding level 2 on the standard scale.

(6) In this section 'authorised officer' means an officer of a licensing authority authorised by the authority for the purposes of this Act.

PART 7

OFFENCES

Unauthorised licensable activities

136 Unauthorised licensable activities

(1) A person commits an offence if –

   (a)   he carries on or attempts to carry on a licensable activity on or from any premises otherwise than under and in accordance with an authorisation, or

(b)   he knowingly allows a licensable activity to be so carried on.

(2) Where the licensable activity in question is the provision of regulated entertainment, a person does not commit an offence under this section if his only involvement in the provision of the entertainment is that he –

(a)   performs in a play,
(b)   participates as a sportsman in an indoor sporting event,
(c)   boxes or wrestles in a boxing or wrestling entertainment,
(d)   performs live music,
(e)   plays recorded music,
(f)   performs dance, or
(g)   does something coming within paragraph 2(1)(h) of Schedule 1 (entertainment similar to music, dance, etc).

(3) Subsection (2) is to be construed in accordance with Part 3 of Schedule 1.

(4) A person guilty of an offence under this section is liable on summary conviction to imprisonment for a term not exceeding six months or to a fine not exceeding £20,000, or to both.

(5) In this Part 'authorisation' means –

(a)   a premises licence,
(b)   a club premises certificate, or
(c)   a temporary event notice in respect of which the conditions of section 98(2) to (4) are satisfied.

137 Exposing alcohol for unauthorised sale

(1) A person commits an offence if, on any premises, he exposes for sale by retail any alcohol in circumstances where the sale by retail of that alcohol on those premises would be an unauthorised licensable activity.

(2) For that purpose a licensable activity is unauthorised unless it is under and in accordance with an authorisation.

(3) A person guilty of an offence under this section is liable on summary conviction to imprisonment for a term not exceeding six months or to a fine not exceeding £20,000, or to both.

(4) The court by which a person is convicted of an offence under this section may order the alcohol in question, and any container for it, to be forfeited and either destroyed or dealt with in such other manner as the court may order.

138 Keeping alcohol on premises for unauthorised sale etc

(1) A person commits an offence if he has in his possession or under his control alcohol which he intends to sell by retail or supply in circumstances where that activity would be an unauthorised licensable activity.

(2) For that purpose a licensable activity is unauthorised unless it is under and in accordance with an authorisation.

(3) In subsection (1) the reference to the supply of alcohol is a reference to the supply of alcohol by or on behalf of a club to, or to the order of, a member of the club.

(4) A person guilty of an offence under this section is liable on summary conviction to a fine not exceeding level 2 on the standard scale.

(5) The court by which a person is convicted of an offence under this section may order the alcohol in question, and any container for it, to be forfeited and either destroyed or dealt with in such other manner as the court may order.

139 Defence of due diligence

(1) In proceedings against a person for an offence to which subsection (2) applies, it is a defence that –

- (a) his act was due to a mistake, or to reliance on information given to him, or to an act or omission by another person, or to some other cause beyond his control, and
- (b) he took all reasonable precautions and exercised all due diligence to avoid committing the offence.

(2) This subsection applies to an offence under –

- (a) section 136(1)(a) (carrying on unauthorised licensable activity),
- (b) section 137 (exposing alcohol for unauthorised sale), or
- (c) section 138 (keeping alcohol on premises for unauthorised sale).

Drunkenness and disorderly conduct

140 Allowing disorderly conduct on licensed premises etc

(1) A person to whom subsection (2) applies commits an offence if he knowingly allows disorderly conduct on relevant premises.

(2) This subsection applies –

- (a) to any person who works at the premises in a capacity, whether paid or unpaid, which authorises him to prevent the conduct,
- (b) in the case of licensed premises, to –
  - (i) the holder of a premises licence in respect of the premises, and
  - (ii) the designated premises supervisor (if any) under such a licence,
- (c) in the case of premises in respect of which a club premises certificate has effect, to any member or officer of the club which holds the certificate who at the time the conduct takes place is present on the premises in a capacity which enables him to prevent it, and
- (d) in the case of premises which may be used for a permitted temporary activity by virtue of Part 5, to the premises user in relation to the temporary event notice in question.

(3) A person guilty of an offence under this section is liable on summary conviction to a fine not exceeding level 3 on the standard scale.

141 Sale of alcohol to a person who is drunk

(1) A person to whom subsection (2) applies commits an offence if, on relevant premises, he knowingly –

  (a) sells or attempts to sell alcohol to a person who is drunk, or
  (b) allows alcohol to be sold to such a person.

(2) This subsection applies –

  (a) to any person who works at the premises in a capacity, whether paid or unpaid, which gives him authority to sell the alcohol concerned,
  (b) in the case of licensed premises, to –
    (i)   the holder of a premises licence in respect of the premises, and
    (ii) the designated premises supervisor (if any) under such a licence,
  (c) in the case of premises in respect of which a club premises certificate has effect, to any member or officer of the club which holds the certificate who at the time the sale (or attempted sale) takes place is present on the premises in a capacity which enables him to prevent it, and
  (d) in the case of premises which may be used for a permitted temporary activity by virtue of Part 5, to the premises user in relation to the temporary event notice in question.

(3) This section applies in relation to the supply of alcohol by or on behalf of a club to or to the order of a member of the club as it applies in relation to the sale of alcohol.

(4) A person guilty of an offence under this section is liable on summary conviction to a fine not exceeding level 3 on the standard scale.

142 Obtaining alcohol for a person who is drunk

(1) A person commits an offence if, on relevant premises, he knowingly obtains or attempts to obtain alcohol for consumption on those premises by a person who is drunk.

(2) A person guilty of an offence under this section is liable on summary conviction to a fine not exceeding level 3 on the standard scale.

143 Failure to leave licensed premises etc

(1) A person who is drunk or disorderly commits an offence if, without reasonable excuse –

  (a) he fails to leave relevant premises when requested to do so by a constable or by a person to whom subsection (2) applies, or
  (b) he enters or attempts to enter relevant premises after a constable or a person to whom subsection (2) applies has requested him not to enter.

(2) This subsection applies –

  (a) to any person who works at the premises in a capacity, whether paid or unpaid, which authorises him to make such a request,

(b)　in the case of licensed premises, to –
  (i)　the holder of a premises licence in respect of the premises, or
  (ii)　the designated premises supervisor (if any) under such a licence,
(c)　in the case of premises in respect of which a club premises certificate has effect, to any member or officer of the club which holds the certificate who is present on the premises in a capacity which enables him to make such a request, and
(d)　in the case of premises which may be used for a permitted temporary activity by virtue of Part 5, to the premises user in relation to the temporary event notice in question.

(3) A person guilty of an offence under subsection (1) is liable on summary conviction to a fine not exceeding level 1 on the standard scale.

(4) On being requested to do so by a person to whom subsection (2) applies, a constable must –

(a)　help to expel from relevant premises a person who is drunk or disorderly;
(b)　help to prevent such a person from entering relevant premises.

Smuggled goods

144　Keeping of smuggled goods

(1) A person to whom subsection (2) applies commits an offence if he knowingly keeps or allows to be kept, on any relevant premises, any goods which have been imported without payment of duty or which have otherwise been unlawfully imported.

(2) This subsection applies –

(a)　to any person who works at the premises in a capacity, whether paid or unpaid, which gives him authority to prevent the keeping of the goods on the premises,
(b)　in the case of licensed premises, to –
  (i)　the holder of a premises licence in respect of the premises, and
  (ii)　the designated premises supervisor (if any) under such a licence,
(c)　in the case of premises in respect of which a club premises certificate has effect, to any member or officer of the club which holds the certificate who is present on the premises at any time when the goods are kept on the premises in a capacity which enables him to prevent them being so kept, and
(d)　in the case of premises which may be used for a permitted temporary activity by virtue of Part 5, to the premises user in relation to the temporary event notice in question.

(3) A person guilty of an offence under this section is liable on summary conviction to a fine not exceeding level 3 on the standard scale.

(4) The court by which a person is convicted of an offence under this section may order the goods in question, and any container for them, to be forfeited

and either destroyed or dealt with in such other manner as the court may order.

Children and alcohol

145 Unaccompanied children prohibited from certain premises

(1) A person to whom subsection (3) applies commits an offence if –

    (a)   knowing that relevant premises are within subsection (4), he allows an unaccompanied child to be on the premises at a time when they are open for the purposes of being used for the supply of alcohol for consumption there, or

    (b)   he allows an unaccompanied child to be on relevant premises at a time between the hours of midnight and 5 am when the premises are open for the purposes of being used for the supply of alcohol for consumption there.

(2) For the purposes of this section –

    (a)   'child' means an individual aged under 16,

    (b)   a child is unaccompanied if he is not in the company of an individual aged 18 or over.

(3) This subsection applies –

    (a)   to any person who works at the premises in a capacity, whether paid or unpaid, which authorises him to request the unaccompanied child to leave the premises,

    (b)   in the case of licensed premises, to –

        (i)   the holder of a premises licence in respect of the premises, and

        (ii) the designated premises supervisor (if any) under such a licence,

    (c)   in the case of premises in respect of which a club premises certificate has effect, to any member or officer of the club which holds the certificate who is present on the premises in a capacity which enables him to make such a request, and

    (d)   in the case of premises which may be used for a permitted temporary activity by virtue of Part 5, to the premises user in relation to the temporary event notice in question.

(4) Relevant premises are within this subsection if –

    (a)   they are exclusively or primarily used for the supply of alcohol for consumption on the premises, or

    (b)   they are open for the purposes of being used for the supply of alcohol for consumption on the premises by virtue of Part 5 (permitted temporary activities) and, at the time the temporary event notice in question has effect, they are exclusively or primarily used for such supplies.

(5) No offence is committed under this section if the unaccompanied child is on the premises solely for the purpose of passing to or from some other place to or from which there is no other convenient means of access or egress.

(6) Where a person is charged with an offence under this section by reason of his own conduct it is a defence that –

    (a) he believed that the unaccompanied child was aged 16 or over or that an individual accompanying him was aged 18 or over, and

    (b) either –

        (i)   he had taken all reasonable steps to establish the individual's age, or

        (ii) nobody could reasonably have suspected from the individual's appearance that he was aged under 16 or, as the case may be, under 18.

(7) For the purposes of subsection (6), a person is treated as having taken all reasonable steps to establish an individual's age if –

    (a) he asked the individual for evidence of his age, and

    (b) the evidence would have convinced a reasonable person.

(8) Where a person ('the accused') is charged with an offence under this section by reason of the act or default of some other person, it is a defence that the accused exercised all due diligence to avoid committing it.

(9) A person guilty of an offence under this section is liable on summary conviction to a fine not exceeding level 3 on the standard scale.

(10) In this section 'supply of alcohol' means –

    (a) the sale by retail of alcohol, or

    (b) the supply of alcohol by or on behalf of a club to, or to the order of, a member of the club.

146 Sale of alcohol to children

(1) A person commits an offence if he sells alcohol to an individual aged under 18.

(2) A club commits an offence if alcohol is supplied by it or on its behalf –

    (a) to, or to the order of, a member of the club who is aged under 18, or

    (b) to the order of a member of the club, to an individual who is aged under 18.

(3) A person commits an offence if he supplies alcohol on behalf of a club –

    (a) to, or to the order of, a member of the club who is aged under 18, or

    (b) to the order of a member of the club, to an individual who is aged under 18.

(4) Where a person is charged with an offence under this section by reason of his own conduct it is a defence that –

    (a) he believed that the individual was aged 18 or over, and

    (b) either –

        (i)   he had taken all reasonable steps to establish the individual's age, or

        (ii) nobody could reasonably have suspected from the individual's appearance that he was aged under 18.

(5) For the purposes of subsection (4), a person is treated as having taken all reasonable steps to establish an individual's age if –

(a)   he asked the individual for evidence of his age, and
(b)   the evidence would have convinced a reasonable person.

(6) Where a person ('the accused') is charged with an offence under this section by reason of the act or default of some other person, it is a defence that the accused exercised all due diligence to avoid committing it.

(7) A person guilty of an offence under this section is liable on summary conviction to a fine not exceeding level 5 on the standard scale.

147 Allowing the sale of alcohol to children

(1) A person to whom subsection (2) applies commits an offence if he knowingly allows the sale of alcohol on relevant premises to an individual aged under 18.

(2) This subsection applies to a person who works at the premises in a capacity, whether paid or unpaid, which authorises him to prevent the sale.

(3) A person to whom subsection (4) applies commits an offence if he knowingly allows alcohol to be supplied on relevant premises by or on behalf of a club –

(a)   to or to the order of a member of the club who is aged under 18, or
(b)   to the order of a member of the club, to an individual who is aged under 18.

(4) This subsection applies to –

(a)   a person who works on the premises in a capacity, whether paid or unpaid, which authorises him to prevent the supply, and
(b)   any member or officer of the club who at the time of the supply is present on the relevant premises in a capacity which enables him to prevent it.

(5) A person guilty of an offence under this section is liable on summary conviction to a fine not exceeding level 5 on the standard scale.

148 Sale of liqueur confectionery to children under 16

(1) A person commits an offence if he –

(a)   sells liqueur confectionery to an individual aged under 16, or
(b)   supplies such confectionery, on behalf of a club –
    (i)   to or to the order of a member of the club who is aged under 16, or
    (ii)   to the order of a member of the club, to an individual who is aged under 16.

(2) A club commits an offence if liqueur confectionery is supplied by it or on its behalf –

(a)   to or to the order of a member of the club who is aged under 16, or

(b) to the order of a member of the club, to an individual who is aged under 16.

(3) Where a person is charged with an offence under this section by reason of his own conduct it is a defence that –

(a) he believed that the individual was aged 16 or over, and
(b) either –
    (i) he had taken all reasonable steps to establish the individual's age, or
    (ii) nobody could reasonably have suspected from the individual's appearance that he was aged under 16.

(4) For the purposes of subsection (3), a person is treated as having taken all reasonable steps to establish an individual's age if –

(a) he asked the individual for evidence of his age, and
(b) the evidence would have convinced a reasonable person.

(5) Where a person ('the accused') is charged with an offence under this section by reason of the act or default of some other person, it is a defence that the accused exercised all due diligence to avoid committing it.

(6) A person guilty of an offence under this section is liable on summary conviction to a fine not exceeding level 2 on the standard scale.

(7) In this section 'liqueur confectionery' has the meaning given in section 191(2).

149 Purchase of alcohol by or on behalf of children

(1) An individual aged under 18 commits an offence if –

(a) he buys or attempts to buy alcohol, or
(b) where he is a member of a club –
    (i) alcohol is supplied to him or to his order by or on behalf of the club, as a result of some act or default of his, or
    (ii) he attempts to have alcohol supplied to him or to his order by or on behalf of the club.

(2) But subsection (1) does not apply where the individual buys or attempts to buy the alcohol at the request of –

(a) a constable, or
(b) a weights and measures inspector,

who is acting in the course of his duty.

(3) A person commits an offence if –

(a) he buys or attempts to buy alcohol on behalf of an individual aged under 18, or
(b) where he is a member of a club, on behalf of an individual aged under 18 he –
    (i) makes arrangements whereby alcohol is supplied to him or to his order by or on behalf of the club, or
    (ii) attempts to make such arrangements.

(4) A person ('the relevant person') commits an offence if –

    (a)   he buys or attempts to buy alcohol for consumption on relevant premises by an individual aged under 18, or

    (b)   where he is a member of a club –

        (i)   by some act or default of his, alcohol is supplied to him, or to his order, by or on behalf of the club for consumption on relevant premises by an individual aged under 18, or

        (ii)   he attempts to have alcohol so supplied for such consumption.

(5) But subsection (4) does not apply where –

    (a)   the relevant person is aged 18 or over,

    (b)   the individual is aged 16 or 17,

    (c)   the alcohol is beer, wine or cider,

    (d)   its purchase or supply is for consumption at a table meal on relevant premises, and

    (e)   the individual is accompanied at the meal by an individual aged 18 or over.

(6) Where a person is charged with an offence under subsection (3) or (4) it is a defence that he had no reason to suspect that the individual was aged under 18.

(7) A person guilty of an offence under this section is liable on summary conviction –

    (a)   in the case of an offence under subsection (1), to a fine not exceeding level 3 on the standard scale, and

    (b)   in the case of an offence under subsection (3) or (4), to a fine not exceeding level 5 on the standard scale.

150 Consumption of alcohol by children

(1) An individual aged under 18 commits an offence if he knowingly consumes alcohol on relevant premises.

(2) A person to whom subsection (3) applies commits an offence if he knowingly allows the consumption of alcohol on relevant premises by an individual aged under 18.

(3) This subsection applies –

    (a)   to a person who works at the premises in a capacity, whether paid or unpaid, which authorises him to prevent the consumption, and

    (b)   where the alcohol was supplied by a club to or to the order of a member of the club, to any member or officer of the club who is present at the premises at the time of the consumption in a capacity which enables him to prevent it.

(4) Subsections (1) and (2) do not apply where –

    (a)   the individual is aged 16 or 17,

    (b)   the alcohol is beer, wine or cider,

(c) its consumption is at a table meal on relevant premises, and
(d) the individual is accompanied at the meal by an individual aged 18 or over.

(5) A person guilty of an offence under this section is liable on summary conviction –

(a) in the case of an offence under subsection (1), to a fine not exceeding level 3 on the standard scale, and
(b) in the case of an offence under subsection (2), to a fine not exceeding level 5 on the standard scale.

151 Delivering alcohol to children

(1) A person who works on relevant premises in any capacity, whether paid or unpaid, commits an offence if he knowingly delivers to an individual aged under 18 –

(a) alcohol sold on the premises, or
(b) alcohol supplied on the premises by or on behalf of a club to or to the order of a member of the club.

(2) A person to whom subsection (3) applies commits an offence if he knowingly allows anybody else to deliver to an individual aged under 18 alcohol sold on relevant premises.

(3) This subsection applies to a person who works on the premises in a capacity, whether paid or unpaid, which authorises him to prevent the delivery of the alcohol.

(4) A person to whom subsection (5) applies commits an offence if he knowingly allows anybody else to deliver to an individual aged under 18 alcohol supplied on relevant premises by or on behalf of a club to or to the order of a member of the club.

(5) This subsection applies –

(a) to a person who works on the premises in a capacity, whether paid or unpaid, which authorises him to prevent the supply, and
(b) to any member or officer of the club who at the time of the supply in question is present on the premises in a capacity which enables him to prevent the supply.

(6) Subsections (1), (2) and (4) do not apply where –

(a) the alcohol is delivered at a place where the buyer or, as the case may be, person supplied lives or works, or
(b) the individual aged under 18 works on the relevant premises in a capacity, whether paid or unpaid, which involves the delivery of alcohol, or
(c) the alcohol is sold or supplied for consumption on the relevant premises.

(7) A person guilty of an offence under this section is liable on summary conviction to a fine not exceeding level 5 on the standard scale.

152 Sending a child to obtain alcohol

(1) A person commits an offence if he knowingly sends an individual aged under 18 to obtain –

   (a)   alcohol sold or to be sold on relevant premises for consumption off the premises, or
   (b)   alcohol supplied or to be supplied by or on behalf of a club to or to the order of a member of the club for such consumption.

(2) For the purposes of this section, it is immaterial whether the individual aged under 18 is sent to obtain the alcohol from the relevant premises or from other premises from which it is delivered in pursuance of the sale or supply.

(3) Subsection (1) does not apply where the individual aged under 18 works on the relevant premises in a capacity, whether paid or unpaid, which involves the delivery of alcohol.

(4) Subsection (1) also does not apply where the individual aged under 18 is sent by –

   (a)   a constable, or
   (b)   a weights and measures inspector,

who is acting in the course of his duty.

(5) A person guilty of an offence under this section is liable on summary conviction to a fine not exceeding level 5 on the standard scale.

153 Prohibition of unsupervised sales by children

(1) A responsible person commits an offence if on any relevant premises he knowingly allows an individual aged under 18 to make on the premises –

   (a)   any sale of alcohol, or
   (b)   any supply of alcohol by or on behalf of a club to or to the order of a member of the club,

unless the sale or supply has been specifically approved by that or another responsible person.

(2) But subsection (1) does not apply where –

   (a)   the alcohol is sold or supplied for consumption with a table meal,
   (b)   it is sold or supplied in premises which are being used for the service of table meals (or in a part of any premises which is being so used), and
   (c)   the premises are (or the part is) not used for the sale or supply of alcohol otherwise than to persons having table meals there and for consumption by such a person as an ancillary to his meal.

(3) A person guilty of an offence under this section is liable on summary conviction to a fine not exceeding level 1 on the standard scale.

(4) In this section 'responsible person' means –

   (a)   in relation to licensed premises –
         (i)   the holder of a premises licence in respect of the premises,

     (ii)   the designated premises supervisor (if any) under such a licence, or

     (iii) any individual aged 18 or over who is authorised for the purposes of this section by such a holder or supervisor,

  (b) in relation to premises in respect of which there is in force a club premises certificate, any member or officer of the club present on the premises in a capacity which enables him to prevent the supply in question, and

  (c) in relation to premises which may be used for a permitted temporary activity by virtue of Part 5 –

     (i)   the premises user, or

     (ii) any individual aged 18 or over who is authorised for the purposes of this section by the premises user.

154 Enforcement role for weights and measures authorities

(1) It is the duty of every local weights and measures authority in England and Wales to enforce within its area the provisions of sections 146 and 147, so far as they apply to sales of alcohol made on or from premises to which the public have access.

(2) A weights and measures inspector may make, or authorise any person to make on his behalf, such purchases of goods as appear expedient for the purpose of determining whether those provisions are being complied with.

Confiscation of alcohol

155 Confiscation of sealed containers of alcohol

(1) In section 1 of the Confiscation of Alcohol (Young Persons) Act 1997 (c 33) (right to require surrender of alcohol) –

  (a) in subsection (1), omit '(other than a sealed container)',

  (b) after that subsection insert –

     '(1A) But a constable may not under subsection (1) require a person to surrender any sealed container unless the constable reasonably believes that the person is, or has been, consuming, or intends to consume, alcohol in any relevant place.', and

  (c) in subsection (6), after 'subsection (1)' insert 'and (1A)'.

(2) In section 12(2)(b) of the Criminal Justice and Police Act 2001 (c 16) (right to require surrender of alcohol), omit '(other than a sealed container)'.

Vehicles and trains

156 Prohibition on sale of alcohol on moving vehicles

(1) A person commits an offence under this section if he sells by retail alcohol on or from a vehicle at a time when the vehicle is not permanently or temporarily parked.

(2) A person guilty of an offence under this section is liable on summary conviction to imprisonment for a term not exceeding three months or to a fine not exceeding £20,000, or to both.

(3) In proceedings against a person for an offence under this section, it is a defence that –

(a)   his act was due to a mistake, or to reliance on information given to him, or to an act or omission by another person, or to some other cause beyond his control, and

(b)   he took all reasonable precautions and exercised all due diligence to avoid committing the offence.

157 Power to prohibit sale of alcohol on trains

(1) A magistrates' court acting for a petty sessions area may make an order prohibiting the sale of alcohol, during such period as may be specified, on any railway vehicle –

(a)   at such station or stations as may be specified, being stations in that area, or

(b)   travelling between such stations as may be specified, at least one of which is in that area.

(2) A magistrates' court may make an order under this section only on the application of a senior police officer.

(3) A magistrates' court may not make such an order unless it is satisfied that the order is necessary to prevent disorder.

(4) Where an order is made under this section, the responsible senior police officer must, forthwith, serve a copy of the order on the train operator (or each train operator) affected by the order.

(5) A person commits an offence if he knowingly –

(a)   sells or attempts to sell alcohol in contravention of an order under this section, or

(b)   allows the sale of alcohol in contravention of such an order.

(6) A person guilty of an offence under this section is liable on summary conviction to imprisonment for a term not exceeding three months or to a fine not exceeding £20,000, or to both.

(7) In this section –

'railway vehicle' has the meaning given by section 83 of the Railways Act 1993;

'responsible senior police officer', in relation to an order under this section, means the senior police officer who applied for the order or, if the chief officer of police of the force in question has designated another senior police officer for the purpose, that other officer;

'senior police officer' means a police officer of, or above, the rank of inspector;

'specified' means specified in the order under this section;

'station' has the meaning given by section 83 of the Railways Act 1993 (c 43); and

'train operator' means a person authorised by a licence under section 8 of that Act to operate railway assets (within the meaning of section 6 of that Act).

False statement relating to licensing etc

158 False statements made for the purposes of this Act

(1) A person commits an offence if he knowingly or recklessly makes a false statement in or in connection with –

    (a) an application for the grant, variation, transfer or review of a premises licence or club premises certificate,

    (b) an application for a provisional statement,

    (c) a temporary event notice, an interim authority notice or any other notice under this Act,

    (d) an application for the grant or renewal of a personal licence, or

    (e) a notice within section 178(1) (notice by freeholder etc conferring right to be notified of changes to licensing register).

(2) For the purposes of subsection (1) a person is to be treated as making a false statement if he produces, furnishes, signs or otherwise makes use of a document that contains a false statement.

(3) A person guilty of an offence under this section is liable on summary conviction to a fine not exceeding level 5 on the standard scale.

Interpretation

159 Interpretation of Part 7

In this Part –

    'authorisation' has the meaning given in section 136(5);
    'relevant premises' means –

        (a) licensed premises, or

        (b) premises in respect of which there is in force a club premises certificate, or

        (c) premises which may be used for a permitted temporary activity by virtue of Part 5;

    'table meal' means a meal eaten by a person seated at a table, or at a counter or other structure which serves the purpose of a table and is not used for the service of refreshments for consumption by persons not seated at a table or structure serving the purpose of a table; and
    'weights and measures inspector' means an inspector of weights and measures appointed under section 72(1) of the Weights and Measures Act 1985 (c 72).

PART 8

CLOSURE OF PREMISES

Closure of premises in an identified area

160 Orders to close premises in area experiencing disorder

(1) Where there is or is expected to be disorder in any petty sessions area, a magistrates' court acting for the area may make an order requiring all premises –

    (a)   which are situated at or near the place of the disorder or expected disorder, and

    (b)   in respect of which a premises licence or a temporary event notice has effect,

to be closed for a period, not exceeding 24 hours, specified in the order.

(2) A magistrates' court may make an order under this section only on the application of a police officer who is of the rank of superintendent or above.

(3) A magistrates' court may not make such an order unless it is satisfied that it is necessary to prevent disorder.

(4) Where an order is made under this section, a person to whom subsection (5) applies commits an offence if he knowingly keeps any premises to which the order relates open, or allows any such premises to be kept open, during the period of the order.

(5) This subsection applies –

    (a)   to any manager of the premises,

    (b)   in the case of licensed premises, to –

        (i)   the holder of a premises licence in respect of the premises, and

        (ii)   the designated premises supervisor (if any) under such a licence, and

    (c)   in the case of premises in respect of which a temporary event notice has effect, to the premises user in relation to that notice.

(6) A person guilty of an offence under subsection (4) is liable on summary conviction to a fine not exceeding level 3 on the standard scale.

(7) A constable may use such force as may be necessary for the purpose of closing premises ordered to be closed under this section.

Closure of identified premises

161 Closure orders for identified premises

(1) A senior police officer may make a closure order in relation to any relevant premises if he reasonably believes that –

    (a)   there is, or is likely imminently to be, disorder on, or in the vicinity of and related to, the premises and their closure is necessary in the interests of public safety, or

    (b)   a public nuisance is being caused by noise coming from the premises and the closure of the premises is necessary to prevent that nuisance.

(2) A closure order is an order under this section requiring relevant premises to be closed for a period not exceeding 24 hours beginning with the coming into force of the order.

(3) In determining whether to make a closure order in respect of any premises, the senior police officer must have regard, in particular, to the conduct of each appropriate person in relation to the disorder or nuisance.

(4) A closure order must –

    (a)   specify the premises to which it relates,

(b) specify the period for which the premises are to be closed,

(c) specify the grounds on which it is made, and

(d) state the effect of sections 162 to 168.

(5) A closure order in respect of any relevant premises comes into force at the time a constable gives notice of it to an appropriate person who is connected with any of the activities to which the disorder or nuisance relates.

(6) A person commits an offence if, without reasonable excuse, he permits relevant premises to be open in contravention of a closure order or any extension of it.

(7) A person guilty of an offence under subsection (6) is liable on summary conviction to imprisonment for a term not exceeding three months or to a fine not exceeding £20,000, or to both.

(8) In this section –

'relevant premises' means premises in respect of which one or more of the following have effect –

(a) a premises licence,

(b) a temporary event notice; and

'senior police officer' means a police officer of, or above, the rank of inspector.

162 Extension of closure order

(1) Where, before the end of the period for which relevant premises are to be closed under a closure order or any extension of it (the 'closure period'), the responsible senior police officer reasonably believes that –

(a) a relevant magistrates' court will not have determined whether to exercise its powers under section 165(2) in respect of the closure order, and any extension of it, by the end of the closure period, and

(b) the conditions for an extension are satisfied,

he may extend the closure period for a further period not exceeding 24 hours beginning with the end of the previous closure period.

(2) The conditions for an extension are that –

(a) in the case of an order made by virtue of section 161(1)(a), closure is necessary in the interests of public safety because of disorder or likely disorder on, or in the vicinity of and related to, the premises,

(b) in the case of an order made by virtue of section 161(1)(b), closure is necessary to ensure that no public nuisance is, or is likely to be, caused by noise coming from the premises.

(3) An extension in relation to any relevant premises comes into force when a constable gives notice of it to an appropriate person connected with any of the activities to which the disorder or nuisance relates or is expected to relate.

(4) But the extension does not come into force unless the notice is given before the end of the previous closure period.

163 Cancellation of closure order

(1) The responsible senior police officer may cancel a closure order and any extension of it at any time –

    (a)   after the making of the order, but

    (b)   before a relevant magistrates' court has determined whether to exercise its powers under section 165(2) in respect of the order and any extension of it.

(2) The responsible senior police officer must cancel a closure order and any extension of it if he does not reasonably believe that –

    (a)   in the case of an order made by virtue of section 161(1)(a), closure is necessary in the interests of public safety because of disorder or likely disorder on, or in the vicinity of and related to, the premises,

    (b)   in the case of an order made by virtue of section 161(1)(b), closure is necessary to ensure that no public nuisance is, or is likely to be, caused by noise coming from the premises.

(3) Where a closure order and any extension of it are cancelled under this section, the responsible senior police officer must give notice of the cancellation to an appropriate person connected with any of the activities related to the disorder (or anticipated disorder) or nuisance in respect of which the closure order was made.

164 Application to magistrates' court by police

(1) The responsible senior police officer must, as soon as reasonably practicable after a closure order comes into force in respect of any relevant premises, apply to a relevant magistrates court for it to consider the order and any extension of it.

(2) Where an application is made under this section in respect of licensed premises, the responsible senior officer must also notify the relevant licensing authority –

    (a)   that a closure order has come into force,

    (b)   of the contents of the order and of any extension of it, and

    (c)   of the application under subsection (1).

165 Consideration of closure order by magistrates' court

(1) A relevant magistrates' court must as soon as reasonably practicable after receiving an application under section 164(1) –

    (a)   hold a hearing to consider whether it is appropriate to exercise any of the court's powers under subsection (2) in relation to the closure order or any extension of it, and

    (b)   determine whether to exercise any of those powers.

(2) The relevant magistrates' court may –

    (a)   revoke the closure order and any extension of it;

    (b)   order the premises to remain, or to be, closed until such time as the relevant licensing authority has made a determination in respect of the order for the purposes of section 167;

    (c)   order the premises to remain or to be closed until that time subject to such exceptions as may be specified in the order;

    (d)   order the premises to remain or to be closed until that time unless such conditions as may be specified in the order are satisfied.

(3) In determining whether the premises will be, or will remain, closed the relevant magistrates' court must, in particular, consider whether –

    (a)   in the case of an order made by virtue of section 161(1)(a), closure is necessary in the interests of public safety because of disorder or likely disorder on the premises, or in the vicinity of and related to, the premises;

    (b)   in the case of an order made by virtue of section 161(1)(b), closure is necessary to ensure that no public nuisance is, or is likely to be, caused by noise coming from the premises.

(4) In the case of licensed premises, the relevant magistrates' court must notify the relevant licensing authority of any determination it makes under subsection (1)(b).

(5) Subsection (2) does not apply if, before the relevant magistrates' court discharges its functions under that subsection, the premises cease to be relevant premises.

(6) Any order made under subsection (2) ceases to have effect if the premises cease to be relevant premises.

(7) A person commits an offence if, without reasonable excuse, he permits relevant premises to be open in contravention of an order under subsection (2)(b), (c) or (d).

(8) A person guilty of an offence under subsection (7) is liable on summary conviction to imprisonment for a term not exceeding three months or to a fine not exceeding £20,000, or to both.

(9) The powers conferred on a magistrates' court by this section are to be exercised in the place required by the Magistrates' Courts Act 1980 (c 43) for the hearing of a complaint and may be exercised by a single justice.

(10) Evidence given for the purposes of proceedings under this section must be given on oath.

166 Appeal from decision of magistrates' court

(1) Any person aggrieved by a decision of a magistrates' court under section 165 may appeal to the Crown Court against the decision.

(2) An appeal under subsection (1) must be commenced by notice of appeal given by the appellant to the justices' chief executive for the magistrates' court within the period of 21 days beginning with the day the decision appealed against was made.

167 Review of premises licence following closure order

(1) This section applies where –

    (a)   a closure order has come into force in relation to premises in respect of which a premises licence has effect, and

    (b)   the relevant licensing authority has received a notice under section 165(4) (notice of magistrates' court's determination), in relation to the order and any extension of it.

(2) The relevant licensing authority must review the premises licence.

(3) The authority must reach a determination on the review no later than 28 days after the day on which it receives the notice mentioned in subsection (1)(b).

(4) The Secretary of State must by regulations –

    (a)   require the relevant licensing authority to give, to the holder of the premises licence and each responsible authority, notice of –
        (i)   the review,
        (ii)   the closure order and any extension of it, and
        (iii) any order made in relation to it under section 165(2);

    (b)   require the authority to advertise the review and invite representations about it to be made to the authority by responsible authorities and interested parties;

    (c)   prescribe the period during which representations may be made by the holder of the premises licence, any responsible authority or any interested party;

    (d)   require any notice under paragraph (a) or advertisement under paragraph (b) to specify that period.

(5) The relevant licensing authority must –

    (a)   hold a hearing to consider –
        (i)   the closure order and any extension of it,
        (ii)   any order under section 165(2), and
        (iii) any relevant representations, and

    (b)   take such of the steps mentioned in subsection (6) (if any) as it considers necessary for the promotion of the licensing objectives.

(6) Those steps are –

    (a)   to modify the conditions of the premises licence,
    (b)   to exclude a licensable activity from the scope of the licence,
    (c)   to remove the designated premises supervisor from the licence,
    (d)   to suspend the licence for a period not exceeding three months, or
    (e)   to revoke the licence;

and for this purpose the conditions of a premises licence are modified if any of them is altered or omitted or any new condition is added.

(7) Subsection (5)(b) is subject to sections 19, 20 and 21 (requirement to include certain conditions in premises licences).

(8) Where the authority takes a step within subsection (6)(a) or (b), it may provide that the modification or exclusion is to have effect only for a specified period (not exceeding three months).

(9) In this section 'relevant representations' means representations which –

(a)   are relevant to one or more of the licensing objectives, and
(b)   meet the requirements of subsection (10).

(10) The requirements are –

(a)   that the representations are made by the holder of the premises licence, a responsible authority or an interested party within the period prescribed under subsection (4)(c),
(b)   that they have not been withdrawn, and
(c)   if they are made by an interested party (who is not also a responsible authority), that they are not, in the opinion of the relevant licensing authority, frivolous or vexatious.

(11) Where the relevant licensing authority determines that any representations are frivolous or vexatious, it must notify the person who made them of the reasons for that determination.

(12) Where a licensing authority determines a review under this section it must notify the determination and its reasons for making it to –

(a)   the holder of the licence,
(b)   any person who made relevant representations, and
(c)   the chief officer of police for the police area (or each police area) in which the premises are situated.

(13) Section 168 makes provision about when the determination takes effect.

(14) In this section 'interested party' and 'responsible authority' have the same meaning as in Part 3.

168 Provision about decisions under section 167

(1) Subject to this section, a decision under section 167 does not have effect until the relevant time.

(2) In this section 'the relevant time', in relation to any decision, means –

(a)   the end of the period given for appealing against the decision, or
(b)   if the decision is appealed against, the time the appeal is disposed of.

(3) Subsections (4) and (5) apply where –

(a)   the relevant licensing authority decides on a review under section 167 to take one or more of the steps mentioned in subsection (6)(a) to (d) of that section, and
(b)   the premises to which the licence relates have been closed, by virtue of an order under section 165(2)(b), (c) or (d), until that decision was made.

(4) The decision by the relevant licensing authority to take any of the steps mentioned in section 167(6)(a) to (d) takes effect when it is notified to the holder of the licence under section 167(12).

This is subject to subsection (5) and paragraph 18(3) of Schedule 5 (power of magistrates' court to suspend decision pending appeal).

(5) The relevant licensing authority may, on such terms as it thinks fit, suspend the operation of that decision (in whole or in part) until the relevant time.

(6) Subsection (7) applies where –

(a)   the relevant licensing authority decides on a review under section 167 to revoke the premises licence, and

(b)   the premises to which the licence relates have been closed, by virtue of an order under section 165(2)(b), (c) or (d), until that decision was made.

(7) The premises must remain closed (but the licence otherwise in force) until the relevant time.

This is subject to paragraph 18(4) of Schedule 5 (power of magistrates' court to modify closure order pending appeal).

(8) A person commits an offence if, without reasonable excuse, he allows premises to be open in contravention of subsection (7).

(9) A person guilty of an offence under subsection (8) is liable on summary conviction to imprisonment for a term not exceeding three months or to a fine not exceeding £20,000, or to both.

169 Enforcement of closure order

A constable may use such force as may be necessary for the purposes of closing premises in compliance with a closure order.

170 Exemption of police from liability for damages

(1) A constable is not liable for relevant damages in respect of any act or omission of his in the performance or purported performance of his functions in relation to a closure order or any extension of it.

(2) A chief officer of police is not liable for relevant damages in respect of any act or omission of a constable under his direction or control in the performance or purported performance of a function of the constable's in relation to a closure order or any extension of it.

(3) But neither subsection (1) nor (2) applies –

(a)   if the act or omission is shown to have been in bad faith, or

(b)   so as to prevent an award of damages in respect of an act or omission on the grounds that the act or omission was unlawful as a result of section 6(1) of the Human Rights Act 1998 (c 42) (incompatibility of act or omission with Convention rights).

(4) This section does not affect any other exemption from liability for damages (whether at common law or otherwise).

(5) In this section, 'relevant damages' means damages awarded in proceedings for judicial review, the tort of negligence or misfeasance in public office.

Interpretation

171 Interpretation of Part 8

(1) This section has effect for the purposes of this Part.

(2) Relevant premises are open if a person who is not within subsection (4) enters the premises and –

    (a) he buys or is otherwise supplied with food, drink or anything usually sold on the premises, or

    (b) while he is on the premises, they are used for the provision of regulated entertainment.

(3) But in determining whether relevant premises are open the following are to be disregarded –

    (a) where no premises licence has effect in respect of the premises, any use of the premises for activities (other than licensable activities) which do not take place during an event period specified in a temporary event notice having effect in respect of the premises,

    (b) any use of the premises for a qualifying club activity under and in accordance with a club premises certificate, and

    (c) any supply exempted under paragraph 3 of Schedule 2 (certain supplies of hot food and drink by clubs, hotels etc not a licensable activity) in circumstances where a person will neither be admitted to the premises, nor be supplied as mentioned in sub-paragraph (1)(b) of that paragraph, except by virtue of being a member of a recognised club or a guest of such a member.

(4) A person is within this subsection if he is –

    (a) an appropriate person in relation to the premises,

    (b) a person who usually lives at the premises, or

    (c) a member of the family of a person within paragraph (a) or (b).

(5) The following expressions have the meanings given –

    'appropriate person', in relation to any relevant premises, means –

        (a) any person who holds a premises licence in respect of the premises,

        (b) any designated premises supervisor under such a licence,

        (c) the premises user in relation to any temporary event notice which has effect in respect of the premises, or

        (d) a manager of the premises;

    'closure order' has the meaning given in section 161(2);

    'extension', in relation to a closure order, means an extension of the order under section 162;

    'manager', in relation to any premises, means a person who works at the premises in a capacity, whether paid or unpaid, which authorises him to close them;

    'relevant licensing authority', in relation to any licensed premises, has the same meaning as in Part 3;

'relevant magistrates' court', in relation to any relevant premises, means a magistrates' court acting for the petty sessions area in which the premises are situated;

'relevant premises' has the meaning given in section 161(8);

'responsible senior police officer', in relation to a closure order, means –

(a)   the senior police officer who made the order, or

(b)   if another senior police officer is designated for the purpose by the chief officer of police for the police area in which the premises are situated, that other officer;

'senior police officer' has the meaning given in section 161(8).

(6) A temporary event notice has effect from the time it is given in accordance with Part 5 until –

(a)   the time it is withdrawn,

(b)   the time a counter notice is given under that Part, or

(c)   the expiry of the event period specified in the temporary event notice,

whichever first occurs.

PART 9

MISCELLANEOUS AND SUPPLEMENTARY

Special occasions

172 Relaxation of opening hours for special occasions

(1) Where the Secretary of State considers that a period ('the celebration period') marks an occasion of exceptional international, national, or local significance, he may make a licensing hours order.

(2) A licensing hours order is an order which provides that during the specified relaxation period premises licences and club premises certificates have effect (to the extent that it is not already the case) as if specified times were included in the opening hours.

(3) An order under this section may –

(a)   make provision generally or only in relation to premises in one or more specified areas;

(b)   make different provision in respect of different days during the specified relaxation period;

(c)   make different provision in respect of different licensable activities.

(4) Before making an order under this section, the Secretary of State must consult such persons as he considers appropriate.

(5) In this section –

'opening hours' means –

(a)   in relation to a premises licence, the times during which the premises may be used for licensable activities in accordance with the licence, and

(b)   in relation to a club premises certificate, the times during which the premises may be used for qualifying club activities in accordance with the certificate;

'relaxation period' means –
- (a) if the celebration period does not exceed four days, that period, or
- (b) any part of that period not exceeding four days; and

'specified', in relation to a licensing hours order, means specified in the order.

Exemptions etc

173 Activities in certain locations not licensable

(1) An activity is not a licensable activity if it is carried on –

- (a) aboard an aircraft, hovercraft or railway vehicle engaged on a journey,
- (b) aboard a vessel engaged on an international journey,
- (c) at an approved wharf at a designated port or hoverport,
- (d) at an examination station at a designated airport,
- (e) at a royal palace,
- (f) at premises which, at the time when the activity is carried on, are permanently or temporarily occupied for the purposes of the armed forces of the Crown,
- (g) at premises in respect of which a certificate issued under section 174 (exemption for national security) has effect, or
- (h) at such other place as may be prescribed.

(2) For the purposes of subsection (1) the period during which an aircraft, hovercraft, railway vehicle or vessel is engaged on a journey includes –

- (a) any period ending with its departure when preparations are being made for the journey, and
- (b) any period after its arrival at its destination when it continues to be occupied by those (or any of those) who made the journey (or any part of it).

(3) The Secretary of State may by order designate a port, hoverport or airport for the purposes of subsection (1), if it appears to him to be one at which there is a substantial amount of international passenger traffic.

(4) Any port, airport or hoverport where section 86A or 87 of the Licensing Act 1964 (c 26) is in operation immediately before the commencement of this section is, on and after that commencement, to be treated for the purposes of subsection (1) as if it were designated.

(5) But provision may by order be made for subsection (4) to cease to have effect in relation to any port, airport or hoverport.

(6) For the purposes of this section –

'approved wharf' has the meaning given by section 20A of the Customs and Excise Management Act 1979 (c 2);
'designated' means designated by an order under subsection (3);
'examination station' has the meaning given by section 22A of that Act;
'international journey' means –
- (a) a journey from a place in the United Kingdom to an immediate destination outside the United Kingdom, or

(b) a journey from a place outside the United Kingdom to an immediate destination in the United Kingdom; and

'railway vehicle' has the meaning given by section 83 of the Railways Act 1993 (c 43).

174 Certifying of premises on grounds of national security

(1) A Minister of the Crown may issue a certificate under this section in respect of any premises, if he considers that it is appropriate to do so for the purposes of safeguarding national security.

(2) A certificate under this section may identify the premises in question by means of a general description.

(3) A document purporting to be a certificate under this section is to be received in evidence and treated as being a certificate under this section unless the contrary is proved.

(4) A document which purports to be certified by or on behalf of a Minister of the Crown as a true copy of a certificate given by a Minister of the Crown under this section is evidence of that certificate.

(5) A Minister of the Crown may cancel a certificate issued by him, or any other Minister of the Crown, under this section.

(6) The powers conferred by this section on a Minister of the Crown may be exercised only by a Minister who is a member of the Cabinet or by the Attorney General.

(7) In this section 'Minister of the Crown' has the meaning given by the Ministers of the Crown Act 1975 (c 26).

175 Exemption for raffle, tombola, etc

(1) The conduct of a lottery which, but for this subsection, would to any extent constitute a licensable activity by reason of one or more of the prizes in the lottery consisting of alcohol, is not (for that reason alone) to be treated as constituting a licensable activity if –

(a) the lottery is promoted as an incident of an exempt entertainment,
(b) after the deduction of all relevant expenses, the whole proceeds of the entertainment (including those of the lottery) are applied for purposes other than private gain, and
(c) subsection (2) does not apply.

(2) This subsection applies if –

(a) the alcohol consists of or includes alcohol not in a sealed container,
(b) any prize in the lottery is a money prize,
(c) a ticket or chance in the lottery is sold or issued, or the result of the lottery is declared, other than at the premises where the entertainment takes place and during the entertainment, or
(d) the opportunity to participate in a lottery or in gaming is the only or main inducement to attend the entertainment.

(3) For the purposes of subsection (1)(b), the following are relevant expenses –

  (a) the expenses of the entertainment, excluding expenses incurred in connection with the lottery,
  (b) the expenses incurred in printing tickets in the lottery,
  (c) such reasonable and proper expenses as the promoters of the lottery appropriate on account of any expenses they incur in buying prizes in the lottery.

(4) In this section –

  'exempt entertainment' has the same meaning as in section 3(1) of the Lotteries and Amusements Act 1976 (c 32);
  'gaming' has the meaning given by section 52 of the Gaming Act 1968 (c 65);
  'money' and 'ticket' have the meaning given by section 23 of the Lotteries and Amusements Act 1976; and
  'private gain', in relation to the proceeds of an entertainment, is to be construed in accordance with section 22 of that Act.

Service areas and garages etc

176 Prohibition of alcohol sales at service areas, garages etc

(1) No premises licence, club premises certificate or temporary event notice has effect to authorise the sale by retail or supply of alcohol on or from excluded premises.

(2) In this section 'excluded premises' means –

  (a) premises situated on land acquired or appropriated by a special road authority, and for the time being used, for the provision of facilities to be used in connection with the use of a special road provided for the use of traffic of class I (with or without other classes); or
  (b) premises used primarily as a garage or which form part of premises which are primarily so used.

(3) The Secretary of State may by order amend the definition of excluded premises in subsection (2) so as to include or exclude premises of such description as may be specified in the order.

(4) For the purposes of this section –

  (a) 'special road' and 'special road authority' have the same meaning as in the Highways Act 1980 (c 66), except that 'special road' includes a trunk road to which (by virtue of paragraph 3 of Schedule 23 to that Act) the provisions of that Act apply as if the road were a special road,
  (b) 'class I' means class I in Schedule 4 to the Highways Act 1980 as varied from time to time by an order under section 17 of that Act, but if that Schedule is amended by such an order so as to add to it a further class of traffic, the order may adapt the reference in subsection (2)(a) to traffic of class I so as to take account of the additional class, and
  (c) premises are used as a garage if they are used for one or more of the following –

(i)   the retailing of petrol,
(ii)   the retailing of derv,
(iii) the sale of motor vehicles,
(iv)   the maintenance of motor vehicles.

177 Dancing and live music in certain small premises

(1) Subsection (2) applies where –

  (a)   a premises licence authorises –
    (i)   the supply of alcohol for consumption on the premises, and
    (ii)   the provision of music entertainment, and
  (b)   the premises –
    (i)   are used primarily for the supply of alcohol for consumption on the premises, and
    (ii)   have a permitted capacity of not more than 200 persons.

(2) At any time when –

  (a)   the premises –
    (i)   are open for the purposes of being used for the supply of alcohol for consumption on the premises, and
    (ii)   are being used for the provision of music entertainment, and
  (b)   subsection (4) does not apply,

any licensing authority imposed condition of the premises licence which relates to the provision of music entertainment does not have effect, in relation to the provision of that entertainment, unless it falls within subsection (5) or (6).

(3) Subsection (4) applies where –

  (a)   a premises licence authorises the provision of music entertainment, and
  (b)   the premises have a permitted capacity of not more than 200 persons.

(4) At any time between the hours of 8 am and midnight when the premises –

  (a)   are being used for the provision of music entertainment which consists of –
    (i)   the performance of unamplified, live music, or
    (ii)   facilities for enabling persons to take part in entertainment within sub-paragraph (i), but
  (b)   are not being used for the provision of any other description of regulated entertainment,

any licensing authority imposed condition of the premises licence which relates to the provision of the music entertainment does not have effect, in relation to the provision of that entertainment, unless it falls within subsection (6).

(5) A condition falls within this subsection if the premises licence specifies that the licensing authority which granted the licence considers the

imposition of the condition necessary on one or both of the following grounds –

(a)   the prevention of crime and disorder,
(b)   public safety.

(6) A condition falls within this subsection if, on a review of the premises licence –

(a)   it is altered so as to include a statement that this section does not apply to it, or
(b)   it is added to the licence and includes such a statement.

(7) This section applies in relation to a club premises certificate as it applies in relation to a premises licence except that, in the application of this section in relation to such a certificate, the definition of 'licensing authority imposed condition' in subsection (8) has effect as if for 'section 18(3)(b)' to the end there were substituted 'section 72(3)(b) (but is not referred to in section 72(2)) or which is imposed by virtue of section 85(3)(b) or 88(3)'.

(8) In this section –

'licensing authority imposed condition' means a condition which is imposed by virtue of section 18(3)(b) (but is not referred to in section 18(2)(a)) or which is imposed by virtue of 35(3)(b), 52(3) or 167(5)(b) or in accordance with section 21;
'music entertainment' means –
(a)   entertainment of a description falling within, or of a similar description to that falling within, paragraph 2(1)(e) or (g) of Schedule 1, or
(b)   facilities enabling persons to take part in entertainment within paragraph (a);
'permitted capacity', in relation to any premises, means –
(a)   where a fire certificate issued under the Fire Precautions Act 1971 (c 40) is in force in respect of the premises and that certificate imposes a requirement under section 6(2)(d) of that Act, the limit on the number of persons who, in accordance with that requirement, may be on the premises at any one time, and
(b)   in any other case, the limit on the number of persons who may be on the premises at any one time in accordance with a recommendation made by, or on behalf of, the fire authority for the area in which the premises are situated (or, if the premises are situated in the area of more than one fire authority, those authorities); and
'supply of alcohol' means –

(a)   the sale by retail of alcohol, or
(b)   the supply of alcohol by or on behalf of a club to, or to the order of, a member of the club.

Rights of freeholders etc

178 Right of freeholder etc to be notified of licensing matters

(1) This section applies where –

   (a)   a person with a property interest in any premises situated in the area of a licensing authority gives notice of his interest to that authority, and

   (b)   the notice is in the prescribed form and accompanied by the prescribed fee.

(2) The notice has effect for a period of 12 months beginning with the day it is received by the licensing authority.

(3) If a change relating to the premises to which the notice relates is made to the register at a time when the notice has effect, the licensing authority must forthwith notify the person who gave the notice –

   (a)   of the application, notice or other matter to which the change relates, and

   (b)   of his right under section 8 to request a copy of the information contained in any entry in the register.

(4) For the purposes of this section a person has a property interest in premises if –

   (a)   he has a legal interest in the premises as freeholder or leaseholder,

   (b)   he is a legal mortgagee (within the meaning of the Law of Property Act 1925 (c 20)) in respect of the premises,

   (c)   he is in occupation of the premises, or

   (d)   he has a prescribed interest in the premises.

(5) In this section –

   (a)   a reference to premises situated in the area of a licensing authority includes a reference to premises partly so situated, and

   (b)   'register' means the register kept under section 8 by the licensing authority mentioned in subsection (1)(a).

Rights of entry

179 Rights of entry to investigate licensable activities

(1) Where a constable or an authorised person has reason to believe that any premises are being, or are about to be, used for a licensable activity, he may enter the premises with a view to seeing whether the activity is being, or is to be, carried on under and in accordance with an authorisation.

(2) An authorised person exercising the power conferred by this section must, if so requested, produce evidence of his authority to exercise the power.

(3) A person exercising the power conferred by this section may, if necessary, use reasonable force.

(4) A person commits an offence if he intentionally obstructs an authorised person exercising a power conferred by this section.

(5) A person guilty of an offence under subsection (4) is liable on summary conviction to a fine not exceeding level 3 on the standard scale.

(6) In this section –

'authorisation' means –
   (a) a premises licence,
   (b) a club premises certificate, or
   (c) a temporary event notice in respect of which the conditions of section 98(2) to (4) are satisfied; and
'authorised person' means an authorised person within the meaning of Part 3 or 4 or an authorised officer within the meaning of section 108(5).

(7) Nothing in this section applies in relation to premises in respect of which there is a club premises certificate but no other authorisation.

180 Right of entry to investigate offences

(1) A constable may enter and search any premises in respect of which he has reason to believe that an offence under this Act has been, is being or is about to be committed.

(2) A constable exercising a power conferred by this section may, if necessary, use reasonable force.

Appeals

181 Appeals against decisions of licensing authorities

(1) Schedule 5 (which makes provision for appeals against decisions of licensing authorities) has effect.

(2) On an appeal in accordance with that Schedule against a decision of a licensing authority, a magistrates' court may –

   (a) dismiss the appeal,
   (b) substitute for the decision appealed against any other decision which could have been made by the licensing authority, or
   (c) remit the case to the licensing authority to dispose of it in accordance with the direction of the court,

and may make such order as to costs as it thinks fit.

Guidance, hearings etc

182 Guidance

(1) The Secretary of State must issue guidance ('the licensing guidance') to licensing authorities on the discharge of their functions under this Act.

(2) But the Secretary of State may not issue the licensing guidance unless a draft of it has been laid before, and approved by resolution of, each House of Parliament.

(3) The Secretary of State may, from time to time, revise the licensing guidance.

(4) A revised version of the licensing guidance does not come into force until the Secretary of State lays it before Parliament.

(5) Where either House, before the end of the period of 40 days beginning with the day on which a revised version of the licensing guidance is laid before it, by resolution disapproves that version –

> (a) the Secretary of State must, under subsection (3), make such further revisions to the licensing guidance as appear to him to be required in the circumstances, and
> (b) before the end of the period of 40 days beginning with the date on which the resolution is made, lay a further revised version of the licensing guidance before Parliament.

(6) In reckoning any period of 40 days for the purposes of subsection (5), no account is to be taken of any time during which –

> (a) Parliament is dissolved or prorogued, or
> (b) both Houses are adjourned for more than four days.

(7) The Secretary of State must arrange for any guidance issued or revised under this section to be published in such manner as he considers appropriate.

183 Hearings

(1) Regulations may prescribe the procedure to be followed in relation to a hearing held by a licensing authority under this Act and, in particular, may –

> (a) require a licensing authority to give notice of hearings to such persons as may be prescribed;
> (b) make provision for expedited procedures in urgent cases;
> (c) make provision about the rules of evidence which are to apply to hearings;
> (d) make provision about the legal representation at hearings of the parties to it;
> (e) prescribe the period within which an application, in relation to which a hearing has been held, must be determined or any other step in the procedure must be taken.

(2) But a licensing authority may not make any order as to the costs incurred by a party in connection with a hearing under this Act.

184 Giving of notices, etc

(1) This section has effect in relation to any document required or authorised by or under this Act to be given to any person ('relevant document').

(2) Where that person is a licensing authority, the relevant document must be given by addressing it to the authority and leaving it at or sending it by post to –

> (a) the principal office of the authority, or
> (b) any other office of the authority specified by it as one at which it will accept documents of the same description as that document.

(3) In any other case the relevant document may be given to the person in question by delivering it to him, or by leaving it at his proper address, or by sending it by post to him at that address.

(4) A relevant document may –

(a) in the case of a body corporate (other than a licensing authority), be given to the secretary or clerk of that body;

(b) in the case of a partnership, be given to a partner or a person having the control or management of the partnership business;

(c) in the case of an unincorporated association (other than a partnership), be given to an officer of the association.

(5) For the purposes of this section and section 7 of the Interpretation Act 1978 (c 30) (service of documents by post) in its application to this section, the proper address of any person to whom a relevant document is to be given is his last known address, except that –

(a) in the case of a body corporate or its secretary or clerk, it is the address of the registered office of that body or its principal office in the United Kingdom,

(b) in the case of a partnership, a partner or a person having control or management of the partnership business, it is that of the principal office of the partnership in the United Kingdom, and

(c) in the case of an unincorporated association (other than a partnership) or any officer of the association, it is that of its principal office in the United Kingdom.

(6) But if a relevant document is given to a person in his capacity as the holder of a premises licence, club premises certificate or personal licence, or as the designated premises supervisor under a premises licence, his relevant registered address is also to be treated, for the purposes of this section and section 7 of the Interpretation Act 1978 (c 30), as his proper address.

(7) In subsection (6) 'relevant registered address', in relation to such a person, means the address given for that person in the record for the licence or certificate (as the case may be) which is contained in the register kept under section 8 by the licensing authority which granted the licence or certificate.

(8) The following provisions of the Local Government Act 1972 (c 70) do not apply in relation to the service of a relevant document –

(a) section 231 (service of notices on local authorities etc),

(b) section 233 (service of notices by local authorities).

185 Provision of information

(1) This section applies to information which is held by or on behalf of a licensing authority or a responsible authority (including information obtained by or on behalf of the authority before the coming into force of this section).

(2) Information to which this section applies may be supplied –

(a) to a licensing authority, or

(b) to a responsible authority,

for the purposes of facilitating the exercise of the authority's functions under this Act.

(3) Information obtained by virtue of this section must not be further disclosed except to a licensing authority or responsible authority for the purposes mentioned in subsection (2).

(4) In this section 'responsible authority' means a responsible authority within the meaning of Part 3 or 4.

General provisions about offences

186 Proceedings for offences

(1) In this section 'offence' means an offence under this Act.

(2) Proceedings for an offence may be instituted –

(a) by a licensing authority,
(b) by the Director of Public Prosecutions, or
(c) in the case of an offence under section 146 or 147 (sale of alcohol to children), by a local weights and measures authority (within the meaning of section 69 of the Weights and Measures Act 1985 (c 72)).

(3) In relation to any offence, section 127(1) of the Magistrates' Courts Act 1980 (information to be laid within six months of offence) is to have effect as if for the reference to six months there were substituted a reference to 12 months.

187 Offences by bodies corporate etc

(1) If an offence committed by a body corporate is shown –

(a) to have been committed with the consent or connivance of an officer, or
(b) to be attributable to any neglect on his part,

the officer as well as the body corporate is guilty of the offence and liable to be proceeded against and punished accordingly.

(2) If the affairs of a body corporate are managed by its members, subsection (1) applies in relation to the acts and defaults of a member in connection with his functions of management as if he were a director of the body.

(3) In subsection (1) 'officer', in relation to a body corporate, means –

(a) a director, member of the committee of management, chief executive, manager, secretary or other similar officer of the body, or a person purporting to act in any such capacity, or
(b) an individual who is a controller of the body.

(4) If an offence committed by a partnership is shown –

(a) to have been committed with the consent or connivance of a partner, or
(b) to be attributable to any neglect on his part,

the partner as well as the partnership is guilty of the offence and liable to be proceeded against and punished accordingly.

(5) In subsection (4) 'partner' includes a person purporting to act as a partner.

(6) If an offence committed by an unincorporated association (other than a partnership) is shown –

(a)   to have been committed with the consent or connivance of an officer of the association or a member of its governing body, or

(b)   to be attributable to any neglect on the part of such an officer or member,

that officer or member as well as the association is guilty of the offence and liable to be proceeded against and punished accordingly.

(7) Regulations may provide for the application of any provision of this section, with such modifications as the Secretary of State considers appropriate, to a body corporate or unincorporated association formed or recognised under the law of a territory outside the United Kingdom.

(8) In this section 'offence' means an offence under this Act.

188 Jurisdiction and procedure in respect of offences

(1) A fine imposed on an unincorporated association on its conviction for an offence is to be paid out of the funds of the association.

(2) Proceedings for an offence alleged to have been committed by an unincorporated association must be brought in the name of the association (and not in that of any of its members).

(3) Rules of court relating to the service of documents are to have effect as if the association were a body corporate.

(4) In proceedings for an offence brought against an unincorporated association, section 33 of the Criminal Justice Act 1925 (c 86) and Schedule 3 to the Magistrates' Courts Act 1980 (c 43) (procedure) apply as they do in relation to a body corporate.

(5) Proceedings for an offence may be taken –

(a)   against a body corporate or unincorporated association at any place at which it has a place of business;

(b)   against an individual at any place where he is for the time being.

(6) Subsection (5) does not affect any jurisdiction exercisable apart from this section.

(7) In this section 'offence' means an offence under this Act.

Vessels, vehicles and moveable structures

189 Vessels, vehicles and moveable structures

(1) This Act applies in relation to a vessel which is not permanently moored or berthed as if it were premises situated in the place where it is usually moored or berthed.

(2) Where a vehicle which is not permanently situated in the same place is, or is proposed to be, used for one or more licensable activities while parked at a particular place, the vehicle is to be treated for the purposes of this Act as if it were premises situated at that place.

(3) Where a moveable structure which is not permanently situated in the same place is, or is proposed to be, used for one or more licensable activities while set in a particular place, the structure is to be treated for the purposes of this Act as if it were premises situated at that place.

(4) Where subsection (2) applies in relation to the same vehicle, or subsection (3) applies in relation to the same structure, in respect of more than one place, the premises which by virtue of that subsection are situated at each such place are to be treated as separate premises.

(5) Sections 29 to 31 (which make provision in respect of provisional statements relating to premises licences) do not apply in relation to a vessel, vehicle or structure to which this section applies.

Interpretation

190 Location of sales

(1) This section applies where the place where a contract for the sale of alcohol is made is different from the place where the alcohol is appropriated to the contract.

(2) For the purposes of this Act the sale of alcohol is to be treated as taking place where the alcohol is appropriated to the contract.

191 Meaning of 'alcohol'

(1) In this Act, 'alcohol' means spirits, wine, beer, cider or any other fermented, distilled or spirituous liquor, but does not include –

  (a) alcohol which is of a strength not exceeding 0.5% at the time of the sale or supply in question,
  (b) perfume,
  (c) flavouring essences recognised by the Commissioners of Customs and Excise as not being intended for consumption as or with dutiable alcoholic liquor,
  (d) the aromatic flavouring essence commonly known as Angostura bitters,
  (e) alcohol which is, or is included in, a medicinal product,
  (f) denatured alcohol,
  (g) methyl alcohol,
  (h) naphtha, or
  (i) alcohol contained in liqueur confectionery.

(2) In this section –

  'denatured alcohol' has the same meaning as in section 5 of the Finance Act 1995 (c 4);
  'dutiable alcoholic liquor' has the same meaning as in the Alcoholic Liquor Duties Act 1979 (c 4);

'liqueur confectionery' means confectionery which –
- (a) contains alcohol in a proportion not greater than 0.2 litres of alcohol (of a strength not exceeding 57%) per kilogram of the confectionery, and
- (b) either consists of separate pieces weighing not more than 42g or is designed to be broken into such pieces for the purpose of consumption;

'medicinal product' has the same meaning as in section 130 of the Medicines Act 1968 (c 67); and

'strength' is to be construed in accordance with section 2 of the Alcoholic Liquor Duties Act 1979.

192 Meaning of 'sale by retail'

(1) For the purposes of this Act 'sale by retail', in relation to any alcohol, means a sale of alcohol to any person, other than a sale of alcohol that –

- (a) is within subsection (2),
- (b) is made from premises owned by the person making the sale, or occupied by him under a lease to which the provisions of Part 2 of the Landlord and Tenant Act 1954 (c 56) (security of tenure) apply, and
- (c) is made for consumption off the premises.

(2) A sale of alcohol is within this subsection if it is –

- (a) to a trader for the purposes of his trade,
- (b) to a club, which holds a club premises certificate, for the purposes of that club,
- (c) to the holder of a personal licence for the purpose of making sales authorised by a premises licence,
- (d) to the holder of a premises licence for the purpose of making sales authorised by that licence, or
- (e) to the premises user in relation to a temporary event notice for the purpose of making sales authorised by that notice.

193 Other definitions

In this Act –

'beer' has the same meaning as in the Alcoholic Liquor Duties Act 1979 (c 4);

'cider' has the same meaning as in that Act;

'crime prevention objective' means the licensing objective mentioned in section 4(2)(a) (prevention of crime and disorder);

'licensed premises' means premises in respect of which a premises licence has effect;

'licensing functions' is to be construed in accordance with section 4(1);

'order', except so far as the contrary intention appears, means an order made by the Secretary of State;

'premises' means any place and includes a vehicle, vessel or moveable structure;

'prescribed' means prescribed by regulations;

'recognised club' means a club which satisfies conditions 1 to 3 of the general conditions in section 62;

'regulations' means regulations made by the Secretary of State;

'vehicle' means a vehicle intended or adapted for use on roads;

'vessel' includes a ship, boat, raft or other apparatus constructed or adapted for floating on water;

'wine' means –

(a) 'wine' within the meaning of the Alcoholic Liquor Duties Act 1979, and

(b) 'made-wine' within the meaning of that Act;

'working day' means any day other than a Saturday, a Sunday, Christmas Day, Good Friday or a day which is a bank holiday under the Banking and Financial Dealings Act 1971 (c 80) in England and Wales.

194 Index of defined expressions

In this Act the following expressions are defined or otherwise explained by the provisions indicated –

Expression	*Interpretation provision*
alcohol	section 191
associate member	section 67(2)
authorised person, in Part 3	section 13
authorised person, in Part 4	section 69
beer	section 193
cider	section 193
club premises certificate	section 60
conviction, in Part 6	section 114
crime prevention objective	section 193
designated premises supervisor	section 15
foreign offence, in Part 6	section 113
given, in relation to a notice, etc	section 184
guest	section 67(1)
interested party, in Part 3	section 13
interested party, in Part 4	section 69
interim authority notice	section 47
late night refreshment	Schedule 2
licensable activity	section 1(1)
licensed premises	section 193
licensing authority	section 3(1)
licensing authority's area	section 3(2)
licensing functions	sections 4(1) and 193
licensing objectives	section 4(2)
order	section 193
permitted temporary activity	section 98
personal licence	section 111(1)
premises	section 193
premises licence	section 11

Expression	Interpretation provision
premises user, in relation to a temporary event notice	section 100(2)
prescribed	section 193
provisional statement	section 29(3)
qualifying club	section 61
qualifying club activity	section 1(2)
recognised club	section 193
regulated entertainment	Schedule 1
regulations	section 193
relevant licensing authority, in Part 3	section 12
relevant licensing authority, in Part 4	section 68
relevant licensing authority, in Part 5	section 99
relevant licensing authority, in Part 6	section 112
relevant offence, in Part 6	section 113
responsible authority, in Part 3	section 13
responsible authority, in Part 4	section 69
sale by retail, in relation to alcohol	section 192
secretary, in Part 4	section 70
supply of alcohol, in Part 3	section 14
supply of alcohol to members or guests, in relation to a club, in Part 4	section 70
temporary event notice	section 100(1)
vehicle	section 193
vessel	section 193
wine	section 193
working day	section 193

Supplementary and general

195 Crown application

(1) This Act binds the Crown and has effect in relation to land in which there is –

(a) an interest belonging to Her Majesty in right of the Crown,
(b) an interest belonging to a government department, or
(c) an interest held in trust for Her Majesty for the purposes of such a department.

(2) This Act also applies to –

(a) land which is vested in, but not occupied by, Her Majesty in right of the Duchy of Lancaster, and
(b) land which is vested in, but not occupied by, the possessor for the time being of the Duchy of Cornwall.

(3) No contravention by the Crown of any provision made by or under this Act makes the Crown criminally liable; but the High Court may declare unlawful any act or omission of the Crown which constitutes such a contravention.

(4) Provision made by or under this Act applies to persons in the public service of the Crown as it applies to other persons.

(5) But nothing in this Act affects Her Majesty in Her private capacity.

196 Removal of privileges and exemptions

No privilege or exemption mentioned in section 199(a) or (b) of the Licensing Act 1964 (c 26) (University of Cambridge and the Vintners of the City of London) operates to exempt any person from the requirements of this Act.

197 Regulations and orders

(1) Any power of the Secretary of State to make regulations or an order under this Act is exercisable by statutory instrument.

(2) Regulations or an order under this Act –

   (a)   may include incidental, supplementary, consequential or transitional provision or savings;
   (b)   may make provision generally or only in relation to specified cases;
   (c)   may make different provision for different purposes.

(3) A statutory instrument containing regulations or an order under this Act, other than one containing –

   (a)   an order under section 5(2) (order appointing start of first period for which statement of licensing policy to be prepared),
   (b)   an order under section 100(8) (alteration of maximum temporary event period),
   (c)   an order under section 107(12) (alteration of limit on number of temporary event notices),
   (d)   an order under section 172 (relaxation of opening hours for special occasions),
   (e)   an order under section 176(3) (order amending definition of 'excluded premises' where alcohol sales are prohibited),
   (f)   an order under section 201 (commencement), or
   (g)   an order under paragraph 4 of Schedule 1 (power to amend meaning of regulated entertainment),

is subject to annulment in pursuance of a resolution of either House of Parliament.

(4) A statutory instrument containing an order within subsection (3)(b), (c), (d), (e) or (g) is not to be made unless a draft of the instrument containing the order has been laid before and approved by a resolution of each House of Parliament.

(5) If a draft of an order within subsection (3)(d) would, apart from this subsection, be treated for the purposes of the Standing Orders of either House of Parliament as a hybrid instrument, it is to proceed in that House as if it were not such an instrument.

198 Minor and consequential amendments

(1) Schedule 6 (which makes minor and consequential amendments) has effect.

(2) The Secretary of State may, in consequence of any provision of this Act or of any instrument made under it, by order make such amendments (including repeals or revocations) as appear to him to be appropriate in –

- (a) any Act passed, or
- (b) any subordinate legislation (within the meaning of the Interpretation Act 1978 (c 30) made,

before that provision comes into force.

199 Repeals

The enactments mentioned in Schedule 7 (which include provisions that are spent) are repealed to the extent specified.

200 Transitional provision etc

Schedule 8 (which makes transitional and transitory provision and savings) has effect.

201 Short title, commencement and extent

(1) This Act may be cited as the Licensing Act 2003.

(2) The preceding provisions (and the Schedules) come into force in accordance with provision made by order.

(3) Subject to subsections (4) and (5), this Act extends to England and Wales only.

(4) Section 155(1) also extends to Northern Ireland.

(5) An amendment or repeal contained in Schedule 6 or 7 has the same extent as the enactment to which it relates.

SCHEDULES

SCHEDULE 1   Section 1

PROVISION OF REGULATED ENTERTAINMENT

PART 1

GENERAL DEFINITIONS

The provision of regulated entertainment

1(1) For the purposes of this Act the 'provision of regulated entertainment' means the provision of –

  (a)   entertainment of a description falling within paragraph 2, or
  (b)   entertainment facilities falling within paragraph 3,

where the conditions in sub-paragraphs (2) and (3) are satisfied.

(2) The first condition is that the entertainment is, or entertainment facilities are, provided –

  (a)   to any extent for members of the public or a section of the public,
  (b)   exclusively for members of a club which is a qualifying club in relation to the provision of regulated entertainment, or for members of such a club and their guests, or
  (c)   in any case not falling within paragraph (a) or (b), for consideration and with a view to profit.

(3) The second condition is that the premises on which the entertainment is, or entertainment facilities are, provided are made available for the purpose, or for purposes which include the purpose, of enabling the entertainment concerned (whether of a description falling within paragraph 2(1) or paragraph 3(2)) to take place.

To the extent that the provision of entertainment facilities consists of making premises available, the premises are to be regarded for the purposes of this sub-paragraph as premises 'on which' entertainment facilities are provided.

(4) For the purposes of sub-paragraph (2)(c), entertainment is, or entertainment facilities are, to be regarded as provided for consideration only if any charge –

  (a)   is made by or on behalf of –
        (i)   any person concerned in the organisation or management of that entertainment, or
        (ii)   any person concerned in the organisation or management of those facilities who is also concerned in the organisation or management of the entertainment within paragraph 3(2) in which those facilities enable persons to take part, and
  (b)   is paid by or on behalf of some or all of the persons for whom that entertainment is, or those facilities are, provided.

(5) In sub-paragraph (4), 'charge' includes any charge for the provision of goods or services.

(6) For the purposes of sub-paragraph (4)(a), where the entertainment consists of the performance of live music or the playing of recorded music, a person performing or playing the music is not concerned in the organisation or management of the entertainment by reason only that he does one or more of the following –

    (a)   chooses the music to be performed or played,
    (b)   determines the manner in which he performs or plays it,
    (c)   provides any facilities for the purposes of his performance or playing of the music.

(7) This paragraph is subject to Part 2 of this Schedule (exemptions).

Entertainment

2(1)The descriptions of entertainment are –

    (a)   a performance of a play,
    (b)   an exhibition of a film,
    (c)   an indoor sporting event,
    (d)   a boxing or wrestling entertainment,
    (e)   a performance of live music,
    (f)   any playing of recorded music,
    (g)   a performance of dance,
    (h)   entertainment of a similar description to that falling within paragraph (e), (f) or (g),

where the entertainment takes place in the presence of an audience and is provided for the purpose, or for purposes which include the purpose, of entertaining that audience.

(2) Any reference in sub-paragraph (1) to an audience includes a reference to spectators.

(3) This paragraph is subject to Part 3 of this Schedule (interpretation).

Entertainment facilities

3(1) In this Schedule, 'entertainment facilities' means facilities for enabling persons to take part in entertainment of a description falling within sub-paragraph (2) for the purpose, or for purposes which include the purpose, of being entertained.

(2) The descriptions of entertainment are –

    (a)   making music,
    (b)   dancing,
    (c)   entertainment of a similar description to that falling within paragraph (a) or (b).

(3) This paragraph is subject to Part 3 of this Schedule (interpretation).

Power to amend Schedule

4 The Secretary of State may by order amend this Schedule for the purpose of modifying –

(a) the descriptions of entertainment specified in paragraph 2, or

(b) the descriptions of entertainment specified in paragraph 3,

and for this purpose 'modify' includes adding, varying or removing any description.

PART 2

EXEMPTIONS

Film exhibitions for the purposes of advertisement, information, education, etc

5 The provision of entertainment consisting of the exhibition of a film is not to be regarded as the provision of regulated entertainment for the purposes of this Act if its sole or main purpose is to –

(a) demonstrate any product,

(b) advertise any goods or services, or

(c) provide information, education or instruction.

Film exhibitions: museums and art galleries

6 The provision of entertainment consisting of the exhibition of a film is not to be regarded as the provision of regulated entertainment for the purposes of this Act if it consists of or forms part of an exhibit put on show for any purposes of a museum or art gallery.

Music incidental to certain other activities

7 The provision of entertainment consisting of the performance of live music or the playing of recorded music is not to be regarded as the provision of regulated entertainment for the purposes of this Act to the extent that it is incidental to some other activity which is not itself –

(a) a description of entertainment falling within paragraph 2, or

(b) the provision of entertainment facilities.

Use of television or radio receivers

8 The provision of any entertainment or entertainment facilities is not to be regarded as the provision of regulated entertainment for the purposes of this Act to the extent that it consists of the simultaneous reception and playing of a programme included in a programme service within the meaning of the Broadcasting Act 1990 (c 42).

Religious services, places of worship etc

9 The provision of any entertainment or entertainment facilities –

(a) for the purposes of, or for purposes incidental to, a religious meeting or service, or

(b) at a place of public religious worship,

is not to be regarded as the provision of regulated entertainment for the purposes of this Act.

Garden fêtes, etc

10(1) The provision of any entertainment or entertainment facilities at a garden fête, or at a function or event of a similar character, is not to be regarded as the provision of regulated entertainment for the purposes of this Act.

(2) But sub-paragraph (1) does not apply if the fête, function or event is promoted with a view to applying the whole or part of its proceeds for purposes of private gain.

(3) In sub-paragraph (2) 'private gain', in relation to the proceeds of a fête, function or event, is to be construed in accordance with section 22 of the Lotteries and Amusements Act 1976 (c 32).

Morris dancing etc

11 The provision of any entertainment or entertainment facilities is not to be regarded as the provision of regulated entertainment for the purposes of this Act to the extent that it consists of the provision of –

   (a) a performance of morris dancing or any dancing of a similar nature or a performance of unamplified, live music as an integral part of such a performance , or
   (b) facilities for enabling persons to take part in entertainment of a description falling within paragraph (a).

Vehicles in motion

12 The provision of any entertainment or entertainment facilities –

   (a) on premises consisting of or forming part of a vehicle, and
   (b) at a time when the vehicle is not permanently or temporarily parked,

is not to be regarded as the provision of regulated entertainment for the purposes of this Act.

PART 3

INTERPRETATION

General

13 This Part has effect for the purposes of this Schedule.

Plays

14(1) A 'performance of a play' means a performance of any dramatic piece, whether involving improvisation or not –

   (a) which is given wholly or in part by one or more persons actually present and performing, and
   (b) in which the whole or a major proportion of what is done by the person or persons performing, whether by way of speech, singing or action, involves the playing of a role.

(2) In this paragraph, 'performance' includes rehearsal (and 'performing' is to be construed accordingly).

Film exhibitions

15 An 'exhibition of a film' means any exhibition of moving pictures.

Indoor sporting events

16(1) An 'indoor sporting event' is a sporting event –

   (a)   which takes place wholly inside a building, and
   (b)   at which the spectators present at the event are accommodated wholly inside that building.

(2) In this paragraph –

      'building' means any roofed structure (other than a structure with a roof which may be opened or closed) and includes a vehicle, vessel or moveable structure,
      'sporting event' means any contest, exhibition or display of any sport, and
      'sport' includes –
         (a)   any game in which physical skill is the predominant factor, and
         (b)   any form of physical recreation which is also engaged in for purposes of competition or display.

Boxing or wrestling entertainments

17 A 'boxing or wrestling entertainment' is any contest, exhibition or display of boxing or wrestling.

Music

18 'Music' includes vocal or instrumental music or any combination of the two.

SCHEDULE 2   Section 1

PROVISION OF LATE NIGHT REFRESHMENT

The provision of late night refreshment

1(1) For the purposes of this Act, a person 'provides late night refreshment' if –

   (a)   at any time between the hours of 11.00 pm and 5.00 am, he supplies hot food or hot drink to members of the public, or a section of the public, on or from any premises, whether for consumption on or off the premises, or
   (b)   at any time between those hours when members of the public, or a section of the public, are admitted to any premises, he supplies, or holds himself out as willing to supply, hot food or hot drink to any persons, or to persons of a particular description, on or from those premises, whether for consumption on or off the premises,

unless the supply is an exempt supply by virtue of paragraph 3, 4 or 5.

(2) References in this Act to the 'provision of late night refreshment' are to be construed in accordance with sub-paragraph (1).

(3) This paragraph is subject to the following provisions of this Schedule.

Hot food or hot drink

2 Food or drink supplied on or from any premises is 'hot' for the purposes of this Schedule if the food or drink, or any part of it, –

  (a) before it is supplied, is heated on the premises or elsewhere for the purpose of enabling it to be consumed at a temperature above the ambient air temperature and, at the time of supply, is above that temperature, or
  (b) after it is supplied, may be heated on the premises for the purpose of enabling it to be consumed at a temperature above the ambient air temperature.

Exempt supplies: clubs, hotels etc and employees

3(1) The supply of hot food or hot drink on or from any premises at any time is an exempt supply for the purposes of paragraph 1(1) if, at that time, a person will neither –

  (a) be admitted to the premises, nor
  (b) be supplied with hot food or hot drink on or from the premises,

except by virtue of being a person of a description falling within sub-paragraph (2).

(2) The descriptions are that –

  (a) he is a member of a recognised club,
  (b) he is a person staying at a particular hotel, or at particular comparable premises, for the night in question,
  (c) he is an employee of a particular employer,
  (d) he is engaged in a particular trade, he is a member of a particular profession or he follows a particular vocation,
  (e) he is a guest of a person falling within any of paragraphs (a) to (d).

(3) The premises which, for the purposes of sub-paragraph (2)(b), are comparable to a hotel are –

  (a) a guest house, lodging house or hostel,
  (b) a caravan site or camping site, or
  (c) any other premises the main purpose of maintaining which is the provision of facilities for overnight accommodation.

Exempt supplies: premises licensed under certain other Acts

4 The supply of hot food or hot drink on or from any premises is an exempt supply for the purposes of paragraph 1(1) if it takes place during a period for which –

  (a) the premises may be used for a public exhibition of a kind described in section 21(1) of the Greater London Council (General Powers) Act 1966 (c xxviii) by virtue of a licence under that section, or

(b)   the premises may be used as near beer premises within the meaning of section 14 of the London Local Authorities Act 1995 (c x) by virtue of a licence under section 16 of that Act.

Miscellaneous exempt supplies

5(1) The following supplies of hot food or hot drink are exempt supplies for the purposes of paragraph 1(1) –

(a)   the supply of hot drink which consists of or contains alcohol,
(b)   the supply of hot drink by means of a vending machine,
(c)   the supply of hot food or hot drink free of charge,
(d)   the supply of hot food or hot drink by a registered charity or a person authorised by a registered charity,
(e)   the supply of hot food or hot drink on a vehicle at a time when the vehicle is not permanently or temporarily parked.

(2) Hot drink is supplied by means of a vending machine for the purposes of sub-paragraph (1)(b) only if –

(a)   the payment for the hot drink is inserted into the machine by a member of the public, and
(b)   the hot drink is supplied directly by the machine to a member of the public.

(3) Hot food or hot drink is not to be regarded as supplied free of charge for the purposes of sub-paragraph (1)(c) if, in order to obtain the hot food or hot drink, a charge must be paid –

(a)   for admission to any premises, or
(b)   for some other item.

(4) In sub-paragraph (1)(d) 'registered charity' means –

(a)   a charity which is registered under section 3 of the Charities Act 1993 (c 10), or
(b)   a charity which by virtue of subsection (5) of that section is not required to be so registered.

Clubs which are not recognised clubs: members and guests

6 For the purposes of this Schedule –

(a)   the supply of hot food or hot drink to a person as being a member, or the guest of a member, of a club which is not a recognised club is to be taken to be a supply to a member of the public, and
(b)   the admission of any person to any premises as being such a member or guest is to be taken to be the admission of a member of the public.

SCHEDULE 3   Section 8

MATTERS TO BE ENTERED IN LICENSING REGISTER

The licensing register kept by a licensing authority under section 8 must contain a record of the following matters –

(a) any application made to the licensing authority under section 17 (grant of premises licence),

(b) any application made to it under section 25 (theft etc of premises licence or summary),

(c) any notice given to it under section 28 (surrender of premises licence),

(d) any application made to it under section 29 (provisional notice in respect of premises),

(e) any notice given to it under section 33 (change of name, etc of holder of premises licence),

(f) any application made to it under section 34 (variation of premises licence),

(g) any application made to it under section 37 (variation of licence to specify individual as premises supervisor),

(h) any notice given to it under section 41 (request from designated premises supervisor for removal from premises licence),

(i) any application made to it under section 42 (transfer of premises licence),

(j) any notice given to it under section 47 (interim authority notice),

(k) any application made to it under section 51 (review of premises licence),

(l) any application made to it under section 71 (application for club premises certificate),

(m) any application made to it under section 79 (theft, loss, etc of certificate or summary),

(n) any notice given to it under section 81 (surrender of club premises certificate),

(o) any notice given to it under section 82 or 83 (notification of change of name etc),

(p) any application made to it under section 84 (application to vary club premises certificate),

(q) any application made to it under section 87 (application for review of club premises certificate),

(r) any notice given to it under section 103 (withdrawal of temporary event notice),

(s) any counter notice given by it under section 105 (counter notice following police objection to temporary event notice),

(t) any copy of a temporary event notice give to it under section 106 (notice given following the making of modifications to a temporary event notice with police consent),

(u) any application made to it under section 110 (theft etc of temporary event notice),

(v) any notice given to it under section 116 (surrender of personal licence),

(w) any application made to it under section 117 (grant or renewal of personal licence),

(x) any application made to it under section 126 (theft, loss or destruction of personal licence),

(y) any notice given to it under section 127 (change of name, etc of personal licence holder),

(z) any notice given to it under section 165(4) (magistrates' court to notify any determination made after closure order),

(zi) any application under paragraph 2 of Schedule 8 (application for conversion of old licences into premises licence),

(zii) any application under paragraph 14 of that Schedule (application for conversion of club certificate into club premises certificate).

SCHEDULE 4   Section 113

PERSONAL LICENCE: RELEVANT OFFENCES

1 An offence under this Act.

2 An offence under any of the following enactments –

(a) Schedule 12 to the London Government Act 1963 (c 33) (public entertainment licensing);

(b) the Licensing Act 1964 (c 26);

(c) the Private Places of Entertainment (Licensing) Act 1967 (c 19);

(d) section 13 of the Theatres Act 1968 (c 54);

(e) the Late Night Refreshment Houses Act 1969 (c 53);

(f) section 6 of, or Schedule 1 to, the Local Government (Miscellaneous Provisions) Act 1982 (c 30);

(g) the Licensing (Occasional Permissions) Act 1983 (c 24);

(h) the Cinemas Act 1985 (c 13);

(i) the London Local Authorities Act 1990 (c vii).

3 An offence under the Firearms Act 1968 (c 27).

4 An offence under section 1 of the Trade Descriptions Act 1968 (c 29) (false trade description of goods) in circumstances where the goods in question are or include alcohol.

5 An offence under any of the following provisions of the Theft Act 1968 (c 60) –

(a) section 1 (theft);

(b) section 8 (robbery);

(c) section 9 (burglary);

(d) section 10 (aggravated burglary);

(e) section 11 (removal of articles from places open to the public);

(f) section 12A (aggravated vehicle-taking), in circumstances where subsection (2)(b) of that section applies and the accident caused the death of any person;

(g) section 13 (abstracting of electricity);

(h) section 15 (obtaining property by deception);

(i) section 15A (obtaining a money transfer by deception);

(j) section 16 (obtaining pecuniary advantage by deception);

(k) section 17 (false accounting);

(l) section 19 (false statements by company directors etc);

(m) section 20 (suppression, etc of documents);

(n) section 21 (blackmail);

(o) section 22 (handling stolen goods);

(p) section 24A (dishonestly retaining a wrongful credit);

(q) section 25 (going equipped for stealing etc).

6 An offence under section 7(2) of the Gaming Act 1968 (c 65) (allowing child to take part in gaming on premises licensed for the sale of alcohol).

7 An offence under any of the following provisions of the Misuse of Drugs Act 1971 (c 38) –

(a) section 4(2) (production of a controlled drug);
(b) section 4(3) (supply of a controlled drug);
(c) section 5(3) (possession of a controlled drug with intent to supply);
(d) section 8 (permitting activities to take place on premises).

8 An offence under either of the following provisions of the Theft Act 1978 (c 31) –

(a) section 1 (obtaining services by deception);
(b) section 2 (evasion of liability by deception).

9 An offence under either of the following provisions of the Customs and Excise Management Act 1979 (c 2) –

(a) section 170 (disregarding subsection (1)(a)) (fraudulent evasion of duty etc);
(b) section 170B (taking preparatory steps for evasion of duty).

10 An offence under either of the following provisions of the Tobacco Products Duty Act 1979 (c 7) –

(a) section 8G (possession and sale of unmarked tobacco);
(b) section 8H (use of premises for sale of unmarked tobacco).

11 An offence under the Forgery and Counterfeiting Act 1981 (c 45) (other than an offence under section 18 or 19 of that Act).

12 An offence under the Firearms (Amendment) Act 1988 (c 45).

13 An offence under any of the following provisions of the Copyright, Designs and Patents Act 1988 (c 48) –

(a) section 107(1)(d)(iii) (public exhibition in the course of a business of article infringing copyright);
(b) section 107(3) (infringement of copyright by public performance of work etc);
(c) section 198(2) (broadcast etc of recording of performance made without sufficient consent);
(d) section 297(1) (fraudulent reception of transmission);
(e) section 297A(1) (supply etc of unauthorised decoder).

14 An offence under any of the following provisions of the Road Traffic Act 1988 (c 52) –

(a) section 3A (causing death by careless driving while under the influence of drink or drugs);
(b) section 4 (driving etc a vehicle when under the influence of drink or drugs);

(c)   section 5 (driving etc a vehicle with alcohol concentration above prescribed limit).

15 An offence under either of the following provisions of the Food Safety Act 1990 (c 16) in circumstances where the food in question is or includes alcohol –

(a)   section 14 (selling food or drink not of the nature, substance or quality demanded);
(b)   section 15 (falsely describing or presenting food or drink).

16 An offence under section 92(1) or (2) of the Trade Marks Act 1994 (c 26) (unauthorised use of trade mark, etc in relation to goods) in circumstances where the goods in question are or include alcohol.

17 An offence under the Firearms (Amendment) Act 1997 (c 5).

18 A sexual offence, within the meaning of section 161(2) of the Powers of Criminal Courts (Sentencing) Act 2000 (c 6).

19 A violent offence, within the meaning of section 161(3) of that Act.

20 An offence under section 3 of the Private Security Industry Act 2001 (c 12) (engaging in certain activities relating to security without a licence).

SCHEDULE 5   Section 181

APPEALS

PART 1

PREMISES LICENCES

Rejection of applications relating to premises licences

1 Where a licensing authority –

(a)   rejects an application for a premises licence under section 18,
(b)   rejects (in whole or in part) an application to vary a premises licence under section 35,
(c)   rejects an application to vary a premises licence to specify an individual as the premises supervisor under section 39, or
(d)   rejects an application to transfer a premises licence under section 44,

the applicant may appeal against the decision.

Decision to grant premises licence or impose conditions etc

2(1) This paragraph applies where a licensing authority grants a premises licence under section 18.

(2) The holder of the licence may appeal against any decision –

(a)   to impose conditions on the licence under subsection (2)(a) or (3)(b) of that section, or
(b)   to take any step mentioned in subsection (4)(b) or (c) of that section (exclusion of licensable activity or refusal to specify person as premises supervisor).

(3) Where a person who made relevant representations in relation to the application desires to contend –

    (a)   that the licence ought not to have been granted, or

    (b)   that, on granting the licence, the licensing authority ought to have imposed different or additional conditions, or to have taken a step mentioned in subsection (4)(b) or (c) of that section,

he may appeal against the decision.

(4) In sub-paragraph (3) 'relevant representations' has the meaning given in section 18(6).

Issue of provisional statement

3(1) This paragraph applies where a provisional statement is issued under subsection (3)(c) of section 31.

(2) An appeal against the decision may be made by –

    (a)   the applicant, or

    (b)   any person who made relevant representations in relation to the application.

(3) In sub-paragraph (2) 'relevant representations' has the meaning given in subsection (5) of that section.

Variation of licence under section 35

4(1) This paragraph applies where an application to vary a premises licence is granted (in whole or in part) under section 35.

(2) The applicant may appeal against any decision to modify the conditions of the licence under subsection (4)(a) of that section.

(3) Where a person who made relevant representations in relation to the application desires to contend –

    (a)   that any variation made ought not to have been made, or

    (b)   that, when varying the licence, the licensing authority ought not to have modified the conditions of the licence, or ought to have modified them in a different way, under subsection (4)(a) of that section,

he may appeal against the decision.

(4) In sub-paragraph (3) 'relevant representations' has the meaning given in section 35(5).

Variation of licence to specify individual as premises supervisor

5(1) This paragraph applies where an application to vary a premises licence is granted under section 39(2) in a case where a chief officer of police gave a notice under section 37(5) (which was not withdrawn).

(2) The chief officer of police may appeal against the decision to grant the application.

Transfer of licence

6(1) This paragraph applies where an application to transfer a premises licence is granted under section 44 in a case where a chief officer of police gave a notice under section 42(6) (which was not withdrawn).

(2) The chief officer of police may appeal against the decision to grant the application.

Interim authority notice

7(1) This paragraph applies where –

  (a) an interim authority notice is given in accordance with section 47, and
  (b) a chief officer of police gives a notice under section 48(2) (which is not withdrawn).

(2) Where the relevant licensing authority decides to cancel the interim authority notice under subsection (3) of section 48, the person who gave the interim authority notice may appeal against that decision.

(3) Where the relevant licensing authority decides not to cancel the notice under that subsection, the chief officer of police may appeal against that decision.

(4) Where an appeal is brought under sub-paragraph (2), the court to which it is brought may, on such terms as it thinks fit, order the reinstatement of the interim authority notice pending –

  (a) the disposal of the appeal, or
  (b) the expiry of the interim authority period,

whichever first occurs.

(5) Where the court makes an order under sub-paragraph (4), the premises licence is reinstated from the time the order is made, and section 47 has effect in a case where the appeal is dismissed or abandoned before the end of the interim authority period as if –

  (a) the reference in subsection (7)(b) to the end of the interim authority period were a reference to the time when the appeal is dismissed or abandoned, and
  (b) the reference in subsection (9)(a) to the interim authority period were a reference to that period disregarding the part of it which falls after that time.

(6) In this paragraph 'interim authority period' has the same meaning as in section 47.

Review of premises licence

8(1) This paragraph applies where an application for a review of a premises licence is decided under section 52.

(2) An appeal may be made against that decision by –

  (a) the applicant for the review,
  (b) the holder of the premises licence, or

(c) any other person who made relevant representations in relation to the application.

(3) In sub-paragraph (2) 'relevant representations' has the meaning given in section 52(7).

General provision about appeals under this Part

9(1) An appeal under this Part must be made to the magistrates' court for the petty sessions area (or any such area) in which the premises concerned are situated.

(2) An appeal under this Part must be commenced by notice of appeal given by the appellant to the justices' chief executive for the magistrates' court within the period of 21 days beginning with the day on which the appellant was notified by the licensing authority of the decision appealed against.

(3) On an appeal under paragraph 2(3), 3(2)(b), 4(3), 5(2), 6(2) or 8(2)(a) or (c), the holder of the premises licence is to be the respondent in addition to the licensing authority.

(4) On an appeal under paragraph 7(3), the person who gave the interim authority notice is to be the respondent in addition to the licensing authority.

PART 2

CLUB PREMISES CERTIFICATES

Rejection of applications relating to club premises certificates

10 Where a licensing authority –

(a) rejects an application for a club premises certificate under section 72, or
(b) rejects (in whole or in part) an application to vary a club premises certificate under section 85,

the club that made the application may appeal against the decision.

Decision to grant club premises certificate or impose conditions etc

11(1) This paragraph applies where a licensing authority grants a club premises certificate under section 72.

(2) The club holding the certificate may appeal against any decision –

(a) to impose conditions on the certificate under subsection (2) or (3)(b) of that section, or
(b) to take any step mentioned in subsection (4)(b) of that section (exclusion of qualifying club activity).

(3) Where a person who made relevant representations in relation to the application desires to contend –

(a) that the certificate ought not to have been granted, or
(b) that, on granting the certificate, the licensing authority ought to have imposed different or additional conditions, or to have taken a step mentioned in subsection (4)(b) of that section,

he may appeal against the decision.

(4) In sub-paragraph (3) 'relevant representations' has the meaning given in section 72(7).

Variation of club premises certificate

12(1) This paragraph applies where an application to vary a club premises certificate is granted (in whole or in part) under section 85.

(2) The club may appeal against any decision to modify the conditions of the certificate under subsection (3)(b) of that section.

(3) Where a person who made relevant representations in relation to the application desires to contend –

  (a)   that any variation ought not to have been made, or
  (b)   that, when varying the certificate, the licensing authority ought not to have modified the conditions of the certificate, or ought to have modified them in a different way, under subsection (3)(b) of that section,

he may appeal against the decision.

(4) In sub-paragraph (3) 'relevant representations' has the meaning given in section 85(5).

Review of club premises certificate

13(1) This paragraph applies where an application for a review of a club premises certificate is decided under section 88.

(2) An appeal may be made against that decision by –

  (a)   the applicant for the review,
  (b)   the club that holds or held the club premises certificate, or
  (c)   any other person who made relevant representations in relation to the application.

(3) In sub-paragraph (2) 'relevant representations' has the meaning given in section 88(7).

Withdrawal of club premises certificate

14 Where the relevant licensing authority gives notice withdrawing a club premises certificate under section 90, the club which holds or held the certificate may appeal against the decision to withdraw it.

General provision about appeals under this Part

15(1) An appeal under this Part must be made to the magistrates' court for the petty sessions area (or any such area) in which the premises concerned are situated.

(2) An appeal under this Part must be commenced by notice of appeal given by the appellant to the justices' chief executive for the magistrates' court

within the period of 21 days beginning with the day on which the appellant was notified by the licensing authority of the decision appealed against.

(3) On an appeal under paragraph 11(3), 12(3) or 13(2)(a) or (c), the club that holds or held the club premises certificate is to be the respondent in addition to the licensing authority.

PART 3

OTHER APPEALS

Temporary event notices

16(1) This paragraph applies where –

(a) a temporary event notice is given under section 100, and
(b) a chief officer of police gives an objection notice in accordance with section 104(2).

(2) Where the relevant licensing authority gives a counter notice under section 105(3), the premises user may appeal against that decision.

(3) Where that authority decides not to give such a counter notice, the chief officer of police may appeal against that decision.

(4) An appeal under this paragraph must be made to the magistrates' court for the petty sessions area (or any such area) in which the premises concerned are situated.

(5) An appeal under this paragraph must be commenced by notice of appeal given by the appellant to the justices' chief executive for the magistrates' court within the period of 21 days beginning with the day on which the appellant was notified by the licensing authority of the decision appealed against.

(6) But no appeal may be brought later than five working days before the day on which the event period specified in the temporary event notice begins.

(7) On an appeal under sub-paragraph (3), the premises user is to be the respondent in addition to the licensing authority.

(8) In this paragraph –

'objection notice' has the same meaning as in section 104; and
'relevant licensing authority' has the meaning given in section 99.

Personal licences

17(1) Where a licensing authority –

(a) rejects an application for the grant of a personal licence under section 120, or
(b) rejects an application for the renewal of a personal licence under section 121,

the applicant may appeal against that decision.

(2) Where a licensing authority grants an application for a personal licence under section 120(7), the chief officer of police who gave the objection

notice (within the meaning of section 120(5)) may appeal against that decision.

(3) Where a licensing authority grants an application for the renewal of a personal licence under section 121(6), the chief officer of police who gave the objection notice (within the meaning of section 121(3)) may appeal against that decision.

(4) Where a licensing authority revokes a personal licence under section 124(4), the holder of the licence may appeal against that decision.

(5) Where in a case to which section 124 (convictions coming to light after grant or renewal) applies –

    (a)   the chief officer of police for the licensing authority's area gives a notice under subsection (3) of that section (and does not later withdraw it), and

    (b)   the licensing authority decides not to revoke the licence,

the chief officer of police may appeal against the decision.

(6) An appeal under this paragraph must be made to the magistrates' court for a petty sessions area in which the licensing authority's area (or any part of it) is situated.

(7) An appeal under this paragraph must be commenced by notice of appeal given by the appellant to the justices' chief executive for the magistrates' court within the period of 21 days beginning with the day on which the appellant was notified by the licensing authority of the decision appealed against.

(8) On an appeal under sub-paragraph (2), (3) or (5), the holder of the personal licence is to be the respondent in addition to the licensing authority.

(9) Sub-paragraph (10) applies where the holder of a personal licence gives notice of appeal against a decision of a licensing authority to refuse to renew it.

(10) The relevant licensing authority, or the magistrates' court to which the appeal has been made, may, on such conditions as it thinks fit –

    (a)   order that the licence is to continue in force until the relevant time, if it would otherwise cease to have effect before that time, or

    (b)   where the licence has already ceased to have effect, order its reinstatement until the relevant time.

(11) In sub-paragraph (10) 'the relevant time' means –

    (a)   the time the appeal is dismissed or abandoned, or

    (b)   where the appeal is allowed, the time the licence is renewed.

Closure orders

18(1) This paragraph applies where, on a review of a premises licence under section 167, the relevant licensing authority decides under subsection (5)(b) of that section –

(a) to take any of the steps mentioned in subsection (6) of that section, in relation to a premises licence for those premises, or

(b) not to take any such step.

(2) An appeal may be made against that decision by-

(a) the holder of the premises licence, or

(b) any other person who made relevant representations in relation to the review.

(3) Where an appeal is made under this paragraph against a decision to take any of the steps mentioned in section 167(6)(a) to (d) (modification of licence conditions etc), the appropriate magistrates' court may in a case within section 168(3) (premises closed when decision taken) –

(a) if the relevant licensing authority has not made an order under section 168(5) (order suspending operation of decision in whole or part), make any order under section 168(5) that could have been made by the relevant licensing authority, or

(b) if the authority has made such an order, cancel it or substitute for it any order which could have been made by the authority under section 168(5).

(4) Where an appeal is made under this paragraph in a case within section 168(6) (premises closed when decision to revoke made to remain closed pending appeal), the appropriate magistrates court may, on such conditions as it thinks fit, order that section 168(7) (premises to remain closed pending appeal) is not to apply to the premises.

(5) An appeal under this paragraph must be commenced by notice of appeal given by the appellant to the justices' chief executive for the magistrates' court within the period of 21 days beginning with the day on which the appellant was notified by the relevant licensing authority of the decision appealed against.

(6) On an appeal under this paragraph by a person other than the holder of the premises licence, that holder is to be the respondent in addition to the licensing authority that made the decision.

(7) In this paragraph –

'appropriate magistrates' court' means the magistrates court for the petty sessions area (or any such area) in which the premises concerned are situated;

'relevant licensing authority' has the same meaning as in Part 3 of this Act; and

'relevant representations' has the meaning given in section 167(9).

SCHEDULE 6   Section 198

MINOR AND CONSEQUENTIAL AMENDMENTS

Universities (Wine Licences) Act 1743 (c 40)

1 The Universities (Wine Licences) Act 1743 ceases to have effect.

Disorderly Houses Act 1751 (c 36)

2 The Disorderly Houses Act 1751 does not apply in relation to relevant premises within the meaning of section 159 of the Licensing Act 2003.

Sunday Observance Act 1780 (c 49)

3 The Sunday Observance Act 1780 ceases to have effect.

Town Police Clauses Act 1847 (c 89)

4 Section 35 of the Town Police Clauses Act 1847 (harbouring thieves or prostitutes at a public venue) ceases to have effect.

Cambridge Award Act 1856 (c xvii)

5 The following provisions of the Cambridge Award Act 1856 cease to have effect –

  (a) section 9 (revocation of alehouse licence by justice of the peace following complaint by Vice Chancellor of the University), and
  (b) section 11 (power to grant wine licence, etc to remain vested in the Chancellor, Masters and Scholars of the University).

Inebriates Act 1898 (c 60)

6 In the First Schedule to the Inebriates Act 1898 (offences by reference to which section 6 of the Licensing Act 1902 operates) –

  (a) omit the entry relating to section 18 of the Licensing Act 1872 and the entry relating to section 41 of the Refreshment Houses Act 1860, and
  (b) after the entries relating to the Merchant Shipping Act 1894 insert –

'Failing to leave licensed premises, etc when asked to do so.	Licensing Act 2003, s 143.'
Entering, or attempting to enter, licensed premises, etc when asked not to do so.	

Licensing Act 1902 (c 28)

7 The Licensing Act 1902 is amended as follows.

8(1) Section 6 (prohibition of sale of alcohol to person declared by the court to be a habitual drunkard) is amended as follows.

(2) For subsection (2) substitute –

  '(2) Subsections (2A) to (2C) apply where a court, in pursuance of this Act, orders notice of a conviction to be sent to a police authority.

  (2A) The court shall inform the convicted person that the notice is to be sent to a police authority.

(2B) The convicted person commits an offence if, within the three year period, he buys or obtains, or attempts to buy or obtain, alcohol on relevant premises.

(2C) A person to whom subsection (2D) applies commits an offence if, within the three year period, he knowingly –

(a) sells, supplies or distributes alcohol on relevant premises, or

(b) allows the sale, supply or distribution of alcohol on relevant premises,

to, or for consumption by, the convicted person.

(2D) This subsection applies –

(a) to any person who works at the premises in a capacity, whether paid or unpaid, which gives him authority to sell, supply or distribute the alcohol concerned,

(b) in the case of licensed premises, to –

(i) the holder of a premises licence which authorises the sale or supply of alcohol, and

(ii) the designated premises supervisor (if any) under such a licence,

(c) in the case of premises in respect of which a club premises certificate authorising the sale or supply of alcohol has effect, to any member or officer of the club which holds the certificate who at the time the sale, supply or distribution takes place is present on the premises in a capacity which enables him to prevent it, and

(d) in the case of premises which may be used for a permitted temporary activity by virtue of Part 5 of the Licensing Act 2003, the premises user in respect of a temporary event notice authorising the sale or supply of alcohol.

(2E) A person guilty of an offence under this section is liable on summary conviction –

(a) in the case of an offence under subsection (2B), to a fine not exceeding level 1 on the standard scale, and

(b) in the case of an offence under subsection (2C), to a fine not exceeding level 2 on the standard scale.'

(3) In subsection (3), for 'licensed persons, and secretaries of clubs registered under Part III of this Act,' substitute 'persons to whom subsection (4) applies'.

(4) After that subsection insert –

'(4) This subsection applies to –

(a) the holder of a premises licence which authorises the sale or supply of alcohol,

(b) the designated premises supervisor (if any) under such a licence,

(c) the holder of a club premises certificate authorising the sale or supply of alcohol, and

(d) the premises user in relation to a temporary event notice authorising the sale or supply or alcohol.

(5) In this section –

"alcohol", "club premises certificate", "designated premises supervisor", "licensed premises", "permitted temporary activity", "premises licence", "premises user" and "temporary event notice" have the same meaning as in the Licensing Act 2003,

"relevant premises" means premises which are relevant premises within the meaning of section 159 of that Act and on which alcohol may be lawfully sold or supplied, and

"the three year period", in relation to the convicted person, means the period of three years beginning with the day of the conviction.'

9 After section 8 (meaning of 'public place') insert –

'8A Interpretation of "licensed premises"

For those purposes, "licensed premises" includes –

    (a) any licensed premises within the meaning of section 193 of the Licensing Act 2003, and

    (b) any premises which may be used for a permitted temporary activity by virtue of Part 5 of that Act.'

Celluloid and Cinematograph Film Act 1922 (c 35)

10 At the end of section 2 of the Celluloid and Cinematograph Film Act 1922 (premises to which the Act does not apply), add 'or which may, by virtue of an authorisation (within the meaning of section 136 of the Licensing Act 2003), be used for an exhibition of a film (within the meaning of paragraph 15 of Schedule 1 to that Act)'.

Sunday Entertainments Act 1932 (c 51)

11 The Sunday Entertainments Act 1932 ceases to have effect.

Children and Young Persons Act 1933 (c 12)

12 The Children and Young Persons Act 1933 is amended as follows.

13 In section 5 (giving alcohol to a child under five) for 'intoxicating liquor' substitute 'alcohol (within the meaning given by section 191 of the Licensing Act 2003, but disregarding subsection (1)(f) to (i) of that section)'.

14 In section 12 (failing to provide for safety of children at entertainments) –

    (a) in subsection (3) omit the words from ', and also' to the end,

    (b) in subsection (5), for paragraph (a) substitute –

       '(a) in the case of a building in respect of which a premises licence authorising the provision of regulated entertainment has effect, be the duty of the relevant licensing authority;', and

    (c) after that subsection, insert –

      '(5A) For the purposes of this section –

> (a) "premises licence" and "the provision of regulated entertainment" have the meaning given by the Licensing Act 2003, and
>
> (b) "the relevant licensing authority", in relation to a building in respect of which a premises licence has effect, means the relevant licensing authority in relation to that building under section 12 of that Act.'

15 In section 107 (interpretation), omit the definition of 'intoxicating liquor'.

Public Health Act 1936 (c 49)

16 In section 226 of the Public Health Act 1936 (power of local authority to close swimming bath and use it instead for other purposes) –

(a) for subsection (3) substitute –

'(3) Nothing in this section shall authorise the use of a swimming bath or bathing place for the provision of regulated entertainment (within the meaning of the Licensing Act 2003), unless that activity is carried on under and in accordance with an authorisation (within the meaning given in section 136 of that Act).', and

(b) omit subsection (4).

London Building Acts (Amendment) Act 1939 (c xcvii)

17 In each of the following provisions of the London Building Acts (Amendment) Act 1939, for 'the premises are so licensed' substitute 'the premises are premises which, by virtue of a premises licence under the Licensing Act 2003, may be used for the supply of alcohol (within the meaning of section 14 of that Act) for consumption on the premises' –

(a) section 11(9)(b) (exemption of licensed premises from provision as to naming of buildings),

(b) paragraph (A) of the proviso to section 13 (offences as to numbering or naming of buildings).

Civic Restaurants Act 1947 (c 22)

18 In section 1(4) of the Civic Restaurants Act 1947 (civic restaurant authority to be subject to law relating to sale of alcohol), for 'the enactments relating to the sale of intoxicating liquor' substitute 'the Licensing Act 2003 and any other enactment relating to the sale of intoxicating liquor'.

London County Council (General Powers) Act 1947 (c xlvi)

19 In section 6(1)(b) of the London County Council (General Powers) Act 1947 (saving in connection with the provision of entertainment for enactments relating to the sale of alcohol), for 'any enactment relating to the sale of intoxicating liquor' substitute 'the Licensing Act 2003 and any other enactment relating to the sale of intoxicating liquor'.

National Parks and Access to the Countryside Act 1949 (c 97)

20 In each of the following provisions of the National Parks and Countryside Act 1949, for 'intoxicating liquor' substitute 'alcohol (within the meaning of the Licensing Act 2003)' –

    (a)   section 12(1)(a) (provision of facilities in National Park),
    (b)   section 54(2) (provision of facilities along long-distance routes).

Reserve and Auxiliary Forces (Protection of Civil Interests) Act 1951 (c 65)

21 The Reserve and Auxiliary Forces (Protection of Civil Interests) Act 1951 is amended as follows.

22 In section 14(2)(a) (protection against insecurity of tenure of place of residence), after 'premises' insert 'in England and Wales which, by virtue of a premises licence under the Licensing Act 2003, may be used for the supply of alcohol (within the meaning of section 14 of that Act) on the premises or in Scotland which are'.

23 In section 18(3)(a) (protection against insecurity of tenure in connection with employment), after 'premises' insert 'in England and Wales which, by virtue of a premises licence under the Licensing Act 2003, may be used for the supply of alcohol (within the meaning of section 14 of that Act) on the premises for consumption on the premises or in Scotland which are'.

24 In section 27(1) (renewal of tenancy expiring during period of service), in the second paragraph (c), for the words 'licensed for the sale of intoxicating liquor for consumption on the premises' substitute 'which, by virtue of a premises licence under the Licensing Act 2003, may be used for the supply of alcohol (within the meaning of section 14 of that Act) for consumption on the premises'.

Hypnotism Act 1952 (c 46)

25 The Hypnotism Act 1952 is amended as follows.

26(1) Section 1 (inclusion in an entertainment licence of conditions in relation to demonstrations of hypnotism) is amended as follows.

(2) In subsection (1) –

    (a)   after 'any area' insert 'in Scotland', and
    (b)   for 'places kept or ordinarily used for public dancing, singing, music or other public entertainment of the like kind' substitute 'theatres or other places of public amusement or public entertainment'.

(3) Omit subsection (2).

27 In section 2 (requirement for authorisation for demonstration of hypnotism) –

    (a)   in subsection (1), for the words from 'in relation' to the end substitute ', unless –

        (a)   the controlling authority have authorised that exhibition, demonstration or performance under this section, or

(b) the place is in Scotland and a licence mentioned in section 1 of this Act is in force in relation to it.',

(b) in subsection (1A) for the words from 'either at premises' to the end substitute 'at premises in Scotland in respect of which a licence under that Act is in force',

(c) after subsection (3) insert –

'(3A) A function conferred by this section on a licensing authority is, for the purposes of section 7 of the Licensing Act 2003 (exercise and delegation by licensing authority of licensing functions), to be treated as a licensing function within the meaning of that Act.', and

(d) for subsection (4) substitute –

'(4) In this section –

"controlling authority" means –
   (a) in relation to a place in England and Wales, the licensing authority in whose area the place, or the greater or greatest part of it, is situated, and
   (b) in relation to a place in Scotland, the authority having power to grant licences of the kind mentioned in section 1 in that area, and
"licensing authority" has the meaning given by the Licensing Act 2003.'

Obscene Publications Act 1959 (c 66)

28(1) Section 2 of the Obscene Publications Act 1959 (prohibition of publication of obscene matter) is amended as follows.

(2) In subsections (3A) and (4A), for 'a film exhibition' in each place it occurs, substitute 'an exhibition of a film'.

(3) For subsection (7) substitute –

'(7) In this section, "exhibition of a film" has the meaning given in paragraph 15 of Schedule 1 to the Licensing Act 2003.'

Betting, Gaming and Lotteries Act 1963 (c 2)

29 The Betting, Gaming and Lotteries Act 1963 is amended as follows.

30 In section 10(1B) (conduct of licensed betting offices) for 'the provision in a licensed betting office of any facility in respect of which a licence under the Licensing Act 1964 or the Licensing (Scotland) Act 1976 is required' substitute –

   '(a) in a licensed betting office in England and Wales, the supply of alcohol (within the meaning of section 14 of the Licensing Act 2003) in circumstances where that supply is a licensable activity (within the meaning of that Act);
   (b) in a licensed betting office in Scotland, the provision of any facility in respect of which a licence is required under the Licensing (Scotland) Act 1976'.

31 In Schedule 4 (rules for licensed betting offices), in paragraph 10(2)(a), for 'intoxicating liquor within the meaning of section 201(1) of the Licensing Act 1964' substitute 'alcohol within the meaning of section 191 of the Licensing Act 2003'.

Children and Young Persons Act 1963 (c 37)

32 For section 37(2)(b) of the Children and Young Persons Act 1963 (restriction on performance by child in licensed premises) substitute –

> '(b) any performance in premises –
> > (i) which, by virtue of an authorisation (within the meaning of section 136 of the Licensing Act 2003), may be used for the supply of alcohol (within the meaning of section 14 of that Act), or
> > (ii) which are licensed premises (within the meaning of the Licensing (Scotland) Act 1976) or in respect of which a club is registered under that Act;'.

Offices, Shops and Railway Premises Act 1963 (c 41)

33 In section 90 of the Offices, Shops and Railway Premises Act 1963 (interpretation), omit the definition of 'place of public entertainment'.

Greater London Council (General Powers) Act 1966 (c xxviii)

34 The Greater London Council (General Powers) Act 1966 is amended as follows.

35 In section 21(1) (licensing of public exhibitions, etc) –

(a) for 'intoxicating liquor' substitute 'alcohol (within the meaning of the Licensing Act 2003)', and
(b) for 'a film exhibition within the meaning of the Cinemas Act 1985' substitute 'an exhibition of a film (within the meaning of paragraph 15 of Schedule 1 to the Licensing Act 2003)'.

36 In section 22 (application to old buildings of provisions for protection against fire in the London Building Acts (Amendment) Act 1939) –

(a) in subsection (1), for the words from 'being in either case' to 'for that purpose' substitute 'which may lawfully be used for the provision of regulated entertainment (within the meaning of the Licensing Act 2003) only by virtue of an authorisation under that Act', and
(b) in subsection (2), for the words from 'where' to 'that licence' substitute 'where a building, or part of a building, is being used for the provision of regulated entertainment by virtue of a premises licence (under the Licensing Act 2003) granted by a borough council, the Common Council, the Sub-Treasurer of the Inner Temple or the Under-Treasurer of the Middle Temple'.

Finance Act 1967 (c 54)

37 In section 5 of the Finance Act 1967 (no requirement for excise licence) –

  (a) in subsection (1), omit paragraph (c), and
  (b) in subsection (3), omit 'which is registered within the meaning of the Licensing Act 1964 or'.

Criminal Appeal Act 1968 (c 19)

38 The Criminal Appeal Act 1968 is amended as follows.

39 In section 10 (appeal against sentence to Crown Court), at the end of subsection (3)(c) add –

>   '(viii) an order under section 129 of the Licensing Act 2003 (forfeiture or suspension of personal licence); or'.

40 In section 31 (powers of Court of Appeal under Part 1 exercisable by single judge), after subsection (2B) insert –

> '(2C) The power of the Court of Appeal, under section 130 of the Licensing Act 2003, to suspend an order under section 129 of that Act may be exercised by a single judge in the same manner as it may be exercised by the Court.'

41 In section 44 (powers of Court of Appeal under Part 2 exercisable by single judge), after subsection (2) insert –

> '(3) The power of the Court of Appeal, under section 130 of the Licensing Act 2003, to suspend an order under section 129 of that Act may be exercised by a single judge, but where the judge refuses an application to exercise that power the applicant shall be entitled to have the application determined by the Court of Appeal.'

42 In section 50 (meaning of 'sentence'), at the end of subsection (1) insert '; and

>   (i)   an order under section 129(2) of the Licensing Act 2003 (forfeiture or suspension of personal licence).'

Theatres Act 1968 (c 54)

43 The Theatres Act 1968 is amended as follows.

44 The following provisions cease to have effect in England and Wales –

  (a) section 1(2) (local authority may not impose conditions on nature of plays),
  (b) sections 12 to 14 (licensing of premises for public performance of plays),
  (c) Schedule 1 (provision about licences to perform plays).

45 In section 15 (warrant to enter theatre where offence suspected) –

  (a) in subsection (1) –
       (i)   paragraph (b) and the word 'or' immediately preceding it, and

(ii)   the words 'or, in a case falling within paragraph (b) above, any police officer or authorised officer of the licensing authority',

    cease to have effect in England and Wales,

(b)   subsections (2) to (5) cease to have effect in England and Wales, and
(c)   subsection (6) is omitted.

46 Section 17 (existing letters patent) ceases to have effect.

47 In section 18(1) (interpretation), in the definition of 'licensing authority', omit paragraphs (a), (b) and (bb).

Gaming Act 1968 (c 65)

48 The Gaming Act 1968 is amended as follows.

49(1) Section 6 (playing games on premises used for sale of alcohol) is amended as follows.

(2) For subsection (2) substitute –

'(2) This section applies to any premises in England and Wales in respect of which there is in force a premises licence authorising the supply of alcohol for consumption on the premises.

(2A)This section also applies to any premises in Scotland in respect of which a hotel licence or public house licence under the Licensing (Scotland) Act 1976 is in force.'

(3) In subsection (3) –

(a)   for paragraph (a) substitute –

'(a) of the holder of the licence which has effect in respect of any premises to which this section applies,', and

(b)   for 'the licensing justices for the licensing district, or, in Scotland, the licensing board for the licensing area, in which the premises are situated' substitute 'the relevant licensing authority, or, in Scotland, the licensing board for the licensing area in which the premises are situated,'.

(4) In subsection (4) –

(a)   for 'the licensing justices for the licensing district, or, in Scotland, the licensing board for the licensing area, in which the premises are situated' substitute 'the relevant licensing authority, or, in Scotland, the licensing board for the licensing area in which the premises are situated,', and

(b)   for 'the justices' substitute 'the authority'.

(5) In subsection (5), for 'licensing justices or a licensing board, the justices or board' substitute 'a licensing authority or a licensing board, the authority or board'.

(6) In subsection (6) –

(a)   for 'the licensing justices or' substitute 'the relevant licensing authority or the',

(b) for paragraph (a) substitute –

'(a) to the holder of the licence,', and

(c) for 'the police area' substitute 'each police area'.

(7) After subsection (7) insert –

'(7A) A function conferred by this section on a licensing authority is, for the purposes of section 7 of the Licensing Act 2003 (exercise and delegation by licensing authority of licensing functions), to be treated as a licensing function within the meaning of that Act.'

(8) For subsection (8) substitute –

'(8) In this section –

"licensing area" has the same meaning as in the Licensing (Scotland) Act 1976,

"licensing authority" and "premises licence" have the same meaning as in the Licensing Act 2003,

"relevant licensing authority", in relation to premises in respect of which a premises licence has effect, means the authority determined in relation to those premises in accordance with section 12 of that Act, and

"supply of alcohol" has the meaning given in section 14 of that Act.'

50 For section 7(2) (offence to allow child to take part in gaming on licensed premises) substitute –

'(2) Neither the holder of the licence which has effect in respect of premises to which section 6 applies, nor anybody employed by him, may knowingly allow a person under 18 to take part on those premises in gaming to which this Part applies.'

51 For section 8(7) (penalty for contravention of section 7(2)) substitute –

'(7) Any person who contravenes section 7(2) is guilty of an offence and –

(a) where the offence is committed in England and Wales, the person is liable on summary conviction to a fine not exceeding level 5 on the standard scale, and

(b) where the offence is committed in Scotland, the provisions of Schedule 5 to the Licensing (Scotland) Act 1976 are to have effect as they have effect in relation to a contravention of section 68(1) of that Act.'

52(1) Schedule 9 (permits in respect of amusement machine premises) is amended as follows.

(2) In paragraph 1 (interpretation), for paragraph (a) substitute –

'(a) in relation to any premises in England and Wales in respect of which there is in force a premises licence authorising the supply of alcohol for consumption on the premises, means the relevant licensing authority in relation to those premises;'.

(3) After that paragraph, insert –

'1A A function conferred by this Schedule on a licensing authority is, for the purposes of section 7 of the Licensing Act 2003 (exercise and delegation by licensing authority of licensing functions), to be treated as a licensing function within the meaning of that Act.'

(4) In paragraph 10A (condition in case of licensed premises, etc that amusement machine must be located in a bar), in sub-paragraph (2)(a), for 'has the same meaning as in the Licensing Act 1964' substitute 'means any place which, by virtue of a premises licence, may be used for the supply of alcohol and which is exclusively or mainly used for the supply and consumption of alcohol'.

(5) In paragraph 11 –

   (a)   in sub-paragraphs (2) and (3) (appeals), for 'proper officer of' substitute 'clerk to', and
   (b)   omit sub-paragraph (5).

(6) Omit paragraph 14 (payment of indemnity out of central funds).

(7) In paragraph 21 (fees), for 'proper officer' substitute 'clerk'.

(8) For paragraph 23 (interpretation of expressions relating to licensing) substitute –

   '23 In this Schedule –

   "alcohol", "licensing authority" and "premises licence" have the same meaning as in the Licensing Act 2003;
   "hotel licence" and "public house licence" have the same meaning as in Schedule 1 to the Licensing (Scotland) Act 1976;
   "relevant licensing authority", in relation to premises in respect of which a premises licence is in force, means the authority determined in relation to those premises in accordance with section 12 of the Licensing Act 2003; and
   "supply of alcohol" is to be construed in accordance with section 14 of that Act.'

(9) Omit paragraph 24 (proper officer of an appropriate authority).

City of London (Various Powers) Act 1968 (c xxxvii)

53 For section 5(3) of the City of London (Various Powers) Act 1968 (entitlement of Corporation of London to apply for and hold licence to sell alcohol in arrangements for catering facilities) substitute –

   '(3) The Corporation of London or any person appointed by them in that behalf may, subject to section 16 of the Licensing Act 2003, for the purposes of this section apply for and hold a premises licence under that Act for the sale by retail of alcohol within the meaning of that Act.'

Finance Act 1970 (c 24)

54 In section 6(2)(b) of the Finance Act 1970 (Angostura bitters) –

   (a)   omit ', the Licensing Act 1964', and
   (b)   for 'either of those Acts' substitute 'that Act'.

Sunday Theatre Act 1972 (c 26)

55 The Sunday Theatre Act 1972 ceases to have effect.

Local Government Act 1972 (c 70)

56 The Local Government Act 1972 is amended as follows.

57 In section 78(1) (supplementary provision relating to changes in local government areas), omit the definition of 'public body'.

58 In section 101 (arrangements for discharge of functions by local authorities), after subsection (14) insert –

'(15) Nothing in this section applies in relation to any function under the Licensing Act 2003 of a licensing authority (within the meaning of that Act).'

59 In section 145(4) (provision of entertainment), for 'intoxicating liquor' substitute 'alcohol'.

60 Section 204 (licensed premises) ceases to have effect.

61(1) Schedule 12 (meetings and proceedings of local authorities) is amended as follows.

(2) In the following provisions, for 'premises licensed for the sale of intoxicating liquor' substitute 'premises which at the time of such a meeting may, by virtue of a premises licence or temporary event notice under the Licensing Act 2003, be used for the supply of alcohol (within the meaning of section 14 of that Act)' –

    (a)   paragraph 10(1) (location of parish council meetings),
    (b)   paragraph 26(1) (location of community council meetings).

(3) In the following provisions, for 'premises licensed for the sale of intoxicating liquor' substitute 'premises which at the time of the meeting may, by virtue of a premises licence or temporary event notice under the Licensing Act 2003, be used for the supply of alcohol (within the meaning of section 14 of that Act)' –

    (a)   paragraph 14(5) (location of parish meetings),
    (b)   paragraph 32(2) (location of community meetings).

Lotteries and Amusements Act 1976 (c 32)

62 Schedule 3 to the Lotteries and Amusements Act 1976 (provision about permits for commercial provision of amusements with prizes) is amended as follows.

63(1) Paragraph 1 (interpretation) is amended as follows.

(2) In sub-paragraph (1), for paragraph (a) substitute –

'(a)   in relation to any premises in England and Wales in respect of which there is in force a premises licence authorising the supply of alcohol for consumption on the premises, the relevant licensing authority in relation to those premises;'.

(3) In sub-paragraph (2) –

   (a)   for the definition of 'justices' on-licence', 'licensing district' and 'Part IV licence' substitute –

    '"alcohol", "licensing authority" and "premises licence" have the same meaning as in the Licensing Act 2003,',

   (b)   omit the definition of 'the proper officer of the authority', and
   (c)   at the appropriate place, insert –

    '"relevant licensing authority", in relation to premises in respect of which a premises licence is in force, means the licensing authority in relation to those premises determined in accordance with section 12 of the Licensing Act 2003;', and
    '"supply of alcohol" has the same meaning as in section 14 of the Licensing Act 2003;'.

(4) After that sub-paragraph insert –

    '(3) A function conferred by this Schedule on a licensing authority is, for the purposes of section 7 of the Licensing Act 2003 (exercise and delegation by licensing authority of licensing functions), to be treated as a licensing function within the meaning of that Act.'

64 In paragraph 8 (appeals) –

   (a)   in sub-paragraphs (2) and (3), for 'proper officer of' substitute 'clerk to', and
   (b)   omit sub-paragraph (4).

65 Omit paragraph 11 (payment of indemnity from central funds).

66 In paragraph 18 (fees), for 'proper officer' substitute 'clerk'.

Rent Act 1977 (c 42)

67 In section 11 of the Rent Act 1977 (tenancy of licensed premises not to be protected or statutory tenancy), for 'premises licensed for the sale of intoxicating liquors' substitute 'premises which, by virtue of a premises licence under the Licensing Act 2003, may be used for the supply of alcohol (within the meaning of section 14 of that Act)'.

Greater London Council (General Powers) Act 1978 (c xiii)

68 The Greater London Council (General Powers) Act 1978 is amended as follows.

69 Section 3 (human posing to be treated as entertainment) ceases to have effect.

70 In section 5(4)(a) (definition of 'booking office') –

   (a)   omit sub-paragraph (ii) and the word 'or' immediately preceding it, and
   (b)   for 'sub-paragraphs (i) and (ii)' substitute 'sub-paragraph (i)'.

Alcoholic Liquor Duties Act 1979 (c 4)

71 The Alcoholic Liquor Duties Act 1979 is amended as follows.

72 In section 4 (interpretation) –

(a)   in the definition of 'justices' licence' and 'justices' on-licence', omit paragraph (a), and

(b)   in the definition of 'registered club', omit 'which is for the time being registered within the meaning of the Licensing Act 1964 or'.

73 In section 71 (exception to penalty for misdescribing alcohol as spirits) –

(a)   after subsection (4) insert –

'(4A) Nothing in this section as it applies to England and Wales shall apply to any alcohol (within the meaning of the Licensing Act 2003) which is prepared on any premises which may be lawfully used for the supply of alcohol (within the meaning of section 14 of that Act) for immediate consumption there.'

(b)   in subsection (5) –
   (i)   omit 'England and Wales or',
   (ii)   omit paragraph (c), and
   (iii) for ', in that club or on board that aircraft, vessel or vehicle,' substitute 'or in that club'.

Licensed Premises (Exclusion of Certain Persons) Act 1980 (c 32)

74 In section 4(1) of the Licensed Premises (Exclusion of Certain Persons) Act 1980 (interpretation), in the definition of 'licensed premises' for the words 'a justices' on-licence (within the meaning of section 1 of the Licensing Act 1964)' substitute 'a premises licence under the Licensing Act 2003 authorising the supply of alcohol (within the meaning of section 14 of that Act) for consumption on the premises'.

Magistrates' Courts Act 1980 (c 43)

75 In Part 3 of Schedule 6 to the Magistrates' Courts Act 1980 (matters to which provision relating to fees taken by clerks to justices does not apply), paragraphs 3 and 5 are omitted.

Local Government, Planning and Land Act 1980 (c 65)

76 The Local Government, Planning and Land Act 1980 is amended as follows.

77 Sections 131 and 132 (licensing in new towns) cease to have effect.

78 In section 133 (miscellaneous provision about new towns), in subsection (1), omit the following definitions –

(a)   'development corporation',
(b)   'the 1964 Act'.

79 In section 146 (disposal of land by urban development corporation) –

(a)   in subsection (3), for 'intoxicating liquor' substitute 'alcohol', and

(b) in subsection (6), for "intoxicating liquor' has the meaning assigned
by section 201 of the Licensing Act 1964' substitute "alcohol' has the
meaning given by section 191 of the Licensing Act 2003'.

Indecent Displays (Control) Act 1981 (c 42)

80 In section 1(4) of the Indecent Displays (Control) Act 1981 (exemptions
from offence of displaying indecent matter) –

(a) for paragraph (d) substitute –

'(d) included in a performance of a play (within the meaning of
paragraph 14(1) of Schedule 1 to the Licensing Act 2003) in
England and Wales or of a play (within the meaning of the
Theatres Act 1968) in Scotland;', and

(b) in paragraph (e) for 'included in a film exhibition as defined in the
Cinemas Act 1985' substitute 'included in an exhibition of a film,
within the meaning of paragraph 15 of Schedule 1 to the Licensing
Act 2003, in England and Wales, or a film exhibition, as defined in the
Cinemas Act 1985, in Scotland'.

New Towns Act 1981 (c 64)

81 In section 18 of the New Towns Act 1981 (disposal by development
corporation of land to occupiers of it before acquisition by corporation), in
subsection (3) for the words 'intoxicating liquor ('intoxicating liquor' having
the meaning given in section 201(1) of the Licensing Act 1964)' substitute
'alcohol (within the meaning of section 191 of the Licensing Act 2003)'.

Local Government (Miscellaneous Provisions) Act 1982 (c 30)

82 The Local Government (Miscellaneous Provisions) Act 1982 is amended
as follows.

83 The following provisions cease to have effect –

(a) section 1 (licensing of public entertainment outside Greater
London),
(b) sections 4 to 6 (controls on take-away food shops),
(c) Schedule 1 (licensing of public entertainment outside Greater
London).

84 In section 10(11) (requirement that apparatus to be installed should be
provided with cut-off switch disapplied in relation to cinemas) for the words
'premises in respect of which a licence under section 1 of the Cinemas Act
1985 is for the time being in force' substitute 'premises in respect of which a
premises licence under the Licensing Act 2003 has effect authorising the use
of the premises for an exhibition of a film, within the meaning of paragraph
15 of Schedule 1 to that Act'.

85(1) Schedule 3 (control of sex establishments) is amended as follows.

(2) In paragraph 3(2) (premises not to be treated as a sex cinema merely
because the exhibition of a film there must be authorised by a licence, etc) –

(a)   for paragraph (a) substitute –

    '(a)   if they may be used for an exhibition of a film (within the meaning of paragraph 15 of Schedule 1 to the Licensing Act 2003) by virtue of an authorisation (within the meaning of section 136 of that Act), of their use in accordance with that authorisation', and

    (b)   in paragraph (b), for 'that Act' substitute 'the Cinemas Act 1985'.

(3) In paragraph 3A (exemption for theatres and cinemas from provisions about sex encounter establishments) for paragraphs (i) and (ii) of the proviso substitute –

    '(i)   for the time being, being used for the provision of regulated entertainment (within the meaning of the Licensing Act 2003), in circumstances where that use is authorised under that Act; or

    (ii)   for the time being, being used for the purposes of late night refreshment (within the meaning of that Act), in circumstances where that use is so authorised; or'.

Representation of the People Act 1983 (c 2)

86 The Representation of the People Act 1983 is amended as follows.

87 In section 185 (interpretation of Part relating to legal proceedings), for the definition of 'Licensing Acts' substitute –

    ' "Licensing Acts" means the Licensing (Scotland) Act 1976 and the Licensing (Northern Ireland) Order 1996 (as that Act or Order may from time to time have effect);'.

88 In Schedule 7 (transitional and saving provision), omit paragraph 4.

Video Recordings Act 1984 (c 39)

89 In section 3(7) of the Video Recordings Act 1984 (exempted supply of video recording) –

(a)   before paragraph (a) insert –

    '(za)   premises in England and Wales which, by virtue of an authorisation within the meaning of section 136 of the Licensing Act 2003, may be used for the exhibition of a film within the meaning of paragraph 15 of Schedule 1 to that Act,', and

(b)   in paragraphs (a) and (c) after 'premises', and in paragraph (b) after the first 'premises', insert 'in Scotland'.

Building Act 1984 (c 55)

90 The Building Act 1984 is amended as follows.

91 In section 24(4) (provision of exits in buildings) for paragraph (c) substitute –

'(c) premises in respect of which a club premises certificate has effect under the Licensing Act 2003,'.

92 In section 74(2) (exemption for certain premises from requirement for local authority's consent for cellars and rooms below subsoil water level), omit paragraph (a) and the word 'or' immediately following it.

Police and Criminal Evidence Act 1984 (c 60)

93 In Schedule 1A to the Police and Criminal Evidence Act 1984 (arrestable offences) at the end there is inserted –

'*Licensing Act 2003*

26. An offence under section 143(1) of the Licensing Act 2003 (failure to leave licensed premises, etc).'

Greater London Council (General Powers) Act 1984 (c xxvii)

94 In section 15(1) of the Greater London Council (General Powers) Act 1984 (exceptions to power of Council to refuse to register sleeping accommodation), at the end insert '; or

    (v) a building –
        (a) in respect of which there is in force immediately before the appointed day a premises licence under the Licensing Act 2003 authorising the supply of alcohol (within the meaning of section 14 of that Act) for consumption on the premises, and
        (b) the use of which for a specified purpose would not contravene the Town and Country Planning Act 1990.'

Cinemas Act 1985 (c 13)

95 The Cinemas Act 1985 ceases to have effect in England and Wales.

Sporting Events (Control of Alcohol etc) Act 1985 (c 57)

96 The Sporting Events (Control of Alcohol etc) Act 1985 is amended as follows.

97 In the following provisions, for 'intoxicating liquor' substitute 'alcohol' –

    (a) section 1(2) and (3) (alcohol on coaches and trains),
    (b) section 1A(2) and (3) (alcohol on certain other vehicles),
    (c) section 2(1) (alcohol at sports grounds).

98 Omit section 2(1A) (application to private rooms of offence of having alcohol at designated sporting event).

99 The following provisions cease to have effect –

    (a) sections 3 and 4 (order about licensing hours in sports grounds),
    (b) section 5 (appeal against such an order),

(c) section 5A (restricted periods in relation to possession of alcohol in private rooms at sports grounds),
(d) section 5B (occasional licences at sports grounds),
(e) section 5C (supply of alcohol by clubs at sports grounds),
(f) section 5D (non-retail sales of alcohol during sporting event),
(g) section 6 (closure of bar during sporting event),
(h) the Schedule (procedure for obtaining order about licensing hours in sports grounds).

100 In section 8 (offences) –

(a) in paragraph (b), for ', 2A(1), 3(10), 5B(2), 5C(3), 5D(2) or 6(2)' substitute 'or 2A(1)', and
(b) omit paragraphs (d) and (e).

101 In section 9 (interpretation) –

(a) omit subsection (5), and
(b) for subsection (7) substitute –

'(7) An expression used in this Act and in the Licensing Act 2003 has the same meaning in this Act as in that Act.'

Housing Act 1985 (c 68)

102 The Housing Act 1985 is amended as follows.

103 In section 11 (provision of board facilities by local housing authority) –

(a) for subsection (3) substitute –

'(3) Where a premises licence under Part 3 of the Licensing Act 2003 authorises the sale by retail of alcohol in connection with the provision of facilities of the kind mentioned in subsection (1)(a), then, notwithstanding the terms of that licence, it does not have effect so as to authorise the sale by retail of alcohol for consumption otherwise than with a meal.',

(b) in subsection (4) after 'the sale of intoxicating liquor' insert 'or the sale by retail of alcohol', and
(c) after that subsection insert –

'(5) An expression used in this section and in the Licensing Act 2003 has the same meaning in this section as in that Act.'

104 In Schedule 1 (tenancies which are not secure tenancies), in paragraph 9, for 'premises licensed for the sale of intoxicating liquor' substitute 'premises which, by virtue of a premises licence under the Licensing Act 2003, may be used for the supply of alcohol (within the meaning of section 14 of that Act)'.

Sex Discrimination Act 1986 (c 59)

105 Section 5 of the Sex Discrimination Act 1986 (discrimination required by public entertainment licence) ceases to have effect.

Fire Safety and Safety of Places of Sport Act 1987 (c 27)

106 After section 33(2) of the Fire Safety and Safety of Places of Sport Act 1987 (requirements of safety certificate to take precedence over conflicting conditions imposed in licence, etc) insert –

'(2A) For the purposes of subsection (2) –

(a) "the licensing of premises" includes the granting of a premises licence or club premises certificate under the Licensing Act 2003, and

(b) "licence" is to be construed accordingly.'

Norfolk and Suffolk Broads Act 1988 (c 4)

107 In paragraph 40(1) of Schedule 3 to the Norfolk and Suffolk Broads Act 1988 (provision of facilities by Broads Authority), in paragraph (b) for 'intoxicating liquor' substitute 'alcohol (within the meaning of the Licensing Act 2003)'.

Housing Act 1988 (c 50)

108 In Schedule 1 to the Housing Act 1988 (tenancies which cannot be assured tenancies), in paragraph 5, for 'premises licensed for the sale of intoxicating liquors' substitute 'premises which, by virtue of a premises licence under the Licensing Act 2003, may be used for the supply of alcohol (within the meaning of section 14 of that Act)'.

Town and Country Planning Act 1990 (c 8)

109 Section 334 of the Town and Country Planning Act 1990 (licensing planning areas) ceases to have effect.

Sunday Trading Act 1994 (c 20)

110(1) Schedule 1 to the Sunday Trading Act 1994 (restrictions on Sunday opening of large shops) is amended as follows.

(2) In paragraph 1 –

(a) for the definition of 'intoxicating liquor' substitute –

'"alcohol" has the same meaning as in the Licensing Act 2003,', and

(b) in paragraph (a) of the definition of 'sale of goods', for 'intoxicating liquor' substitute 'alcohol'.

(3)   In paragraph 3(1)(b) for 'intoxicating liquor' substitute 'alcohol'.

Criminal Justice and Public Order Act 1994 (c 33)

111 In section 63 of the Criminal Justice and Public Order Act 1994 (power to remove persons attending raves, etc), for subsection (9)(a) substitute –

'(a) in England and Wales, to a gathering in relation to a licensable activity within section 1(1)(c) of the Licensing Act 2003 (provision of certain forms of entertainment) carried on under and in accordance with an authorisation within the meaning of section 136 of that Act;'.

Deregulation and Contracting Out Act 1994 (c 40)

112 Section 21 of the Deregulation and Contracting Out Act 1994 (Sunday Observance Act 1780 not to apply to sporting events) ceases to have effect.

London Local Authorities Act 1995 (c x)

113 In section 14 of the London Local Authorities Act 1995 (interpretation of Part relating to near beer premises), in the definition of 'near beer premises' –

(a) for 'intoxicating liquor is provided exemption or saving from the provisions of the Act of 1964 by virtue of section 199 of that Act' substitute 'alcohol is not a licensable activity under or by virtue of section 173 of the Licensing Act 2003',

(b) for paragraph (A) substitute –

'(A) a premises licence under Part 3 of that Act which authorises the supply of alcohol (within the meaning of section 14 of that Act) for consumption on the premises;',

(c) in paragraph (B) –
   (i) omit 'Schedule 12 to the London Government Act 1963,' and 'or the Private Places of Entertainment (Licensing) Act 1967', and
   (ii) at the end insert 'or a premises licence granted under Part 3 of the Licensing Act 2003 which authorises the provision of any form of regulated entertainment (within the meaning of Schedule 1 to that Act)',

(d) omit paragraphs (C) to (E),

(e) for paragraphs (F) and (G) substitute –

'(F) a temporary event notice under the Licensing Act 2003, by virtue of which the premises may be used for the supply of alcohol (within the meaning of section 14 of that Act);',

(f) for the words from 'during the hours' to 'licence:' substitute 'during the hours permitted by such licence or notice:', and

(g) for 'such licence; and' substitute 'such licence or notice; and'.

Employment Rights Act 1996 (c 18)

114 In section 232(7) of the Employment Rights Act 1996 (definition of 'catering business') –

(a) in paragraph (a) for 'intoxicating liquor' substitute 'alcohol', and

(b) for '"intoxicating liquor" has the same meaning as in the Licensing Act 1964' substitute '"alcohol" has the same meaning as in the Licensing Act 2003'.

Confiscation of Alcohol (Young Persons) Act 1997 (c 33)

115(1) Section 1 of the Confiscation of Alcohol (Young Persons) Act 1997 (confiscation of alcohol) is amended as follows.

(2) In subsection (1) –

   (a)   for 'intoxicating liquor', in each place it occurs, substitute 'alcohol',
   (b)   in paragraph (b) for 'liquor' substitute 'alcohol', and
   (c)   for 'such liquor' substitute 'alcohol'.

(3) For subsection (7) substitute –

   '(7) In this section –

      "alcohol" –

         (a)   in relation to England and Wales, has the same meaning as in the Licensing Act 2003;
         (b)   in relation to Northern Ireland, has the same meaning as "intoxicating liquor" in the Licensing (Northern Ireland) Order 1996; and

      "licensed premises" –

         (a)   in relation to England and Wales, means premises which may by virtue of Part 3 or Part 5 of the Licensing Act 2003 (premises licence; permitted temporary activity) be used for the supply of alcohol within the meaning of section 14 of that Act;
         (b)   in relation to Northern Ireland, has the same meaning as in the Licensing (Northern Ireland) Order 1996.'

Police Act 1997 (c 50)

116 In section 115(5) of the Police Act 1997 (enhanced criminal record certificates), after paragraph (d) insert –

   '(da) a personal licence under the Licensing Act 2003;'.

London Local Authorities Act 2000 (c vii)

117 In section 32 of the London Local Authorities Act 2000 (interpretation of provisions about the licensing of buskers), in the definition of 'busking', for paragraph (b) substitute –

   '(b)   under and in accordance with a premises licence under Part 3 of the Licensing Act 2003, or a temporary event notice having effect under Part 5 of that Act, which authorises the provision of regulated entertainment (within paragraph 2(1)(e) to (h) or 3(2) of Schedule 1 to that Act (music and dancing));'.

Private Security Industry Act 2001 (c 12)

118(1) Paragraph 8 of Schedule 2 to the Private Security Industry Act 2001 (door supervisors etc for licensed premises) is amended as follows.

(2) In sub-paragraph (2), for paragraphs (a) to (d) substitute –

'(a) any premises in respect of which a premises licence or temporary event notice has effect under the Licensing Act 2003 to authorise the supply of alcohol (within the meaning of section 14 of that Act) for consumption on the premises;

(b) any premises in respect of which a premises licence or temporary event notice has effect under that Act to authorise the provision of regulated entertainment;'.

(3) For sub-paragraph (3) substitute –

'(3) For the purposes of this paragraph, premises are not licensed premises –

(a) if there is in force in respect of the premises a premises licence which authorises regulated entertainment within paragraph 2(1)(a) or (b) of Schedule 1 to the Licensing Act 2003 (plays and films);

(b) in relation to any occasion on which the premises are being used –

(i)   exclusively for the purposes of a club which holds a club premises certificate in respect of the premises, or

(ii) for regulated entertainment of the kind mentioned in paragraph (a), in circumstances where that use is a permitted temporary activity by virtue of Part 5 of that Act;

(c) in relation to any occasion on which a licence is in force in respect of the premises under the Gaming Act 1968 (c 65) and the premises are being used wholly or mainly for the purposes of gaming to which Part 2 of that Act applies; or

(d) in relation to any such other occasion as may be prescribed for the purposes of this sub-paragraph.'

(4) After sub-paragraph (5) insert –

'(6) Sub-paragraphs (2)(a) and (b) and (3)(a) and (b) are to be construed in accordance with the Licensing Act 2003.'

Criminal Justice and Police Act 2001 (c 16)

119 The Criminal Justice and Police Act 2001 is amended as follows.

120 In section 1(1) (offences leading to penalties on the spot), at the end of the Table insert –

'Section 149(4) of the Licensing Act 2003	Buying or attempting to buy alcohol for consumption on licensed premises, etc by child'

121 In section 12 (alcohol consumption in designated public place) –

(a) in subsections (1) and (2), for 'intoxicating liquor', in each place it occurs, substitute 'alcohol', and

(b) in subsection (2) for 'such liquor' substitute 'alcohol'.

122 In section 13 (designated public places), in subsection (2) for 'intoxicating liquor' substitute 'alcohol'.

123(1) Section 14 (places which are not designated public places) is amended as follows.

(2) In subsection (1) –

    (a)   for paragraphs (a) to (d) substitute –

        '(a) premises in respect of which a premises licence or club premises certificate, within the meaning of the Licensing Act 2003, has effect;

        (b) a place within the curtilage of premises within paragraph (a);

        (c) premises which by virtue of Part 5 of the Licensing Act 2003 may for the time being be used for the supply of alcohol or which, by virtue of that Part, could have been so used within the last 20 minutes;', and

    (b)   in paragraph (e), for 'intoxicating liquor' substitute 'alcohol'.

(3) Omit subsection (2).

124 In section 15(1)(a) (byelaw prohibiting consumption of alcohol), for 'intoxicating liquor' substitute 'alcohol'.

125 In section 16(1) (interpretation of sections 12 to 15) –

    (a)   before the definition of 'designated public place' insert –

    '"alcohol" has the same meaning as in the Licensing Act 2003;',

    (b)   omit the definition of 'intoxicating liquor', and the word 'and' immediately following it, and

    (c)   after the definition of 'public place' insert '; and

    '"supply of alcohol" has the meaning given by section 14 of the Licensing Act 2003'.

126 In each of the following provisions, for 'unlicensed sale of intoxicating liquor' substitute 'unauthorised sale of alcohol' –

    (a)   section 19(1) and (2) (service of closure notice by constable or local authority),

    (b)   section 20(3)(a) (no application for closure order where unauthorised sale of alcohol has ceased),

    (c)   section 21(1)(b) and (2)(b) (closure order),

    (d)   section 27(6) (fixing notice on premises where personal service cannot be effected).

127 In section 28 (interpretation of provisions relating to closure of unlicensed premises) –

    (a)   before the definition of 'closure notice' insert –

    '"alcohol" has the same meaning as in the Licensing Act 2003;',

    (b)   omit the definition of 'intoxicating liquor', and

    (c)   for the definition of 'unlicensed sale' substitute –

    '"unauthorised sale", in relation to any alcohol, means any supply of the alcohol (within the meaning of section 14 of the Licensing Act 2003) which –

(a)   is a licensable activity within the meaning of that Act, but

(b)   is made otherwise than under and in accordance with an authorisation (within the meaning of section 136 of that Act).'

128 In Schedule 1 (powers of seizure) –

(a)   at the end of Part 1 insert –

'*Licensing Act 2003*

74. The power of seizure conferred by section 90 of the Licensing Act 2003 (seizure of documents relating to club).', and

(b)   at the end of Part 3 insert –

'*Licensing Act 2003*

110. The power of seizure conferred by section 90 of the Licensing Act 2003 (seizure of documents relating to club).'

SCHEDULE 7 Section 199

REPEALS

Short title and chapter	Extent of repeal
Universities (Wine Licences) Act 1743 (c 40)	The whole Act.
Sunday Observance Act 1780 (21 Geo. 3 c 49)	The whole Act.
Metropolitan Police Act 1839 (c 47)	Section 41.
Town Police Clauses Act 1847 (c 89)	Section 35.
Cambridge Award Act 1856 (c xvii)	Sections 9 and 11.
Inebriates Act 1898 (c 60)	In the First Schedule – the entry relating to section 18 of the Licensing Act 1872, and the entry relating to section 41 of the Refreshment Houses Act 1860.
Sunday Entertainments Act 1932 (c 51)	The whole Act.
Children and Young Persons Act 1933 (c 12)	In section 12(3), the words from ', and also' to the end. In section 107, the definition of 'intoxicating liquor'.
Public Health Act 1936 (c 49)	Section 226(4).

Short title and chapter	*Extent of repeal*
Common Informers Act 1951 (c 39)	In the Schedule – the entry relating to section 11 of the Universities (Wine Licences) Act 1743, and the entry relating to the Sunday Observance Act 1780.
Hypnotism Act 1952 (c 46)	Section 1(2).
London Government Act 1963 (c 33)	Section 52(3). Schedule 12.
Offices, Shops and Railway Premises Act 1963 (c 41)	In section 90, the definition of 'place of public entertainment'.
Licensing Act 1964 (c 26)	The whole Act.
Administration of Justice Act 1964 (c 42)	In Schedule 3, paragraph 31.
Refreshment Houses Act 1964 (c 88)	The whole Act.
Private Places of Entertainment (Licensing) Act 1967 (c 19)	The whole Act.
Licensing (Amendment) Act 1967 (c 51)	The whole Act.
Finance Act 1967 (c 54)	In section 5 – in subsection (1),the words '; and accordingly as from that date –' and paragraphs (c) and (e), and in subsection (3), the words 'which is registered within the meaning of the Licensing Act 1964 or'. Section 45(4). Schedule 7.
Theatres Act 1968 (c 54)	Section 15(6). Section 17. In section 18(1), in the definition of 'licensing authority', paragraphs (a), (b) and (bb). In Schedule 2 – the entries relating to the Licensing Act 1964, and the entry relating to the Private Places of Entertainment (Licensing) Act 1967.

Short title and chapter	Extent of repeal
Gaming Act 1968 (c 65)	In Schedule 9 – paragraph 11(5), paragraph 14, and paragraph 24. In Schedule 11, in Part 3, the entries relating to the Licensing Act 1964.
Greater London Council (General Powers) Act 1968 (c xxxix)	Sections 47 to 55.
Late Night Refreshment Houses Act 1969 (c 53)	The whole Act.
Finance Act 1970 (c 24)	In section 6(2)(b), the words ', the Licensing Act 1964'.
Courts Act 1971 (c 23)	In Schedule 6, paragraphs 7 and 13. In Schedule 8, paragraph 42. In Schedule 9, in Part 1, the entries relating to – the London Government Act 1963, the Licensing Act 1964, the Private Places of Entertainment (Licensing) Act 1967, the Theatres Act 1968, and the Late Night Refreshment Houses Act 1969.
Sunday Theatre Act 1972 (c 26)	The whole Act.
Local Government Act 1972 (c 70)	In section 78(1), the definition of 'public body'. Section 204. In Schedule 25, paragraphs 1 to 9.
Local Government Act 1974 (c 7)	In Schedule 6, paragraph 24.
Licensing (Amendment) Act 1976 (c 18)	The whole Act.
Lotteries and Amusements Act 1976 (c 32)	In Schedule 3 – in paragraph 1(2), the definition of 'the proper officer of the authority', and paragraphs 8(4) and 11.
Licensing (Scotland) Act 1976 (c 66)	In Schedule 7, paragraphs 9(a), (b), (d) and (f), 10, 11 and 12.

Short title and chapter	*Extent of repeal*
Greater London Council (General Powers) Act 1976 (c xxvi)	Sections 5 to 8.
Licensing (Amendment) Act 1977 (c 26)	The whole Act.
Greater London Council (General Powers) Act 1978 (c xiii)	Sections 3 and 4. Section 5(4)(a)(ii) and the word 'or' immediately preceding it.
Customs and Excise Management Act 1979 (c 2)	In Schedule 4, in paragraph 12, in the Table, the entry relating to the Licensing Act 1964.
Alcoholic Liquor Duties Act 1979 (c 4)	In section 4 – in the definition of 'justices' licence' and 'justices' on-licence', paragraph (a), and in the definition of 'registered club', the words 'which is for the time being registered within the meaning of the Licensing Act 1964 or'. In section 71(5) – the words 'England and Wales or', and paragraph (c). In Schedule 3, paragraph 5.
Greater London Council (General Powers) Act 1979 (c xxiii)	Section 3.
Licensing (Amendment) Act 1980 (c 40)	The whole Act.
Magistrates' Courts Act 1980 (c 43)	In Schedule 6, in Part 3, paragraphs 3 and 5. In Schedule 7, paragraphs 45 to 48 and 50.
Local Government, Planning and Land Act 1980 (c 65)	Sections 131 and 132. In section 133(1), the definitions of 'development corporation' and 'the 1964 Act'.
Highways Act 1980 (c 66)	In Schedule 24, paragraph 12.
Finance Act 1981 (c 35)	In Schedule 8, paragraphs 24 and 25.
Licensing (Amendment) Act 1981 (c 40)	The whole Act.
Supreme Court Act 1981 (c 54)	In section 28(2)(b), the words 'the Licensing Act 1964,'.

Short title and chapter	Extent of repeal
New Towns Act 1981 (c 64)	In Schedule 2, paragraph 2. In Schedule 12, paragraphs 1 and 29(a)(i).
Local Government (Miscellaneous Provisions) Act 1982 (c 30)	Section 1. Sections 4 to 7. Schedule 1. In Schedule 2, paragraphs 1 to 6.
Greater London Council (General Powers) Act 1982 (c i)	Section 7.
Representation of the People Act 1983 (c 2)	In Schedule 7, paragraph 4. In Schedule 8, paragraphs 7 to 10.
Licensing (Occasional Permissions) Act 1983 (c 24)	The whole Act.
Building Act 1984 (c 55)	In section 74(2), paragraph (a) and the word 'or' immediately following it.
Greater London Council (General Powers) Act 1984 (c xxvii)	Section 4(1) and (3). Sections 19 to 22.
Cinemas Act 1985 (c 13)	Section 3(1A). Section 9. Sections 17 and 18. In section 19(3), paragraph (a) and the word 'or' immediately following it. In Schedule 2, paragraphs 2, 3, 6, 7, 8, 14, 15 and 16(a) and the word 'and' immediately following it.
Licensing (Amendment) Act 1985 (c 40)	The whole Act.
Local Government Act 1985 (c 51)	In Schedule 8 – paragraph 1(1), in paragraph 1(3), the words following paragraph (c), and paragraphs 2 to 5.
Sporting Events (Control of Alcohol etc) Act 1985 (c 57)	Section 2(1A). Sections 3 to 6. Section 8(d) and (e). Section 9(5). The Schedule.
Insolvency Act 1985 (c 65)	In Schedule 8, paragraph 12.
Insolvency Act 1986 (c 45)	In Schedule 14, the entries relating to the Licensing Act 1964.

Short title and chapter	*Extent of repeal*
Sex Discrimination Act 1986 (c 59)	Section 5.
Public Order Act 1986 (c 64)	In Schedule 1, paragraphs 4, 5, 7(5) and 8.
Greater London Council (General Powers) Act 1986 (c iv)	Section 3.
Fire Safety and Safety of Places of Sport Act 1987 (c 27)	Sections 42, 43, 45 and 46. Schedule 3. In Schedule 5 – in paragraph 1, the definition of 'the 1963 Act' and the definition of 'the 1982 Act' and the word 'and' immediately preceding it, and paragraphs 8 to 10.
Licensing Act 1988 (c 17)	The whole Act.
Licensing (Retail Sales) Act 1988 (c 25)	The whole Act.
Licensing (Amendment) Act 1989 (c 20)	The whole Act.
Employment Act 1989 (c 38)	In Schedule 6, paragraph 30.
Town and Country Planning Act 1990 (c 8)	Section 334.
Entertainments (Increased Penalties) Act 1990 (c 20)	Section 1.
Licensing (Low Alcohol Drinks) Act 1990 (c 21)	Section 1.
Broadcasting Act 1990 (c 42)	In Schedule 20, paragraphs 7 and 8.
London Local Authorities Act 1990 (c vii)	Sections 4 to 17, 19 and 20.
London Local Authorities (No 2) Act 1990 (c xxx)	Section 6.
Finance Act 1991 (c 31)	In Schedule 2, in paragraph 1, the words ', the Licensing Act 1964'.
London Local Authorities Act 1991 (c xiii)	Sections 18 to 21.
Sporting Events (Control of Alcohol etc) (Amendment) Act 1992 (c 57)	The whole Act.
Charities Act 1993 (c 10)	In Schedule 6, paragraph 27.

Short title and chapter	Extent of repeal
Local Government (Wales) Act 1994 (c 19)	In Schedule 2, paragraph 2. In Schedule 15, paragraph 41. In Schedule 16, paragraphs 22, 29, 32, 36, 69 and 73.
Coal Industry Act 1994 (c 21)	In Schedule 9, paragraph 8.

Criminal Justice and Public Order Act 1994 (c 33)	In section 63 –
	    in subsection (10), the definitions of 'entertainment licence' and 'local authority', and
	    subsection (11).

Deregulation and Contracting Out Act 1994 (c 40)	Section 18(1). Section 19. Section 21. Schedule 7. In Schedule 11, paragraph 1.
London Local Authorities Act 1994 (c xii)	Section 5.
Licensing (Sunday Hours) Act 1995 (c 33)	The whole Act.
London Local Authorities Act 1995 (c x)	In section 14 – in paragraph (B), the words 'Schedule 12 to the London Government Act 1963,' and 'or the Private Places of Entertainment (Licensing) Act 1967', and paragraphs (C) to (E). Section 28. Sections 45 and 46.
London Local Authorities Act 1996 (c ix)	Sections 20 to 23.
Justices of the Peace Act 1997 (c 25)	In Schedule 4, in paragraph 17(3), the words ', other than any duties as secretary to a licensing planning committee under Part VII of the Licensing Act 1964'.
Confiscation of Alcohol (Young Persons) Act 1997 (c 33)	In section 1(1), the words '(other than a sealed container)'.
Public Entertainments Licences (Drug Misuse) Act 1997 (c 49)	The whole Act.

Short title and chapter	Extent of repeal
Access to Justice Act 1999 (c 22)	In Schedule 10, paragraphs 23 to 29 and 31. In Schedule 11, paragraph 17. In Schedule 13, paragraphs 36 to 56, 61, 62, 87, 124 and 132.
Greater London Authority Act 1999 (c 29)	In Schedule 29, paragraphs 6, 67, 70 and 71.
Licensing (Young Persons) Act 2000 (c 30)	The whole Act.
Freedom of Information Act 2000 (c 36)	In Schedule 1, paragraph 17.
London Local Authorities Act 2000 (c vii)	Sections 22 to 26. Schedule 1.
Criminal Justice and Police Act 2001 (c 16)	In section 1(1), in the Table, the entry relating to section 169C(3) of the Licensing Act 1964. In section 12(2)(b), the words '(other than a sealed container)'. Section 14(2). In section 16(1), the definition of 'intoxicating liquor' and the word 'and' immediately following it. Sections 17 and 18. In section 28, the definition of 'intoxicating liquor'. Sections 30 to 32. In Schedule 1, paragraphs 7 and 90.

SCHEDULE 8

Section 200

TRANSITIONAL PROVISION ETC.

PART 1

PREMISES LICENCES

Introductory

1(1) In this Part –

'canteen licence' has the same meaning as in section 148 of the 1964 Act (licences for seamen's canteens);

'children's certificate' has the same meaning as in section 168A of that Act;

'existing licence' means –

(a) a justices' licence,

(b) a canteen licence,

(c) a licence under Schedule 12 to the London Government Act 1963 (c 33) (licensing of public entertainment in Greater London),

(d) a licence under the Private Places of Entertainment (Licensing) Act 1967 (c 19),

(e) a licence under the Theatres Act 1968 (c 54),

(f) a licence under the Late Night Refreshment Houses Act 1969 (c 53),

(g) a licence under Schedule 1 to the Local Government (Miscellaneous Provisions) Act 1982 (c 30) (licensing of public entertainments outside Greater London),

(h) a licence under section 1 of the Cinemas Act 1985 (c 13), or

(i) a licence under Part 2 of the London Local Authorities Act 1990 (c vii) (night cafe licensing);

'existing licensable activities', under an existing licence, are –

(a) the licensable activities authorised by the licence, and

(b) any other licensable activities which may be carried on, at the premises in respect of which the licence has effect, by virtue of the existence of the licence (see sub-paragraph (2));

'first appointed day' means such day as may be specified as the first appointed day for the purposes of this Part;

'new licence' has the meaning given in paragraph 5(1);

'relevant existing licence', in relation to an application under paragraph 2, means an existing licence to which the application relates;

'relevant licensing authority' has the same meaning as in Part 3 of this Act (premises licences);

'second appointed day' means such day as may be specified as the second appointed day for the purposes of this Part; and

'supply of alcohol' means –

(a) sale by retail of alcohol, or

(b) supply of alcohol by or on behalf of a club to, or to the order of, a member of the club.

(2) In determining, for the purposes of paragraph (b) of the definition of 'existing licensable activities', the other licensable activities which may be carried on by virtue of a licence –

(a) section 182 of the 1964 Act (relaxation of law relating to music and dancing licences) is to be disregarded so far as it relates to public entertainment by way of music and singing provided by not more than two performers, and

(b) in the case of an existing licence granted under the Theatres Act 1968 (c 54), the reference in that paragraph to the licence is to be read as including a reference to any notice in force under section 199(c) of the 1964 Act (notice of intention to sell alcohol by retail at licensed theatre premises) in relation to that licence.

(3) In the application of section 12 (relevant licensing authority in Part 3 of this Act) for the purposes of this Part, the reference in subsection (4)(a) of that section to an applicant for a premises licence is to be read as a

reference to an applicant under paragraph 2 for the grant of a licence under paragraph 4.

Application for conversion of existing licence

2(1) This paragraph applies where, in respect of any premises, one or more existing licences have effect on the first appointed day.

(2) A person may, within the period of six months beginning with the first appointed day, apply to the relevant licensing authority for the grant of a licence under paragraph 4 to succeed one or more of those existing licences.

(3) But an application may be made under this paragraph in respect of an existing licence only if –

  (a)   it is held by the applicant, or
  (b)   the holder of the licence consents to the application being made.

(4) An application under this paragraph must specify –

  (a)   the existing licensable activities under the relevant existing licence or, if there is more than one, the relevant existing licences,
  (b)   if any relevant existing licence authorises the supply of alcohol, specified information about the person whom the applicant wishes to be the premises supervisor under the licence granted under paragraph 4, and
  (c)   such other information as may be specified.

(5) The application must also be in the specified form and accompanied by –

  (a)   the relevant documents, and
  (b)   the specified fee.

(6) The relevant documents are –

  (a)   the relevant existing licence or, if there is more than one, each of them (or a certified copy of the licence or licences in question),
  (b)   a plan in the specified form of the premises to which the relevant existing licence or licences relate,
  (c)   if any relevant existing licence authorises the supply of alcohol, any children's certificate in force in respect of the premises (or a certified copy of any such certificate),
  (d)   a form of consent in the specified form, given by the individual (if any) named in the application in accordance with sub-paragraph (4)(b),
  (e)   a form of consent in the specified form, given by any person who is required to consent to the application under sub-paragraph (3), and
  (f)   such other documents as may be specified.

(7) In this paragraph any reference to a certified copy of a document is a reference to a copy of that document certified to be a true copy –

  (a)   in the case of a justices' licence, children's certificate or canteen licence, by the chief executive of the licensing justices for the licensing district in which the premises are situated,

(b) in any other case, by the chief executive of the local authority which issued the licence,

(c) by a solicitor or notary, or

(d) by a person of a specified description.

(8) A document which purports to be a certified copy of an existing licence or children's certificate is to be taken to be such a copy unless the contrary is shown.

Police consultation

3(1) Where a person makes an application under paragraph 2, he must give a copy of the application (and any documents which accompanied it) to the chief officer of police for the police area (or each police area) in which the premises are situated no later than 48 hours after the application is made.

(2) Where –

(a) an appeal is pending against a decision to revoke, or to reject an application for the renewal of, the relevant existing licence or, if there is more than one such licence, a relevant existing licence, and

(b) a chief officer of police who has received a copy of the application under sub-paragraph (1) is satisfied that converting that existing licence in accordance with this Part would undermine the crime prevention objective,

he must give the relevant licensing authority and the applicant a notice to that effect.

(3) Where a chief officer of police who has received a copy of an application under sub-paragraph (1) is satisfied that, because of a material change in circumstances since the relevant time, converting the relevant existing licence or, if there is more than one such licence, a relevant existing licence in accordance with this Part would undermine the crime prevention objective, he must give the relevant licensing authority and the applicant a notice to that effect.

(4) For this purpose 'relevant time' means the time when the relevant existing licence was granted or, if it has been renewed, the last time it was renewed.

(5) The chief officer of police may not give a notice under sub-paragraph (2) or (3) after the end of the period of 28 days beginning with the day on which he received a copy of the application under sub-paragraph (1).

Determination of application

4(1) This paragraph applies where an application is made in accordance with paragraph 2 and the applicant complies with paragraph 3(1).

(2) Subject to sub-paragraphs (3) and (5), the relevant licensing authority must grant the application.

(3) Where a notice is given under paragraph 3(2) or (3) in respect of an existing licence (and not withdrawn), the authority must –

    (a)   hold a hearing to consider it, unless the authority, the applicant and the chief officer of police who gave the notice agree that a hearing is unnecessary, and

    (b)   having regard to the notice –

        (i)   in a case where the application relates only to that licence, reject the application, and

        (ii)   in any other case, reject the application to the extent that it relates to that licence,

if it considers it necessary for the promotion of the crime prevention objective to do so.

(4) If the relevant licensing authority fails to determine the application within the period of two months beginning with the day on which it received it, then, subject to sub-paragraph (5), the application is to be treated as granted by the authority under this paragraph.

(5) An application must not be granted (and is not to be treated as granted under sub-paragraph (4)) –

    (a)   if the relevant existing licence has or, if there is more than one, all the relevant existing licences have ceased to be held by the applicant before the relevant time, or

    (b)   where there is more than one relevant existing licence (but paragraph (a) does not apply), to the extent that the application relates to an existing licence which has ceased to be held by the applicant before the relevant time.

(6) For the purposes of sub-paragraph (5) –

    (a)   where, for the purposes of paragraph 2(3)(b) a person has consented to an application being made in respect of a relevant existing licence, sub-paragraph (5)(a) and (b) applies in relation to that licence as if the reference to the applicant were a reference to –

        (i)   that person, or

        (ii)   any other person to whom the existing licence has been transferred and who has given his consent for the purposes of this paragraph, and

    (b)   'the relevant time' is the time of the determination of the application or, in a case within sub-paragraph (4), the end of the period mentioned in that sub-paragraph.

(7) Section 10 applies as if the relevant licensing authority's functions under sub-paragraph (3) were included in the list of functions in subsection (4) of that section (functions which cannot be delegated to an officer of the licensing authority).

Notification of determination and issue of new licence

5(1) Where an application is granted (in whole or in part) under paragraph 4, the relevant licensing authority must forthwith –

    (a)   give the applicant a notice to that effect, and

    (b)   issue the applicant with –

(i)   a licence in respect of the premises (a 'new licence') in accordance with paragraph 6, and

(ii) a summary of the new licence.

(2) Where an application is rejected (in whole or in part) under paragraph 4, the relevant licensing authority must forthwith give the applicant a notice to that effect stating the authority's reasons for its decision to reject the application.

(3) The relevant licensing authority must give a copy of any notice it gives under sub-paragraph (1) or (2) to the chief officer of police for the police area (or each police area) in which the premises to which the notice relates are situated.

The new licence

6(1) This paragraph applies where a new licence is granted under paragraph 4 in respect of one or more existing licences.

(2) Where an application under paragraph 2 is granted in part only, any relevant existing licence in respect of which the application was rejected is to be disregarded for the purposes of the following provisions of this paragraph.

(3) The new licence is to be treated as if it were a premises licence (see section 11), and sections 19, 20 and 21 (mandatory conditions for premises licences) apply in relation to it accordingly.

(4) The new licence takes effect on the second appointed day.

(5) The new licence must authorise the premises in question to be used for the existing licensable activities under the relevant existing licence or, if there is more than one relevant existing licence, the relevant existing licences.

(6) Subject to sections 19, 20 and 21 and the remaining provisions of this paragraph, the new licence must be granted subject to such conditions as reproduce the effect of –

(a)   the conditions subject to which the relevant existing licence has effect at the time the application is granted, or

(b)   if there is more than one relevant existing licence, all the conditions subject to which those licences have effect at that time.

(7) Where the new licence authorises the supply of alcohol, the new licence must designate the person named in the application under paragraph 2(4)(b) as the premises supervisor.

(8) The new licence must also be granted subject to conditions which reproduce the effect of any restriction imposed on the use of the premises for the existing licensable activities under the relevant existing licence or licences by any enactment specified for the purposes of this Part.

(9) In determining those restrictions, the relevant licensing authority must have regard to any children's certificate which accompanied (or a certified copy of which accompanied) the application and which remains in force.

(10) Nothing in sub-paragraph (6) or (8) requires the new licence to be granted for a limited period.

(11) But, where the application under paragraph 2 includes a request for the new licence to have effect for a limited period, the new licence is to be granted subject to that condition.

Variation of new licence

7(1) A person who makes an application under paragraph 2 may (notwithstanding that no licence has yet been granted in consequence of that application) at the same time apply –

   (a)   under section 37 for any licence so granted to be varied so as to specify the individual named in the application as the premises supervisor, or
   (b)   under section 34 for any other variation of any such licence,

and for the purposes of an application within paragraph (a) or (b) the applicant is to be treated as the holder of that licence.

(2) In relation to an application within sub-paragraph (1)(a) or (b), the relevant licensing authority may discharge its functions under section 35 or 39 only if, and when, the application under paragraph 2 has been granted.

(3) Where an application within sub-paragraph (1)(a) or (b) is not determined by the relevant licensing authority within the period of two months beginning with the day the application was received by the authority, it is to be treated as having been rejected by the authority under section 35 or 39 (as the case may be) at the end of that period.

Existing licence revoked after grant of new licence

8(1) This paragraph applies where the relevant licensing authority grants a new licence under this Part in respect of one or more existing licences.

(2) If sub-paragraph (4) applies to the existing licence (or each of the existing licences) which the new licence succeeds, the new licence lapses.

(3) If –

   (a)   where the new licence relates to more than one relevant existing licence, sub-paragraph (4) applies to one or more, but not all, of those licences, or
   (b)   sub-paragraph (4) applies to a children's certificate in respect of the premises,

the licensing authority must amend the new licence so as to remove from it any provision which would not have been included in it but for the existence of any existing licence or certificate to which sub-paragraph (4) applies.

(4) This sub-paragraph applies to an existing licence or children's certificate if –

   (a)   it is revoked before the second appointed day, or
   (b)   where an appeal against a decision to revoke it is pending immediately before that day, the appeal is dismissed or abandoned.

(5) Any amendment under sub-paragraph (3) takes effect when it is notified to the holder of the new licence by the relevant licensing authority.

(6) The relevant licensing authority must give a copy of any notice under sub-paragraph (5) to the chief officer of police for the police area (or each police area) in which the premises to which the new licence relates are situated.

Appeals

9(1) Where an application under paragraph 2 is rejected (in whole or in part) by the relevant licensing authority, the applicant may appeal against that decision.

(2) Where a licensing authority grants such an application (in whole or in part), any chief officer of police who gave a notice in relation to it under paragraph 3(2) or (3) (that was not withdrawn) may appeal against that decision.

(3) Where a licence is amended under paragraph 8, the holder of the licence may appeal against that decision.

(4) Section 181 and paragraph 9(1) and (2) of Schedule 5 (general provision about appeals against decisions under Part 3 of this Act) apply in relation to appeals under this paragraph as they apply in relation to appeals under Part 1 of that Schedule.

(5) Paragraph 9(3) of that Schedule applies in relation to an appeal under sub-paragraph (2).

False statements

10(1) A person commits an offence if he knowingly or recklessly makes a false statement in or in connection with an application under paragraph 2.

(2) For the purposes of sub-paragraph (1) a person is to be treated as making a false statement if he produces, furnishes, signs or otherwise makes use of a document that contains a false statement.

(3) A person guilty of an offence under this section is liable on summary conviction to a fine not exceeding level 5 on the standard scale.

Opening hours

11(1) This paragraph applies where –

   (a) within such period (of not less than six months) as may be specified, the holder of a justices' licence for any premises applies, in accordance with Part 3 of this Act, for the grant of a premises licence in respect of those premises, and
   (b) the licence, if granted in the form applied for, would authorise the sale by retail of alcohol.

(2) In determining the application for the premises licence under section 18, the relevant licensing authority may not, by virtue of subsection (3)(b) of that section, grant the licence subject to conditions which prevent the sale of alcohol on the premises during the permitted hours.

(3) But sub-paragraph (2) does not apply where –

(a)   there has been a material change in circumstances since the relevant time, and

(b)   the relevant representations made in respect of the application include representations made by the chief officer of police for the police area (or any police area) in which the premises are situated advocating that, for the purposes of promoting the crime prevention objective, the premises licence ought to authorise the sale of alcohol during more restricted hours than the permitted hours.

(4) In this paragraph –

'permitted hours' means the permitted hours during which the holder of the justices' licence is permitted to sell alcohol on the premises under Part 3 of the 1964 Act;
'relevant representations' has the meaning given in section 18(6); and
'relevant time' means the time when the justices' licence was granted or, if it has been renewed, the last time it was renewed.

Provisional licences

12(1) Where –

(a)   during such period as may be specified the relevant licensing authority receives an application in accordance with Part 3 of this Act for the grant of a premises licence in respect of any premises ('the relevant premises'),

(b)   under section 6 of the 1964 Act, a provisional grant of a justices' licence has been made for –
  (i)   the relevant premises or a part of them, or
  (ii) premises that are substantially the same as the relevant premises or a part of them, and

(c)   the conditions of sub-paragraph (2) are satisfied,

the licensing authority must have regard to the provisional grant of the justices' licence when determining the application for the grant of the premises licence.

(2) The conditions are –

(a)   that the provisional grant of the justices' licence has not been declared final, and

(b)   that the premises to which the provisional grant relates have been completed in a manner which substantially complies with the plans deposited under the 1964 Act or, as the case may be, with those plans with modifications consented to under section 6(3) of that Act.

PART 2

CLUB PREMISES CERTIFICATES

Introductory

13(1) In this Part –

'existing club certificate' means a certificate held by a club under Part 2 of the 1964 Act for any premises;

'existing qualifying club activities' means the qualifying club activities authorised by the relevant existing club certificate in respect of those premises;

'first appointed day' means such day as may be specified as the first appointed day for the purposes of this Part;

'relevant existing club certificate', in relation to an application under paragraph 14, means the existing club certificate to which the application relates;

'relevant licensing authority' has the same meaning as in Part 4 of this Act (club premises certificates); and

'second appointed day' means such day as may be specified as the second appointed day for the purposes of this Part.

(2) In the application of section 68 (relevant licensing authority in Part 4 of this Act) for the purposes of this Part, the reference in subsection (4) of that section to an applicant for a club premises certificate is to be read as a reference to an applicant under paragraph 14 for the grant of a certificate under paragraph 16.

Application for conversion of existing club certificate

14(1) This paragraph applies where, in respect of any premises, a club holds an existing club certificate on the first appointed day.

(2) The club may, within the period of six months beginning with the first appointed day, apply to the relevant licensing authority for the grant of a certificate under paragraph 16 to succeed the existing club certificate so far as it relates to those premises.

(3) An application under this Part must specify the existing qualifying club activities and such other information as may be specified.

(4) The application must also be in the specified form and accompanied by –

(a)   the relevant documents, and
(b)   the specified fee.

(5) The relevant documents are –

(a)   the relevant existing club certificate (or a certified copy of it),
(b)   a plan in the specified form of the premises to which that certificate relates, and
(c)   such other documents as may be specified.

(6) In this paragraph any reference to a certified copy of a document is a reference to a copy of that document certified to be a true copy –

(a)   by the chief executive of the licensing justices for the licensing district in which the premises are situated,
(b)   by a solicitor or notary, or
(c)   by a person of a specified description.

(7) A document which purports to be a certified copy of an existing club certificate is to be taken to be such a copy unless the contrary is shown.

Police consultation

15(1) Where a person makes an application under paragraph 14, he must give a copy of the application (and any documents which accompany it) to the chief officer of police for the police area (or each police area) in which the premises are situated no later than 48 hours after the application is made.

(2) Where –

    (a)   an appeal is pending against a decision to revoke, or to reject an application for the renewal of, the relevant existing club certificate, and

    (b)   a chief officer of police who has received a copy of the application under sub-paragraph (1) is satisfied that converting that existing club certificate in accordance with this Part would undermine the crime prevention objective,

he must give the relevant licensing authority and the applicant a notice to that effect.

(3) Where a chief officer of police who has received a copy of the application under sub-paragraph (1) is satisfied that, because of a material change in circumstances since the relevant time, converting the relevant existing club certificate in accordance with this Part would undermine the crime prevention objective, he must give the relevant licensing authority and the applicant a notice to that effect.

(4) For this purpose 'the relevant time' means the time when the relevant existing club certificate was granted or, if it has been renewed, the last time it was renewed.

(5) The chief officer of police may not give a notice under sub-paragraph (2) or (3) after the end of the period of 28 days beginning with the day on which he received a copy of the application under sub-paragraph (1).

Determination of application

16(1) This paragraph applies where an application is made in accordance with paragraph 14 and the applicant complies with paragraph 15(1).

(2) Subject to sub-paragraphs (3) and (5), the licensing authority must grant the application.

(3) Where a notice is given under paragraph 15(2) or (3) (and not withdrawn), the authority must –

    (a)   hold a hearing to consider it, unless the authority, the applicant and the chief officer of police who gave the notice agree that a hearing is unnecessary, and

    (b)   having regard to the notice, reject the application if it considers it necessary for the promotion of the crime prevention objective to do so.

(4) If the relevant licensing authority fails to determine the application within the period of two months beginning with the day on which it received

it, then, subject to sub-paragraph (5), the application is to be treated as granted by the authority under this paragraph.

(5) An application must not be granted (and is not to be treated as granted under sub-paragraph (4)) if the existing club certificate has ceased to have effect at –

(a)   the time of the determination of the application, or
(b)   in a case within sub-paragraph (4), the end of the period mentioned in that sub-paragraph.

(6) Section 10 applies as if the relevant licensing authority's functions under sub-paragraph (3) were included in the list of functions in subsection (4) of that section (functions which cannot be delegated to an officer of the licensing authority).

Notification of determination and issue of new certificate

17(1) Where an application is granted under paragraph 16, the relevant licensing authority must forthwith –

(a)   give the applicant a notice to that effect, and
(b)   issue the applicant with –
    (i)   a certificate in respect of the premises ('the new certificate') in accordance with paragraph 18, and
    (ii)   a summary of the new certificate.

(2) Where an application is rejected under paragraph 16, the relevant licensing authority must forthwith give the applicant a notice to that effect containing a statement of the authority's reasons for its decision to reject the application.

(3) The relevant licensing authority must give a copy of any notice it gives under sub-paragraph (1) or (2) to the chief officer of police for the police area (or each police area) in which the premises to which the notice relates are situated.

The new certificate

18(1) The new certificate is to be treated as if it were a club premises certificate (see section 60), and sections 73, 74 and 75 apply in relation to it accordingly.

(2) The new certificate takes effect on the second appointed day.

(3) The new certificate must authorise the premises to be used for the existing qualifying club activities.

(4) Subject to sections 73, 74 and 75, the new certificate must be granted subject to such conditions as reproduce the effect of the conditions subject to which the relevant existing club certificate has effect at the time the application is granted.

(5) The new certificate must also be granted subject to conditions which reproduce the effect of any restriction imposed on the use of the premises for

the existing qualifying club activities by any enactment specified for the purposes of this Part.

(6) Nothing in sub-paragraph (4) or (5) requires the new certificate to be granted for a limited period.

Variation of new certificate

19(1) A person who makes an application under paragraph 14 may (notwithstanding that no certificate has yet been granted in consequence of that application) at the same time apply under section 84 for a variation of the certificate, and, for the purposes of such an application, the applicant is to be treated as the holder of that certificate.

(2) In relation to an application within sub-paragraph (1), the relevant licensing authority may discharge its functions under section 85 only if, and when, the application under this Part has been granted.

(3) Where an application within sub-paragraph (1) is not determined by the relevant licensing authority within the period of two months beginning with the day the application was received by the authority, it is to be treated as having been rejected by the authority under section 85 at the end of that period.

Existing club certificate revoked after grant of new certificate

20 Where the relevant licensing authority grants a new certificate under this Part, that certificate lapses if and when –

   (a) the existing club certificate is revoked before the second appointed
        day, or
   (b) where an appeal against a decision to revoke it is pending
        immediately before that day, the appeal is dismissed or abandoned.

Appeals

21(1) Where an application under paragraph 14 is rejected by the relevant licensing authority, the applicant may appeal against that decision.

(2) Where a licensing authority grants such an application, any chief officer of police who gave a notice under paragraph 15(2) or (3) (that was not withdrawn) may appeal against that decision.

(3) Section 181 and paragraph 15(1) and (2) of Schedule 5 (general provision about appeals against decisions under Part 4 of this Act) apply in relation to appeals under this paragraph as they apply in relation to appeals under Part 2 of that Schedule.

(4) Paragraph 15(3) of that Schedule applies in relation to an appeal under sub-paragraph (2).

False statements

22(1) A person commits an offence if he knowingly or recklessly makes a false statement in or in connection with an application under paragraph 14.

(2) For the purposes of sub-paragraph (1) a person is to be treated as making a false statement if he produces, furnishes, signs or otherwise makes use of a document that contains a false statement.

(3) A person guilty of an offence under this section is liable on summary conviction to a fine not exceeding level 5 on the standard scale.

PART 3

PERSONAL LICENCES

Introductory

23(1) Paragraphs 24 to 27 apply where –

    (a) during the transitional period, the holder of a justices' licence applies to the relevant licensing authority for the grant of a personal licence under section 117,

    (b) the application is accompanied by the documents mentioned in sub-paragraph (3), and

    (c) the applicant gives a copy of the application to the chief officer of police for the relevant licensing authority's area within 48 hours from the time the application is made.

(2) In this paragraph 'transitional period' means such period (of not less than six months) as may be specified for the purposes of this Part.

(3) The documents are –

    (a) the justices' licence (or a certified copy of that licence),

    (b) a photograph of the applicant in the specified form which is endorsed, by a person of a specified description, with a statement verifying the likeness of the photograph to the applicant, and

    (c) where the applicant has been convicted of any relevant offence or foreign offence on or after the relevant date, a statement giving details of the offence.

(4) In this paragraph any reference to a certified copy of a justices' licence is to a copy of that licence certified to be a true copy –

    (a) by the chief executive of the licensing justices for the licensing district concerned,

    (b) by a solicitor or notary, or

    (c) by a person of a specified description.

(5) A document which purports to be a certified copy of a justices' licence is to be taken to be such a copy, unless the contrary is shown.

Section 120 disapplied

24 Section 120 (determination of application for grant) does not apply in relation to the application.

Police objections

25(1) Sub-paragraph (2) applies where –

    (a)   the applicant has been convicted of any relevant offences or foreign offences on or after the relevant date, and

    (b)   having regard to –

        (i)   any conviction of the applicant for a relevant offence, and

        (ii) any conviction of his for a foreign offence which the chief officer of police considers to be comparable to a relevant offence,

whether occurring before or after the relevant date, the chief officer of police is satisfied that the exceptional circumstances of the case are such that granting the application would undermine the crime prevention objective.

(2) The chief officer of police must give a notice stating the reasons why he is so satisfied (an 'objection notice') –

    (a)   to the relevant licensing authority, and

    (b)   to the applicant.

(3) The objection notice must be given no later than 28 days after the day on which the chief officer of police receives a copy of the application in accordance with paragraph 23(1)(c).

(4) For the purposes of this paragraph –

    (a)   'relevant offence' and 'foreign offence' have the meaning given in section 113, and

    (b)   section 114 (spent convictions) applies for the purposes of this paragraph as it applies for the purposes of section 120.

Determination of application

26(1) The relevant licensing authority must grant the application if –

    (a)   it is satisfied that the applicant holds a justices' licence, and

    (b)   no objection notice has been given within the period mentioned in paragraph 25(3) or any notice so given has been withdrawn.

(2) Where the authority is not satisfied that the applicant holds a justices' licence, it must reject the application.

(3) Where the authority is so satisfied, but sub-paragraph (1)(b) does not apply, it –

    (a)   must hold a hearing to consider the objection notice, and

    (b)   having regard to the notice, must –

        (i)   reject the application if it considers it necessary for the promotion of the crime prevention objective to do so, and

        (ii) grant the application in any other case.

(4) If the authority fails to determine the application within the period of three months beginning with the day on which it receives it, then, the application is to be treated as granted by the authority under this paragraph.

(5) Section 10 applies as if the relevant licensing authority's functions under sub-paragraph (3) were included in the list of functions in subsection (4) of that section (functions which cannot be delegated to an officer of the licensing authority).

(6) In the application of section 122 (notification of determinations) to a determination under this paragraph, the references to an objection notice are to be read as references to an objection notice within the meaning of paragraph 25(2).

Appeals

27(1) Where a licensing authority rejects an application under paragraph 26, the applicant may appeal against that decision.

(2) Where a licensing authority grants an application for a personal licence under paragraph 26(3), the chief officer of police who gave the objection notice may appeal against that decision.

(3) Section 181 and paragraph 17(6) and (7) of Schedule 5 (general provision about appeals relating to personal licences) apply in relation to appeals under this paragraph as they apply in relation to appeals under paragraph 17 of that Schedule.

(4) Paragraph 17(8) of that Schedule applies in relation to an appeal under sub-paragraph (2) above.

Interpretation of Part 3

28 For the purposes of this Part –

'relevant date', in relation to the holder of a justices' licence, means –

(a)   the date when the licence was granted, or
(b)   where it has been renewed, the last date when it was renewed, or
(c)   where it has been transferred to the holder and has not been renewed since the transfer, the date when it was transferred; and

'relevant licensing authority', in relation to an application for a personal licence under section 117, means the authority to which the application is made in accordance with that section.

PART 4

MISCELLANEOUS AND GENERAL

Consultation on licensing policy

29 Until such time as section 59 of the 1964 Act (prohibition of sale, etc of alcohol except during permitted hours and in accordance with justices' licence etc) ceases to have effect in accordance with this Act, section 5(3) of this Act (licensing authority's duty to consult before determining licensing policy) has effect as if for paragraphs (c) to (e) there were substituted –

'(c)   such persons as the licensing authority considers to be
       representative of holders of existing licences (within the
       meaning of Part 1 of Schedule 8) in respect of premises situated
       in the authority's area,

(d)   such persons as the licensing authority considers to be
       representative of clubs registered (within the meaning of the
       Licensing Act 1964 (c 26)) in respect of any premises situated in
       the authority's area,'.

Meaning of 'methylated spirits' (transitory provision)

30 Until such time as an order is made under subsection (6) of section 5 of the
Finance Act 1995 (c 4) (denatured alcohol) bringing that section into force,
section 191 of this Act (meaning of 'alcohol') has effect as if –

(a)   for subsection (1)(f) there were substituted –

       '(f)   methylated spirits,', and

(b)   in subsection (2), the definition of 'denatured alcohol' were omitted
       and at the appropriate place there were inserted –

       '"methylated spirits" has the same meaning as in the Alcoholic Liquor
       Duties Act 1979 (c 4);'.

Savings

31 Notwithstanding the repeal by this Act of Schedule 12 to the London
Government Act 1963 (c 33) (licensing of public entertainment in Greater
London), or of any enactment amending that Schedule, that Schedule shall
continue to apply in relation to –

(a)   licences granted under section 21 of the Greater London Council
       (General Powers) Act 1966 (c xxviii) (licensing of public exhibitions
       in London), and

(b)   licences granted under section 5 of the Greater London Council
       (General Powers) Act 1978 (c xiii) (licensing of entertainments
       booking offices in London),

as it applied before that repeal.

32(1) In Schedule 3 to the Local Government (Miscellaneous Provisions) Act
1982 (c 30) (control of sex establishments), paragraph (ii) of the proviso to
paragraph 3A (as substituted by paragraph 85(3) of Schedule 6 to this Act)
does not apply in relation to a borough of a participating council (within the
meaning of section 2 of the London Local Authorities Act 1990 (c vii)) which
has appointed a day under section 3 of that Act for the coming into force of
section 18 of that Act (repeal of paragraph (ii) of the proviso to paragraph 3A
of Schedule 3 to that Act).

(2) On or after the coming into force of paragraph 85(3) of Schedule 6 to this
Act, the reference in section 18 of that Act to paragraph (ii) of the proviso to
paragraph 3A of Schedule 3 to that Act is to be read as a reference to that
paragraph as substituted by paragraph 85(3) of Schedule 6 to this Act.

33 Notwithstanding that by virtue of this Act the Cinemas Act 1985 (c 13) ceases to have effect in England and Wales, section 6 of that Act (other than subsection (3)), and sections 5, 20 and 21 of that Act so far as relating to that section, shall continue to have effect there for the purposes of –

(a) paragraph 3(2)(b) of Schedule 3 to the Local Government (Miscellaneous Provisions) Act 1982 (definition of 'sex cinema'), and

(b) section 3(6)(b) of the Video Recordings Act 1984 (c 39) (exempted supplies).

Interpretation

34 In this Schedule –

'justices' licence' means a justices' licence under Part 1 of the 1964 Act; 'specified' means specified by order; and 'the 1964 Act' means the Licensing Act 1964 (c 26).

INDEX

References are to paragraph numbers.

Admission, public
  licensing hearing   13.8.1,
    13.8.2
Advertising
  club premises certificate
    application   8.2.3
    review application   8.10.3,
      8.10.5
    variation   8.9.1
  film   4.5.2
  premises licence
    application   7.5.5, 7.10.1
    review application   7.21.9
Age limit
  child, access to licensed
    premises   11.8.1
  child, supply of alcohol to
    2.3.20, 11.7.1
    belief that over 16   11.8.5
    belief that over 18   11.7.2,
      11.7.3, 11.7.12
    clubs   2.3.18, 11.7.5
  legislative background   1.2.5,
    1.2.14
  personal licence, for   2.3.11,
    10.3.1
Alcohol
  children and, *see* Children and
    alcohol
  club, supply in, *see* Club premises
    certificate
  definition   4.3.1, 15.5.2
  entertainment, supplied with
    4.5.11
  excluded (disqualified)
    premises   7.23
  excluded substances   4.3.1
  expulsion of drunk person,
    constable's duty   11.5.6
  hot drink containing   4.7.4

late night refreshment   4.7.4,
  4.7.5
legislative background
  1.1–1.3
offences   11.1.5, 11.4–11.7
  background   1.2
  child, supply to, buying or
    consuming, *see* Children
    and alcohol
  disorderly conduct, relating
    to   11.5.2, 11.5.5
  drunkenness/failure to leave
    premises   11.5.1, 11.5.5
  exposure for sale by retail
    11.4.1
  false statement   11.11
  penalties   11.4.1, 11.4.3,
    11.5, 11.6.1, 11.7.7
  'place of sale'   11.1.6
  possession or control for sale
    purposes   11.4.3
  sale to/obtaining for drunk
    person   1.2.6, 11.5.3,
    11.5.4
  smuggled goods   11.6.1,
    11.6.2
  train, sale while prohibited
    11.10.3
  vehicle, sale from   11.10.1,
    11.10.2
personal licence requirement, *see*
  Personal licence
premises licence supervisor
  requirement, *see* Premises
  licence
'sale by retail'   4.3.2, 4.3.3,
  11.4.1
small-scale temporary event, at,
  see Temporary event
smuggled   11.6.1, 11.6.2

Alcohol – *cont*
  supplies within Act   2.3.21,
    4.1.1, 4.2.1, 4.3
  telephone/internet/fax sales,
    place of   4.3.5
All-day opening   1.2.13
Appeal
  background   14.1.1–14.1.7
  closure order   12.6.10, 12.7.8–
    12.7.10
    'aggrieved person'   12.6.10
  club premises certificate   14.4
    circumstances for   14.4.1
    magistrates' court for
      14.4.2
    notice   14.4.2
    respondents   14.4.3
    review decision, and appeal
      period   8.10.9
  consultation failure   6.3.6,
    6.3.7
  conversion of existing licence
    refusal, against   15.2.15
    club premises   15.3.10
  conversion of justices' licence to
    personal licence   15.4.8
  costs discretion   14.2.9,
    14.2.10
  Crown Court   2.2.3, 12.6.10,
    14.1.3, 14.1.6
  evidence   14.2.7
  'final' decisions   14.1.5
  Guidance invalidity, as to
    6.6.4
  Guidance on hearings   6.3.7
  judicial review, interaction with,
    see Judicial review
  licensing statement   6.3.6,
    6.3.7, 6.7.2–6.7.4
  magistrates' court powers on
    6.7.3, 6.7.4, 14.2, 14.7.2
    dismissal   14.2.1
    Guidance   14.2.4
    power to remit and give
      directions   14.2.1,
      14.2.2
    substitution of decision
      14.2.1
  personal licence   10.8.7, 14.6

  chief officer of police, right
    of   14.6.2
  circumstances for   14.6.1,
    14.6.2
  forfeiture or suspension,
    against   14.6.4
  order that continues pending
    appeal   14.6.3
  time-limit   14.6.3
  police right   7.14.5, 14.3.1,
    14.3.3, 14.6.2
  premises licence   14.3
    circumstances for   14.3.1
    determination   7.14.5
    interim authority notice
      14.3.3
    magistrates' court for
      14.3.2
    notice   14.3.2
    respondents   14.3.3, 14.3.4
    review determination
      7.21.12, 7.21.13
    review following closure
      order   14.7.1–14.7.3
  reasons   14.2.8
  rehearing, as   14.2.3, 14.2.7
  review of decision making
    process, whether is
    14.2.2–14.2.6
  right   2.2.3, 14.1 *et seq*
  temporary event notice counter
    notice   9.5.8, 9.5.9, 14.5
    no right against service of
      counter notice   14.5.3
    rights of appeal   14.5.1
    time-limit   14.5.2
  time-limit   14.1.6, 14.3.2,
    14.4.2, 14.6.3
Application *see* Club premises
  certificate; Personal licence;
  Premises licence
  consideration on merits   2.3.6
  matters for consideration, *see*
    Objectives, licensing
Art gallery
  educational, etc, film in   4.5.2
Association
  offence by   11.2.3–11.2.5
'Authorised person'/officer
  entry powers   7.22.3, 8.11.2,
    11.1.3

'Authorised person'/officer – *cont*
  entry powers – *cont*
    evidence of authority of
        officer   11.1.3
    obstruction offence   7.22.2,
        9.6.2, 11.1.3
Authorities, *see* Local authority
    licensing body

Bazaar   9.1.1
Beer tent   7.3.1, 9.1.1
Betting and gaming
  control of   2.2.1, 4.5.7
  definition   4.1.3
Boxing   4.1.1, 4.4.1, 11.3.2
Broadcasts   4.5.5
Burger van   2.3.15
Business, continuation
  authority for, *see* Premises licence

Charge
  goods or services, for   4.1.6
Charity
  hot food/drink supplied by
      4.7.4
  premises licence applicant
      7.4.1, 7.4.2
Child
  see also Age limit
  alcohol offences/restrictions
      relating to, *see* Children and
      alcohol
  employment in licensed/club
      premises   11.7.15
  film classification   7.12.3
  protection from harm, licensing
      objective   3.2.1
  music entertainment   7.24.7
  responsible body for service
      relating to   7.5.6
  unaccompanied, prohibition on
      entry to premises   11.8
    age limit   11.8.1
    defence   11.8.5, 11.8.6
    offence/persons liable
        11.8.2, 11.8.3
    passing through premises
        11.8.4

    penalty   11.8.7
    premises   11.8.1
Children and alcohol
  buying/attempting to buy
    child   11.7.9
    consumption on premises,
        for   11.7.11, 11.7.18
    offences   11.7.9–11.7.12
    on behalf of child   11.7.10,
        11.7.11
    see also 'sale or supply to' *below*
  consuming on premises,
      offence   11.7.14, 11.7.16
  enforcement   11.7.13, 11.7.17
  entry etc into licensed premises/
      club etc, premises
    delivery of alcohol to child by
        worker on   11.7.16
    employment in, offence
        11.7.15
    sending child to obtain
        alcohol   11.7.17
    unaccompanied child entry
        prohibition   11.8, *see
        also* Child
  sale by, unsupervised
      11.7.18
    exemption for table meals
        11.7.18, 11.7.19
  sale or supply to   11.7
    age, minimum   2.3.20,
        11.7.1, *see also* Age limit
    background   1.2.5
    belief that not under age
        11.7.2, 11.7.3, 11.7.12,
        11.8.5
    club, in   2.3.18, 11.7.5,
        11.7.9–11.7.12
    defences   11.7.2–11.7.4,
        11.7.12
    due diligence defence
        11.7.4
    liqueur confectionery
        11.7.8
    offences relating to   11.7.1,
        11.7.5, 11.7.8, 11.7.9–
        11.7.18
    penalty   11.7.7, 11.7.9,
        11.7.11

Children and alcohol – *cont*
  sale or supply to – *cont*
    prosecution of offence
        11.1.5
    restrictions　　11.7, *see also*
        Age limit
    test purchases　　11.7.13,
        11.7.17
    surrender, constable's power
        11.9
    table meals exemption
        11.7.11, 11.7.18, 11.7.19
Church　　13.4.9, *see also*
    Interested party; Religious
    service; Worship, place of
Cinema, *see* Film; Sex cinema
Closure order　　2.3.12, 9.6.6,
    12.1 *et seq*
  appeal　　14.1.3
  background, legal　　12.1.1–
      12.1.3
  cancellation of order　　12.5
    discretion　　12.5.1
    notice of　　12.5.3
    obligation　　12.5.2
    officer for　　12.5.1, 12.5.2
  extension of order　　12.4
    belief and ground　　12.4.2,
        12.4.3
    officer for　　12.4.1
    time effective and duration
        12.4.4
  general order　　12.2
    applicant, senior police
        officer　　12.2.1
    constable's power to
        enforce　　12.2.6
    ground　　12.2.2–12.2.4
    magistrates' court power
        12.2.1
    offence/liable persons
        12.2.5
    premises subject to　　12.2.3
  police immunity from damages
    awards　　12.8
    exceptions　　12.8.2, 12.8.3
  review of premises licence
    following　　2.3.13
    appeal　　14.7.1–14.7.3
  scope　　12.1.2

specific order　　12.3
  'appropriate person', notice
      to　　12.3.6, 12.3.7
  constable's power to
      enforce　　12.3.10
  contents of　　12.3.5
  duration　　12.3.5
  extension, *see* 'extension of
      order' *above*
  grounds　　12.3.2, 12.3.3
  magistrates' court review
    powers　　12.3.1, 12.6, *see
        also* Review
  notification of licensing
      authority　　12.6.1
  offence and penalty
      12.3.8–12.3.10
  revocation　　12.6.3, 12.7.8
  review by authority
    following　　12.3.1, 12.7,
        see also Review
  senior police officer's
      decision　　12.3.1–12.3.4
  time effective　　12.3.6
Club　　8.1 *et seq*
  alcohol supply in　　4.3.4,
      10.1.1, 10.2.3
  child, to/on behalf of
      2.3.18, 11.7.5, 11.7.9–
      11.7.12
  club premises certificate for, *see*
      Club premises certificate
  background　　8.1.1–8.1.6
  conversion of existing certificate,
      see Transitional
  entertainment in　　4.1.1, 4.1.4,
      8.4
    censorship of plays
        prohibited　　8.6.5
  late night refreshments in
      4.7.1
  member, review of certificate
      request　　8.10.2
  offence by, liability for, *see*
      Association
  opening hours without qualifying
      activities　　7.6.13
  personal licence not required
      10.1.1

Club – *cont*
  premises licence   7.22.1, 8.3.3,
    8.4.6
  recognition cessation, effect
    of   7.16.2
  regulation of, *see* Club premises
    certificate
Club premises certificate
  alcohol supply   4.3.4, 8.3.1,
    8.4.1–8.4.3
    associate member   8.4.5
    guest, to   4.3.4, 8.4.1, 8.4.5
    off premises consumption
      8.4.3, 8.4.4
    sale   8.3.2, 8.4.1
  appeal, *see* Appeal
  application   8.2.1
    advertisement of   8.2.3
    determination   8.6
    documents with   8.2.2
    licensing authority for
      8.2.1, 8.2.2
    operating schedule   8.2.2,
      8.2.4
    representations   8.2.3
  background   1.2.11, 2.3.18,
    8.1.1–8.1.5
  conditions   8.6.1, 8.6.4, 8.6.5
    changes   8.9.7
    justification   8.6.5, 13.6.4
    modification   8.10.7
    prohibited conditions   8.6.5
  display   8.7.1, 8.7.6
  duration   8.8
  failure to produce   8.7.3, 8.7.6
  fee   8.2.2
  form of   8.7
    contents   8.7.1
  good faith test   8.3.1, 8.5
    factors   8.5.1
    failure of, notification and
      reasons   8.5.2
  grant   8.6.1, 8.6.4
  hours   8.2.4
  inspection and entry powers
    8.2.5, 8.9.1, 8.11
    drugs suspected   8.11.1
    limited right generally
      8.11.2
    reasonable force   8.11.1

    who may exercise   8.11.1,
      8.11.2
  issue   5.5.4
  keeping/producing   8.7.3,
    8.7.5
  lapse   8.8.2
  licensing objectives, promotion
    by licensing authority
    8.6.2, 8.9.4, 8.9.5
  lost, damaged etc, copy on
    8.7.2
  meaning   8.1.6
  minimum membership   8.3.1,
    8.4.8
  nominated person   8.7.5,
    8.7.6
  notifications
    change of name/rules/
      address   8.7.4
    determination by licensing
      authority   8.6.6
    variation application
      determination   8.9.5
  plan of premises   8.2.2, 8.7.1
  'qualifying club'   8.2.1, 8.3,
    8.12
    conditions   8.3.1
    review failure disqualifies
      8.8.1
  'qualifying club activities'   8.4
  regulated entertainment
    8.4.1, 8.4.7
  rejection of application   8.6.4
  'relevant club activities'   8.2.4,
    8.4
    change to   8.9.7,
      8.10.9
    exclusion from certificate
      8.6.4
    list   8.4.1
    removal from certificate
      8.10.7, 8.10.9
  representations   8.6.2
    hearing   8.6.2
    none received   8.6.1
    reasons for decision   8.6.6
    'relevant'   8.6.3
    variation application, as to, *see*
      'variation' *below*

Club premises certificate – *cont*
  review   8.10
    advertisement of
        application   8.10.3,
        8.10.5
    form of notice   8.10.3
    hearing   8.10.5
    licensing authority
        determination options
        8.10.7
    period between   8.10.4
    rejection grounds   8.10.4
    relevance to objectives
        8.10.1
    repeated requests   8.10.4
    representations   8.10.5–
        8.10.7
    request for   8.10.2
    suspending effect of   8.8.1,
        8.10.7
  secretary, duties   8.7.3–8.7.5
  summary   5.5.4, 5.5.5, 8.7.1,
      8.7.6
  supervisor, circumstances for
      8.3.3, 8.4.6
  'supply to members or
      guests'   4.3.4
  surrender   8.8.1, 8.8.2
  suspension   8.8.1, 8.10.7,
      8.10.9
  update/reissue   5.5.5
  variation   8.9
    advertisement and
        notification   8.9.1
    appeal   8.10.9
    certificate with application
        8.9.2
    frivolous or vexatious
        representation   8.9.6,
        13.7.2–13.7.6
    grant   8.9.4, 8.10.8
    hearing   8.9.3
    notification duties of licensing
        authority   8.9.5, 8.10.8
    rejection of application
        8.10.7, 8.10.8
    relevant representations
        8.9.3, 8.9.4
    responsible authority
        8.10.2, 8.10.10
    scope of   8.9.7

withdrawal   8.4.8, 8.8.1,
    8.10.7, 8.10.9
Committee, *see* Local authority
    licensing body
Company
  dissolution or insolvency
      7.16.2, 7.16.5, 17.16.6
  offence by, officer's liability
      11.2.1
Conditions, *see* Club premises
    certificate; Premises licence
Consent
  premises supervisor   7.5.4,
      7.8.1
Construction, premises under
    7.13.2
Consultation   6.3
  see also Licensing statement
  transitional provisions   15.5.1
Conversion, *see* Transitional
Costs   13.2.2
  appeal, award on   14.2.9,
      14.2.10
Councillor
  interest in matter, *see* Local
      authority licensing body
Credit sales   1.2.7
Crime and disorder prevention
  see also Police
  licensing objective   3.2.1, 3.2.5
  personal licence decision,
      relevance to   2.3.11,
      10.3.7, 10.8.1
Criminal conviction
  justices' licence holder applying
      for personal licence
      15.4.2, 15.4.3
  personal licence holder, *see*
      Personal licence
Criminal offences under Act, *see*
    Children and alcohol; Offences
Crown Court
  appeal to   12.6.10, 14.1.3

Damages
  closure order, police
      immunity   12.8
Dance, *see* Music and dancing
Death
  premises licence holder
      7.16.2, 7.16.5, 7.16.6, 7.20.10

Defences, *see* Offences

Designated premises supervisor, *see* Premises licence: supervisor

Destruction or damage of licence, *see* Lost/stolen certificate or licence

Directory requirements 3.1.4, 3.1.5

Disability, person with condition relating to 7.1.2.6

Disclosure
  criminal conviction
    justices' licence holder applying for personal licence 15.4.2, 15.4.3
    personal licence holder, *see* Personal licence
  information provided to authority, further disclosure restrictions 13.8.3
  interest in matter, *see* Local authority licensing body

Discretion, *see* Local authority

Disorder
  see also Crime and disorder prevention
  disorderly conduct, offences relating to 11.5.2, 11.5.5
  prevention of
    general closure order ground 12.2.2
    sale of alcohol on train prohibition for 11.10.3
    specific closure order ground/ extension ground 12.3.2, 12.4.3

Display
  club premises certificate 8.7.1, 8.7.6
  premises licence 7.15.5
  temporary event notice 9.6.3, 9.6.4

Drama, *see* Play

Drinking-up time 1.2.9

Drugs, search for 8.11.1

Drunkenness 1.2.6, 11.5.1– 11.5.5

Due diligence defence 11.1.7– 11.1.9, 11.3.1, 11.7.4

Employee
  bar, club, etc
    age restriction, introduction of 1.2.8
    child, current prohibition 11.7.15
    late night refreshments for 4.7.1
  disclosure of interest by councillor 13.3.1
  security staff 7.12.4

Entertainment
  meaning for licensing purposes, *see* 'regulated' *below*
  private places of entertainment 1.3.2, 4.1.1, 4.4, *see also* Club
  public entertainments 2.3.17, 4.1.1, 4.4, 7.24.1
  regulated entertainment 4.2.1, 4.4
    alcohol supply combined with 4.5.11
    audience, entertainment of 4.4.1
    club, qualifying activity 4.1.1, 8.4.1
    definition 4.4.1
    exemptions 4.3.6, 4.5, 9.1.1
    films, *see* Film
    licensable activity 4.2.1, 4.4.1
    licensing/certification of, *see* Club premises certificate; Premises licence; Temporary event
    music/dancing, *see* Music and dancing
    plays, *see* Play
    review of provisions 6.6.5
    sport, *see* Boxing; Sports event; Wrestling
    unauthorised activity offence exemption 11.3.2

Entertainment facilities 4.4.2

Entry powers
  'authorised person' 7.22.3, 8.11.2, 11.1.3
  club 8.11.1, 8.11.2, 11.1.3

Entry powers – *cont*
  constable   7.22.2, 8.11.1, 9.6.2,
    11.1.4
  evidence of authority for
    11.1.3
  obstruction offence   7.22.2,
    9.6.2, 11.1.3
  premises licence   7.22
    circumstances for exercise
      7.22.2
    who may exercise   7.22.2
  reasonable force   7.22.2,
    11.1.3
  temporary event premises
    9.6.1
Environmental health department
  authorised person for entry,
    officer as   11.1.3
  review request   8.10.2
  service on   7.5.6
Evidence   13.2.1
  appeal   14.2.7
Excluded premises
  alcohol supply/sale   7.23
    garage   4.3.7, 7.23.1–7.23.4
    service station, motorway
      4.3.7, 7.23.1
Exemptions
  late night refreshments, *see* Late
    night refreshments
  licensable activities   4.5, 4.7,
    5.1.2
  regulated entertainment
    4.3.6, 4.5, 9.1.1
  table meals, *see* Meals, table
Exhibition hall   4.7.3
Existing licence conversion, *see*
  Transitional
Extension of licence   2.3.8
  human rights issues   13.4.8

Fair hearing
  adjournment to ensure
    13.4.10
  closure order review   12.6.8,
    12.8.3
  local authority as 'public
    authority'   13.1.3
  right   13.4
    licensing proceedings
      13.4.2

    review and compatibility
      with   13.4.3
False statement   11.11
Fax sale, place of   4.3.5
Fees   2.3.22, 7.9, 8.2.2
Festival, *see* Temporary event
Fete
  alcohol supply at   4.5.11, 9.1.1
  exemption from regulated
    entertainment   4.5.7
  limited period licence   7.6.14
  'private gain', for   4.5.7
Film
  see also Premises licence
  advertising, educational or
    information   4.5.2
  background, legal   1.3.4
  cinema licence abolished
    2.3.16
  classification   7.12.3
  door staff   7.12.4
  'exhibition of a film'   4.4.1
  meaning   4.4.1
  showing, as regulated
    entertainment   4.1.1,
    4.4.1
Fire authority
  'authorised person' for entry,
    officer as   7.22.3,
    11.1.3
  consultation with   6.3.1
  service on   7.5.6
Fit and proper person test
  end of   2.3.11
Food, *see* Burger van; Hot-dog
    stand; Late night refreshments;
    Meals, table
Football, *see* Sports event
Force, use of reasonable, *see* Entry
    powers
Forfeiture, *see* Personal licence
Friendly society   8.12
Frivolous or vexatious
    representation
  club premises certificate, relating
    to
    application   8.6.3
    variation   8.9.6, 13.7.2–
      13.7.6

Frivolous or vexatious
   representation – *cont*
   premises licence, relating to
      application   7.11.3, 7.11.4,
         7.17.3, 7.17.6, 13.7.2–
         13.7.6
      variation   7.17.2, 7.17.3,
         7.17.6
Fundraising event, *see* Temporary
   event

Gaming, *see* Betting and gaming
Garage, *see* Excluded premises
Geographical area   5.1.3
Good faith test, *see* Club premises
   certificate: alcohol supply
Guest, *see* Club premises certificate
Guidance   6.6
   appeals   6.7.4
   draft, approval of   6.6.1,
      13.6.1
   forward to   2.1.2, 3.1.1
   invalidity
      assertion of   6.6.4
      ultra vires rules   6.6.3
   local authority duty to have
      regard to   3.2.2–3.2.4,
      5.2.2, 13.6.2
   principles underpinning Act
      7.5.1
   requirement for   6.6.1, 13.6
   revision/review   6.6.2
   status of   3.2.4, 5.2.3

Harm, protection of child from
   licensing objective, *see* Child
Health and Safety Executive
   'authorised person' from
      7.22.3
   service on   7.5.6
Hearing   13.1 *et seq*
   costs   13.2.2
   deprivation of   13.4.5
   disclosure of interest by
      councillor, *see* Local
      authority licensing body
   discretion, proper exercise of, *see*
      Local authority

duty to hold unless
   agreement   13.4.6
evidence   13.2.1
expedited   13.2.1
fair hearing right, *see* Fair hearing
Guidance on   13.6.3
licensing objectives, promotion
   of   13.6.3–13.6.5
natural justice   13.1.5, 13.4.1,
   13.4.7
   breach   13.4.10
   deprivation of right to earn a
      living   13.4.7
none   13.4.4
notice   13.2.1
   failure   13.4.10
procedural variety   13.1.1,
   13.1.2
public access   13.8.1, 13.8.2
   exclusion grounds   13.8.2
regulatory power   13.1.4,
   13.2.1, 13.8.1
scope of   13.2.1
representations   13.4.9, 13.7,
   see also Interested party
review hearing, Guidance
   13.6.5–13.6.7
   criminal convictions, approach
      to   13.6.6–13.6.8
High Court, *see* Judicial review
Hot-dog stand   2.3.15
'premises'   7.3.1
Hotel
   late night refreshments in
      4.7.1
Hours
   all day opening   1.2.13
   club   7.6.13, 8.2.4
   extension   2.3.8, *see also*
      Temporary event
   permitted hours concept
      abolished   2.3.7
   premises licence, *see* Premises
      licence
   temporary event   9.3.3
   without licensing activities,
      opening times   7.6.13
Human rights issues
   closure orders   12.6.8, 12.8.3,
      see also Fair hearing

Human rights issues – *cont*
  licence extension   13.4.8
  licence removal 'in accordance
    with law', etc   13.4.7
  reasons for decision   15.4.7
    appeal   14.2.8

Industrial and provident society
  8.12
Insolvency   7.16.2, 7.16.5, 7.16.6
Inspection of premises
  club premises certificate, relating
    to   8.2.5, 8.9.1, *see also*
    Entry powers
  premises licence, *see* Entry powers
Interested party
  closure order review
    representations   12.7.6
  club premises certificate
    representations   8.6.3,
    8.9.3
  club premises certificate review
    representations   8.10.6
    request   8.10.2
  frivolous or vexatious
    representations, *see* Frivolous
    or vexatious representation
  meaning   13.4.9, 13.7.1
  premises licence application
    appeal right   7.14.5
    representations   7.11.2–
    7.11.4, 7.14.5
  premises licence review
    request   7.21.4
  premises licence variation,
    representations   7.17.3,
    7.21.6
  'relevant' representations
    7.17.3, *see also*
    Representations
  vicinity, living etc in   7.11.5,
    13.7.1
Internet sales, place of   4.3.5

Judicial review
  appeal alternative, use of
    14.1.4
  decisions subject to   2.2.3
  final appeal decisions   14.1.5

licensing policy statement
  challenge   6.3.6, 6.7.2,
  13.5.4
temporary event notice counter
  notice   9.5.9
variation of premises licence
  determination   7.17.6
Justices, *see* Licensing justices;
  Magistrates; Magistrates' court
Justices licence
  conversion   10.1.4, 15.1.1,
  15.4, *see also* Transitional

Keeping and producing, *see* Club
  premises certificate; Display;
  Nominated person; Personal
  licence; Premises licence

Lap dancer   11.3.2
Lapse, *see* Club premises certificate;
  Premises licence
Late night refreshments
  alcohol   4.7.4, 4.7.5
  background   1.3.5
  charity provision   4.7.4
  deemed provision   4.6.2
  definition   4.6.1
  exemptions   4.7
    employees   4.7.2
    exhibition halls   4.7.3
    hotels etc   4.7.1
    types of food and drink/no
      charge made   4.7.4
  'hot food/drink'   4.6.3, 4.6.3
  licensable activity   2.3.15,
    4.1.1, 4.2.1, 4.6
  previous provisions brought
    together   2.3.15
  vehicle, from   4.7.4
  vending machine, from   4.7.4
Legal representation   13.2.1
Legislative background
  basic principles, establishment
    of   1.2.4
  current Act (1964)   1.2.10
  historical   1.1–1.3
  introduction of annual
    licensing   1.2.2

Legal representation – *cont*
  new Act (2003)   2.1 *et seq*
    activities within scope, *see*
      Licensable activities
    aim of   1.3.7
    Bill, introduction speech in
      HL   2.1.1
    deregulation and self-
      regulation   2.1.6
    excluded activities   4.1.3
    flexible system   1.3.8, 2.1.2
    ill-considered provisions
      2.1.4
    local decision-making, based
      on   2.1.5
    repealed statutes   2.1.7,
      4.1.2
    significant changes in   2.3
    system under   1.3.8
    wholesale change   2.1.3
  off-licences   1.2.3
  purposes of legislation   1.1.1
Licensable activities   4.1 *et seq*
  alcohol retail sale/supply of, *see*
    Alcohol; Club
  consideration, provided for
    4.1.1, 4.1.5–4.1.7
    'charge'   4.1.6
    with a view to profit   4.1.7
  definition   4.2.1
  exclusions   4.1.3, 4.4.3
  exemptions   4.5, 4.7, 5.1.2
  late night refreshments, *see* Late
    night refreshments
  list   4.1.1, 4.2.1
  premises licence, *see* Premises
    licence
  regime for   4.2
  regulated entertainment, *see*
    Entertainment
  temporary/fundraising etc, *see*
    Temporary event
  unauthorised
    exemption, regulated
      entertainment performer/
      participant   11.3.2
    offences   11.3, *see also*
      Offences
Licensed premises
  see also Alcohol; Premises licence

  delivery of alcohol to child by
    worker on   11.7.16
  employment of child, offence
    11.7.15
  personal licence holder
    10.1.2, 10.1.3, *see also*
    Personal licence
  sending child to obtain alcohol
    from   11.7.17
  unaccompanied child prohibited,
    see Child
Licensing body
  Inns of Court etc   5.1.2
  local authority, *see* Local authority
    licensing body
Licensing guidance, *see* Guidance
Licensing justices
  role abolished   2.2.1, 2.3.1
Licensing objectives, *see* Objectives,
  licensing
Licensing proceedings, *see*
  Hearings; Local authority
  licensing body
Licensing qualification   10.4.1
Licensing statement
  appeal   6.3.6, 6.3.7, 6.7.2–
    6.7.4
  challenge (judicial review)
    6.3.6, 6.7.2, 13.5.4
  consultation duty   6.3
    conduct of, 'Sedley' rules
      6.3.5, 6.3.6, 6.3.8
    failure   6.3.6, 6.3.7
    guidance on   6.3.4
    persons to be consulted
      6.3.1, 6.3.3
    representations right   6.3.5,
      6.3.8
    time for   6.3.2
  discretion and exceptions
    6.7.2
  duty to have regard to   3.2.3,
    3.2.4, 5.2.2
  law on, summary   6.7.2
  licensing authority regard to
    3.2.2
  preparation and publication
    duty   6.2.1, 6.3
  regulation power   6.5.1
  review   6.3, 6.3.2

Licensing statement – *cont*
  revision   6.4.1
  time for   6.2.1
Limited period, licence for, *see*
  Temporary event
Liqueur confectionery   11.7.8
Local authority
  see also Environmental health
    department; Planning
    authority
  'authorised person'   7.22.3
  code of conduct   13.2.4
  costs award against   14.2.9,
    14.2.10
  discretion, exercise of   13.5
    fetter on   13.5.5
    Guidance, effect of, *see*
      Guidance
    Wednesbury
      unreasonableness
      13.5.2, 13.5.3
  licensing body, *see* Local authority
    licensing body
  standing orders   13.2.3
  ward councillor, dual roles
    prohibited   5.3.5, 13.2.4
Local authority licensing body
  'authorised person'   7.22.3, *see*
    also 'Authorised person'/
    officer
  committee   5.3
    delegation by, to officer
      5.4.1–5.4.4
    delegation by, to sub-
      committee   5.4.1–5.4.4
    delegation to   5.3.2
    membership   5.3.1, 5.3.4–
      5.3.6
    proceedings   5.6, 13.1.4
    quorum etc   13.1.5, 13.8.1
  conflict of interest   5.3.5,
    13.2.4
  council is   5.1.1
  duties   3.2.2, 3.2.3, 5.2.1
    licensing functions   5.2.2
    promotion of objectives
      3.1.3, 3.2.2, 5.2.3, 13.6.3
  geographical area   5.1.3
  Guidance, duty to have regard,
    see Guidance

hearings, *see* Hearing
interest of member, disclosure
    and effect of   13.3
  advice to councillors   13.3.4
  disregards   13.3.3
  non-disclosure makes void
    13.3.5
  non-pecuniary   13.3.4
  pecuniary interest   13.3.1–
    13.3.3
  pecuniary interest of
    spouse   13.3.2
  share interest   13.3.3
licensing statement, *see* Licensing
    statement
overlap with another
    function   5.3.3
policy   6.2.1, 6.5.1, 6.7
  law, summary   6.7.2
  unlawful, challenge for
    6.7.4, 13.5.4, 13.5.5
  see also Licensing statement
premises licence, for, *see* Premises
    licence
register   5.5
  inspection   5.5.3
sub-committee   5.4, 13.1.5
summary of licence or certificate,
    see Summary
transfer of functions to   2.2.1–
    2.2.3
  appeal safeguard   2.2.3
Local weights and measures
  authority
  enforcement duty   11.7.13
  proceedings institution   11.1.5
  test purchases   11.7.13
London
  'near beer' premises   4.7.3
  night café   2.3.15
  transitional   15.5.3
Lost/stolen certificate or licence
  club premises certificate   8.7.2
  personal licence   10.5.2
  premises licence   7.15.2
  temporary event notice   9.6.5
Lotteries   4.1.3, 4.3.6
Lucky dip   9.1.1

Magistrates
  betting and gaming licensing
    2.2.1
Magistrates' court
  appeal to/from, *see* Appeal
  closure order
    general order, power
      12.2.1
    specific order, review of
      12.3.1, 12.6, *see also* Review
Mandatory requirements   3.1.4,
  3.1.5
Meals, table   11.7.11, 11.7.18,
  11.7.19
Medical practice
  interested party   13.4.9
Member
  club, *see* Club; Club premises
    certificate
  licensing body, *see* Local authority
    licensing body
Miners welfare institute   8.12
Mortgagee
  'aggrieved person', for closure
    order review decision
    12.6.10
  interim authority application
    7.20.10
  registration of interest in
    property   7.20.8, 7.20.9
Motor vehicle, *see* Excluded
    premises; Vehicle
Motorway service station, *see*
    Excluded premises
Museum
  educational etc film shown in
    4.5.2
Music and dancing
  broadcast   4.5.5
  club, in   4.1.1, 4.2.1, 4.4.1,
    8.4.1, *see also* Club premises
    certificate
  incidental music   4.5.3, 4.5.4
  licensing under Act   2.3.17,
    4.1.1, 4.2.1, 4.4
    licensable activity   4.2.1,
      4.4.1
  see also Club premises
    certificate; Premises
    licence

limited period licence   7.6.14
Morris dancing   4.5.8
'music'   4.4.1
performance of music or
    dance   4.4.1, 7.24.5
playing of recording of   4.4.1
regulation   4.4
  background   1.3.1
  definition for   4.4.1
  exemptions   4.5.3, 4.5.4,
    4.5.8
  performer/disc jockey offence
    exemption   11.3.2
small premises, live music
    7.24.4–7.24.7

Natural justice, *see* Hearing
New Year   1.2.13
Noise, *see* Public nuisance
Nominated person
  club premises certificate
    8.7.5, 8.7.6
  premises licence   7.15.4
Notice
  club premises certificate
    determination   8.6.6
  hearing   13.2.1
    failure   13.4.10
  personal licence
    determination   10.3.8
  premises licence
    changes   7.15.3
    determination   7.14.1
    review determination
      7.21.11
    variation application
      determination   7.17.5
    variation of supervisor
      determination   7.18.4
  temporary event notice, *see*
    Temporary event

Objections, *see* Police
Objectives, licensing   3.2
  background   3.1.1–3.1.3
  closure order review, promotion
    steps   12.7.5
  club premises certificate
    application, promotion
    8.6.2, 8.9.4, 8.9.5

Objectives, licensing – *cont*
  conditions, imposition only if
    necessary to promote
    13.6.4
  crime prevention, *see* Crime and
    disorder prevention
  licensing authority general duty
    to promote   3.1.3, 3.2.2,
    5.2.3
    hearing, in   13.6.3–13.6.5
  list   3.2.1, 5.2.1
  personal licence
    determination   2.3.11
  premises licence application
    2.3.6
    promotion steps in   7.6.17,
    7.10.3, 7.10.4
  protection of children, *see* Child
  public nuisance prevention, *see*
    Public nuisance
  public safety, *see* Public safety
Occasional permission/licence
  see also Temporary event
  introduction of power   1.2.13
  replacement of   2.3.9
Offences   11.1 *et seq*
  alcohol, relating to, *see* Alcohol;
    Children and alcohol
  association   11.2.3–11.2.5
  body corporate   11.2.1, 11.2.5
  child, relating to, *see* Children
    and alcohol
  defences
    belief that child not under
      age   11.7.2, 11.7.3,
      11.7.12, 11.8.5
    due diligence defence
      11.1.7–11.1.9, 11.3.1,
      11.7.4
  entry to premises on
    suspicion   11.1.3, 11.1.4,
    see also Entry powers
  institution of proceedings for
    11.1.5
  old offences, replacement/
    abolition   2.3.19
  overview   11.1.1, 11.1.2
  partnership   11.2.2
  strict liability   11.1.7–11.1.10,
    11.3.1

  tax evasion, relating to   11.6
  time-limit for prosecution
    11.1.5
  unauthorised licensing
    activities   11.3
    carrying on without licence,
      etc   11.3.1
    exemption for performers/
      participants   11.3.2
    'knowingly' allowing activity to
      be carried on   11.3.3,
      11.3.4
    penalty   11.3.5
Officer, *see* 'Authorised person'/
  officer
Off-licence/sales
  background law   1.2.3
  club   8.4.3, 8.4.4
Operating schedule
  club premises certificate
    application   8.2.2, 8.2.4
  premises licence application, *see*
    Premises licence
Owner of property
  'aggrieved person', for closure
    order review decision
    12.6.10
  interim authority application
    7.20.10
  registration of interest in
    property   7.20.8, 7.20.9

Partner
  disclosure of interest by
    councillor   13.3.1
  offence, prosecution for
    11.2.2
Permitted hours
  see also Hours
  abolition of concept   2.3.7,
    7.6.8
  protection on conversion
    15.2.6, 15.2.17
Personal licence   10.1 *et seq*
  age of holder   2.3.11, 10.3.1
  alcohol sale by retail, for
    10.1.1, 10.1.2, 10.2.2
  appeal provisions, *see* Appeal
  application   10.2
    applicant   10.2.1

Personal licence – *cont*
  application – *cont*
    crime prevention objective
        2.3.11, *see also* 'criminal
        convictions' *below*
    determination   10.3
    licensing authority for
        10.2.4
    procedure   10.2.1
    suitability considerations
        2.3.11, *see also*
        'qualification' *below*
  background   10.1
  change of address etc,
      notification   10.5.3
  club, not needed for   10.1.1
  criminal convictions   10.3.2–
      10.3.5, 10.9
    after application   10.3.5,
        10.9.2
    court powers as to existing
        licence   10.10
    'foreign offence'   10.3.3
    Guidance on   13.6.6–13.6.8
    licence, in   10.5.1
    notification by court to
        authority   10.10.3
    notification duty of holder to
        court   10.3.5, 10.9.1–
        10.9.4
    notification duty of holder to
        authority   10.10.4
    reference to police   10.3.2,
        10.3.6
    'relevant offence'   10.3.3
    renewal, relevance to
        10.8.2–10.8.4
    spent   10.3.4
  database of   5.5.6, 5.5.7,
      10.1.6
  definition   10.2.2
  designated supervisor of premises
      to hold   7.12.2
  duration and validity   10.6,
      10.7.4
    appeal period, during
        14.6.3
  forfeiture   10.10.1, 10.10.2,
      14.6.4
  form and contents   10.1.7,
      10.5–10.5.4

  grant   10.3.1, 10.3.7
  justices' licence conversion
      into   15.4
  keeping and showing, *see*
      'production on demand'
      below
  licensed premises   10.1.2,
      10.1.3
  licensing authority
    accurate record, duty
        10.11.1–10.11.3
    responsible for   10.1.5
  lost, damaged, etc, copy on
      10.5.2
  notice of grant/rejection
      10.3.8
  objection of police   10.3.6,
      10.8.4, *see also* Police
  one licence restriction   10.2.5
  production on demand
      10.5.4, 10.11.2
  qualification   10.1.4, 10.3.1,
      10.4
    age limit   2.3.11, 10.3.1
    'licensing qualification'
        10.4.1
  rejection of application
      10.3.2, 10.3.7, 10.3.8
    crime prevention objective
        10.3.7
  renewal   10.6.3, 10.7, 10.8
    application   10.7.1, 10.7.2
    crime prevention objective
        10.8.1, 10.8.6
    determination of
        application   10.8
    grant   10.8.4, 10.8.5
    reference to police   10.8.2–
        10.8.4
    rejection   10.8.6
    time for   10.7.3
    transitional provision
        10.6.3, 10.7.4
  requirement for   2.3.10
  residence of holder   10.1.5
  revocation   10.3.5, 10.8.3,
      10.9.3
    refusal, police appeal right
        14.6.2

Personal licence – *cont*
  surrender   10.9.3, 10.12,
    14.6.4
    notice of   10.12.1
    time of   10.12.2
  suspension   10.10.1, 10.10.2,
    14.6.4
  temporary event premises user,
    whether holds   9.4.5,
    9.4.6
Plan of premises
  club premises certificate, for
    8.7.1
  premises licence, for   7.7.1
Planning authority
  service on   7.5.6
Play
  background   1.3.3, 1.3.4
  censorship conditions
    prohibited   7.12.7, 8.6.5
  club, in   4.1.1, 4.2.1, 4.4.1,
    8.4.1, *see also* Club premises
    certificate
  door staff   7.12.4
  licensable activity   4.2.1, 4.4.1
  meaning   4.4.1
  old licences abolished   2.3.16,
    see now Premises licence
  'performance of a play',
    regulated entertainment
    4.4.1
    performer, offence
      exemption   11.3.2
  regulated entertainment
    4.4.1, *see also* Club; Premises
    licence
Poetry reading   4.4.3
Police
  appeal right   7.14.5, 14.3.1,
    14.3.3, 14.6.2
  conversion applications,
    relating to   15.2.15,
    15.3.10, 15.4.8
  closure powers, *see* Closure order
  confiscation of alcohol from
    child   11.9
  consultation with   6.3.1
  conversion of club registration
    certificate, objection to
    15.3.4, 15.3.5

hearing of application
  15.3.5
conversion of existing licence,
  objection to   15.2.7–
  15.2.9
  hearing of application
    15.2.11
  limitations   15.2.8–15.2.10
conversion of justices' licence to
  personal licence, objection
  to   15.4.3, 15.4.7
  hearing of application
    15.4.7
costs award against   14.2.9,
  14.2.10
entry to premises, *see also* Entry
  powers
lost/stolen licence, etc, report to
  club premises certificate
    8.7.2
  personal licence   10.5.2
  premises licence   7.15.2
  temporary event notice
    9.6.5
notification of determinations to
  club premises certificate
    8.6.6, 8.9.5
  premises licence   7.14.1,
    7.17.5
  transfer of premises licence
    7.20.5
obstruction of constable, *see* Entry
  powers
personal licence objection
  10.3.6
  hearing   10.3.6, 10.8.4
  notice of grant/rejection
    following   10.3.8
  reference for   10.3.2, 10.3.6
  renewal application, reference
    for   10.8.2–10.8.4
premises licence objections
  change of designated
    supervisor   7.18.2
  delegation prohibited on
    5.4.2
  interim authority, to
    7.17.6, 7.16.7
  transfer of premises licence,
    to   7.20.2, 7.20.4

Police – *cont*
  representations by (premises
      licence)
    'relevant'   7.11.1
    statement with   7.11.6
  service on   7.5.6
  temporary event notice
    appeal against counter notice
        refusal   9.5.8
    copy to   9.3.7
    counter notice copy to
        9.4.8
    modification of   9.5.6, 9.5.7
    objection notice   9.5.2,
        9.5.3
Policy
  local authority, *see* Licensing
      statement
'Premises'   7.3.1
Premises licence   7.1 *et seq*
  alcohol supply   7.6.16, 7.8.1,
      7.12.2
    retail sale requires   4.3.2,
        4.3.3
  appeal right, *see* Appeal
  applicant
    bodies, definitions given
        7.4.1
    list of possible   7.4.1
  application   2.3.6, 7.5 *et seq*
    advertising of   7.5.5, 7.10.1
    determination   7.10, 7.14
    documents, etc, with   7.5.4,
        7.6–7.9, *see also* 'operating
        schedule' *below*
    form   7.5.4
    Guidance   7.5.1, 7.5.2
    provisional statement, by, *see*
        Provisional statement
    service   7.5.6, 7.10.1
  background   7.1.1–7.1.3
  changes, notification duty
      7.15.3
  circumstances for, *see* 'licensable
      activities' *below*
  closure of premises, *see* Closure
      order
  conditions   7.12
    alcohol sale   7.12.2
    breach of   7.6.2

    changes   7.17.7
    flexibility   7.12.1
    Guidance on   7.6.3, 7.12.5,
        7.12.6
    justification for   7.12.1,
        7.12.5, 13.6.4
    mandatory   7.6.4, 7.10.1–
        7.12.3
    modification of   2.3.13,
        7.21.10, 12.7.5
    opening hours, as to   2.3.7
    operating schedule, stemming
        from   7.6.2–7.6.4,
        7.10.1
    security staff, relating to
        7.12.4
  consent, *see* 'supervisor' *below*
  criteria for grant   2.3.6
  definition   7.1.4
  display   7.15.5
  duration   2.3.2, 7.16
  entry powers, *see* Entry powers
  failure to produce   5.5.5,
      7.15.5
  fee   7.9
  form   7.15
    contents   7.15.1
  grant   7.5.3, 7.6.1, 7.10.1,
      7.10.4
    reasons for, where
        representations   7.14.2
  hearing   7.10.2, 7.10.3
  holder
    death   7.16.2, 7.16.5, 7.16.6,
        7.20.10
    duties   7.15.3–7.15.5
    incapacity   7.16.6
    see also 'supervisor' below
  hours   2.3.7, 7.6.8–7.6.12
    Guidance on   7.6.9, 7.6.12
    separate, for different
        activities   7.6.11
    without licensable activities
        7.6.13
  inspection powers, *see* Entry
      powers
  interim authority to continue
      business   7.16.6, 7.20.10
    example   7.16.9

Premises licence – *cont*
  interim authority to continue
      business – *cont*
    lapse and appeal right
        7.16.8
    police objection   7.16.8
    procedural rules   7.16.7
    time-limit for application
        7.16.7
  issue   5.5.4, 7.14.4
  keeping and producing, duty
      7.15.4
  nominated person   7.15.4
  lapse   2.3.4, 5.5.5, 7.16.2,
      7.16.4
  licensable activities   4.2.1,
      7.6.6, 7.6.7
    change to   7.17.7, 7.21.10
    exclusion from licence
        7.10.4, 12.7.5
  licensing objectives, steps to
      promote
    applicant, by   7.6.17
    local authority, by, 7.10.3,
        7.10.4
  limited period   7.6.14, 7.16.1
  local authority licensing body
      for   7.2.1, 7.5.4
  lost, damaged etc, copy licence
      on   7.15.2
  notice
    determination of
        application   7.14.1
    variation application
        determination   7.17.5
  operating schedule   7.5.4, 7.6
    contents   7.6.5–7.6.17
    incorporation in licence
        7.6.2, 7.6.3
    liaison over preparation
        7.6.1, 7.12.5
    nature of   7.6.1
  'permanent' nature of   2.3.2
  personal licence holder, *see*
      Personal licence
  plan of premises   7.7.1, 7.15.1
  'premises'   7.3.1
  principles for   7.5.1
  reinstatement   7.16.5
  reissue/update   5.5.5

  rejection of application
      7.10.4, 7.14.3
  representations   7.11
    effect of   7.5.3, 7.6.4, 7.10.2,
        7.10.3
    frivolous or vexatious
        7.11.3, 7.11.4, 7.17.3,
        7.17.6, 13.7.2–13.7.6
    'interested party'   7.11.2,
        7.11.5
    none   7.5.3
    police, by, *see* Police
    'relevant'   7.10.2, 7.11.1
  review   2.3.13, 7.21
    advertising of application
        7.21.9
    appeal and effect of
        lodging   7.21.12,
            7.21.13
    background to provision
        7.21.1, 7.21.2
    entry powers exercisable
        on   7.22.2
    following closure order
        2.3.13, 14.7
    hearing   7.21.9
    licensing authority
        determination options
        7.21.10
    licensing objectives, relevance
        to   7.21.3, 7.21.10
    notice   7.21.5
    notification of
        determination   7.21.11
    period between   7.21.8
    rejection grounds   7.21.6,
        7.21.7, 7.21.12
    repeated request   7.21.6–
        7.21.8
    request for   7.21.4, 7.21.14
    suspending effect of   7.16.3
  revocation   7.16.1, 7.21.10,
      12.7.5
  small premises, live music in, *see*
      Small premises
  summary   5.5.4, 5.5.5, 7.14.4,
      7.15.1
    display   7.15.5
  supervisor
    alcohol supply, necessary
        for   7.12.2, 7.18.3

Premises licence – *cont*
  supervisor – *cont*
    change of   2.3.4, 7.15.3,
      7.18, *see also* Variation
    consent of, in application
      7.5.4, 7.8.1
    consent of, to variation
      7.18.1
    information on, in
      application   7.6.15
    information on, in licence
      7.6.15, 7.15.1
    qualification   7.12.2
    refusal to specify   7.10.4
    removal of   7.21.10, 12.7.5
    removal request, *see* Removal
      request by supervisor
  surrender   7.16.1, 7.16.4
  suspension   2.3.13, 7.16.3,
    7.21.10, 12.7.5
  transfer   2.3.3, 7.16.5, 7.16.6,
    7.16.9, 7.20
    applicant   7.20.1
    application procedure
      7.20.1
    consent to   7.20.3, 7.20.7
    grant   7.20.3, 7.20.4
    hearing   7.20.4
    notification of determination/
      reasons   7.20.5
    notification of supervisor of
      application   7.20.6
    police objections   7.20.2,
      7.20.4
    registration of interest in
      property   7.20.8, 7.20.9
    rejection   7.20.3
  variation   7.17
    application procedure
      7.17.1
    grant   7.17.2, 7.17.4, 7.17.5
    hearing   7.17.2, 7.17.4
    notification of   7.17.5
    rejection   7.17.4, 7.17.5
    relevant representations
      7.17.2, 7.17.3, 7.17.6
    scope/restrictions   7.17.7
Private places of entertainment, *see*
  Entertainment
Prize   4.3.6

Protection order   2.3.4
Provisional statement
  premises licence application
    by   7.13
  advantage of   7.13.4
  effect of   7.13.5
  fee   7.13.3
  form   7.13.3
  premises under construction/
    alteration   7.13.2
  procedural provisions
    7.13.6
  representations   7.13.4,
    7.13.5
  schedule of works   7.13.3
Public admission
  licensing hearing   13.8.1,
    13.8.2
Public entertainments, *see*
  Entertainment
Public nuisance
  closure order for   12.3.2
    extension   12.4.3
  prevention, licensing
    objective   3.2.1, 3.2.5
  music entertainments
    7.24.7
  'public nuisance'   3.2.5, 3.2.6,
    12.3.3
Public safety
  closure order extension
    consideration   12.4.3
  licensing objective   3.2.1, 3.2.5
Public transport, role of   7.6.10
Publicity, *see* Advertising; Display

Qualification
  personal licence holder, *see*
    Personal licence
  supervisor of premises
    licence   17.12.2
Qualifying activities, *see* Club
  premises certificate

Raffle   4.3.6, 9.1.1
Records   5.5
Register
  central database of personal
    licences   5.5.6, 5.5.7,
    10.1.6

Register – *cont*
  licensing authority   5.5.1–
    5.5.3
Regulated entertainment, *see*
  Entertainment
Reinstatement, *see* Premises licence
'Relevant' representations, *see*
  Representations
Religious service   4.5.6
Removal of licence
  abolition   2.3.5
Removal request by supervisor
  7.19
  notices
    effect of   7.19.3
    holder of licence   7.19.2
    licensing authority   7.19.1
Renewal
  see also Personal licence
  human rights issues   13.4.7
  premises licence as
    'permanent'   2.3.2
Representations
  see also Interested party
  closure order review before
    authority   12.7.4,12.7.6
  club premises certificate, as to, *see*
    Club premises certificate
  consultation, during   6.3.5,
    6.3.8
  delegation prohibited after
    5.4.2
  premises licence application/
    variation, as to, *see* Premises
    licence
  'relevant'   7.17.3, 13.7.2
    club premises certificate
      8.6.3, 8.9.3
    delegated powers, for   5.4.3,
      5.4.4
    'frivolous or vexatious' are not,
      see Frivolous or vexatious
      representation
    Guidance   13.7.6
    premises licence   7.10.2,
      7.11.1
Residents' association   13.4.9, *see*
  also Interested party
Responsible authority   7.5.6
  review request by

club premises certificate
  8.10.2, 8.10.10
premises licence   7.21.4,
  7.21.14
Retail sale   4.3.2, 4.3.3, 10.1,
  10.2, 11.4.1
Review
  see also Appeal; Judicial review
  closure order, licensing authority
    powers   12.3.1, 12.7
  appeal, position pending
    12.7.8–12.7.10
  hearing   12.7.4
  licensing objectives, steps for
    promotion of   12.7.5
  notice of determination
    12.7.7
  offence   12.7.11
  procedure   12.7.3
  representations   12.7.4,
    12.7.6
  revocation   12.7.8
  suspension of
    determination   12.7.9,
    12.7.10
  time-limit for
    determination   12.7.2
  trigger for   12.3.1, 12.7.1
  closure order, magistrates'
    powers   12.3.1, 12.6
  'aggrieved person'   12.6.10
  appeal   12.6.10
  constitution of court   12.6.5
  fair hearing requirement
    12.6.8, 12.6.9
  grounds for exercise   12.6.4
  hearing required   12.6.2,
    12.6.3, 12.6.6
  notification of licensing
    authority   12.6.5, 12.7.1
  police duty to apply   12.6.1
  powers available   12.6.3
  procedure   12.6.7
  club premises certificate
    2.3.13, 8.10
  criminal convictions, approach
    to   13.6.6, 13.6.7
  fair hearing right, and   13.4.3
  following closure order
    2.3.13, 14.7

Review – *cont*
hearing, Guidance   13.6.5–
13.6.7
premises licence, *see* Premises
licence
Revocation
closure order   12.6.3, 12.7.8
human rights issues   13.4.7
personal licence, *see* Personal
licence
premises licence, *see* Premises
licence
provision for   2.3.13
Risk assessment
premises licence grant
application, for   7.5.1–
7.5.3
Royal palaces   5.1.2

Search, *see* Entry powers
Secretary of State
guidance to licensing authorities,
see Guidance
licensing statement, regulation
power   6.5.1
policy review, regulation
power   6.5.1
Security Industry Authority
7.12.4
Security staff   7.12.4
Service
conversion to premises licence
application, of   15.2.7
premises licence application,
of   7.5.6, 7.10.1
Service station, *see* Excluded
premises
Sex cinemas   15.5.4
Sex establishments   4.1.3
Shares
disclosure of interest   13.3.3
Small premises   7.24
music entertainment in
7.24.4–7.24.7
Act provision for   7.24.5
public nuisance   7.24.7
'two-in-a-bar' rule   7.24.1–
7.24.3
Small scale temporary event, *see*
Temporary event

Smuggled goods   11.6.1, 11.6.2
Sports event
indoor   4.1.1
definition   4.4.1
participant offence
exemption   11.3.2
licensable activity   4.2.1, 4.4.1
outdoor   4.1.3
prevention of alcohol sale
introduced   1.2.13,
12.2.3, *see also* Closure order
Stand-up comedians   4.4.3
Statement, licensing, *see* Local
authority licensing body
Strip-tease artist   11.3.2
Summary, *see* Club premises
certificate; Premises licence
Supervisor, *see* Premises licence
Surrender
club premises certificate
8.8.1, 8.8.2
personal licence   10.9.3, 10.12
premises licence   7.16.1,
7.16.4
Suspension, *see* Club premises
certificate; Personal licence;
Premises licence

Takeaways
see also Late night refreshments
background   1.3.5
'premises'   7.3.1, *see also*
Premises licence
Telephone sales, place of   4.3.5
Television and radio
live broadcasts   4.5.5
Temporary event   9.1 *et seq*
alcohol sale or supply, etc
9.3.3, 9.3.4
child, offences relating to
11.7.15–11.7.19, 11.8.1
see also Children and alcohol
background   9.1.1–9.1.3
closure order power   9.6.6,
12.1.2, 12.2.1, *see also* Closure
order
counter notice
appeal and challenge   9.5.8,
9.5.9, 14.5

Temporary event – *cont*
 counter notice – *cont*
  following police objection
   9.5.3, 9.5.4, 9.5.8
  use and effect 9.4.8
 duration, maximum 9.3.1,
  9.3.3
 entry powers 9.6.1
  obstruction offence 9.6.2
 fee 9.3.6
 gap between events 9.4.1
 hours 9.3.3
 introduction of concept, and
  purpose 9.1.4, 9.1.5
 maximum number and premises
  use in year 9.4.4
 notice 2.3.8, 2.3.9, 9.2.1, 9.3
  copies 9.3.5, 9.3.7
  delivery of 9.3.5
  display and production
   9.6.3, 9.6.4
  effect of 9.3.1
  form and contents 9.3.3
  individual giving 9.3.2
  licensable activities 9.3.3
  lost or damaged, copy on
   9.6.5
  receipt acknowledgement
   9.5.1
  time for 9.3.5
  two authorities, to 9.2.2,
   9.5.5
  two years, straddling 9.4.7
  withdrawal 9.3.8
 objections by police 9.5
  decision and notices 9.5.3–
   9.5.5
  hearing 9.5.3
  modification of notice
   alternative 9.5.6, 9.5.7
  procedure 9.5.2, 9.5.3
 permitted temporary
  activities 9.2
 'premises user' 9.3.2
  business colleagues and
   associates 9.4.3, 9.4.9
  maximum notices per year
   9.4.5, 9.4.6
  notice publicity, duty as to
   9.6.3, 9.6.4

 restrictions and limits 9.4
 same premises, events in
  9.4.2
Test purchases 11.7.13, 11.7.17
Theatre, *see* Play
Time of licensable activities, *see*
 Hours
Time-limit
 appeal 14.1.6, 14.5.2
 conversion application
  15.1.1, 15.2.4, 15.3.2, 15.4.1
 hearings 13.2.1
Tombola 4.3.6, 9.1.1
Trader
 retail alcohol sale 4.3.2
Train
 alcohol sale, prohibiting
  order 11.10.3
 not a 'vehicle' 4.3.8
Transfer application
 premises licence, *see* Premises
  licence
Transitional 15.1 *et seq*
 alcohol definition 15.5.2
 club certificates 15.1.4, 15.3
  appeal 15.3.10
  application 15.3.3
  'existing club certificate'
   15.3.1
  grant/deemed grant 15.3.6
  issue of new certificate and
   summary 15.3.8
  notice to police 15.3.4
  police objection 15.3.4,
   15.3.5
  rejection 15.3.10
  revocation appeal pending
   15.3.7
  time-limit 15.3.2
  variation application
   combined 15.3.9
  consultation and
   representations 15.5.1
 conversion to personal
  licence 15.4
  appeal right 15.4.8
  application 15.4.2
  criminal conviction since
   grant/last renewal etc
   15.4.2, 15.4.3

Transitional – *cont*
  conversion to personal licence – *cont*
    deemed grant   15.4.6
    determination issues   15.4.4
    grant   15.4.5
    hearing, circumstances for   15.4.7
    justices' licence holder's right   15.4.1
    notice to police   15.4.3
    police objection   15.4.3, 15.4.7
    rejection   15.4.7
    time-limit   15.4.1
  conversion to premises licences   15.1.2, 15.1.3, 15.2
    appeal right   15.2.15
    application   15.2.3–15.2.6
    consent of holder, circumstances   15.2.5
    'existing licence'   15.2.1
    failure consequences   15.1.8
    grant/deemed grant   15.2.12
    'new licence'   15.2.2, 15.2.13
    notice to police   15.2.7
    police objection   15.2.7–15.2.9, 15.2.11
    premises supervisor, designation of   15.2.6, 15.2.13
    rejection   15.2.15
    renewal refusal appeal pending   15.2.10
    revocation appeal pending   15.2.9, 15.2.10
    service of application copy   15.2.7
    time-limit   15.2.4
    variation application combined   15.2.14
  justices' licences   15.1.1, 15.1.5, 15.2, 15.4
    provisional grant, premises licence after   15.2.18

London special provisions   15.5.3
no provisions   15.1.7
overview   15.1
permitted hours protection   15.2.16, 15.2.17
protective provisions   15.1.6
six-month period for replacements   15.1.1, 15.2.4, 15.3.2, 15.4.1

Ultra vires   6.6.3

Variation
  club premises certificate, *see* Club premises certificate
  conversion, on
    existing licence   15.2.14
    existing club certificate   15.3.9
  premises licence, *see* Premises licence
  premises supervisor   7.18
    application   7.18.1
    immediate effect, request for   7.18.3
    notification of decision   7.18.4
    police objection   7.18.2
Vehicle
  definition   4.3.8, 11.10.2
  not permanently/temporarily parked
    alcohol sale from   4.7.5, 11.10.1, 11.10.2
    entertainment provision on   4.5.9
    hot food/drink supplied on   4.7.4
    licensable activities on   4.5.9, 7.3.1, 11.10, *see also* Premises licence
  parked/parking locations   4.5.9, 7.3.1
  'premises'   7.3.1
Vending machine
  hot drink from, late night refreshment exemption   4.7.4

Vessel
  'authorised person'   7.22.3
  not a 'vehicle'   4.3.8
  not permanently moored
    4.5.10
  premises   4.5.10, 7.3.1
  responsible bodies, service on
    7.5.6
Vexatious representation, *see*
  Frivolous or vexatious
  representation
Vicinity, person in, *see* Interested
  party

Wales
  Sunday closing   2.3.14

Website
  internet sales   4.3.5
  use of   7.5.5
Weights and measures, *see* Local
  weights and measures
  authority
White Paper 2000   1.3.6
Wholesale supplies   2.3.21, 4.3.3
Wine broker   4.3.3
Worship, place of   4.5.6
Wrestling   4.1.1, 4.4.1,
  11.3.2
Written order, place of sale
  4.3.5

Zoning   2.3.7, 7.6.9